1993

Justice and Modern Moral Philosophy

Justice and Modern Moral Philosophy

Jeffrey Reiman

Yale University Press
New Haven and London

Designed by James J. Johnson
and set in Bodoni Book types
by Brevis Press, Bethany, Connecticut.
Printed in the United States of America by
BookCrafters, Inc., Chelsea, Michigan.

Library of Congress Cataloging-in-Publication Data

Reiman, Jeffrey H.
    Justice and modern moral philosophy / Jeffrey Reiman.
    p.   cm.
    Bibliography: p.
    Includes index.
    ISBN 0–300–04518–2 (cloth)
          0–300–05234–0 (pbk.)
    1. Justice (Philosophy)   2. Ethics.   3. Social ethics.   I. Title.
B105.J87R45   1990
172'.2—dc20   89–8965
                                                              CIP

The paper in this book meets the guidelines for
permanence and durability of the Committee on
Production Guidelines for Book Longevity of the
Council on Library Resources.

10   9   8   7   6   5   4   3

For my parents,
Max and Shirley Reiman

There is but one essential justice which cements
society, and one law which establishes this justice.
This law is right reason, which is the true rule of all
commandments and prohibitions.
　　—Cicero, *The Laws*

For remember that you were once slaves in Egypt; that
is why I command you to observe this rule.
　　—Deuteronomy 24:22

Contents

Contents

Preface

In this book I aim to present and defend a complete theory of justice, starting from an account of its source, its obligatory force, and its primacy over other moral ideals and ending with a set of principles of natural and social justice that are binding on all rational individuals. I hope thereby to vindicate the widely held belief—recently doubted by philosophers—that the most important truths of morality can be identified by the natural reasoning faculties of human beings. But the stakes here are greater than vindication of a popular belief. Unless truths of morality can be identified by reason, moral conflicts are only clashes between people with different unverifiable beliefs. Then, victory goes to the side with the power (of arms, numbers, persuasion, habit, or tradition) to prevail, and right becomes indistinguishable from might. The theory of justice as reason's answer to subjugation described in this book seeks a cure for this danger in the threat itself. It explores the frontier between right and might to find the materials for a satisfactory theory of justice.

Digging along the border between right and might yields a surprisingly rich lode. Whatever else can be said about what is right, we know that it must be different from might. Because philosophical attempts to identify what is right have generally failed to achieve wide agreement, this book starts off in the opposite direction—trying to find what is right by determining what is not might. I argue that those requirements that it is reasonable for people to regard as protecting them against subjugation, when subjugation is understood in a fittingly wide sense, amount to a full and satisfying system of principles of justice. The vulnerability of all rational human beings to subjugation and our interest in preventing it account not only for our concern for justice but also for our natural rational capacity to recognize it. I go on to argue, moreover, that reason requires us to refrain from subjugating one another and, thus, that the requirements of justice are requirements of reason.

I argue further that the idea that justice can be found by looking for what prevents subjugation expresses the inner wisdom of the social contract tradition in moral philosophy and accounts for the abiding appeal of that tradition—indeed, for the substantial quantum of truth that the tradition carries forth. Consequently, interwoven with the argument for justice as reason's answer to subjugation is an interpretation of the history of contractarian moral theory from Hobbes to Rawls. The theory defended here shows what is correct in John Rawls's widely and rightly acclaimed *A Theory of Justice* and suggests that where the theory goes wrong it does so for lack of what justice as reason's answer to subjugation provides.

Justice and Modern Moral Philosophy has taken about fifteen years to bring from the first stirrings to the present book. During that period and more, I have been on the faculty of the American University in Washington, D.C. I am grateful to the university for providing me with a stimulating and supportive atmosphere in which to develop this project and, in particular, for two sabbatical years that made possible the uninterrupted reflection that is the lifebreath of philosophy. Though I am currently a full-time member of the Department of Philosophy and Religion of American University, during the period in which most of the work on this book was done, I held an appointment in the School of Justice of the university (now called the Department of Justice, Law, and Society). There, I had the opportunity, rare for a philosopher, to practice my abstract craft in the midst of a lively and diverse group of inquirers from many disciplines all aiming to understand that part of the world occupied by the criminal justice system. I hope that these fine colleagues will see how deeply this book is influenced by my experience with them. The idea of looking at moral philosophy from the place where might meets right, which shapes the book from start to finish, I attribute to my years in the School of Justice.

I am grateful to Kai Nielsen of Calgary University and to Hugo Bedau of Tufts University for their helpful comments on parts of an early version of the book and, in particular, to Jan Narveson of the University of Waterloo, who gave me extensive and extremely challenging comments on one complete draft of the book. I thank also the anonymous reviewers who have read my work over the years, from the first bits and pieces that I tried to publish separately to the final draft. I have learned a great deal from these named and unnamed philosophers, and I have incorporated many of their suggestions in what follows, but since I have also not heeded many of their warnings, they cannot be blamed for my errors.

For most of the years I was working on this book, I was a member of a philosophical discussion group made up of American University faculty members, Charley Hardwick and Phillip Scribner (of the Department of Philosophy and Religion), Jon Wisman (of the Department of Economics), and Barry Chabot (then of the Department of Literature, though now at Miami University of Ohio). In addition to contributing generally to my continuing education, the group read an early draft of the book and discussed its ideas and arguments. Much that I learned from that and other discussions with them has found its way into the book. Moreover, each of them has left his special imprint on what follows. Barry Chabot helped me immeasurably on the writing. Jon Wisman stimulated me to reflect deeply on my views about economics and psychology. Charley Hardwick gave me detailed comments on several drafts right down to the final one and jogged many enjoyable miles with me discussing the eternal questions of philosophy. My greatest philosophical debt, however, is owed to Phillip Scribner, with whom I engaged in an intensive philosophical conversation lasting more than a decade. When I form my own views, his are never far from my mind.

I am grateful to Jeanne Ferris, my editor at Yale University Press, for her efforts to bring this book into existence and her wise counsel, and to Stacey Mandelbaum, manuscript editor at Yale, for her thorough and thoughtful work.

I cannot thank my wife, Sue Headlee, for proofreading my manuscript, or even for putting up with my long hours in front of the word processor. She was busy at her own word processor getting herself a Ph.D. in economics at the time. I thank her, instead, for surrounding me with beauty, moral passion, and intellectual excitement, without which this book, and my life, would be a duller and paler thing.

Finally, for reasons set out in the fourth section of chapter 3, this book is dedicated to my parents, Max and Shirley Reiman, who first taught me about justice.

Key to Abbreviated References in the Text

ASU   Robert Nozick. *Anarchy, State, and Utopia*. New York: Basic, 1974.

BN   Jean-Paul Sartre. *Being and Nothingness*. New York: Philosophical Library, 1956; originally published 1943.

BT   Martin Heidegger. *Being and Time*. New York: Harper & Row, 1962; originally published 1927.

C   Karl Marx. *Capital*. 3 vols. New York: International Publishers, 1967; originally published 1867, 1885, 1894.

CGP   Karl Marx. *Critique of the Gotha Program*. In *Marx-Engels Reader*, 2d ed., ed. Robert C. Tucker. New York: Norton, 1978; originally published 1891.

CPR   Immanuel Kant. *Critique of Practical Reason*. Indianapolis, Ind.: Bobbs-Merrill, 1956; originally published 1788.

DOI   Jean-Jacques Rousseau. *A Discourse on the Origin of Inequality*. In *The Social Contract and Discourses*. London: Dent & Sons, 1973; originally published 1755.

DPE   Jean-Jacques Rousseau. *A Discourse on Political Economy*. In *The Social Contract and Discourses*. London: Dent & Sons, 1973; originally published 1758.

EC   Peter Singer. *The Expanding Circle: Ethics and Sociobiology*. New York: Farrar, Straus & Giroux, 1981.

ECG   John Locke. *An Essay Concerning the True Original, Extent and End of Civil Government*. In *Two Treatises of Government*. London: Dent & Sons, 1924; originally published 1690.

EPM   David Hume. *An Enquiry Concerning the Principles of Morals*. Indianapolis, Ind.: Hackett, 1983; originally published 1751.

FMM   Immanuel Kant. *Foundations of the Metaphysics of Morals*, ed. Robert P. Wolff. Indianapolis, Ind.: Bobbs-Merrill, 1969; originally published 1785.

FS   Joseph Butler. *Fifteen Sermons*. London: Bell & Sons, 1953; originally published 1726.

L   Thomas Hobbes. *Leviathan*, parts 1 and 2. Indianapolis, Ind.: Bobbs-Merrill, 1958; originally published 1651.

LE   Immanuel Kant. *Lectures on Ethics*. Indianapolis, Ind.: Hackett, 1963; originally published 1924.

LLJ   Michael Sandel. *Liberalism and the Limits of Justice*. New York: Cambridge University Press, 1982.

LM   R. M. Hare. *The Language of Morals*. Oxford: Oxford University Press, 1952.

M   René Descartes. *Meditations on First Philosophy*. In *A Discourse on Method, etc.* London: Dent & Sons, 1912; originally published 1641.

MBA   David Gauthier. *Morals by Agreement*. Oxford: Oxford University Press, 1986.

MJ   Immanuel Kant. *The Metaphysical Elements of Justice*. Part 1 of *The Metaphysics of Morals*. Indianapolis, Ind.: Bobbs-Merrill, 1965; originally published 1797.

MPV   Kurt Baier. *The Moral Point of View*. Abr. ed. New York: Random House, 1965.

MV   Immanuel Kant. *The Metaphysical Principles of Virtue*. Part 2 of *The Metaphysics of Morals*, in *Ethical Philosophy*. Indianapolis, Ind.: Hackett, 1983; originally published 1797.

NE   Aristotle. *The Nicomachean Ethics*. London: Longmans, Green, 1879.

OL   John Stuart Mill. *On Liberty*. In *Utilitarianism, Liberty and Representative Government*. London: Dent & Sons, 1964; originally published 1859.

PE   G. E. Moore. *Principia Ethica*. Cambridge: Cambridge University Press, 1962; originally published 1903.

PR   G. W. F. Hegel. *Philosophy of Right*. Oxford: Oxford University Press, 1942; originally published 1821.

RM   Alan Gewirth. *Reason and Morality*. Chicago: University of Chicago Press, 1978.

SC   Jean-Jacques Rousseau. *The Social Contract*. In *The Social Contract and Discourses*. London: Dent & Sons, 1973; originally published 1762.

T   Gilbert Harman. *Thought*. Princeton, N.J.: Princeton University Press, 1973.

TJ   John Rawls. *A Theory of Justice*. Cambridge: Harvard University Press, 1971.

U   John Stuart Mill. *Utilitarianism*. In *Utilitarianism, Liberty and Representative Government*. London: Dent & Sons, 1964; originally published 1861.

VFN   Thomas Nagel. *The View from Nowhere*. New York: Oxford University Press, 1986.

Introduction: *The Theory of Justice as Reason's Answer to Subjugation*

> Unjust social arrangements are themselves
> a kind of extortion, even violence.
> —John Rawls, *A Theory of Justice*

The current sorry state of moral philosophy—in particular, prevailing skepticism about the possibility of establishing any moral principles as true or valid beyond a reasonable doubt—has an immensely troubling implication, namely, that we are unable to identify the difference between right and might; because all moralities depend on this difference, such skepticism threatens the very possibility of morality. Moral principles are commonly invoked in interpersonal transactions in which people disagree about how to act, with one person invoking a principle and (at least, implicitly) asserting that it has higher authority than another's decision about how to act. If the assertion prevails and the other alters his earlier decision and complies, that must be either because the asserted principle should prevail over his decision or because it somehow is in fact able to prevail. To show that the former is the case, we must be able to show that the other person is mistaken if he persists in his earlier decision about how to act. For that, we must be able to show that the principle invoked is somehow true or valid beyond a reasonable doubt. If we cannot show this, as the prevailing skepticism holds, then we cannot know whether the transaction has been resolved according to right or to might. And if we cannot know this, then we cannot know that the very project of trying to get our fellows to act morally is anything more than just pushing people around.

This situation is not changed when the moral principle with which the other complies is widely or deeply believed. Neither the commonsense complacency that mistakes numbers of believers for reasons to believe nor the shrill dogmatism that mistakes strength of conviction for force of argument can overcome the inherent questionability of current moral beliefs. No matter how widely believed an asserted moral principle happens to be, until we know that it *should* override contrary judgments, any attempt to persuade   1 another to act according to that principle is rightly suspect as a possible case of *subjugation*—with this term understood very broadly to characterize any case in which the judgment of one person prevails over the contrary judgment of another simply because it can and thus without adequate justification for believing that it should.

A successful justification must refute the suspicion of subjugation. However, nothing in our mental arsenal except reason has a chance of refuting this suspicion, because nothing but reason can (if anything can) distinguish between the beliefs we should hold and those that we do hold. If we cannot discern this difference using reason, we cannot know whether we are acting morally or merely imposing our judgments on others we get to comply with a principle. If reason can do the job, it will give us the principles that are truly justified in overriding contrary judgments, and these must be the true principles of justice. We should be able to reach these principles if through reason we can identify the conditions under which the charge of subjugation can be answered and the suspicion overcome. This idea guides the theory of justice as reason's answer to subjugation.

The theory views the crucial problem for moral philosophy as distinguishing between right and might. Since attempts to define right first and take might as the residue have not been widely convincing, this theory proceeds in the opposite way—defining might first and taking right as what is left. It aims first to determine the way in which subjugation arises as a threat to rational human beings and then to work back to justice by identifying the conditions under which rational human beings should be persuaded that they are not being subjugated. Principles that satisfy these conditions have a special status not shared by any other moral belief: They are the only ones that can withstand the charge of being might not right. I shall, however, go further and argue that reason requires us not to subjugate our fellows and thus that these principles are required by reason.

Moreover, I contend that the idea that we can reach justice by finding the conditions under which subjugation has been eliminated is the inner wisdom of the social contract tradition in moral thinking. Accordingly, the theory presented here is equally a theory of the social contract theory, and the defense of the theory of justice as reason's answer to subjugation is intertwined with an interpretation of the history of social contractarian moral theorizing from Hobbes to Rawls.

This approach leads to a conception of justice embodied in the following two summary principles of justice:

1. *Whether or not* people *cooperate* to produce benefits, they owe each other noninterference, easy rescue, respect for natural ownership, trust-

worthiness, intergenerational solicitude, and punishment no greater than lex talionis and deterrence require—and these are owed to everyone equally.

2. Where people *do cooperate* to produce benefits, they owe each other distribution of the benefits and efforts that went into producing them according to the difference principle—that inequalities must work to maximize the share of everyone in society starting from the worst-off individual.

The first principle sums up the requirements of natural justice, stating what all sane adult human beings owe to all other sane adult human beings, whether or not they are members of the same social structure. The second principle sums up the requirements of social justice, stating what all sane adult human beings owe to any other sane adult human being with whom they share a social structure. Thus, it determines the conditions for the design of just social structures.

Those familiar with John Rawls's theory of justice will surely note a resemblance between the two summary principles stated here and Rawls's own two principles of justice, which hold, first, that everyone is entitled to equal maximum liberty, and, second, that goods (primarily economic) should be distributed according to the difference principle. The resemblance is here to be sure, but it should not be allowed to overshadow the differences, which are at least as great as the similarities. Most important, Rawls's two principles are distinguished by the *nature* of the benefits they distribute (the first principle distributes liberty, the second goods), whereas the two summary principles are distinguished by the *source* of the benefits distributed (the first distributing what does not arise from cooperation, the second distributing what does). And although the difference principle turns up in both Rawls's second principle and the second of the summary principles, it does not mean exactly the same thing in both places. In the fourth section of chapter 5, I offer an interpretation of the difference principle inspired by (though not tied to) the Marxian labor theory of value. This transforms the difference principle from one that divides up goods into one that determines the proportions in which people should work for each other. My second principle is thus as directed toward protecting against subjugation as the first and is only secondarily a principle for dividing up goods. Moreover, I shall argue in the fifth section of chapter 5 that a logical deduction of the difference principle—a goal voiced and just as soon despaired of by Rawls—can be accomplished. For all these differences, it is nonetheless a major implication of my argument that much in Rawls's theory is correct and can be defended on stronger grounds than Rawls presents.

3

All of these issues will be discussed at length in what follows. I offer these few hints simply to give readers an idea of where the theory of justice as reason's answer to subjugation leads. In the remainder of this introductory chapter, I shall first sketch the arguments for five theses that represent the core of the theory and then outline the structure of the book.

1. *Justice is the set of principles regulating behavior that it would be reasonable for all human beings to accept to best protect themselves against the threat of subjugation each poses to the others.* Because human beings are rational, they normally act on the basis of some judgment of what, in light of their desires and beliefs (including moral beliefs), they should do. This is not itself a moral *should*, nor is the judgment a moral judgment, since it includes whether they should do what they believe they morally should do. It is rather the final "all things considered" executive judgment that rational agents make before they initiate action, although *action* should be understood quite broadly to include even doing nothing and the judgment may be unconscious and only implicit in the chosen action. Whatever their judgment, human beings naturally view with hostility any action of another that blocks their ability to execute it. When confronted with such action, they can be expected to demand from the other some reason that they should tolerate it. That is to say, they can be expected to ask for what we normally call a *justification*. And despite what people will accept as justification, when they demand justification they are demanding something that truly justifies, something that supplies good reasons—reasons that ought to persuade—for why they should willingly endure action that stymies execution of their judgments. Principles that truly justify are the *true principles of justice*. We set out upon the search for the principles of justice, then, by looking for the principles that should persuade rational beings to endure willingly actions of others that block their ability to execute their own judgments.

Imagine a conflict between two people who have reached incompatible judgments about how to act, such that if both act on their judgments one will be blocked in executing his judgment and one will prevail. Call this the "outcome" or "resolution" of their conflict, and call the one who is blocked the "loser" and the one who prevails the "winner." For our purposes, it does not matter whether the outcome is already produced, currently in the making, or anticipated. Assume further that both winner and loser are able reasoners, such that each can recognize whatever reasons there are for him or her to prevail and can expect the other to be persuaded if he or she really ought to be persuaded. If the winner can offer no good reasons to the loser for allowing her to prevail, then the winner prevails because she has whatever capacity or resources are necessary to prevail. In that case, one person's judgment has been overridden by another's because of the sheer ability to override.

It should be clear that if the winner offers as justification no more than that she has judged that she should act the way she did, this will not justify. This merely establishes that her judgment conflicts with the loser's and provides no good reason that either judgment should prevail. More likely, however, the winner will appeal to some moral principle that allegedly requires the loser to accept this resolution of the conflict between them. The loser may, in fact, accept this appeal; he may even share the belief in that moral principle. But if appeal to this moral principle truly justifies, then it will *require* the loser to accept the resolution of the conflict, even if the loser does not share the belief in this principle. We cannot appeal to the loser's agreement to show that the principle truly justifies. To test whether the principle truly justifies, we should assume that it is not shared by the loser. We should think of our conflict as one between people who have reached incompatible moral judgments about how to act.

In what follows, I shall look for the conditions of true justifications by considering conflicts between people who offer competing moral principles to justify their desired outcomes. But if we are successful in finding the conditions of true justifications, these conditions will apply with equal force to any situation of conflicting judgments about how to act, whether or not moral principles are cited by either of the conflicting parties.

If some moral principle could be proven true beyond a reasonable doubt, then anyone who disagreed with that principle would be mistaken. If the winner has appealed to that principle, then the winner prevails because she is right, not simply because she can. Otherwise, the two still confront each other as two people with incompatible judgments, and one prevails because he or she is able to. Let us assume provisionally (later I shall argue against this assumption) what most contemporary moral philosophers tend to believe is the case—namely, that no moral principles can be proven true beyond a reasonable doubt. Call this the *assumption of moral inconclusivity.* This assumption does not imply that there are no true moral beliefs, only that there are none we can prove true in a way that would show that any reasonable person who disagrees is mistaken. Given the assumption of moral inconclusivity, no appeal to a moral principle can show that the resolution of a conflict between people with differing moral beliefs is not a case of one person simply being able to impose her moral belief on the other. No appeal to a moral principle can, then, overcome the suspicion of subjugation and truly justify.

Even under the assumption of moral inconclusivity, however, there remains a way in which the demand for justification can be answered. Since every human being reaches judgments about how he will live, the ability of other human beings to block the execution of those judgments poses a threat to all human beings. Because human beings are rational, each can recognize this threat as it applies both to him as an individual and to everyone else. For the same reason, if there is some set of principles that it would be reasonable for all to agree to as a way of protecting themselves against this threat, all human beings can be expected to recognize the unique status of those principles: Though these principles require thwarting the execution of some judgments, they do so precisely in the name of mutual protection against the thwarting of individuals' judgments.

One way of characterizing the uniqueness of such principles is that they would be intrinsically self-justifying, in the sense that complaints against them would be self-refuting. Look again at the conflict between individuals with incompatible moral judgments. Suppose that the loser complains about his fate (actual or anticipated) at the hands of the winner. Given the assumption of moral inconclusivity, the loser is no more able to support his complaint by appeal to his moral belief than the winner was able to justify her action by appeal to hers. The loser's complaint then boils down to an objection to having his judgment thwarted. If the loser wants to gain agreement from others, he must go further and grant the general wrongness of thwarting people's judgments. It might seem enough that the loser endorse any widely shared aversion, so that, for example, he could expect agreement with his complaint about being hurt by granting the general wrongness of hurting people. But people differ in the things they are averse to, and more importantly, they differ in their judgments about what justifies imposing such things on people. What they do not differ in, however, is their desire to live according to their judgments, no matter how different. To be effective, then, any complaint must grant the legitimacy of protecting people against the thwarting of their judgments and thus endorse the principles needed for that protection. It follows that a complaint against such actions is either reducible to the assertion that one does not desire to have his judgments blocked or must endorse the principles on which those actions are based. In either case, the complaint self-destructs. Here, the demand for justification answers itself.

Given moral inconclusivity, it follows that only appeal to the principles that it would be reasonable for all to adopt as protection against having their judgments thwarted can answer the call for justification and thus overcome the suspicion of subjugation. I shall argue at length that the two summary principles stated at the outset of this chapter meet this test. These principles of justice sum up reason's answer to subjugation. But as long as we remain under the assumption of moral inconclusivity, it cannot be shown that we are required to act on these principles. These principles define actions that are justifiable, but I have not shown that we are required to act justifiably. For the moment, the principles are reason's *weak* answer to subjugation.

But the weak answer is far from powerless. These principles represent the only set of terms upon which people who differ on their moral beliefs (or who question their moral beliefs, take seriously the fallibility of their moral beliefs, recognize that their moral beliefs may change, or agree that subjugation is wrong) can agree that their relations are not characterized by subjugation. Moreover, I shall show that these principles correspond to the most widely held and most important of existing beliefs about justice. The theory of justice as reason's (weak) answer to subjugation will show how those beliefs arose: They represent the implicit terms of peaceful coexistence among people who differ in their moral beliefs but who are alike in their vulnerability to, and hostility to, having their judgments about how to live blocked. The principles of justice as reason's answer to subjugation represent an equilibrium solution toward which conflicts over moral principles and beliefs about how to live should tend and have tended.

Later, I argue that the assumption of moral inconclusivity is false, but only because the very principles needed to prevent subjugation can be proven true beyond a reasonable doubt. These principles amount to reason's *strong* answer to subjugation and spell out requirements of justice binding on any rational human being.

2. *Justice has primacy over all other moral beliefs.*   The claim that justice is preeminent over other moral beliefs strikes many as dubious, since justice is a meager notion, concerned with restraining people from interfering with each other rather than with promoting the full flowering of human solidarity; a jealous notion, concerned with dividing up people's shares in the common stock of things rather than with generosity; and a harsh notion, concerned with punishing people for wrongly interfering or for taking more than their share rather than with improving them. So meager, jealous, and harsh a notion seems to underestimate drastically human capabilities and thus is hardly an attractive candidate for primacy when compared to ideals of human flourishing, solidarity, virtue, or mercy. But the comparison is inappropriate. The thesis that justice has primacy over other moral beliefs should not be interpreted as claiming that justice is a more worthy moral ideal than any other. Justice's primacy is strictly functional: It reflects the special moral task that justice is assigned.

From the vantage point of justice as reason's answer to subjugation, we always view moral beliefs in the role they play in human interactions, chiefly interactions in which some people are trying to get other people to act in certain ways by urging them to believe that they are required to so act (or to refrain from so acting, or from resisting some other action, and so on). Call such interactions "moralizing." Moralizing is morality as an active human enterprise. But if justice is the opposite of subjugation, then justice determines generally the morally permissible terms under which people can rightly require anything of others, and these include the morally permissible means by which holders of some moral belief can get others to adopt or conform to that belief. Thus, justice necessarily has authority over other moral beliefs because its task is to determine the things that can be done in the name of other moral beliefs. Justice's authority is not a matter of its alleged higher worth, like the authority of a noble over commoners, but of what is necessary to its unique function, like the authority of a police officer over other citizens. The analogy is apt because justice polices the border between might and right. It has authority over all moral ideals because anyone urging moral ideals must keep to the right side of this border to be moral at all. Justice is moralizing's morality.

It may be countered that this argument for justice's primacy over other moral beliefs only applies under the assumption of moral inconclusivity, since if some moral belief could be proven true beyond a reasonable doubt, then appeal to it would show the resolution of some conflict to be nonsubjugating even if other parties to the conflict did not share the moral belief. But even if the assumption of moral inconclusivity is false (as, in fact, I shall argue), the requirement that moral beliefs be proven true beyond a reasonable doubt if they are to dispel the suspicion of subjugation is itself a requirement of justice when justice is understood as the conditions necessary to overcome the suspicion of subjugation. Even if moral inconclusivity is false, the primacy of justice obtains.

3. *Only reason can require in a nonsubjugating way. If there are requirements of justice, therefore, they must be requirements of reason that are not based on assuming in advance the truth of any unproven moral principle.* The winner asserts that her conflict with the loser has been resolved in conformity to some moral requirement. The loser disagrees. He doubts that the principle asserted by the winner is truly a moral requirement and charges that the conflict has been resolved simply by the winner imposing her moral beliefs on him—that is, by subjugation. It should be obvious that no argument that assumes the truth of the moral requirement asserted by the winner can work to refute this charge, as that only reproduces the conflict that occasions the charge.

But there is a more general point to be made—namely, that no argument that starts by assuming the truth of *any* particular moral principle, stating *any* moral requirement, can work. If, after asserting some moral principle that the loser does not share, the winner appeals to some other principle as the deeper basis for the requirement she asserts, only two outcomes are possible. Either the loser subscribes to the newly identified principle, or he does not. If he does, then the original condition in which the loser's judgment was contrary to the winner's is replaced by one in which they agree. This may show that no subjugation occurred, but only by showing that there really was no conflict. If, however, there are real moral requirements, they will bind even those who hold conflicting moral beliefs. Since we are looking for the conditions under which an asserted moral requirement justifies the resolution of a real conflict, we should assume that the loser does not subscribe to any moral principle from which the asserted requirement can be derived. But then the winner's appeal to a new moral principle simply reproduces the conflictual situation that originally brought us to this pass. It follows that the suspicion of subjugation haunts every moral principle that may be asserted to justify the outcome of a conflict, and thus the suspicion can only be rebutted from a starting point of neutrality toward the truth of all moral beliefs. Suspicion of subjugation forces morality into the arms of reason.

By *reason*, I mean the faculty of rational thought rather than some abstract relationship between propositions. And by this faculty, I mean the capacity to make correct inferences from propositions, to size up facts for what they are and what they imply, and to identify the best means to some end, and, in general, to distinguish what we should believe from what we merely do believe. Note here that I define reason by its product rather than by its process, and I assume that normally functioning rational thought is capable of producing this product. This is adequate for our purposes because this is a book on moral philosophy not epistemology and because a variety of accounts of how reason works are probably compatible with my view so long as they lead to the appropriate product. This notwithstanding, I accept broadly Gilbert Harman's notion that rational thought works by maximizing coherence (*T*, 158–59). Theoretical reason works by maximizing the coherence of one's explanatory beliefs about the world. Practical reason works by maximizing the coherence of one's ends and planned actions with the explanatory beliefs about the world that theoretical reason certifies (*T*, 168). With the proviso that other accounts of the machinery of rational thought may also support the moral theory defended here, I shall in what follows suggest how this account supports my view.

It must be confessed that these are hard times for reason, since twentieth-century philosophers have done much to challenge the claims traditionally made in reason's name. My response to this is the following: Either reason can distinguish between what we do believe and what we should believe, or it cannot. If it cannot, then nothing can, as any alternative must start from something we simply *do* believe, such as the testimony of faith or feeling, intuition or inspiration, custom or convention. From this, it follows that only reason can (if anything can) give us the requirements of justice, because nothing but reason can show us that a conflict between people who hold different moral beliefs is actually a relationship between one who is correct in his moral beliefs and one who is mistaken. Thus, only reason can overcome the suspicion that one person has simply succeeded in imposing his moral beliefs on the other. Either reason can distinguish justice from subjugation, or nothing can. The fate of justice is tied to the fate of reason.

My argument implies, therefore, that the costs of giving up on reason are great. And it implies that those who resist paying these costs should think twice before giving up on reason. There is, however, an even deeper reason why only reason can give us the requirements of justice. I assume the truth of the account about to be sketched and leave it to metaphysicians to prove it.

Philosophers distinguish between freedom of the will and freedom of action. Freedom of the will is the capacity to make decisions that are (in a notoriously obscure sense) one's own—not simply preprogrammed in one's DNA or blindly compelled by one's desires—and to initiate action on those decisions. Freedom of action is a matter of the degree to which individuals or institutions allow rather than hamper the performance of the actions one has freely willed to perform. I maintained earlier that, because human beings are rational, they act on the basis of some final executive judgment about what they should do. Subjugation occurs when a person is blocked in his ability to act on such a judgment by another without true justification—that is, without some principle that truly requires that outcome. Thus, we can say that subjugation happens when a person exercises free will to reach a judgment about how to act but is denied, without true justification, the freedom of action to execute that judgment.

The process of arriving at such a judgment is reasoning. I believe that the best way of elucidating the obscure sense of free will is as the capacity to reason about how one should act and to perform an action *because* this reasoning indicates that this action is what one should do. A being with this double capacity has the leverage over her desires and compulsions needed to count as free her decisions and the actions that execute those decisions. Further, since to be free one must be able to act *because* reason shows an act to be the one that should be done, this implies that such a showing by reason must be sufficient to get the individual to decide and act. And that implies that a free being must regard the conclusions of reason

10

as requirements. A being then has a free will to the extent that for her the conclusions of reason are effective requirements upon her decisions and actions.

It follows that the requirements of reason are not in conflict with freedom of the will. But a person can, either knowingly or unknowingly, act contrary to the requirements of reason. Is he subjugated if he is deprived by his fellows of the freedom of action to do so? If the requirements of reason bind a person's free will without subjugating him and if free will is the capacity to arrive at judgments about how to act by reasoning, then the requirements of reason require a person to bring his judgments into conformity with those requirements without subjugating him. A person who is deprived of the freedom of action to act contrary to reason's requirements is not subjugated, because he is nonsubjugatingly required to judge that he should not so act. No one else's judgment is imposed on him. It follows that the requirements of reason run parallel, not perpendicular, to the lines of freedom and thus do not subjugate. We are free—as the Greeks already knew—precisely because we are subject to the authority of reason.

Only arguments that appeal to reason itself—and only such facts or beliefs as reason can certify from a morally neutral position—can work to rebut the suspicion of subjugation. Appeals by the winner to faith, revelation, tradition, or intuition will not do, since these simply stack one fact against another, with no warrant to show that overriding the loser's judgment in their name is nonsubjugating.

4. *The social contract theory works as a theory of justice because—whatever the understandings of its proponents—the theory effectively poses the question of justice as that of determining the conditions under which social interactions are nonsubjugating.* Justice as reason's answer to subjugation is a member of the extended family of social contract theories. But it is also *a theory of* the social contract theory. It offers an explanation of the philosophical power of the social contract as a model of reasoning about justice. I contend that the idea that justice can be found by looking for the conditions under which the suspicion of subjugation can be rebutted is the inner wisdom that guides—and accounts for the continuing appeal of—the modern contractarian tradition of moral theorizing that was begun by Hobbes, matured by Locke and further by Rousseau, deepened by Kant, and shaken by Marx, and that continues to beckon us in the work of Rawls. The argument for justice as reason's answer to subjugation is thus intertwined with an interpretation of the history of social contract theories—from Hobbes to Rawls—as if it were a progression of increasingly successful attempts to work out the implications of this guiding notion.

11

I emphasize that I do not offer my interpretation of the history of social contract theorizing as an argument about what the social contractarians actually thought. Thus, I do not aim to enter (and even less to resolve) the scholarly debates on the subject. I claim only that *in effect* the history of the social contract is a history of formulations of the question of justice as the question of eliminating subjugation and that—irrespective of what the contractarians thought—this accounts for the appeal of contractarianism and its perennial capacity to come up with convincing answers to the question of justice. This is what I mean in speaking of justice as reason's answer to subjugation as a theory of the social contract theory. After tracking the history of the social contract from Hobbes to Rawls, I shall show that Rawls has much of the correct approach to the problem of justice in place but that his theory is vulnerable to devastating critique because it lacks a theoretical foundation that explains why the social contract is the proper way to arrive at justice. Justice as reason's answer supplies the needed foundation.

I consider the core of social contractarian theorizing the attempt to find legitimate authority by formulating some situation in which people's inclinations and judgments are thought to be in conflict and no moral principle is assumed to be valid—the "state of nature" or the "original position"—and then asking what rules it would be reasonable for all to agree to. Justice as reason's answer to subjugation is itself a contractarian theory because, since subjugation is a threat to all rational agents and no moral principle can be assumed in advance to be immune from suspicion, the suspicion of subjugation can only be rebutted on terms to which it would be reasonable for all human beings to agree, even across their moral disagreements and their conflicting inclinations. And this can work (if anything can) because, as our discussion of the previous thesis suggests, what it would be reasonable for people to agree to (under some suitably described conditions) is not subjugating.

An important feature of justice as reason's answer to subjugation is that it arrives at contractarianism from an unexpected direction. In so doing, it allows a novel derivation of the features of social contract theory. To see this, return to our imagined conflict between two individuals with incompatible moral judgments. Suppose that one asserts his judgment that there is a moral requirement binding on the other and that he somehow gets the other to comply with that requirement. How do we formulate the question of whether subjugation has occurred? With the suspicion of subjugation raised, we cannot start by assuming that the moral assertion is true. Nor can we appeal to some other moral principle, from which the asserted one could be derived, as true. Consequently, we have to answer the question of whether subjugation occurred without assuming that any moral requirements are true ones.

What is more, since the assertion of a moral requirement claims that the recipient is bound even if her desires and judgments are to the contrary, we should not assume that the recipient has desires or judgments supportive of the asserted requirement. She may, of course, but if the requirement is valid, it will override her contrary desires and judgments. Thus, to determine unambiguously whether the requirement is valid, we assume the absence of supportive desires and judgments. Accordingly, to pose the question of whether subjugation has occurred, we must imagine the parties to the suspect moral transaction as sharing a world in which no moral requirement is assumed to be true and as having potentially conflicting desires and judgments about how to act—that is, as standing in a relationship whose basic features are those of the state of nature.

We "enter" the state of nature simply by viewing moral conflicts as conflicts between people trying (consciously or unconsciously) to impose their moral judgments on each other. We "leave" the state of nature when we prove that this is not the case. Thus, the state of nature is a way of thinking about present moral transactions, rather than some imagined pre-civilized human condition. It is the way the present social world looks when the truth of conflicting moral assertions is doubted: Moral transactions appear in the harsh light of the suspicion of subjugation. The state of nature is the structure of potential subjugation "beneath" rather than "before" present social arrangements that comes into view when the curtain of moral certainties is drawn away. And the social contract captures the logic of the solution to the problem of justice—not as an imaginary agreement of dubious relevance to current arrangements, but as the implicit shape of a satisfactory answer to the question of whether current arrangements subjugate the people who actually participate in them.

Justice as reason's answer to subjugation is unique as a contractarian theory, because we do not start by characterizing the contracting situation as an imaginary place and then work back to current reality. We start from current reality and derive the features of the contracting situation from the conditions necessary to pose the question of whether subjugation is occurring currently. Once this question is formulated, we can apply it to possible as well as actual situations.

This reversal of normal procedure has several advantages. First, it encapsulates a theory of how the social contract works to model moral reasoning and to yield valid conclusions about justice. Second, by starting with a question posed about actual arrangements, this route to the contract shows   13 us clearly the present relevance of an agreement that never actually occurs—something that remains mysterious when the state of nature is presented as an imagined past (as in Hobbes) or as simply imaginary (as in Rawls). Third, by starting with a theory of how the social contract works to model moral reasoning, we have a clue to guide us in the proper characterization of the state of nature, the parties in it, and the agreement they are to reach—where prior theorists have generally designed these in the way that struck them intuitively as most appropriate. I call the version of the state of nature that emerges from following this clue "the natural context." Later we shall see that one benefit of such a clue is that the natural context is free of a devastating problem that turns up in Rawls's version of the contracting situation—the so-called gambler problem. With this problem eliminated, we shall see that Rawls's hope for a logical deduction of the principles of justice from contractarian premises can be realized.

Tracing the history of contractarian theorizing, one sees that in the hands of such early theorists as Hobbes and Locke the contract is used to arrive at legitimate political authority, whereas later—say with Kant and Rawls—it is used to reach binding morality. A further virtue of the approach used here is that it elucidates the links between these uses. The underlying appeal of the contract is that it represents a way of posing the problem of subjugation. If the suspicion of subjugation haunts every current moral transaction, then there is a subterranean political dimension of morality. Every moral assertion is potentially an alteration of the relative power of individuals to execute their judgments, an attempt at "governing" one's fellows. A true morality spells out the conditions under which human beings may rightly govern other human beings. The question of whether asserted moral requirements are true, then, becomes the question of whether the governing they aim to do represents legitimate authority or subjugation. It follows that a device designed originally to test claims to legitimate political authority is simultaneously a machine for testing the credentials of claims to binding morality. The suspicion of subjugation is the underground passage that links the political and the moral uses of the contract.

5. *Reason requires that we refrain from subjugating our fellow human beings. Therefore, the requirements of justice are requirements of reason.*   The third thesis stated that only reason *can* give us the requirements of justice. The fifth thesis states that reason *does* give us the requirements of justice. More precisely, reason requires that we act according to principles that all can reasonably accept. This is equivalent to requiring that we refrain from subjugating one another. Since the principles of justice are those that eliminate subjugation from human interactions, reason requires that we act ac-

cording to those principles. The argument for this thesis is surely the most unorthodox and speculative in the book. Drawing upon the insights of existentialist authors, I try to show that human subjectivity is a special kind of fact in that recognition of its nature implies the truth of the normative requirement that human beings not be subjugated. With this, the hostility of human beings to subjugation is elevated from natural fact to rational imperative, and the requirements of justice are, then, reason's own requirements. Very briefly, the argument for the fifth thesis is as follows.

If, as the third thesis contends, only reason can give us the requirements of justice, this can happen in one of only two ways: formally or substantively. Formally, reason would give us the requirements of justice if those requirements could be derived from logic. This is the strategy of those, such as Alan Gewirth, who appeal to the principle of universalizability. Universalizability is the notion that if I affirm that something is true or appropriate in one case, I must—to avoid logical contradiction—grant that it is true or appropriate in any relevantly similar case. If I affirm that my interests should be served, I must affirm that the interests of others (who are similar to me in that they are people with purposes they care about, and so on) should be served as well. Otherwise, I both affirm and deny that people's interests should be served and thus contradict myself. I shall consider Gewirth's argument in detail later and conclude that it cannot work for the simple reason that logical requirements are not moral requirements. If we are required to be just by the law of noncontradiction, then the unjust person, say, a murderer, is no worse than anyone who contradicts himself, for example, by asserting that a bachelor is married. Moral requirements then must be different from logical requirements.

If the formal approach cannot work, all that remains is the substantive approach. In this approach, there must be some fact for which the recognition of its nature implies the truth of the requirements of justice. And this indeed is what I try to prove. Starting with an account of fundamental human psychology that is essentially Heideggerian, I contend that knowledge of our mortality makes us care about how we live our lives in an urgent and ultimate way. We find ourselves confronted with an imperative to live a life whose worth to us compensates for the endless nothingness to follow. Since this is true of all human beings, it is the natural ground of human equality. And it is not just an inclination or a blind compulsion. That a being cares about his life in this way is a compelling reason for him to try to live the life that answers to this care. There is, then, for each person a rational imperative of self-interest. But this is not yet a requirement on anyone else, and thus not yet a requirement that we not subjugate our fellows.

I argue further that human subjectivity is an unusual fact—what it is,   15 is what it is like to be it. We do not get a better view of our subjectivity from our first-person positions; being a subject is something that only happens in the first person. What it is like to be a subject is to occupy, in the first person, a practical partisan attitude. A subject does not just *have* this attitude. Subjectivity is the *inhabiting of* that attitude. It occurs and can only be grasped in the first person. Accordingly, to know subjectivities other than one's own, observation alone will not do. One must identify with them. To identify with them requires inhabiting imaginatively the partisan practical attitude that constitutes being them. I contend that such identifying is a cognitive act, not mere empathy or sympathy. But doing it as faithfully as is necessary to obtain accurate knowledge of the subjects around one constrains one to judge one's actions and disposes one to act in ways that are reasonable in light of those subjects' practical attitudes.

The key notion here—that subjectivity is not captured by the ordinary objectifying awareness typical of observation but must instead be known by being it oneself or imaginatively projecting oneself into being it, in the case of others—has been a staple of European philosophy since at least the turn of the century, when thinkers like Husserl and Bergson made it a crucial feature of their doctrines. It has only recently been endorsed in Anglo-American philosophy, however, most notably by Thomas Nagel (*VFN*, 18). I mention this only to purchase tolerance for the notion, since I shall use it in ways that would probably surprise Husserl, Bergson, and Nagel. I shall use it to argue that a contractarian-like morality is required by reason. I do this by coupling the notion about subjectivity to another notion—namely, that it is a requirement of reason that one direct one's acts to the world as it really is and thus that one obtain accurate knowledge of the situation in which one acts. Since identification is how one obtains accurate knowledge of other human subjects, it is a requirement of reason that one identify with all the human subjects who may be affected by one's action. Therefore, it is a requirement of reason that one reason about one's action as if it had to be acceptable to everyone affected by it.

Put in terms of the account of reason as maximizing coherence, in maximizing the coherence of his beliefs about the world, a rational individual arrives at the recognition that other human beings are subjects like him and that being a subject is something that can only be adequately understood by identification. Accordingly, he identifies with the subjects around him. Since this is part of maximizing the coherence of his beliefs about the world, it plays a role in his maximizing the coherence of his plans and ends. Identifying has, however, the effect of bringing into his view the demands of others for coherence with *their* ends, not as facts to be observed from without but with that particular first-person urgency they bear for those whose demands they are. Identifying with the first-person reality of others puts ends and goals into one's field of reflection with a strange charge, a kind of other-directed valence that eludes one's attempt to render them coherent from one's own individual standpoint. A person can ignore this or try to forget it, but these will be no more successful ways of maximizing coherence than willful ignorance ever is. It follows that he can only maximize the coherence of his plans by making sure that they are coherent from the standpoint of all the people affected by his planned actions. In short, what I add to the notion that reason is a matter of maximizing coherence is the claim that, as one does this in a social context, one encounters a class of unique facts—other subjects—whose nature is to force one to shift the perspective from which one aims at coherence. This means that one can only maximize coherence by reasoning in the form depicted in the social contract.

This transforms reason's weak answer into reason's strong answer. It shows that it is a requirement that reasoning about how to act take a form like that depicted in the social contract theory. And since our reasoning develops by adapting itself to the tasks of knowing the world around us, this requirement is also a natural tendency of reason. Moreover, by so adapting itself, reason is brought to see what I think is the simple truth of morality— namely, that the fact that human beings care about their mortal lives in the way they do is reason enough to allow them, each and all, to make the best of them. Recognizing this truth is discovering that reason requires human beings to refrain from subjugating one another.

In addition to transforming the principles needed to protect everyone against the danger of subjugation from reason's weak answer into reason's strong answer to subjugation, this thesis has other important implications. It gives deeper meaning to the primacy of justice. That primacy turns out to be reason's own authority over rational beings. Justice is reason's own test of the credentials of any moral ideal that is pressed on people against their wills. Moreover, this thesis extends our account of the power of the social contract theory. Where previously I argued that justice as reason's answer to subjugation accounts for the appeal of the social contract, the implication of the present thesis is that justice as reason's answer shows how contractarianism can yield true and binding conclusions about the requirements of justice.

Defending the fifth thesis requires arguing that there is a fact, knowledge of which entails certain evaluative judgments and the related practical dispositions. I am aware that much of modern moral philosophy is devoted to proving that this sort of argument cannot possibly work. That facts and values must be rigidly separated and knowledge of facts cannot entail eval-   17 uative decisions or dispositions is held to be a truth built into our concepts. But if there is such a fact, then so much the worse for our concepts. No philosopher is allowed to forget that Zeno proved that motion through space was conceptually impossible, and Parmenides that change itself was. Their arguments were invitations to refutation. Arguments against them, however, had an advantage that mine does not. No one could seriously doubt that motion or change took place, and so it was evident that Zeno's and Parmenides's arguments had to be wrong. But few who have thought about it believe that there is a fact that spans the fact-value divide, and thus my task requires exhibiting this fact in a convincing way. I shall argue that subjectivity is just such a fact, and that it has eluded philosophers because its nature as something that spans the fact-value divide can only be grasped in the first person. If that is granted, then it will be easy to show that the conceptual arguments proving its impossibility are mistaken. These arguments take as the model for facts those objects that can be observed and fail to include the one fact, subjectivity, that must be identified with to be known.

In sum, I contend that the solution to the problem of facts and values is that there is one type of fact that can only be known by being it (or identifying with being it), and that being it (or identifying with being it) entails a valuation. I shall try to show that this account can withstand the charge that it commits the so-called naturalistic fallacy. Nonetheless, as I have suggested, this is the most unorthodox argument in the book, and I am sure that many readers will be skeptical about it. I ask only that it be considered with an open mind, because my other arguments up to this point strongly suggest that, unless the substantive approach to establishing the requirements of justice as requirements of reason can work, nothing can work to distinguish right from might. For those who remain skeptical nonetheless, I hasten to add that the rest of the argument can still be defended in the more modest ways characteristic of contemporary moral philosophy. For example, those who doubt that the principles of justice defended here are required by reason may still be able to see that these principles match many of our firmest moral convictions and arise from a coherent and appealing way of formulating the test of justice.

The five theses and the arguments for them just sketched are not a capsule version of the book to follow. They are rather a logical digest of the book. They represent in trim and logically ordered form the underlying structure of what will now emerge piecemeal in the course of a more luxuriant journey through the history of moral philosophy. My purposes in presenting this are several. First, although the meandering process that we shall follow henceforth is, I believe, rich enough in historical details and philosophical surprises to make it worth the trip, readers will be aided by a logical roadmap with which to keep their bearings.

But this digest has an even more important purpose: All the issues of moral philosophy are currently in dispute. As a result, each of the steps in the construction of a whole moral theory, such as I am to present here, is likely to be greeted with skepticism. But if one could see how the individual steps add up to make a philosophically satisfying whole, this in itself would count against that skepticism and in favor of the steps. Thus moral philosophers face a catch-22; they need to present their whole theory as part of the argument for accepting the steps, but they can only build up to the whole by arguing for each step one at a time. I have tried to outflank this problem by presenting, as far as possible, the whole theory first. Having done this, I shall now briefly outline the course that the defense of the theory will take in the remainder of the book.

The book is divided into two parts. The first part, I call, borrowing a phrase from Hobbes, "The Science of Natural Justice" (*L*, chap. 31). Chapter 1, "Subjugation and the Natural Test of Morality," begins with an analysis of the Hobbesian and Lockean versions of the social contract theory, which I take to be responses to a challenge implicit in Descartes's philosophy. This chapter attempts to show that the theoretical significance of the state of nature lies in its embodiment of a morally neutral test for the presence of subjugation in human relations and that the wisdom of state of nature theorists lay in their recognition of this as the naturally appropriate test of morality. This is easily missed because of the vividness with which the state of nature is portrayed as a primitive condition existing either only in the imagination or far in the past, and thus of dubious relevance to the present. The point, however, is that the philosophic work that the state of nature is meant to accomplish requires only that we think of it as representing present arrangements, with belief in the validity of moral principles subtracted. I offer a version of the state of nature, the natural context, designed strictly to be understood as the present minus belief in the validity of moral assertions. To understand what would be reasonable for people to agree to in the natural context, I defend a conception of fundamental human psychology and of the normative nature of self-interested practical reasoning. I close this chapter by demonstrating how the social contract represents reason's weak answer to subjugation.

In chapter 2, "Reason and the Internal Social Contract," I pick up the line that runs from Hobbes to Locke and follow it through Rousseau to Kant, and on into the contemporary philosophical world. I try to show that the logic of the social contract theory requires the move from believing that   19 morality is something like a contract between individuals to believing that the social contract is a natural and necessary structure built into each individual's reason. This recognition occurs most fully in the ethical theory of Kant—but I shall show that it is already a clear tendency in Hobbes's theory and thus that a straight line joins him to Kant. In this chapter, I consider the currently popular attempts to establish moral requirements on a rational basis—utilitarianism, universalizability, neo-Hobbesianism, and others—and argue that they are fatally flawed. I argue that recognition of the fact of human subjectivity entails the principle that each should act according to principles that all can accept and thus that the social contract models the necessary and natural structure of every rational individual's moral reasoning. The social contract represents reason's strong answer to subjugation.

Once we have the structure of reason's answer to subjugation, we move on to part 2, "The Principles of Justice," and try to spell out the basic principles of justice—the requirements of any kind of requiring. In chapter 3, "Natural Justice and the Natural Covenant," I spell out the implications of the science of natural justice for the obligations that human beings owe all other human beings independent of any social arrangements they may share with them. In this chapter, I also answer the objection that justice as reason's answer to subjugation commits the so-called naturalistic fallacy, and I present the argument for the primacy of justice over other moral ideals. Contrary to those who think that emphasis on justice slights the value of community, I show that the reverse is the case: Justice is the precondition of community.

I trace the connection between natural and social justice in chapter 4, "From Natural Justice to Social Justice." The question of social justice emerges as a complex variation on the original question of subjugation. I lay out the implications of the science of natural justice for the design of just social arrangements in chapter 5, "Social Justice and the Social Contract." Posing the question of social justice will take us further along the contractarian road, to consider Rousseau and Rawls, as well as the challenges to contractarianism from Marxism and libertarianism. I shall defend a moral version of Marx's labor theory of value and argue that, with it, the Marxian challenge has real import that no theory of social justice can ignore. I contend further that the social contract can be formulated in a way that meets the challenge. I shall argue that Rawls's version of the social contract theory is largely correct. But Rawls's theory is designed to accommodate our moral intuitions reflectively considered, not to arrive at moral principles required by reason. Rawls has constructed his theory by cutting it so that

its conclusions match the edges of our moral convictions, rather than by laying a foundation under it that would enable its conclusions to be called truths. Consequently, Rawls's defense of his principles of justice, lacking solid foundation, is somewhat makeshift and precarious, leaving the principles hanging in midair, easy prey to opponents, and the theory itself wide-open to devastating attack at crucial points (particularly concerning the so-called gambler problem). The theory of justice as reason's answer to subjugation provides Rawls's theory with the necessary foundation and indicates the changes that must be made in his theory to make it stand up to attack. Moreover, on this basis, I shall argue that the general structure of social justice is provided by the difference principle and, further, that a logical deduction can be supplied for this principle. I close this chapter with a presentation of the specific principles of social justice, which I call "the articles of the social contract."

There is a kind of historical structure in these last three chapters. I take the principles of natural justice to be those that would be seen by people whose social structure was simple, even transparent—say, a nomadic tribe or a people only recently settled, such as the Israelites in the latter half of the second millennium before the birth of Christ. It is no accident that these people made use of the covenant as a metaphor for the visible mutual reasonableness of their obligations. I shall argue that the principles of natural justice correspond to the secular elements of the Ten Commandments. I take the principles of social justice to be those that would occur to settled territorial peoples with a complex social structure based on differential access to resources secured by a public enforcement apparatus, who come to see that their social structure is not a natural landscape, but something that they could change and thus for which they are morally responsible—such as were the Europeans at the time of the birth of capitalism in the latter half of the second millennium after Christ. It is no accident that these people made use of the contract as a metaphor for the possibility of taking responsibility for the structure of society. And I shall argue that, while the difference principle understood quite broadly provides the abiding structure of social justice, its particular requirements change as conditions change in history. Thus, it shows the conditions under which a capitalist society would be just, as well as those under which a socialist or communist society would be. I shall leave it to others to determine which conditions currently obtain.

I conclude the book with some suggestions about how the moral theory here defended stands in relation to the other large and abiding concerns of philosophy: metaphysics and religion.

If my arguments are sound, then the principles defended in the third and fifth chapters will emerge as requirements of reason and constitute moral knowledge that issues from the social contract. This will have its full force for those who are persuaded by the argument that reason requires us to refrain from subjugation. Readers should bear in mind, however, that the principles in chapters 3 and 5 also hold on the basis of a weaker thesis: They provide the mutually reasonable conditions of peace among people who are hostile to subjugation, and they spell out those ways in which people who acknowledge that they ought not to subjugate one another should treat each other. These principles are reason's answer to subjugation whether (on the weak thesis) we bring the question to reason, or (on the strong thesis) reason brings the answer to us.

PART ONE

The Science of Natural Justice

Chapter 1: *Subjugation and the Natural Test of Morality*

> Amongst men, however, there is a
> kind of natural justice.
> —Aristotle, *Nicomachean Ethics*

Authority and Reason: Descartes, Hobbes, and Locke

"I think, therefore, I am," wrote Descartes, taking for the thinking human subject the name of God, revealed in the biblical commandment to Moses: "Thus shalt thou say unto the children of Israel, *I am* hath sent me unto you" (Exod. 3:13). In this way, Descartes announced the demise of the medieval worldview and the birth of modernity.

Descartes formulated the ontology of the modern scientific outlook. He rejected the Thomistic-Aristotelian notion that physical things had purposes built into them, essences striving to be realized, and replaced it with the mechanistic notion that matter is just extended stuff and physical objects are just matter in motion. This had the effect of evicting all purposes, including moral ones, from the physical world, and consigning them to a purgatory of uncertain location. At the same time, Descartes realized that rational thought is not an indifferent medium into which beliefs are received, but a kind of testing, an examining of credentials in which only what it found worthy of belief is believed. To think something true is not to swallow a belief, but to proclaim its victory over the possibility of its falsehood. Thinking does not proceed directly to belief, but indirectly via the overcoming of doubt. Thus Descartes replaced the dominant mental attitude of the medieval period, faith, with its opposite, doubt. The implications of this shift are momentous: If the movement of thinking involves overcoming of doubt, then a thinker will resist all authority unless and until he judges its credentials in order. His own reason becomes a thinker's highest authority.

Descartes proceeded by subjecting all his beliefs to systematic and extreme doubt, in order to see which beliefs could survive this pressure. To doubt the things that seemed most evident, he entertained the possibility that an *evil demon* existed, bent on deceiving him even where he felt most certain. Eventually, Descartes arrived at the famous *cogito ergo sum*, "I   25 think therefore I am," recognizing that he could not doubt that he existed, since to doubt he must exist. Even an evil demon could not deceive on this. From there he proceeded to prove the existence of a God who is too good to deceive him where he is most certain. Accordingly, Descartes concluded that, at least regarding those things of which he had "clear and distinct" ideas, he could be sure.

Descartes went on, however, to confess that, God being infinite, "I must not be surprised if I am not always capable of comprehending the reasons why God acts as He does" (*M*, iv, 113). This is an essential ingredient in Descartes's argument against the appeal to purposes or "final causes" in natural science: "This consideration alone is sufficient to convince me, that the whole class of final causes is of no avail in physical or natural things; for it appears to me that I cannot, without exposing myself to the charge of temerity, seek to discover the impenetrable ends of Deity" (*M*, iv, 113). This statement undermines Descartes's argument for certainty from God's goodness. Indeed, God's impenetrability turns Him into as great a threat to certainty as the evil demon. We cannot know that there is not some good purpose of God's that would lead Him to deceive us. And the implication of this is that we can never arrive at certainty by accepting authority beyond our comprehension.

Not only is Descartes's argument for God not being a deceiver doubtful, his argument for the existence of God is (as any argument must be) already based on trusting his own reason and is therefore circular as an attempt to justify that trust. That circularity is the real lesson of the argument: It shows that a reasoner cannot find a basis for trusting reason that does not already presuppose that trust. Descartes's argument for that trust is tucked away in the Third Meditation prior to the argument for God, where he writes that "what the natural light [of reason] shows to be true can be in no way doubtful . . . : inasmuch as I possess no other faculty . . . , which can teach me the falsity of what the natural light declares to be true, and which is equally trustworthy" (*M*, iii, 99). Finding a reason for doubting the natural light presupposes trust either in the natural light itself or in a faculty more trustworthy than it. Since we have no more trustworthy faculty, doubting the natural light must presuppose trust in the natural light, and thus render such doubting nugatory. Descartes, after all, never simply doubts; he always looks for some reason to doubt—be it the possibility of dream or of divine deceit. Doubt itself presupposes trust in reason, and thus that trust cannot be doubted.

Descartes proved that, for a rational creature, knowledge based on faith in authority is indistinguishable from ignorance. Faith is unwarranted certainty—doubt ignored, not doubt overcome. Knowledge is only possible for us, then, if, in the clarity and distinctness of our ideas, we can be the warrant for our own certainty. The human thinker takes the place of God as the ultimate authority because there can be no authority for a rational being unless the validity of that authority can be proved to that rational being. And though Descartes showed this for scientific authority, it is in principle a challenge to all forms of authority.

The social contract theory was an attempt to meet this challenge with respect to political authority. No less than scientific authority, legitimate political authority—the right to make and enforce rules of conduct—must be proved valid for the rational beings over whom it is asserted. Much as authority in the realm of knowledge is indistinguishable from ignorance unless it is shown worthy of rational assent, so authority in the political realm is indistinguishable from oppression unless it is shown worthy of rational assent. But to prove political authority worthy of rational assent requires imagining a world without political authority and showing that it would be rational for people in that world to assent to some form of political authority. This was the contractarian strategy.

The state of nature corresponds to Cartesian doubt in the political realm by representing the world with political authority eliminated. Descartes held that true beliefs had to be built up anew after doubting them wholesale; the social contractarians aimed to build the case for political authority after eliminating it in the state of nature. Moreover, the social contract was the Cartesian solution to the problem in the political realm. As Descartes held that the thinking subject must provide the warrant for her own beliefs, the social contractarians aimed to show that the thinking subject provides the warrant for her own political obligations by agreeing to them in the state of nature.

The social contractarians realized that people do not normally see their political duties as self-imposed, much less as having been agreed to. If political obligations were to be understood as issuing from an agreement made by those subject to them, it had to be an agreement inscribed in the tendency of their reasoning itself, not an actual signing on the dotted line. Thus, the contractarians realized that they had to prove to the thinking subjects that political authority was already theirs, that their reason was the source of its life, that it was what they would rationally choose if they had the opportunity, even though the very factors that made the choice of political authority rational meant that people could not wait to choose it. If political authority did not exist to provide a stable social life, few would reach the maturity needed to be capable of choosing. Thus, it was necessary to construct approximations of the choice in thought, in order to prove the warrant of political authority in reality.   27

The entire exercise of imagining the state of nature is pointless unless it is a way of showing that the choice for political authority is a rational one in the present. Because the state of nature must be imagined, it is easy to miss the contemporary relevance of the exercise. The only way the rationality of the choice for political authority could be tested in a present already shaped by the existence of such authority is by imagining the present without that authority. The formulations of this test by the contractarian theorists, their characterization of the state of nature, and thus their results, were no doubt shaped, even distorted, by their own moral prejudices, as well as by the ideological needs of the new world of capitalism being born around them. Nonetheless, I contend that the fundamental insight is sound, that the test can be formulated in an undistorted way, and that the result is a rational standard to which any system of rules—political or moral—must conform if it is to justify its *current* claim to authority. But first let us consider the most radical of the classical contractarians, Thomas Hobbes.

On July 21, 1683, the University of Oxford held a convocation in which several subversive propositions were solemnly condemned, and the books containing them burned. The first of the condemned propositions was: "All civil authority is derived originally from the people"; the second: "There is a mutuall compact, tacit or express, between a prince and his subjects, and if he perform not his duty, they are discharged from theirs." Among the books burned was Thomas Hobbes's *Leviathan*, published thirty-two years earlier.[1]

Though Hobbes held the first of these subversive propositions and argued as well that governments were established by compact, he did not subscribe to the second. Hobbes maintained that authority derived from the people by virtue of a covenant they entered into to create a sovereign power over them, but that the sovereign himself was not a party to the agreement and thus could not be accused of breaching its terms (*L*, chap. 18). Indeed, Hobbes considered the covenant in its very nature a perpetual and nonrescindable grant that, rather than giving the people a way out of their obligation to obey civil authority, committed them to it forever: "They that have already instituted a commonwealth, being thereby bound by covenant to own [that is, authorize and thus obey] the actions and judgments of one [sovereign], cannot lawfully make a new covenant among themselves to be obedient to another, in anything whatsoever, without his permission" (*L*, chap. 18).

Hobbes did not invent the theory that civil authority was established by compact. The Pilgrims, for instance, landing in Massachusetts in November 1620, had proclaimed: "We do solemnly and mutually, in the presence of God and of one another, covenant and combine ourselves together into a

28

civil body politic." The theory had roots in the medieval coronation oaths
of the Germanic kings, in which justice and good government were pledged
in return for the people's assent to their accession, and in the contractual
relations between feudal lords and their vassals. The coronation oaths were
occasionally referred to explicitly as "compacts," and the term *feudalism*
derives from the Latin *foedus*, which in some interpretations means contract.
The covenants harked back still further to the Old Testament, in which God
is said to have a covenant with Abraham and his descendants and it is
found, as well, for example, that "Jehoiada made a covenant between the
Lord and the king and people, that they should be the Lord's people; and
also between the king and the people" (2 Kings 11:17). But whereas,
throughout its history, the theory had generally been invoked to limit the
power of sovereigns, Hobbes used it to establish the legitimacy of absolute
political authority, not subject to the judgment of the citizenry.[2]

No one took up the Cartesian challenge to authority in the political
realm more radically than Hobbes, who was a contemporary and an ac-
quaintance of Descartes. Hobbes attempted to establish the legitimacy of
political authority without any appeal to God's will, indeed without assuming
any already-existing binding moral obligations. Whereas Locke, writing
about half a century after Hobbes, imagined the state of nature as a condition
in which people were under moral obligations because they belonged to God
and thus could not dispose of themselves or others simply as they wished,
Hobbes understood people in the state of nature to be under no obligation
whatsoever, fully at liberty to take the lives and possessions of their fellows
as they saw fit. In his *Essay Concerning the True Original, Extent and End
of Civil Government*, Locke wrote: "The state of Nature has a law of Nature
to govern it, which obliges every one, and reason, which is that law, teaches
all mankind who will but consult it, that being all equal and independent,
no one ought harm another in his life, health, liberty or possessions; for
men being all the workmanship of one omnipotent and infinitely wise Maker;
all the servants of one sovereign Master, sent into the world by His order
and about His business; they are His property, whose workmanship they
are made to last during His, not one another's pleasure" (*ECG*, sec. 6).

Compare Hobbes in the *Leviathan*: "And because the [natural] condition
of man . . . is a condition of war of every one against every one—in which
case everyone is governed by his own reason and there is nothing he can
make use of that may not be a help unto him in preserving his life against
his enemies—it follows that in such a condition every man has a right to
everything, even to one another's body" (*L*, chap. 14). Hobbes's strategy
was to start with an amoral state of nature, in which human beings are bent

29

only on preserving themselves, and to establish the credentials of political authority from nothing but what is rational for them to agree to in light of their interest in preservation.

The all-consuming interest in self-preservation has two consequences. First, since the state of nature has no binding morality, each person has by default a right to anything he deems necessary to his preservation. But this makes everyone a threat to everyone else. And each person's attempt to protect himself against the rest renders everyone all the more threatened—creating a kind of "war of all against all," the very opposite of a condition conducive to self-preservation.

Hobbes's argument for the inevitable tendency of the state of nature to become a war of all against all is, he admitted, "an inference made from the passions" (*L*, chap. 13), which, he felt, "are commonly more potent than [men's] reason" (*L*, chap. 19). He maintained that people do not merely desire to possess the objects of their current desires but the objects of *all* their desires; thus, their overriding goal is to be assured of the means to satisfy their desires permanently. But since the threats to one's permanent satisfaction are limitless, the goal of desire must be limitless power to secure that satisfaction. Defining *power* as "present means to obtain some future apparent good" (*L*, chap. 10), Hobbes wrote, "I put for a general inclination of all mankind a perpetual and restless desire of power after power that ceases only in death" (*L*, chap. 11). Therefore, "if any two men desire the same thing, which nevertheless they cannot both enjoy, they become enemies," and, in the state of nature, "where an invader has no more to fear than another man's single power, if one plant, sow, build, or possess a convenient seat, others may probably be expected to come prepared with forces united to dispossess and deprive him, not only of the fruit of his labor, but also of his life or liberty" (*L*, chap. 13).

The likelihood of this is enough to make it reasonable for each to protect himself in advance: "from this diffidence of one another there is no way for any man to secure himself so reasonable as anticipation" (*L*, chap. 13). Waiting until he is attacked gives the attacker an advantage, so it is reasonable to strike preemptively. Since everyone knows that others will be inclined to preemptive strikes, such strikes become, in a spiraling fashion, all the more imperative for everyone—even those who "otherwise would be glad to be at ease within modest bounds." Hobbes concluded, "It is manifest that, during the time men live without a common power to keep them all in awe, they are in that condition which is called war, and such a war is of every man against every man" (*L*, chap. 13).

Even when it does not erupt into actual battle, this war exists in the disposition to battle, and thus in the constant presence of danger and the all-consuming need to protect oneself in advance. Thus, there is "no place for industry, because the fruit thereof is uncertain: and consequently no culture of the earth; . . . no knowledge of the face of the earth; no account of time; no arts; no letters; no society; and, which is worst of all, continual fear and danger of violent death; and the life of man solitary, poor, nasty, brutish, and short" (*L*, chap. 13).

While Hobbes allowed that the condition of war may never have existed, he did not treat it as merely imaginary. The war of all against all is confirmed in the present, in the hostile relations between states above which there is no higher political authority and in the dangers perceived within states, presumably due to the imperfect reach of public power. These are evidence that the war of all against all expresses real tendencies in actual people, the real direction in which their passions would lead them were they not impeded by greater power. If someone wishes to have this "confirmed by experience," writes Hobbes, "Let him therefore consider with himself— when taking a journey he arms himself and seeks to go well accompanied, when going to sleep he locks his doors, when even in his house he locks his chests, and this when he knows there be laws and public officers, armed, to revenge all injuries shall be done him—what opinion he has of his fellow subjects when he rides armed, of his fellow citizens when he locks his doors, and of his children and servants when he locks his chests" (*L*, chap. 13).

It might be objected that Hobbes's notion of people's desires as unlimited and self-centered is extreme and that the state of nature would not lead to the war of all against all. But Hobbes could admit that people were often benevolent and limited in their desires. To make his argument, he need maintain only that they were not universally and dependably so, implying that people leave themselves unnecessarily vulnerable if they do not protect themselves against others in the state of nature. That would be enough to get the cycle of threat, defense, and preemptive strike going, right up to the war of all against all.

Hobbes concludes further that the interest in self-preservation results in a "shadow morality," projected, so to speak, beyond the war of all against all. Since war is a threat to self-preservation, the interest in self-preservation dictates, as a "law of nature," that individuals seek peace. This gives rise to an entire "morality" requiring actions conducive to peace that, in fact, turns out to be a full table of nineteen laws of nature requiring fairness and nonaggression and the like. Most important, these laws compel people to try to get out of the state of nature. From the fundamental law of nature that counsels people to seek peace, a second law of nature follows: *"that a man be willing, when others are so too . . . , to lay down this right to all things, and be contented with so much liberty against other men as he would*   31 *allow other men against himself.* For as long as every man holds this right of doing anything he likes, so long are all men in the condition of war" (*L*, chap. 14). Hobbes maintains that this and the remaining laws of nature can be summed up in the Golden Rule (*L*, chap. 15).

These laws of nature constitute only a shadow morality, however, because until people can be confident that others would do the same, these laws do not bind their actions. To act on them would be contrary to self-preservation, which is the source of the laws themselves: "If other men will not lay down their right as well as he, then there is no reason for anyone to divest himself of his, for that were to expose himself to prey, which no man is bound to, rather than to dispose himself to peace" (*L*, chap. 14). Since mere promises will not give the assurance necessary to reduce this risk, the shadow morality remains in the shadows until people leave the state of nature by establishing a sovereign who can enforce everyone's surrender of his right to do anything he likes.

This argument implies not only the need for a sovereign, but for an *absolute* sovereign. The sovereign's power cannot be subject to the approval of his subjects, since dependence on their approval would render that power as uncertain and unpredictable as the judgments of his subjects and thus make it still irrational for anyone to restrain himself voluntarily. The war of all against all is not over as long as people's actions toward one another are governed by their own private judgments and not subordinated to a public judgment that effectively overrides them. This means that the citizens cannot be the judges of whether their sovereign is exercising his power legitimately.

Accordingly, when people in Hobbes's state of nature contract to establish a sovereign, the sovereign himself is not a party to that contract—since that would imply that he could be held by the other parties to its terms. Nor is he even held to be bound by the laws he will make—since that would imply that the citizens could judge whether or not he was acting lawfully. Since it is rational for people to do what is necessary to end the war of all against all, and nothing less will do the trick, it is rational for them to agree to absolute authority.

Ironically, starting from the Cartesian notion that political authority must be justified to the reason of those who are subject to it, Hobbes ends up claiming that the authority that is so justified is a sovereign whose power is not subject to the rational judgment of his subjects!

But reason balks, as Locke realized. Inasmuch as the sovereign is not subject to the contract, and thus to the judgments of his subjects as to how he is fulfilling its terms, his subjects, like people in the state of nature, are unprotected from him, and, as Locke noted, agreement to that is irrational:

"As if when men, quitting the state of Nature, entered into society, they agreed that all of them but one should be under restraint of laws; but that he should retain all the liberty of the state of Nature, increased with power, and made licentious with impunity. This is to think that men are so foolish that they take care to avoid what mischiefs may be done to them by polecats or foxes, but are content, nay, think it safety, to be devoured by lions" (*ECG*, sec. 93). Rather than getting people out of the state of nature, Hobbes left them in it, at least with respect to their sovereign.

If it be countered that, at least, under Hobbes's sovereign, people are subject only to the power of one whereas previously they had been subject to the power of everyone, it must be replied that the sovereign has power equivalent to that of everyone who surrendered their power to him. Insofar as people are still in the state of nature with their sovereign, they are subject to just as much unbridled power as ever, and, given the advantages of centralization, arguably more, as Locke recognized: "he being in a much worse condition that is exposed to the arbitrary power of one man who has the command of a hundred thousand than he that is exposed to the arbitrary power of a hundred thousand single men" (*ECG*, sec. 137).

Hobbes's theory cannot explain why a person in the state of nature should prefer the establishment of a sovereign to the war of all against all. Indeed, nothing in his theory shows how these could be distinguished. There is no reason to assume that the sovereign would be more likely to leave the subject in possession of the fruits of his labor than, say, an ordinary pirate might. The right of the sovereign to his subject's property is the same as the pirate's right to it in the state of nature, only writ large (*L*, chaps. 24, 29; cf. *ECG*, secs. 138, 140).

Nor is there good reason in Hobbes's theory to assume that the sovereign will be more likely to leave the subject in possession of his life than an ordinary pirate would. There are no effective limits on the sovereign's power to take his subjects' lives or his right to judge his subjects deserving of capital punishment (cf. *ECG*, sec. 137). The subject is entitled to resist this, argued Hobbes, but he cannot even, as he might versus a pirate, expect his fellows to help him resist. "In the making of the commonwealth, every man gives away the right of defending another, but not of defending himself" (*L*, chap. 28). Furthermore, with pirates, violence can generally be avoided by giving in to their material demands. Hobbes gives us no way of knowing that the peace thereby achieved would be any different from that achieved by the establishment of a sovereign. Hobbes was quite consistent, then, in allowing that commonwealths established by conquest—where subjects promise obedience in return for the victor sparing their lives—are as much the product of covenants as any voluntarily created commonwealth (*L*, chap. 20).

It would seem that Hobbes could only have offered the *Leviathan* as a more secure place than the state of nature, on the assumption that the sovereign would exercise just that voluntary moral restraint, the undependability of which makes the state of nature lead to war. Thus Hobbes's faith in his sovereign smacks of just the sort of faith that he finds foolish unless enforced by some common power, which in this case would have to be above the sovereign. Hobbes's argument begs the very question he posed. Actually, as we shall see in chapter 2, the problem goes even deeper.

For the moment, it suffices to note that Locke stands Hobbes's argument on its head. Hobbes has argued that there can be no binding morality without the prior existence of political authority to end the war of all against all. That is, without such authority, each person is subject to the relative power of others to get their way, and this is a state of war. But if, as Locke argues, the state of war can exist even after the sovereign is installed, then the state of war is defined by a certain power relation between people, not by the absence of a sovereign. Consequently, the remedy for the state of war is not the establishment of a sovereign but the establishment of limits to everyone's power vis-à-vis everyone else. Since these limits must restrict everyone, they must limit the sovereign as well and thus cannot depend on his existence. This is the reverse of Hobbes's view, in which the sovereign is the condition of the limits. It implies, as Locke saw, that the opposite of the state of war is not peace but justice: "Want of a common judge with authority," Locke wrote, "puts all men in a state of Nature; force without right upon a man's person makes a state of war both where there is, and is not, a common judge" (*ECG*, sec. 19). The establishment of a commonwealth under political authority is the opposite of the state of nature, but it is not the opposite of the state of war, which can exist in or out of a commonwealth—wherever just limits on the exercise of power between people do not exist.

This recognition will naturally incline us more toward Locke's account of the establishment of political authority than Hobbes's. Locke perceived a valid and binding moral law in the state of nature that people could be expected to know. For him, political (or civil) authority is established because people have a tendency to be biased in their own cases, and so there is need for a way of determining definitively what the law requires in individual cases: "For though the law of Nature be plain and intelligible to all rational creatures, yet men, being biased by their interest . . . , are not apt to allow of it as a law binding to them in the application of it to their particular cases" (*ECG*, sec. 124). Moreover, leaving enforcement to the private judgments and efforts of individuals is inefficient and insecure (*ECG*, secs. 125 and 126). Thus, for Locke the sovereign has a far more limited mandate—as a trustee of the power of individuals to execute the law of nature, he is hired, so to speak, to do this job more efficiently, and thus, unlike Hobbes's sovereign, subject to the citizens' judgments about how well he is performing.

But Locke's theory depends on people actually recognizing a single moral law—without a sovereign to enforce it. Otherwise, subjecting the sovereign's authority to the citizens' judgments will render that authority unreliable, and the specter of conflict and chaos that Hobbes took to require a sovereign looms again. What is missing from Locke's theory is a satisfactory account of why we can depend on others to recognize the same moral law. His own explanation is all too closely tied to the belief in the existence of God and the belief that all can easily see what it is that God meant for humanity. This second belief was already dubious in Locke's own lifetime, and the first will no longer secure universal assent today. If people's belief in the existence of moral law and their beliefs about its contents are as variable as their beliefs about God's existence and what He requires, then they are hardly dependable. Without a satisfactory account of why we can depend on people recognizing a single moral law, we are returned to Hobbes's view that an absolute sovereign is necessary to prevent war.

Thus, the Cartesian challenge seems to hurl us into an endless circle: We need political authority because we cannot depend on people's rational judgments, and we can only depend on political authority if it is subject to people's rational judgments. The way out of the circle lies in showing that we can depend on people's rational judgments to hit upon the structure of valid moral authority. To accomplish this, we must show that something like Hobbes's laws of nature—summed up in the Golden Rule—are inscribed in human reason as its requirement and natural tendency. We shall take this up in chapter 2, where we shall see that Hobbes himself believed something of the sort.

There is another implication of this argument, although whether the participants recognized it is unclear. Hobbes took morality to be based on political authority. Tracing his argument, however, led us to the conclusion that political authority could not win the rational assent of its subjects unless it was based on morality, since any other political authority would leave them just as vulnerable to subjugation as before, if not more so. But if morality is the cure to the vulnerability to subjugation, then moral relations must be the opposite of relations of subjugation. This was already recognized by St. Augustine in the famous question posed by him, in *The City of God*, more than a thousand years earlier: "Justice being taken away, what are kingdoms but great robberies?"[3]

The implication of Augustine's rhetorical question is that justice makes the difference between legitimate authority and subjugation. There are two ways to proceed from this. One is to look first for the requirements of justice and then to hold that what conforms to them is not subjugation. This is Locke's strategy. It involves reliance on revelation, and, after Descartes, is no longer satisfactory. The other alternative is to look first for the requirements of nonsubjugating relations and then to hold that what conforms to them is just. Since relations of subjugation are imposed on people against their wills, we can find nonsubjugating relations by asking what it would be reasonable for people willingly to accept. This is the strategy of Hobbes, who took the covenants people make to be "the fountain and original of justice" (*L*, chap. 15).

Being more radical than any of his predecessors (and most of his successors), Hobbes rejected the notion that justice has some prior content independent of what people have reason to agree to. Consequently, he reversed the traditional order of question and answer: Instead of asking, What is justice? in order to determine what all have reason to agree to, he asked What have all reason to agree to comply with? in order to determine what justice is. This question makes sense if justice can be found by looking for the conditions that make human relations nonsubjugating. This clue to justice is, I believe, the social contractarians' fundamental contribution to moral philosophy.

Entering the Natural Context: Doubting Moral Authority

In the remainder of this chapter, I shall argue that the social contract theory provides a satisfactory test of the validity of moral principles, and I shall try to formulate that test. As in the introduction, I refer to moral principles as they are used—not just philosophized about—and thus as functioning (actually or potentially) in the human enterprise of moralizing. Consequently, I understand "testing the validity of a moral principle" as determining whether that moral principle can function in a true assertion of a moral requirement. Looking for the validity of moral principles as used, we will ultimately be led to formulate the valid principles of justice.

I shall not assume that the conclusions reached in our discussion of Hobbes and Locke are true, but take them instead as clues. We shall start again, trying now to build a version of social contract theory acceptable by modern standards. To the extent that we arrive at points anticipated in our discussion of the classical theory, our reconstruction will make explicit and defend the wisdom of the classical theory. The danger in the contractarian strategy is that, in constructing the state of nature by subtraction, too much will be cut away, so that the authority found reasonable will be distorted by the impoverished nature of the baseline against which it is shown to be reasonable. No doubt Hobbes fell victim to this danger. This is not reason to despair of the strategy, but to improve it. Remember that the point of the strategy is to test the reasonableness of present assertions of moral requirements. Once the strategy is formulated for this end, however, we can easily apply it to any conceivable assertion of a moral requirement by asking whether it could play a role in a valid present moral assertion. What I call the "natural context" is designed to subtract from present reality the least amount necessary to perform this test.

Think of present social reality as a series of situations in which people are held to be required, on moral grounds, to act in certain ways. The standard case will be one in which one person asserts a moral requirement to another, but this is not the only type of case. Cases in which, for example, people comply with rules in order to avoid penalties, or have become so habituated to compliance that it is done automatically without thought of the penalty, or comply because the rules were pounded into them as children are all effectively cases in which some people have managed to get others to conform with moral requirements. To simplify matters, we can think of all of these on the model of the standard case, since all are easily reducible to the standard case.

Let us then think of present social reality as if it were a series of moral transactions involving two persons, an asserter of a moral requirement and a recipient to whom it is asserted. By a *moral requirement*, I mean a moral principle stating an act that people must freely choose to do, whether or not they judge that they should. *Act*, here, includes inaction or refraining from certain actions, and *judge* refers to that final, all-things-considered executive decision about what they should do (including whether they should do what they believe they morally should do) that precipitates action. *Judgment*, then, is generally equivalent to *will*, and it includes both self-interested and moral judgment.

Because moral requirements bind the recipient, even against his will, a requirement may or even should be forced on someone who refuses to comply freely. Such force may take the form of physical restraint, violence, or the so-called moral sanctions—intentional application of such painful treatments as contempt, obloquy, withdrawal of trust, ostracism, as penalties for noncompliance. Resort to force in any of these forms, however, is not how the requirements require in the first instance. Uses or threats of force respond to anticipated or actual failures of free compliance with what is already held to be required. Moral requirements license force as their "back-up." They aim in the first instance for free compliance.

A variety of linguistic forms—*duty* or *obligation, right* or *wrong*—can be used in asserting moral requirements. Since we are considering in very

37

general terms how anyone can be truly required to do anything he is not inclined to do, the differences in the connotations of these words or phrases are irrelevant for our present purposes. I shall therefore use these terms interchangeably. Whatever else is to be said of moral terms like *duty* or *requirement*, their meanings must suit them for influencing action without recourse to force. And they do, because calling an action a moral duty or requirement is asserting that a person should or must freely choose the action, so that if the assertion is believed there results a strong impulsion to follow it. It should be noted here that as requirements and duties are asserted in varying strengths, so the *shoulds* and *musts* that correspond to them come in varying strengths and likewise the impulsions to action they generate.

Crucial for our purposes is that an asserted moral requirement implicitly claims to override the contrary judgment of the recipient. Otherwise moral requirements would not really *require*. Bear in mind that the contrary judgment of the recipient is her final judgment when the asserter enters the picture. This is important because if, say, the asserter threatens the recipient with force or penalty for not complying, the recipient may then judge that she should comply. We would still say that she has been compelled to act against her judgment—meaning the earlier judgment against which the requirement was asserted. The same holds if the recipient goes against her earlier judgment as a result of hypnosis, trickery, fraud, or susceptibility to the asserter's power to influence her thinking.

This claim to override people's judgments makes every assertion of a moral requirement an invocation of authority over the recipient. I shall call the authority invoked in assertions of a moral requirement, "moral authority," and I shall call such assertions made by one person to another with the aim of influencing the other's behavior, "assertions of moral authority" or "attempts to exercise moral authority." Consider for a moment what this moral authority is.

When a person invokes authority over another by insisting that the other has a duty to act contrary to how she may judge, the asserter is not invoking his personal authority. He invokes the authority of some impersonal principle, one that holds some action as required independently of who makes the assertion. To be sure, people do assert personal authority, as when a person claims the right to command because of his office. Such cases are invariably parasitic upon some implicit appeal to the authority of an impersonal principle. Even the assertion of personal authority by some individual—a parent or a police officer—invokes the authority of the principle that provides occupants of his role with the right to command. Though such 38 a principle refers to characteristics possessed only by some people (perhaps even only one), it implicitly claims that anyone who possessed those characteristics would have that right. Accordingly, when anyone claims personal authority, his claim can be factored into two assertions: (1) the impersonal principle asserting a right to command for any possessors of certain characteristics, and (2) an instantiation assertion to the effect that he possesses those characteristics. Though the joint effect of these two assertions, if true, is that the asserter in particular is owed obedience, the first assertion is the specifically moral claim. The invocation of authority for such impersonal principles is what is at issue in the analysis of the validity of assertions of moral authority. The instantiation assertions merely tie that authority down to a particular person.

In this respect, claims to personal authority are no different from more obviously impersonal assertions of moral authority, such as, "you should do such-and-such because you promised." When one person asserts this to another, the assertion can be factored into the impersonal principle asserting that anyone should keep his promises and the instantiation assertion to the effect that one person has made a particular promise to another person. This example shows that instantiation assertions work both sides of the street. They may tie authority down to some particular possessor of characteristics or tie a specific obligation down to some particular person based on past actions (such as having said "I promise" under the appropriate conditions) or any other characteristics possessed by only some or even only one person. Here, too, the principle invoked implicitly holds that anyone who possessed the characteristics in question would have the obligation and then adds instantiation assertions to the effect that some person in particular does.

In any assertion of duty, an impersonal principle that could be urged by anyone and that is implicitly addressed to anyone can be separated out for analysis from the instantiation assertions. I shall accordingly treat assertions of moral duty as invoking the authority of a principle that applies to everyone, though they may contain conditions that, in fact, make them apply uniquely to particular persons.

What I have said about assertions of moral duty applies with equal force to assertions of moral rights. I will not try to settle the thorny problem of whether there is a duty correlated to every right (or vice versa). It is evident that any assertion that the recipient should act some way because the asserter (or some third party) has a right to it invokes the authority of an impersonal principle overriding the recipient's inclinations. This principle, which is implicitly addressed to everyone, can be distinguished from the instantiation assertions that give it a particular force in these particular circumstances. I shall speak of assertions of moral rights and of moral duties as, equally, assertions of moral authority.

The assertion of moral requirements (in the form of rights or duties) is not the only sort of assertion that occurs in moral discourse. There are also what might be called moral recommendations. These can take the form of presenting someone with a vivid portrayal of some action or state of affairs in the hope that he will become (or discover himself already) inclined to do the action or promote the state of affairs. Examples of virtue, descriptions of imaginary utopias, and much that is morally uplifting in art work this way. Since such assertions call only for action the individual is inclined to do, they do not invoke authority over him and thus are not part of the moral authority with which we are primarily concerned. Only assertions of moral requirements invoke moral authority.

The distinction I make here between moral requirements and moral recommendations corresponds broadly but not exactly to a classification common in moral discussion. Those actions people are required to perform are commonly referred to as their duties, and those that are not required but urged as valuable are commonly referred to as "beyond the call of duty," and, by philosophers, as "supererogatory." Of duties, we are normally condemned for failing in them, though rarely praised for succeeding, while just the reverse is the case with supererogatory actions. Part of the explanation for this is that the acts that are beyond the call of duty depend in large measure for their value on our freely wanting to perform them; these actions are transformed if they are forced. A person forced to be charitable gives not charity but ransom, and a person forced to be courageous only runs from what scares him most. With respect to duties, by contrast, although it is thought better to refrain from murdering and theft out of a desire to do so, we hold people responsible for refraining irrespective of their motives. Thus, duties can be forced or exacted from people and are commonly the subject of punishment.

If this were all there were to it we could identify duties with moral requirements, and supererogatory actions with moral recommendations. But the issue is more complicated because several distinctions are at work in the classification scheme I have just described. In addition to the distinction between what is required and what is recommended, there is also the distinction between what is required whenever the opportunity is present and what is required in the general sense that enough of it must get done in some time period. Take charity, for example. Charity is not required in any particular case, nor is its failure in any particular case sanctioned, and thus it might be said to be a moral recommendation. But people do speak of a duty to be charitable, and this is more than loose talk. It conveys the notion that there is a general requirement to be charitable in at least some number of the fitting occasions that present themselves and that someone who is not has failed morally in some way. Such a person is liable to some kind of sanction, such as contempt from the normally charitable members of the community. This makes it more than a recommendation.

Charity, so understood, straddles the distinction between moral requirement and moral recommendation. It is not something we are required to do independent of our desires—it would not be charity if it did not reflect a spontaneous inclination to give. But we are nonetheless required to try to become a person who has charitable desires—and this requirement is placed on us independent of our desires. Thus, we do not fail in our duty to be charitable in any given instance of stinginess, but we would surely fail if we were stingy all our lives. Philosophers have noted this strange straddling position of such duties as charity (or courage) and called them "imperfect duties." We do not owe these to anyone in particular or at any particular time, but we owe them generally nonetheless.

For our purposes, what matters is not *what* is urged (charity, courage, honesty, or nonviolence), but *how*. The same ideal might then be the subject of a moral requirement and a moral recommendation. When something like charity is urged as a noble and beautiful ideal with the hope that its appeal will be contagious, it is a moral recommendation and not an invocation of moral authority. When it is urged as a duty, as something we are to shape our inclinations toward, whether or not we so judge (with the implied suggestion that one who refuses renders himself deserving of some intentionally applied sanction), then I take it as a moral requirement, and the assertion of it as an assertion of moral authority.

The justification of moral authority is the most pressing concern of moral philosophy. In the name of this authority, substantial sacrifices may be demanded of people, indeed, exacted from them by the use of force now or the threat of force after. No doubt, people may voluntarily make great sacrifices beyond the call of duty, as well. But they, at least, have the consolation of acting according to their own judgments. Their actions, no matter how painful, are at least part of their becoming the persons they think they should be. In this respect, virtue is its own reward, even if the reward is only a consolation prize. Such reward need not accompany the exaction of duties. This not only makes justification of moral authority pressing but also sets its agenda: Justifying moral authority requires establishing the validity of the implicit claim of such authority to override people's judgments.

How is this justification to be found? Though the two-person moral transaction is the basic unit for analysis, we have seen that assertions of moral authority appeal to principles that can be invoked by or addressed to anyone. Everyone is the potential asserter and recipient of any asserted moral requirement; thus, their authority must be proven to every human being.   41

Proving their authority in this way requires at least proving to human beings that it would be rational for them to move from doubting the validity of assertions of moral authority to granting it. Doing so requires imagining every human being in a situation in which the validity of these assertions is doubted—the natural context—and then looking for grounds that would overcome this doubt.

In the natural context, there is no assumption that people have unlimited desires, or self-interested rather than altruistic ones, only that their desires are their own, whatever their objects. There is no assumption that people's passions will overcome their reason. It is even allowed that people may be spontaneously moved to embrace and desire to act on moral ideals. There is no inevitable war of all against all. The natural context is the totality of present (and possible) social interactions with one qualification: assertions of moral authority are doubted.

What remains is the verbal shell of the assertions, moves in interpersonal transactions. Such moves attempt to persuade that there is a course of action that must be freely chosen. We can call this "moral pressure." In the natural context, we do not subtract moral pressure as such. The point of imagining the natural context is not to test the rationality of allowing people to utter assertions of moral authority, but rather to test the rationality of assent to the validity of such assertions. What we imagine is the absence of belief in the validity of assertions of moral authority, not the absence of the assertions themselves. People in the natural context still have ideas about how they and their fellows should behave, and they still urge one another to act in certain ways by asserting that there is a duty to do so. The difference, to put it somewhat crudely, is that no one believes them. All are practicing Cartesians who doubt the validity of claims to moral authority. Instead, they understand such claims to express only the judgments of those who urge them and thus to lack authority to override their own judgments.

Although the natural context includes many cases in which people's judgments agree, I shall treat it as if it included only cases in which they do not agree, since it is in these cases that we can test the real power of asserted moral requirements.

It is crucial that the necessity of imagining the natural context not be allowed to distract us from its reality in the present. That it takes an effort of imagination to picture the terrain under the streets and buildings of Manhattan makes it no less the real and current natural context of that city. Indeed, the analogy with the terrain underlying a city is helpful. It is a corrective to the tendency to think of the state of nature as a different imaginary city. The natural context is present *under* current assertions of moral duty. We see it not by imagining some other place, but by looking at

42

the place where we are and imagining away our normal grant of validity to moral assertions. All cases of people asserting moral requirements then become nothing but cases in which two people confront each other with conflicting judgments. To see what is revealed when we make this effort of imagination, we must consider, in turn, the fundamental psychology of being human and the nature of nonmoral practical reasoning.

Psychology in the Natural Context: Subjectivity, Identity, Equality, and Sovereignty

Absence of valid moral authority implies the existence of personal sovereignty in the way that absence of valid international governing authority implies the existence of national sovereignty. By *personal sovereignty*, I mean the assertion and sincere belief that one's own judgment about how to act is the highest authority for oneself. I take personal sovereignty to indicate a natural fact about human beings, consideration of which will lead us to the natural ground of equality between human beings and (in the following section) to the natural ground of the normative force of practical reasoning.

A personal imperative enters the natural world with the emergence of creatures like us who have desires and sufficient rationality to recognize that their desires may fail to be satisfied and who have, above all, knowledge of their mortality. This happens because knowledge of our death transforms living into living *a life*. The recognition—however dimly present to consciousness, however concealed by belief in immortality or the like—that we live but once and then no more, that this brief life is not something that *happens to* us as if we existed before and after it happened, but that it *is* us, brings into our awareness the distinction between living well and living poorly and confronts us with an urgent command to do the former. "Living well" here means that an individual lives a life whose worth to him—measured in terms he finds appropriate—compensates for the endless darkness on the other side. Naturally, what constitutes this worth will vary with individuals and different times in history. In one period, it may be living out the duties inscribed in one's caste, whereas in another, it may be fulfilling one's potential or achieving peak experiences. One person may want an active life, and another a passive life. Since it is in every case an individual who knows that he will end and never be again, that individual must be satisfied that he has lived well.

Each person's need to live well produces an urgent interest not only in living but in living some way. As a result, a kind of doubling takes place: A biological individual identifies its being with that of a certain biographical   43 individual. It is no accident that we use the term *life* to refer to both biological survival and biographical trajectory.

Because a human being identifies his biological existence with a biographical one, he comes to have an identity. But this identity is not just a flat logical identity of "I = I." It is a charged existential identity—not "I am who I am," but "I must be who I am." This is because human identity is a response to human mortality. The finitude of our lives casts infinite value on how we lead those lives. Knowing that we are mortal biologically, our biographies become matters of life and death. Since my whole life is my once-in-eternity chance to be, I cannot help caring about how I live that whole life and how it fares in each moment. In each moment what is at stake is not this or that desire or goal, but me, my being as something stretching from birth and death.

Heidegger expresses this by saying, "Human being is an entity for which, in its being, that being is an issue," and, consequently, human being is "an entity whose being must be defined as 'care'" (*BT*, 236–38). At the same time, Heidegger characterizes human being as "being-toward-death" (*BT*, 293–96), which refers not merely to the death that awaits us at the end of biological life but to how that future end permeates our present to shape the way we live from moment to moment. All of this is grasped in the first person. Says Heidegger, human being "is *in each case mine*" (*BT*, 67). In the third person, death happens to people at the end of their lives; in the first person, it is ever present, raising the stakes in everything one does. Human being is not like the being of chairs and tables. To be human is not just to be something, but to have to be something, to find one's being as a job to be done—an inescapable and all-mattering task that is, in each case, for each individual, *my* task. Human being is *mine* in a way different from, even opposite from, the way in which ordinary possessions are mine. It is not mine in the way my house is mine, but in the way my fate is mine—not because it belongs to me but because I belong to it.

I contend, then, that first-person knowledge of our mortality leads us to want to live our lives in some way that answers the endless silence on the other side. No utilitarian formula can give us the shape of this answer in advance. All that can be said at a general level is that, as first-person knowledge of my mortality challenges me to live a life with worth that compensates for the eternal absence ahead, so nothing can meet this challenge unless I recognize it as having that worth. This may take the form of seeking satisfactions, but it need not. And if it does, the value to me of those satisfactions will lie not in their being satisfactions, but in their doing whatever it is that I recognize as giving my life worth. Indeed, it is precisely this that turns pleasing into counting, hurting into losing, and that transforms my satisfactions from mere matter in motion into motions that matter. This sets us apart from other sentient creatures, who to be sure experience satisfaction and pain as we do, but not losing and mattering. It is precisely this, I shall argue later, that brings morality into the natural world.

Let us reserve the term *individual* for the living biological entity and use the term *self* for the biographical trajectory—the cluster of projects the realization of which will make the difference between living well and living poorly for that individual. We should not think of this cluster of projects as if the individual knew them completely in advance. That knowledge is changeable and emerges in the course of experience. But, however gradually it comes to be known, this cluster of projects amounts to the shape of a whole worthwhile life, and thus the term self is appropriate for it. I mean this latter term to convey the notion of a being who is the same over time (my self is selfsame for the duration) and has a particular shape (my self is that of which my self-image is the image). The claim I am making, then, is that it is a feature of first-person subjective experience that each individual identifies his very being with the being of some self (however dimly conceived and slowly emerging his conception of this self is). This identity is not static but dynamic, not "individual equals self," but "individual must equal self."

I use the term *subjectivity* for this dynamic relation of individual to self. Being a human subject is being an individual impelled to be and become some self. Though subjectivity is tied to some specific individual and self, the term subjectivity refers to something that occurs in every human individual. Thus, we can speak of subjectivity as a universal trait distinguishable (in thought) from any individual or self. I shall use the term *person* to point to specific cases of subjectivity. A person is an individual identified with being and becoming a particular self. It is human subjectivity tied to specific projects and possibilities for achieving them. Accordingly, a person has an urgent desire to live some particular life and is the agent by which efforts to realize that desire are organized. *Personal identity* is this dynamic investment of an individual's being in the lifelong project of being some self. The personal identity represented on passports and birth certificates, as well as the identity of the person over time and in the face of physical and psychological change, only matter because a human being is a creature that stakes out the whole of its life as the arena of its being.

The claim I am making is very general. It is meant to describe a universal feature of being human. Thus, it does not describe particular personality types. I am not saying that everyone is interested in achievements or accomplishments or that everyone takes the long view into consideration in making decisions. Rather, my claim is that whatever kind of life a person is invested in, be it a life of activity or passivity, of prudential calculation

45

or impulsiveness, it is some kind of life. Even passive people are committed to achieving a life of passivity, and impulsive people to building a whole life of a certain kind in living from moment to moment. Each is challenged by his mortality and understands his life in some way as a response to that challenge, and thus cannot help caring about the success of that response—however passive or carefree it may be. Nor is the generality of my claim limited by the belief of many people in their own immortality. In my view, such people not only believe in an illusion, but one for which there is no supporting evidence and much contrary evidence. Consequently, I take the widespread belief in immortality to confirm my view: It shows how far people will go to cope with their mortality.

I agree, then, with Charles Taylor and Harry Frankfurt, both of whom argue that we do not only evaluate options against an existing body of desires but evaluate our desires in light of some conception of the kind of being we really want to be. I agree with Frankfurt that being able to determine effectively, on the basis of rational evaluation, which of our desires we will act upon is freedom of the will. But I think I go beyond both in insisting—following Heidegger, with whom Taylor allies his view to some measure—that such fundamental evaluation is inescapable for us as we recognize our mortality. Even those who push such things from their minds live their lives, all the while, as answers to the question: What kind of being do I really want to be?[4]

Human subjectivity is not passive or neutral, but a practical and partisan attitude lived toward the world. I grasp this reality in myself directly, in my first-person sense of the finitude of my life and the infinite difference made to me by how I live that finite life. I can grasp it in others by participating imaginatively in their first-person reality. This is important, because we tend to think of human subjectivity as a kind of object that could be observed in a third-person way. Consider the following.

At the close of an essay entitled "Imagination and the Self," Bernard Williams takes up the intriguing puzzle of how I can imagine that I am someone else, say Napoleon, which it seems I can.[5] This is a puzzle for the following reason. The natural way to describe imagining that I am Napoleon is to think that some ghostlike version of me is inserted into Napoleon's brain as his pilot. But, on reflection, this will not do, since Napoleon had no tiny Reiman in his brain. The creature I would be imagining myself to be would not be Napoleon but Napoleon's body with a brain implant. Let us call this the Frankensteinian interpretation. It is obviously not satisfactory, since according to it I can never really imagine being someone else. Avoiding this seems to require that I describe the process as imagining Napoleon as he is, or, rather, was. We can call this the Leibnizian interpretation. Leibniz

46

is said to have held that someone who wished to be the king of China was wishing only that he (the wisher) would cease to exist and that there would be a king of China. But the Leibnizian interpretation is also not very satisfactory, since any time I imagine historical personages who lived before I was born, I imagine them existing and me not. And I seem to be doing something quite different when I imagine that I am them.

The Frankensteinian interpretation implies that I can never imagine being someone else, and the Leibnizian that I am doing it far more frequently than I think I am. Neither seems correct. Perhaps we delude ourselves when we think we are imagining being someone else, but Williams assumes it is possible and so do I. Williams does not attempt a full-scale solution. He considers the problem at the end of an article in which he earlier argued that we can visualize unseen things, because visualizing something is not the same as visualizing ourselves seeing it. At least, we can distinguish these two, as when I visualize what is happening on the stage and visualize myself in the theater watching what is happening on the stage. On this basis, he concludes that in imagining that I am Napoleon I do not imagine that I am there having the experience of Napoleon, I just imagine being Napoleon. While this avoids the Frankensteinian interpretation, it does not adequately distinguish itself from the Leibnizian one. How is imagining being Napoleon different from just imagining Napoleon existing? How does it count as my imagining being Napoleon without my imagining me inside Napoleon?

The Frankensteinian and Leibnizian views make a similar error. Both take the subjective reality of the one I am to imagine myself being as if that reality were an object to be observed in my imagination. Then there are only two alternatives, depending on whether I imagine that the Napoleon-object is me or Napoleon. If I imagine that the Napoleon-object is me, then it is not Napoleon; if I think that the Napoleon-object is Napoleon, then it is not me. In neither case do I succeed in imagining me being Napoleon. Assuming that the subjectivity of Napoleon is a kind of object predictably either distorts the other (into a Frankenstein) or distorts my act of imagination (into mere thinking of another, per Leibniz).

The solution lies in seeing that subjectivity is not an object to be observed, but a partisan practical attitude taken up. Imagining being Napoleon is imagining his existence in the first person. I do that by taking up (in imagination) a certain attitude toward the features of his existence— namely, the attitude of caring that I take normally toward the features of my own life about those features of his life. This is different from just thinking about Napoleon existing because, rather than observing him caring about those features, I participate imaginatively in that caring. Yet, it is not   47 imagining that some me is inside Napoleon, because what I participate in imaginatively is just the caring that one who was Napoleon would experience. I do not imagine Reiman caring about the features of Napoleon's existence; I imagine caring about them as if I were Napoleon.

What this shows is that human subjectivity is an attitude that an individual has toward his own self, toward the life that he must live. It shows that subjectivity is an attitude grasped in the first person, rather than an object observable in a third-person way. But it also shows (on the assumption that I can imagine being another) that subjectivity is a universal trait, an attitude that each individual has toward his self, but that can be imagined in separation from the particular individual to whom it is attached in any case. I can imagine being another person because, since I am a person, I can separate in my imagination the subjectivity that is tied to the self I must be and imagine it tied to the self that another person must be. This fact—that subjectivity is shared by all persons and thus separable from the particulars of each person—is what enables me to imagine being Napoleon. I can identify with Napoleon by, so to speak, imaginatively separating the subjectivity that is mine from the self I aim to be and reattaching it to the self Napoleon aims to be. This amounts to allowing myself to experience the way in which the difference between the success and failure of his projects makes an inescapably crucial difference—as if my life depended on them.

I say "inescapably" here, because that is central to imagining caring about those projects as if I were Napoleon. Observing—albeit in my imagination—how Napoleon cares about these projects does not quite make it. I am still keeping them at arm's length, not where they are for Napoleon. Napoleon does not have his fate—he is it. To imagine being Napoleon, I must imagine that I am his fate. I must participate in Napoleon's mortality, in that first-person sense that this life is everything that he is and has, that his projects are his only chance to be at all.

The universal first-person sense of mortal life as the only chance to be at all makes the lives that human beings live into their fates. By *fate*, I do not mean to suggest that human lives are predetermined. Having a fate is caring not only that one lives: it is caring about the particular life that one lives. It is living not just in the space between breath and stillness, but between hope and destiny, between the life one wants and the life one gets. This latter space is not neutral but charged, not indifferent but directional, polarized. To occupy it is to want to act to bring about a certain life.

Accordingly, I understand subjectivity as the inhabiting of the partisan practical attitude of an individual toward the self in whom it is invested. Note that the claim that subjectivity can only be grasped in the first person and eludes third-person observation is not based on a dualistic metaphysics, as if subjectivity were made of mental or spiritual substance wholly other than bodies and objects made of matter. The claim I am making is metaphysically neutral. It requires only believing that subjectivity is real, but it takes no sides on whether it is real because it is a property of physical systems or of some nonphysical substance (see *VFN*, 29, for a concurring view).

Because subjectivity is a universal trait, we reach here the natural equality of human beings. All human beings are equal in living their lives as their one and only chance in eternity to live the life they want to live. All human beings (meaning, of course, all those who are sufficiently normal and developed beyond infancy to count as actually rational) are equal in caring ultimately about this project (though the project itself may be one of self-abnegation or self-sacrifice) and in being vulnerable to its unredeemable failure. All human beings are equal in being persons. This equality is a natural fact about human beings.

The desire to live out some biographical life is an ongoing fact about any person, much like the desire to stay alive, even during sleep. It is a dispositional desire evidenced in the person's choices and efforts, much as the desire to be rational is evidenced in thinkers by their efforts to be consistent with their beliefs and to reflect on those beliefs, though they need not explicitly feel or be conscious of acting on the desire. And of course it is a desire that may be quite specific (like wanting to be like Napoleon or Jesus) or quite vague (like wanting to live pleasurably or traditionally).

Because the life one wants is made up of desires (including needs) and their fulfillments, the desire to live the life one wants is a kind of "meta-desire"—a desire for how all one's particular desires are to be satisfied. Though the shape of this meta-desire only emerges progressively over the course of one's life, I shall, for simplicity's sake, speak of it as if it were available in its fully specified form. This form is the implicit target of the meta-desire as it exists at any point in one's life.

To distinguish it from the particular desires out of which a life is made, I shall call this meta-desire an "interest." This is fitting since the aim of the meta-desire is not some particular object or quantity of satisfaction. Its aim is for the person to be a certain self. This is captured by the notion of interest, which derives from *inter esse*, meaning "that in which one has one's being." Note that the term interest has both a subjective and an objective meaning. It can mean the desire for that in which one has one's being (as when we speak of having an interest in literature), or it can mean the object of that desire (as when we speak of protecting financial interests). Since the two meanings are strictly correlative, the second being the reflection of the first in the world, I shall use the term to mean both, though the first meaning is fundamental.

Because people have an interest in living a particular life, the satisfaction of their particular desires matters in a way that is not reducible to the satisfaction itself. This interest bestows importance on particular desires by assigning them a role in the enduring project of a life and thereby assigns all other desires their index of importance as reasons for acting. Accordingly, I call the meta-desire the *sovereign interest*, where "sovereignty" connotes three things: hierarchy, command, and exclusive jurisdiction.

People's desires are organized hierarchically, such that some desires may be restrained in the name of others, and any desire may be restrained in the name of the desire to live the life one wants. In assigning each desire its index of importance as a reason for acting, the sovereign interest establishes a hierarchical ordering among the individual's desires. In this ordering, biological necessities naturally occupy a prominent place, because they are conditions of being any self at all. Nonetheless, a person may sacrifice even such necessities in order to live the life he wishes (say, a hunger-striker) and may bestow upon conditions that are not biological necessities (say, independence or artistic expression) the status of needs. A young writer is said to have sent his poems to Rilke asking Rilke to tell him if he was really a poet; Rilke sent the poems back unread, telling the young writer that he would know himself that he was a poet when he thought that unless he wrote poetry he would die.

The sovereign interest is my real self-interest: my interest in being the self with whom my very being is identified. We can separate ourselves from particular desires, frustrate them intentionally, even work to eradicate them—but the sovereign interest is inescapable; it constitutes the "who" in who one is. Thus, it speaks to the individual in a commanding voice, delegating authority to the most important desires (including needs) so that they, too, come to speak in commanding voices and constitute compelling reasons to act.

Desires are nonfungible. As far as the desirer is concerned, the satisfaction of someone else's desire cannot be substituted for his satisfaction of his own desire. This is a fortiori true of the desire to live the life one wants. Because of the commanding nature of the desire to live the life one wants, nonfungibility is felt most urgently with regard to this desire. Insofar as this commanding and nonfungible desire sits atop the hierarchy of one's desires, giving to each its index of importance (which may be a negative index) as a ground for action, the desire to live the life one wants naturally crowds out any competing claim for determining what actions are reasonable for an individual. Since the sovereign interest is just this particular individual's interest in his being, the fulfillment of that interest is not interchangeable. No fulfillment of any other person's sovereign interest can satisfy it. Thus, at least in the absence of valid moral authority, no reason for action other than those given by the individual's own sovereign interest is a reason for him to act. Consequently, the sovereign interest asserts exclusive jurisdiction.

It is important to note that an individual does not just act on her sovereign interest directly, but on her judgment about that interest, and that judgment is a fallible one. A person might turn out to have different desires than she thinks, or her desires might have more or less importance to her than she anticipated, once they are satisfied (or sacrificed). She might, in new circumstances, come to have desires she did not anticipate. Thus, though I speak of people acting on their desire for the life they want to live, this is a shorthand way of saying that they act on their judgment, implicit or explicit, of what serves this desire, a judgment that is fallible and revisable.

It is equally important, however, not to exaggerate the gap between what a person truly desires and what she judges that she desires. Except in very extreme circumstances, the gap is not large enough for other people to insert their own judgments as superior to hers. This is because a mistake about what one truly desires is different from other mistakes. It is not like a mistake about the number of moons around Jupiter, which could be corrected and confirmed without consulting the mistaken one. A mistake about what I truly desire is basically an incorrect prediction about what will best satisfy me. Every hypothesis about what an individual really desires is always aimed at predicting what the individual herself would (assuming she is conscious and sane) actually come to judge that she desires when presented with accurate knowledge about herself and the world. Accordingly, while it is in principle always possible, and in fact common enough, that other people are able to form better judgments about what an individual truly desires than she is, their judgments are predictions about what she will judge, and they depend upon her judgments for their confirmation. In general, such judgments made by other people have what credit they have only as short-term loans taken out against the individual's own judgment.

But even this misses something crucial. I satisfy my desires as steps toward becoming the self that I (the individual I am) aim to be. And though I may change my idea of the self I aim to be, merely satisfying my particular desires has no point unless I can eventually embrace the resulting life as the life I want as mine. Since mortality challenges me through my recognition of it, I must ultimately live a life that I recognize as meeting that challenge. 51

Ultimately, satisfaction of what an individual really desires must be satisfaction of what he judges that he desires, or it misses its target. Treating a person in terms of desires he does not recognize as his own for any length of time imposes on him a life other than the life he desires to live, no matter how reasonable it would be, in theory, for him to desire these things. It is, for example, often enough the case that a person was mistaken in his choice of a spouse, and that other people, friends or family, knew better. From this, however, it does not follow that it would have been better if those people had selected his spouse for him, since in the choice of a mate, it is not only important to have the one that one truly desires, but also the one that one thinks one desires.

My sovereign interest is, accordingly, not simply an interest in having some set of desires satisfied independent of my judgment; it is an interest in having the desires that I judge to be my own satisfied. That such judgments may be false suggests not that they stand apart from my desires, but that I am in a dynamic process of self-discovery that—as we noted earlier—occurs progressively in time rather than all at once. Thus, the ambiguity in personal sovereignty: It claims the sovereignty of both the individual's desires and his judgment about those desires, even though the two may diverge. Analogously, claims to national sovereignty assert both that the nation's own constitution is the highest law of the land and that the nation is the final judge of what that constitution requires, even though that judgment may be mistaken.

This feature of sovereign interest is intertwined with another. Because we are active beings who live our lives by introducing changes in the world and ourselves, our sovereign interests do not present themselves to us as menus of desired experiences to be passively undergone, but primarily (if not exclusively) as accomplishments to be actively performed. "It is," says Kant, exaggerating the case somewhat, "by his activities and not by enjoyment that man feels that he is alive" (*LE*, 160). Just as satisfying desires does not satisfy me unless I judge the desires satisfied to be mine, so too, performing desired actions does not satisfy me unless I can embrace the actions as my own. This requires not just that they be caused by my muscles, but that as much as possible they be direct expressions of my sovereign interest. Aristotle writes that "their own existence is a thing which all beings alike hold choice-worthy, and which they, consequently, love; and existence, in its highest sense, consists in the manifestation of our inner self in some external act" (*NE*, ix:7, 274). I do not just want to live my life, but to lead it.[6] Thus, in much the same way that it is central to my sovereign interest that I be the judge of my desires, it is of central importance to me that I be the author of my actions. And this latter shares an ambiguity like that of the former, since it is always in principle possible that by being forced to act against my will I will more effectively realize my sovereign interest than by acting as I am spontaneously moved. But such coerced actions cannot really serve my sovereign interest unless I come to embrace them as my own.

That personal sovereignty is not only of desires but of judgments, and that it aims not only at actions but at authorship of actions, indicates something essential to sovereign interests. The sovereign interest is the meta-desire to live the life that one wants, where that life is itself a pattern of desires. Note that *desire* occurs twice in this formulation, secondly in the pattern of desires that make up one's life and firstly in the meta-desire itself. If I am correct about the importance of judgment and authorship, then they ought not to be thought of under the second occurrence of desire, but under the first. The desire to be judge of my desires and author of my actions is not among the desires that make up the life I want. Rather, it is part of the structure of the meta-desire itself. The meta-desire is my desire to author, or lead, the life that I judge I desire.

Since this meta-desire exists for me dynamically in an ongoing process of self-discovery, there may always be a disjunction between my sovereign interest and either the life I lead or the desires I judge to be mine—but the disjunction is always temporary and, more importantly, only to be healed within me. So understood, I shall treat the meta-desire to author, or lead, the life I judge that I desire and the meta-desire to live the life I want as equivalent expressions of the sovereign interest, and I shall take for granted that this is a shorthand way of speaking of the implicit target of an interest whose content is revealed only progressively.

Nothing is said here about the kind of life aimed at by a sovereign interest, nor about the objects of the particular desires that make it up. Sovereign interest is not the same as selfishness or egotism, since the desires that are sovereign may be for the well-being of others. It may take the form of wanting to live without a plan. It does not presuppose that people are prudential rather than impulsive, only that even wanting to live impulsively is also wanting a certain kind of life. Likewise, the desires that make up a sovereign interest are not necessarily unlimited, nor does everyone claiming personal sovereignty imply that people will live in hostile relations, or even that their desires will conflict. Moreover, the desire to live the life one wants may be unreasonable, either in the sense of being more than the world can possibly provide (such as a desire to live forever) or in the sense of being for mutually exclusive ends (such as desiring both adventure and security). But as it is a desire aimed at the real world, we can take it as desiring the closest possible approximation of the life desired.

I take it then that in the natural context, in the absence of moral authority, people will act on their judgment of what is their sovereign interest. They will be moved above all to become the selves they aim to be, as they judge this. They will treat that task as their highest imperative and act on it as far as their power permits. They will act as if they thought themselves personal sovereigns, above whom no higher jurisdiction exists. The absence of moral authority implies the existence of personal sovereignty in the way that the absence of international governing authority implies the existence of national sovereignty. There was more than met the eye in the fact that both Hobbes and Locke likened the relations between people in the state of nature to the relations among nations (*L*, chap. 13; *ECG*, sec. 14).

Reason in the Natural Context: The Nonmoral "Ought" and the Personal Imperative of Self-Interest

Because individuals have sovereign interests, they have an interest in knowing how to live the life they desire. Thus they reason about the conditions in which they live. This is theoretical reason. And they reason about how to act in those conditions. This, in the absence of valid moral authority, is self-interested practical reason—though self-interest here means whatever serves the person's interest in becoming the self he wants to be. This implies that the nature of human existence impels us to question and test the beliefs upon which we act: "I am, therefore, I doubt" is also true, which shows that our Cartesian starting point has its roots in the nature of human subjectivity. Moreover, that human subjectivity is a first-person partisan practical attitude explains why self-interested practical reasoning yields normative—albeit, nonmoral—conclusions about what a person ought to do. I shall argue that personal identity has a normative structure, such that persons are not only inclined to make self-interested judgments about what they ought to do, but such that some of those judgments are true. Consider, first, why this nonmoral "ought" is something of a mystery.

Individuals engaging in self-interested practical reasoning commonly arrive at nonmoral normative conclusions of the sort: "I ought to (or should or must) take my pills." That practical reasoning can come up with nonmoral normative conclusions is mysterious because reasoning is normally identified with determining what is the case, what is an effective means to what, and so on—that is, with theoretical reason. So understood, the business of reasoning proper is done when it has been determined that taking my pills will, compared with the alternatives, most effectively prevent illness. Reason, it is usually thought, cannot tell me that I ought to prevent illness, and so it cannot go the further step and conclude that I ought to take my pills. To reach this conclusion, there must be some nonrational thing, a desire or feeling or inclination to stay healthy, and practical reason is simply theoretical reason in the service of this nonrational thing. Reason, said Hume, is the slave of the passions.

On this view, the conclusion that I should take my pills is a shorthand form for the conjunction of two theoretical statements: "I desire to stay healthy" and "Taking the pills is the most effective means thereto." But this does not dispel the mystery, since it is not clear how two theoretical claims about what is the case can add up to a practical claim about what should be. Either I am compelled to act on the desire to be healthy, or I am not; that is, either I have a choice as to whether I act on it, or I do not. If I have a choice, then, from the existence of the desire it cannot follow that I should do what is most effective for it, unless it has already been established as true that I should act on the desire. And if I have no choice, then it is pointless to tell myself that I should take my pills (or even that I must), since merely discovering that they are the most effective means to staying healthy will suffice.

Nor will it do to reply that the ought is a counsel of consistency—that is, that I ought to choose means consistent with my choice of ends. For if the question is only one of consistency, then I can satisfy it equally well by giving up the end. Then the ought amounts to be advice: "Either take your pills or give up wanting to be healthy," and this still leaves open whether I ought to take my pills. On this view, what I ought to do is not take my pills but be consistent—which at very least is something different from what the practical conclusion seemed to be. Moreover, it is not at all obvious that I ought to be consistent. For example, if I have some end that I wish I did not have, or one that I even suspect I should not have, then my best course of action may be to avoid the means to it or even to choose actions that will frustrate my achievement of it. Again, then, unless I ought to adopt the end, it does not follow that I ought to adopt the means to it, and so the practical conclusion remains a mystery.

Nor is my desire to be healthy sufficient to carry the weight of this ought. My desires are just facts, any one of which I might ignore. Indeed, philosophers have questioned whether one's desires ever must be reasons to act. Since one can regard any of one's desires with indifference—indeed, even take its existence as reason for acting against its satisfaction—there appears to be nothing logically impossible about being indifferent or even antipathetic to one's desires. This logical point must be granted. There is nothing logically self-contradictory in the idea of someone regarding all his desires as facts to be ignored. But for the purposes of moral philosophers, who are not concerned, as logicians are, with what is true in any possible world, but with what is true in this actual one, the issue is not settled by logic. It is a question of the kind of creatures we are in fact. We could only ignore our desires if powered by a desire, the desire to live a certain life. We could not ignore our particular desires without embracing the meta-desire to live a life of indifference to our particular desires. Understood, then, as a human undertaking rather than as a proposition, even ignoring desires is pursuing a sovereign interest. Because we are bent on realizing our sovereign interests, our practical reasoning is naturally in the service of our sovereign interests, as Kant recognized. "Man is a being of needs," wrote Kant, and thus "his reason . . . has an inescapable responsibility" (*CPR*, 61).

But even this suggests too great a divide between my practical reason and my sovereign interest, as if the former were a tool used by the latter. Practical reason cannot be a tool, since using tools is already a product of practical reason. Practical reasoning is not something my sovereign interest uses; it is my sovereign interest's coherent voice translating itself into possible actions in the world. The ought of practical reasoning is the imperative tone in which my sovereign interest speaks. Having a sovereign interest, I cannot help reasoning practically, and I cannot help experiencing the conclusions of that reasoning in the first person as commands. I live the ought of practical reason before I reflect on it.

Because reasoning can be expressed in propositions, it is all too easy, particularly for philosophers, to fall into thinking that reasoning is just operating on and moving among propositions. Then reason tends to look like a neutral tool, and worse, to be the enemy of the warmer, fleshier aspects of life. But even the most impulsive person reasons. As soon as he judges which among various alternatives will best realize his desire of the moment— a judgment he may make instantly and wordlessly—he reasons. Having a sovereign interest, one cannot look at the world without reasoning, without transforming the things in it into means or obstacles to one's ends, the spaces in it into paths and distances. One cannot help but aim to maximize the coherence of one's beliefs about the world with one's goals and plans. The practical reasoning that operates on propositions is the linguistic distillate of this more primitive process. But since the ought lives in that primitive process, it cannot be found in the linguistic distillate. This is why the ought has proven so elusive to philosophers.

I live the ought of practical reason in the first person because it is derived from an even more urgent imperative, which I live in the first person: the must of sovereign interest. If my account of personal identity is correct, then at any given moment a person lives in the tension between the individual she is and the self she must be. From the outside, in the third person, a human being is just what she is, so many molecules and so on. Fulfilling her sovereign interest looks like adding on to what she already is. There is no imperative to add. From the inside, in the first person, however, a human being lives her being as if it were just out ahead of her. Her self stands before her as herself and as a task to be accomplished. This fact gives personal identity a normative structure. In the first person, fulfilling my sovereign interest is not adding to what I am, it is becoming what I am. That my sovereign interest is identified with my being, my inter esse, gives it imperative force. What stands to me as the very condition of my being is what I must do or bring about. Writes Nietzsche in *The Gay Science*: "What does your conscience say?—You must become who you are."[7]

The notion that we live the ought of practical reason in the first person dovetails with the assumption about the relation between free will and reason voiced in the introduction. There I claimed that free will is the capacity to reason about how one should act and then to perform an action because this reasoning dictates that the action is, all things considered, what one should do. I maintained further that this means that to have free will a being must regard the conclusions of his reasoning as sufficient to move him to action, and thus he must regard those conclusions as requirements. But then such reasoning cannot be something that a free being freely uses since doing something freely already involves doing it because it is judged required by reason. Rather, reasoning is being free. The notion of human beings as reasoning beings must be understood in a strong sense: Reasoning is our being. "It is," wrote Aristotle, "his reason that really constitutes each man's self" (*NE*, ix:8, 278). What I recognize as me is just this inner reasoning about what to do and what to believe, and I am free insofar as I can engage in this reasoning and be required to act on its conclusions. At the same time, however, as this me is vulnerable to the requirements of reason, I may also fail to act on them. They are at once necessities and not necessitated for me. This, I contend, is because, as a subject, I live in the tension between the biological life that I have and the biographical life that I must live. Because I must live this life, the conclusions of my practical reasoning are necessities for me; and because I live in a tension with that life, live it as a task at which I may fail, they are not necessitated.

Here I think is the solution to one of the puzzling features of practical talk. When we attempt to distinguish between "must" and "should" and "ought," it becomes evident that the first of these is the most enigmatic of the three. The reason is that "must" seems to signify necessity, that over which I have no choice. And yet when used in prudential (or moral) talk, "You must take your pills" (or "You must tell the truth"), it is directed to things that it is within one's freedom to avoid. I think the explanation of this is that, in the first person, human beings confront imperatives that are at once necessary and subject to choice. They are necessary because they are the conditions of their very being, and they are subject to choice because, in the first person, human beings experience their being as a task to be accomplished and thus one that they may fail to take on.

The must of sovereign interest is the natural imperative for persons. The ought of self-interested practical reason is a derivative of the must of sovereign interest. The must is a particularly unyielding imperative. It is not, as are shoulds and oughts, restricted to what one can do. Philosophers normally hold that 'ought' implies 'can': It is only true that one ought to do something if one can do it. If one never could do it, it was never true that one ought to have done it. But the must of sovereign interest is not like that. Whether or not he can, a person must realize his sovereign interest in the sense that, if he fails, no matter what the cause, he fails at being in the distinctive human sense: He fails to be the self he must be. When this unyielding must translates itself into actions within the power of the individual person, it speaks in the milder tones of should and ought. The ought of practical reason is the must of sovereign interest applied to the alternatives actually possible for the person whose sovereign interest is at stake.

Practical reasoning yields an ought because it is reasoning that occurs within the inner tension that characterizes first-person human being as mine—my own being that must be realized. Since that "mine-ness" signifies not that it belongs to me but that I belong to it, I find myself owned by my interest in being the person I aim to be and owing it service. "We are," writes Bishop Butler, "in a peculiar manner . . . intrusted with ourselves" (*FS*, 194). Since my practical reasoning is just the way I line up my options in order to accomplish this service, this "owing," by which I owe myself the task of becoming myself is the source of the ought of practical reasoning.

Here it is worth pausing to note that even disinterested theoretical reason yields conclusions with normative force. It tells me what I ought or should or even must believe. This ought also has its source in my sovereign interest. Since I cannot reason about how to act in the world without correct beliefs about the world, the reason that is the voice of my sovereign interest is theoretical in addition to being practical. Consequently, all reasoning—theoretical and practical—carries an ought with it, which cannot be found among its propositions. It is found rather in the imperative tones in which my sovereign interest speaks, tones audible only in the first person. To engage in reasoning—theoretical or practical—is to feel the pull of that ought in the first person, commanding me about what to believe or what to do. The difference between theoretical and practical reason is that practical reason is tied to my particular sovereign interest and thus casts its ought only toward me, whereas theoretical reason is tied to the interest in knowing the world that I share with all other rational creatures and accordingly casts its ought more broadly. Practical reasoning, then, is inherently subjective, commanding only me. By contrast, theoretical reasoning is inherently objective or aims to be. Anyone seeing it to be correct will be pulled toward believing what it indicates he ought to believe. In both cases, human subjectivity is the natural ground of the ought—and it has proven elusive to philosophers because human subjectivity can only be known in the first person. It vanishes when we look for it with the third-person eye of observation.

So far, it might seem that the ought of self-interested practical reason is a brute fact, a kind of compulsion that grabs hold of the reasoning faculties of a human being once she learns of her mortality and its implications. There is truth in this, but if that were all there were, then self-interested practical reason would still be the slave of the passions and we could still ask whether an individual ought to do what her practical reason tells her she ought to do. If the ought is just a brute fact, it is blind and thus carries no warrant with it. Our thinking we ought to pursue our sovereign interests would no more entail that we really and truly ought to, than some people's thinking the world owes them a living entails that they are truly owed one.

But the ought of practical reasoning is more than a brute fact, because it derives from the must of sovereign interest. And the must of sovereign interest represents a true first-person nonmoral normative claim: "I must realize my sovereign interest" is—in the absence of valid moral claims—necessarily true, though it is true only for the individual whose sovereign interest it is. "I must realize my sovereign interest" is true because—in the absence of valid moral authority—a rational human being, who knows he has a once-in-eternity chance to live the life he wants to live, who cares ultimately about being the self he aims to be, must bring that self into being or fail in an ultimate way at being at all. *Must is now's answer to never again.* The infinite darkness and silence on the other side of my death makes how I live on this side so important to me as to give realizing my sovereign interest the unyielding imperative force of must, and being so important to me, that imperative is true.

Because personal identity is dynamic, each individual human being finds in himself a true nonmoral normative claim: "I must realize my sovereign interest." I call this *the personal imperative of self-interest*, or, for short, *the personal imperative*. The personal imperative of self-interest bestows normative force on the particular desires that compose my sovereign interest. That this imperative is true shows that the normative structure of personal identity, though itself a natural fact about human subjects, is the   59 ground of normative judgments of practical reason that are themselves true, not mere brute facts. "I must realize my sovereign interest," entails "I ought to promote my sovereign interest as far as possible." And from the truth of the latter follow the particular (accurately drawn) conclusions of self-interested practical reason and their truth.

That a being cares ultimately about whether or not it lives the life it wants to live, that it recognizes that it stands before a finite lifespan in which success in that project must register or never happen, is—in the absence of valid moral authority—reason enough to make it true that he must succeed in that project. But, as the truth of the personal imperative is a truth heard and verified only in the first person, so the accurate conclusions of self-interested practical reason are inherently subjective—true only for the individual whose self-interest it is.

Here it will be helpful to distinguish my claim from one to which it bears surface resemblance. In *Reason and Morality*, Alan Gewirth argues that human action has a normative structure, in that every prospective agent (that is, every being like us that acts for purposes or expects to) must affirm a "deontic judgment" to the effect that she has rights to the conditions of effective action, namely, rights to freedom and minimum well-being (*RM*, 48–103). Gewirth goes on to argue that, via the logical requirement of universalizability, every prospective agent must affirm that every prospective agent has such rights. In chapter 2, I shall take up this feature of Gewirth's theory and show that it does not, contrary to his claims, establish a moral requirement to respect the rights of others to freedom and well-being. For the present, however, I want to point out how the personal imperative, "I must realize my sovereign interest," a first-person normative claim like Gewirth's deontic judgment, is profoundly different from the latter; similarly, what I mean by the normative structure of personal identity is profoundly different from Gewirth's notion of the normative structure of action.

The most important difference is that Gewirth claims that agents must make a deontic judgment addressed to others, whereas I hold that "I must realize my sovereign interest" is addressed only to the individual whose sovereign interest it is. This is not to say that Gewirth's deontic judgment is moral while the personal imperative is nonmoral. Both are nonmoral. Gewirth says of his deontic judgment that it is "not moral but rather prudential." He contends that a prospective agent must make the nonmoral claim that others owe him noninterference with his "freedom and well-being as his prudential due" (*RM*, 71). Gewirth starts his argument for this contention by claiming that every agent must affirm the goodness of the purposes for which he acts, and thus the goodness of his action and the goodness of the conditions—freedom and well-being—necessary for his action (*RM*,

48–51, 57). This is a purely evaluative judgment, which says nothing about the behavior of others, and I have no quarrel with this part of Gewirth's argument. But Gewirth goes on to claim that this necessary evaluative judgment entails a deontic judgment addressed to others: "the agent's statement, 'My freedom and well-being are necessary goods [to me],' entails his further statement, 'I have rights to freedom and well-being [from others]'" (*RM*, 64).

I shall deal only briefly with Gewirth's defense of this entailment, since I am more concerned to distinguish my claim from his than to refute his. Nonetheless, it is worth seeing that his claim becomes implausible at the point at which it steps beyond mine. One way in which Gewirth argues for the entailment is this: A prospective agent must affirm that freedom and well-being are necessary goods. Given this, says Gewirth, an agent who did not affirm that he had rights to freedom and well-being would be granting that it was "permissible that other persons interfere with or remove his freedom and well-being," and that would show that "he regards his freedom and well-being with indifference or at least as dispensable," and that would deny that these were necessary goods. Such an agent "would be in the position of affirming and denying that his freedom and well-being are necessary goods" (*RM*, 80–81).

But this argument is not persuasive. Suppose a starving person, minutes from death, recognizes that food is a necessary good for her. Must she affirm that others owe her food? Must she go beyond asserting that she needs food in the strongest terms, to asserting that she has a right to it? Would it follow from her not asserting that she has a right to that food, that she was accepting that she does not need it, that she was regarding food "with indifference or at least as dispensable"? Needless to say, such a starving person might affirm that she had a right to food, and if it were likely to be believed, it would probably be smart of her to do so. And she will surely (perhaps even necessarily) want others to act as if she had a right to food. But none of this requires her to affirm that she has that right. And none of it shows that not affirming that she has that right implies that she is indifferent to whether or not she eats. Likewise, that freedom and well-being are necessary goods for me implies that it is necessary for me that others not interfere with those goods or that it is necessary for me that others act as if they owed me that noninterference. None of this requires me to affirm that they do owe it to me or means that my refusal to affirm that they owe it is tantamount to my regarding their interference with indifference. After all, people in Hobbes's state of nature regard interference with their freedom and well-being with anything but indifference, but they make no claim that they are owed non-interference. Surely this is logically possible.

Like Gewirth, then, I contend that each individual makes a normative judgment about his own purposes; but unlike Gewirth, I take that judgment to be directed only to that individual and assert nothing about what anyone else ought to do. But there is another difference. I contend that the personal imperative of self-interest is true, and derivatively, the accurately drawn conclusions of self-interested practical reason are true as well—at least in the absence of valid moral authority. Gewirth does not and cannot claim that his deontic judgment is true. It is rather something that an actor is committed to as a feature of his very action. As such, it is a brute fact, a kind of compulsion that grabs hold of the reasoning faculties of a prospective agent. But then the ought in Gewirth's deontic judgment is just a brute fact—it is blind and thus carries no warrant with it. Thus, by the normative structure of action, Gewirth means that acting commits a person to other-directed normative judgments as a matter of sheer inescapable fact. By the normative structure of personal identity, I mean that being a person commits one to self-directed normative judgments as a matter of fact while at the same time providing warrant for the truth of those judgments.

This account of the normative structure of personal identity has two further virtues. First, it explains the paradoxical fact that I can have duties to myself. We normally think that whoever is owed a duty has the right to release the ower from performance. If I owed a duty to myself, accordingly, I would be free to release myself from it, and thus it would lack the binding quality that is a necessary feature of duty. But I can have a duty to myself because I am a biological individual identified with becoming a biographical self as the very condition of my being. As such, it is true that I must realize my sovereign interest and that I ought to promote my sovereign interest as far as possible. But, then, it is true, as well, that I have duties—from which I cannot release myself though I can fail to perform them—to do those things in my power that are necessary to realize my sovereign interest.

Second, this account explains the point of three of Plato's four "cardinal" virtues. Leaving the virtue of justice aside for the moment (we shall return to it at the end of this chapter), the three are prudence (the disposition to weigh equally all the moments of my whole life in judging how to act), temperance (the disposition to weigh appropriately all of my desires in judging my plan of life, rather than allow any particular desire to overpower the rest), and fortitude (the strength to carry out these judgments in the face of adversity). What is curious about these virtues is that they do not seem to be among the pattern of desires that constitute the life that everyone desires to live. Thus, they seem to reflect particular preferences for one kind of life over others and consequently to be disqualified from the exalted status of "the virtues" for want of universality. Their universality, however, lies in

62

the fact that they are capacities (or, as the word *virtue* suggests, powers) that serve the meta-desire to lead whatever life one judges that one desires. My sovereign interest commands these as duties, though not as moral duties.

In the previous section, I argued that human beings are persons, and thus as a matter of psychological fact, they find themselves pursuing a sovereign interest that is commanding, exclusive, and nonfungible and that, in the absence of valid moral authority, gives them compelling reasons for acting. In the present section, I have argued that as persons, it is true—again, in the absence of valid moral authority—that they should act on the practical reasons emanating from their sovereign interests, since this is their chance at being the selves they must be and time is running out. Accordingly, the natural context is a realm of personal sovereignty because, in it, people will be moved above all to act according to the judgments about their sovereign interest that issue from their practical reasoning—and, for each person, it will be true that he should.

The Evil Demon in the Natural Context:
The Suspicion of Subjugation

Picture now current social reality with all the cases in which people are confronted with moral requirements, either in the form of assertions voiced by one person to another or in the form of laws, customs, conditioning, or indoctrination. Think of all of these latter cases as if they were actually voiced assertions, since they could be at any time and almost surely were at some time. Because we want to test whether these asserted moral requirements really require, imagine that they are asserted to people whose own sovereign judgments on how to act are contrary to the requirements asserted. Since the requirements are, if valid, appropriately backed up with force, remember that such force, in the form of some threatened penalty, always stands in the wings. If, to this picture of current social reality, we add doubt about the validity or truth of the moral requirements asserted, we are "in" the natural context.

The natural context is the context of morality because it is the framework to which we are reduced when we doubt morality, and thus it is the framework into which morality returns if the doubt is answered. Moreover, it is the natural context of morality because it is the setting within which the practice of morality occurs and matters: It indicates where the balance that morality tips is set and thus what hangs in the balance. It provides a medium independent of morality in which the weight of moral claims must be measured. But in so doing, it sets questions that any morality must answer, tests that a morality must pass. As a result, looking at morality as an undertaking inserted in the natural context opens the way to moral knowledge. But not until the evil demon appears.

It is of great importance here to bear in mind that the natural context is not imaginary. To be sure, since it is a world without belief in the validity of moral authority and since we know of no society without this belief, it can only be conceived imaginatively. But it also takes an effort of imagination to think, say, of the normal pattern of natural growth that is everywhere deflected by accident, disease, or idiosyncrasy, or of the forward thrust of the earth's flight through space that is everywhere deflected by the sun's gravity. In each of these cases an effort of imagination is needed not because the object of thought is imaginary, like Cinderella's carriage, but because as it exists in actuality it is altered by forces that must be eliminated in thought to grasp it. The trajectory of human behavior in the absence of moral authority is no less real than the trajectory of the earth's forward motion in the absence of deflecting forces.

Imagining the natural context requires picturing social reality as made up of many separate individuals striving to realize their sovereign interests (as they judge them) as fully as possible, coexisting loosely next to one another and even bobbing up and down relative to one another, like the separate molecules that make up a liquid. We may think of their relative up-and-down positions as representing the relative power of each to realize the objects of his sovereign interest. In this picture, the only values are things that come to matter to individuals by being objects of the desires that comprise their sovereign interests. And there is no preordained location for each on the up-and-down scale that represents her power to get what she wants out of life, since that would amount to accepting as true some moral belief about how people should act irrespective of their inclinations. But there is nothing unreal in what is pictured here; indeed, there is nothing that is not presently real in it.

When I speak of the natural context, I ask the reader to picture present social reality as if it were a set of relations among individuals, each pressing for the realization of his sovereign interest as he judges it. As in present reality, people in the natural context still assert to others that they are morally required to act in some way. All that is different is that these assertions are not believed.

To "enter" the natural context, we need only picture present social relations and assume that everyone doubts the moral assertions that are being made expressly, or implicitly in the form of laws and customs. What we see then is asserters invoking a kind of moral authority over recipients, and recipients doubting that the authority is valid. With the validity of that authority doubted, what remains is people expressing and acting on their judgments. Accordingly, an asserted moral requirement appears as an expression of the asserter's judgment aimed at getting the recipient to act in some other way than she (the recipient) judges she should. When—without true justification—one person succeeds in getting another to act the way the first judges, at the expense of what the second judges she should do, I call that "subjugation." Accordingly, if an assertion of moral authority is false but succeeds, it is subjugation because the moral authority that the asserter invokes is precisely authority to override the judgment of the recipient. In the natural context, assertions of moral authority are not false but doubted. Such assertions appear as possible attempts by the asserter to subjugate the recipient's sovereign interest to his (the asserter's) own. In the natural context, assertions of moral authority evoke the suspicion of subjugation.

Note that in speaking of subjugation, I use the term in an uncommonly broad sense. It is normally used to refer to such grosser forms of imposition of power by one person over another as slavery or political oppression. My contention is not that every action, including verbal action, that alters the relations between individuals' sovereign interests in the way that a successful (though unproven) moral assertion would is subjugation—rather, my contention is that every such action may be subjugation, and it is this suspicion that must be overcome to show the validity of invocations of moral authority. Accordingly, once we grant the validity of some system of moral authority, only those actions that violate the principles of that system will be identified as subjugation. Our normal use of this term reflects our general belief in valid moral authority, and so the term is only applied to actions that grossly violate it. But what is wrong with these actions is that they alter the relations between people in unjustified ways. Thus, it is reasonable to think of all actions that alter those relations as potential acts of subjugation until proven justified. Hence, when all moral assertions are subjected to Cartesian doubt, the broader-than-normal use of the term is fitting.

I take it that a moral assertion always in some degree states what the asserter truly judges that the recipient should do. It is, I guess, conceivable that people might make moral assertions indifferently, affectlessly mouthing moral principles that others have taught them. In that case, asserters function as a kind of conduit for some earlier asserter—parents or teachers, or their parents or teachers—as far back as it takes to reach whoever believed in the principle enough to get the ball rolling. Then the current asserter serves, so to speak, as that earlier asserter's representative. Likewise, an insincere asserter (say, one who merely wants to manipulate the recipient) can be thought of asserting what another would assert sincerely. Subjugation occurs equally whether one's subjugator acts on one directly or through intermediaries. Since what is crucial for us is that the judgment of someone other than the recipient is asserted to override the recipient's, nothing is lost by speaking of these indirect cases as what the asserter judges.

What I am calling subjugation does not rest on assuming anything about the asserter's motives, for instance, that he in any way intends to control the behavior of the recipient. If subjugation occurs, it is simply a fact about the relationship of the wills of the asserter and the recipient that results from a successful, though not true, moral assertion. Thus, when I speak of a moral asserter as possibly trying to subjugate a recipient, I do not mean that he is intentionally attempting to bring about the suppression of the other. I mean he is trying to act in a way whose outcome is subjugation—irrespective of what is in the asserter's mind at the time. If people in the natural context naturally resist the assertion of moral authority over them by others, it is not the others' intentions that are the ground of their resistance. Their concern is with the effect that granting the validity of the authority would have on their pursuit of their sovereign interests.

Thus, the suspicion that moral principles may be means to subjugate people to whom they are addressed should be kept separate from the Nietzschean view that morality (by which Nietzsche meant Christian-style alms-giving other-cheek-turning morality) represents a conscious or subconscious desire to dominate the strong-willed members of the race. Nietzsche's thesis is an empirical claim about the actual contents of the consciousness or subconsciousness of moralizers, whereas mine is a claim about the potential effect of moralizing, independent of those contents. Nonetheless, Nietzsche stands as a powerful reminder that even the most generous-sounding of moral principles may be means of subjugation. And the force of Nietzsche's reminder is not weakened if those who actually assert a principle have no desire for subjugation. Once a principle is widely and effectively taught, people may press it on others with no shady subconscious motivation and yet function as conduits for the motives of those who originated the principle.

As soon as the recipient of moral pressure dissents from the claim to moral authority that the pressurer asserts, the recipient implicitly asserts her right to act on her own judgment, where *right* means the absence of any requirement that she do otherwise. Indeed, the natural sovereignty of people's judgments about their sovereign interests is equivalent to the assertion of this right. As such, the asserter and the recipient stand to each other in the relation of individuals in the natural context. Indeed, this is another way of seeing the reality to which the natural context corresponds: It is the relationship in which people who disagree on what is morally required really stand before there is a way to determine who is right. But we need not wait for actual dissent from the recipients. Since suspension of belief in the validity of all moral claims is appropriate if we are to test the validity of any, the natural context is the way in which the present real human situation must be perceived if moral philosophy is to do its job. Enter, the evil demon.

People tend to resist the assertion by others of authority to override their own judgments. Indeed, their sovereignty is the natural demand not to be subjugated, not to have others' judgments override their own without justification. With moral authority doubted, assertions of it appear as assertions of authority to override people's judgments with dubious justification. Thus, such assertions appear as possible means to subjugate recipients. In the natural context, then, where we view people as asserting the sovereignty of their own judgments, the doubt of moral authority becomes the suspicion of subjugation. The demand to resolve the doubt and prove the validity of an asserted moral requirement becomes equivalent to proving that it is not merely a means to subjugation. Only by proving that an asserted moral requirement does in truth override the recipient's sovereign interest can one prove that it is not merely a means to subjugation. And proving that it is not merely a means to subjugation is proving that an asserted moral requirement does in truth override the recipient's sovereign interest. Overcoming suspicion of subjugation is the natural test of moral requirements. The conditions that overcome the suspicion of subjugation are the requirements of moral requiring, and thus of any morally acceptable requiring at all.

Once the suspicion of subjugation is raised, its tendency is to grow. It naturally spreads beyond the clash of judgments to cases where asserter and recipient agree. Even where the recipient agrees with the asserter's principle, that is no proof against subjugation, as her agreement may be an artifact of her upbringing. Deep conditioning tailors a child's psyche to fit the shape of the social world before the child has resources to resist or criticize it and makes the group's traditions and customs feel like sensibility itself, much as it makes the group's language feel like sense itself. A person's agreement with a moral principle may be no more than a sign of successful conditioning. And that means that a person, finding himself believing that he is required to do something, can test the requirement by asking whether, if he did not subscribe to it, an assertion of it to him by another could be defended against the suspicion of subjugation.

It is worth noting that any asserter has available to him one automatic way of escaping the suspicion of subjugation: He need only add (sincerely, of course, and so that recipient clearly understands) that the recipient do the act urged only if she thinks she should. But this effectively turns the assertion into a moral recommendation, no longer a requirement. And such an assertion is no form of subjugation of its recipient, since she is not asked   67 to subordinate her judgment to that of anyone else. Indeed, she is not asked to refrain from action on her judgment at all, but to consider changing her judgment.

Call to mind the picture of the natural context described earlier. Like imagining away the buildings and streets of Manhattan, imagining away the validity of moral authority gives us the real natural substratum below. We saw this as a kind of fluid relation among coexisting centers of sovereign interest, whose relative up-and-down positions represent their relative power to obtain the objects of their sovereign interests. The natural context is a war of all against all in the attenuated sense that it is a realm in which people stand in relation to one another limited only by the balance of their relative powers; each person presses toward the achievement of his sovereign interest as far as he can, subject to the power of the rest to achieve theirs. Any attempt to apply moral pressure in this context by asserting moral authority is effectively an attempt to alter the relations of power among these individuals. "Entering the natural context" amounts to seeing moral assertions as just that, attempts to rearrange power relations between people. If we take the term *political* to refer to the relations of power in which people stand, the natural context shows the substratum of morality to be political. Part of the abiding appeal of the social contract theory is that it continually reminds us of this political substratum of morality.

If we combine these ideas with the notion that the natural context is not another place, but present reality minus moral authority, what we get is this: The natural context is not found by looking away from current reality toward a different one, but by looking at current reality in a different way. Mainly, it is a way of seeing moral relations as power relations. This view is achieved by squinting at present reality, much as one might squint at a painting to shut out its meaningful content, the better to see the balance of its colors or the geometry of its shapes. Here the squinting shuts out the halo of legitimacy surrounding actually accepted moral principles, the better to see the balance of personal fates and the geometry of relative power that remains. Since all moralities claim to be more than power, right rather than might, seeing moral relations as power relations throws into sharp relief what must be proven if moral claims are to be made good.

The Social Contract and Reason's Weak Answer to Subjugation

Having entered the natural context, all assertions of moral requirements are suspect as attempts at subjugation. This is not to say that they are attempts at subjugation, only that they may be. We exit the natural context if we can show that some moral requirements are not attempts at subjugation. To do that, we must show that it is unreasonable to view certain requirements as doing no more than getting some people to subordinate their sovereign interests to those of others. Until this is shown, no one need treat an asserted moral requirement as binding on him. It remains just an assertion and the assertion of moral authority is no more authoritative than the assertion that it is warm is warm. Moreover, an assertion of moral authority is not a harmless assertion. Its effect, if complied with, is to reduce the recipient's ability to achieve his sovereign interest.

If no assertion of moral authority can be binding unless it is more than an attempt at subjugation, then none can be proven binding by appeal to some other unproven assertion of moral authority, since that assertion might itself be no more than an attempt at subjugation. To be obligatory, moral requirements must be proven nonsubjugating without assuming in advance the validity of any moral requirements that have not themselves been proven nonsubjugating. This means no strategy that appeals to moral principles taken as axiomatic, intuitive, revealed by God, or embedded in tradition can overcome the suspicion of subjugation, since these appeals are all equivalent to assuming in advance the validity of moral requirements that have not been proven nonsubjugating. The natural test of morality must appeal strictly to rational considerations—facts, logic, and inferences from these—that do not depend upon prior moral assumptions. The widely held notion that moral conclusions can only be derived from moral premises must be wrong, at least if the conclusions are to be morally obligatory. When reason looks for the credentials of moral authority, it must find itself, un-mixed with any moral belief not already warranted by it—as the social contractarians realized. Nothing less can dispel the suspicion of subjugation.

This outcome was already prefigured in the Cartesian challenge. Social contractarianism is moral Cartesianism: recognition in the moral realm that nothing can be accepted as authority by reason unless it proves the validity of its authority to reason, which amounts to recognizing that reason is the ultimate moral authority. In the realm of knowledge, authority without rational warrant is indistinguishable from ignorance; in the realm of morality, authority without rational warrant is indistinguishable from subjugation. The state of nature is the moral equivalent of the Cartesian doubt. Whether people in the state of nature are regarded as positively hostile or merely as undependably benevolent is as irrelevant to the outcome as whether doubt comes from the blatant mischief of the evil demon or the inscrutable good-ness of the benevolent God. Just as the certainty of clear and distinct ideas is reason's recognition of itself as the determiner of knowledge, so the social   69 contract is reason's recognition of itself as the determiner of morality. If moral authority must prove itself to reason, reason must be the ultimate moral authority.

It would be a mistake, however, to think that this conclusion is merely a creature of the formulation of the problem. Only reason can establish valid moral authority. Only rational proof of its validity can lift one person's assertion of another's duty above the status of being a mere judgment of his about how the other should live. Anything else is just an assertion that carries the day, if it does, because somehow, through the strength of its advocates or the vulnerabilities of its targets, it prevails. The simple fact is that we want moral principles to do a job that only reason can perform: override our judgments without subjugating us.

As I said at the outset, I believe that reason can do this because freedom of the will is just the capacity to reason about how to act and then to perform an action because reasoning indicates it is the appropriate thing to do. Freedom of the will is not the ability to do what one wants, since one's wants might themselves be compulsions. It is the ability to want what one wants. When a free person does what she wants, it will not be because she has been swept along by the force of her desires, but because she has reviewed and evaluated them and then determined that some action in their service is appropriate. The capacity to perform such a review and evaluation, and then to act on its outcome because it is the product of such an assessment, gives an individual the leverage over her desires (as well as over her habits, neurotic compulsions, and the rest) that is needed to count her decisions as free, her wants as what she truly wants, her actions as her own. I think that this account of freedom is compatible with the determinism that natural science implies about the world, but, as I said earlier, I leave such things to metaphysicians. My concern is to indicate that reason's requirements are not freedom's enemies.

If to be free one must act because reason shows an act to be appropriate, such a showing by reason must be sufficient grounds for the individual to act. If reason simply recommended an action and left it undetermined whether this was sufficient grounds to do the action, then the individual's decision to do it would not occur because reason showed the act to be appropriate—but because of whatever nonrational thing had to be added to reason's recommendation to yield sufficient grounds. But in that case the action would be the product of the blind force of that nonrational thing and lose its claim to be free. If, however, reason's conclusions must be sufficient, they must be requirements. And that implies not only that reason is no enemy of freedom, but also that complying with reason's requirements is being free. As the Greeks well knew, freedom is conformity to reason, not violation of it. Violation of reason would be not freedom, but chance, randomness, whimsy, pointlessness—what the ancients understood as chaos. Freedom is self-possession, not the abandonment of self to caprice.

This is why only reason can do the job that we ask of morality—and our language testifies to the link. Nonmoral practical reason shares a vocabulary with morality: ought, should, must, right, and wrong all occur in both prudential judgments of self-interest and moral judgments. Indeed, these terms occur in theoretical reason as well, where conclusions should or must be believed and answers are right or wrong. The link between morality and reason is that rational compulsion is the only sort that can override an individual's judgments and acquit itself of the charge of subjugation at the same time. The force of reason is the only force that runs along rather than counter to the lines of force of human freedom.

How can reason refute the suspicion of subjugation? There seem to be two possibilities. If reason could directly and conclusively prove that compliance with a particular moral principle is required of all human beings, then that would rebut the suspicion of subjugation regarding that principle in the strongest way. I leave this possibility aside until the next chapter. For the moment, we operate under the assumption of moral inconclusivity.

The other possibility is to show that some requirements are needed to protect everyone from subjugation. It would be unreasonable to suspect these requirements as attempts at subjugation, if we are to protect everyone against subjugation. I shall develop this possibility in this section. It is reason's weak answer to subjugation, because it depends on the assumption that we must protect everyone against subjugation. Without this assumption, it is within reason for a person to claim that the requirements that keep him from subjugating others are themselves subjugating of him. The weak answer identifies the requirements of protecting everyone against subjugation, but it is weak because it does not entail that everyone is required to comply with these requirements. To turn this into a requirement, it is necessary to assume that subjugation is a general evil against which everyone is to be protected. Call this the *antisubjugation assumption*—at this point at least, it is not itself required by reason.

In the next chapter, I shall develop reason's strong answer by showing that reason does, in fact, require that everyone be protected against subjugation. But since subjugation is a threat to all rational beings, the assumption that everyone should be protected against subjugation as much as possible is a plausible and appealing one. Since no one is likely to complain about subjugation while denying this assumption (if he wishes to be taken seriously), the weak answer is far from impotent.

Earlier we saw that the suspicion of subjugation arises when one person   71 succeeds in getting another to act contrary to his judgment of his sovereign interest, and we saw that the effect of this success rather than the intention was crucial. This effect is essentially a reduction in the recipient's ability to pursue his sovereign interest as he judges it. The occurrence of this reduction effect is not equivalent to subjugation; it is only suspected as such. If there is a valid moral requirement that justifies this effect, then it is not subjugation. The mere presence of the reduction effect is not itself sufficient to establish the existence of subjugation. This is important, as the effect itself is inevitable whenever individuals' wills conflict, a circumstance that must be understood very broadly. The assertion of a moral requirement is only one way in which the reduction effect that evokes the suspicion of subjugation can be produced. If you want to wear red in my presence and I want to see only green, however we act, only one of us can get what he or she wants. The reduction effect is produced by any action that people undertake when their wills or judgments are in conflict.

One implication of this is that whatever will stop one person from subjugating another will itself raise the suspicion of subjugation. Stopping subjugation must also have the effect of blocking someone in her pursuit of her sovereign interest. It follows that we cannot hope to eliminate totally the reduction effect that raises the suspicion of subjugation. The most we can hope for is to distinguish the cases in which the reduction effect should count as subjugation from those that are necessary to block subjugation. If subjugation is an evil against which everyone is to be protected, then those restrictions necessary to block subjugation are valid ones and should not count as subjugation. It follows from the antisubjugation assumption that everyone must accept as nonsubjugating those restrictions necessary to keep him from subjugating others.

Because we do not start with any moral principle that could tell us what these necessary restrictions are, we must find them by looking at what makes subjugation objectionable in the first place. What makes subjugation objectionable is that it limits people in the pursuit of their sovereign interest. The requirements that would protect each person's ability to pursue her sovereign interest to the greatest extent possible compatible with everyone else having like ability are those necessary to reduce the threat of subjugation as far as possible for everyone. These requirements escape the suspicion of subjugation because they are invoked by that suspicion, to do battle with subjugation. Anyone who complains that these requirements subjugate him is claiming that what keeps him from subjugating others is subjugation, and given the antisubjugation assumption, that undermines his complaint that he is being subjugated.

What would protect each person's ability to pursue her sovereign interest to the greatest extent possible is equivalent to what it would be reasonable for each person to accept in light of her sovereign interest. Factoring in that this must be compatible with everyone else having a like ability, we get what it would be reasonable for everyone to agree to in light of their sovereign interests, when each can get no more than what everyone else would reasonably agree to. For simplicity's sake, I shall restate this last idea as what it would be reasonable for everyone to agree to together—where it is understood that people's reasonable judgments are made in light of their sovereign interests and that each is limited in what he can insist on as a condition of his agreement because it must be reasonable for the rest to agree to it as well. Accordingly, the requirements that it would be reasonable for everyone to agree to together are those necessary to reduce the threat of subjugation to the greatest extent possible for everyone and, thus, are not subjugating. With this, the outlines of the social contract come into view.

To find the requirements that overcome the suspicion of subjugation, then, we must ask whether there are any requirements that it would be reasonable for all to agree to together in light of their sovereign interests. But how to ask this is far from a simple matter, and since differences in how we pose the question will yield differences in the answers, it is of great importance that we formulate the question properly. We are in the natural context, looking with a duly suspicious eye at present reality, including all the moral requirements that people expressly or implicitly assert to one another, and we are trying to formulate the question in a way that asks whether these actual assertions are attempts at subjugation. If we have this, we can easily extend it to possible assertions by imagining them being asserted in the present.

In light of this orientation to present reality, it might seem that the way to pose our question is to ask the actual people we see before us (perhaps after weeding out those who are certifiably irrational) whether they agree to the requirements that are urged on them. But this will not do, for several important reasons. First, since requirements are asserted as overriding the recipient's judgment, they are normally asserted when the recipient disagrees. If the only requirements that were not subjugating were those that people actually agreed with, there would be no real requiring at all. Second, even among normal rational people actual agreement may be a function of successful conditioning to accept some principle, and then actual agreement might tell us how deeply effective some means of subjugation had been, instead of showing that it was not a means to subjugation. Third, actual agreement will be a function of people's knowledge of the implications of that agreement, and if people's knowledge (or reasoning capacity) is faulty, then their actual agreement will be contaminated. They will think they are agreeing to one thing when, in fact, they are agreeing to something else. Fourth, even the most reasonable actual agreement will be a function of the initial condition in which alternatives are offered up for possible acceptance. What will be rational to me now will be a function of how much it is an improvement over my present situation. But my current situation may be the result of my accepting (or of people having imposed on me) other requirements, which themselves may be means of subjugation. If I am already the victim of extreme subjugation, a lesser subjugation may be enough of an improvement to make it my rational choice—but then my agreement to it would not show it to be nonsubjugating, only less subjugating. Fifth, any actual agreement a person is likely to make will be dictated by the specific desires indexed according to his current judgment of his sovereign interest. Those desires may change over the course of an individual's life, such that what he actually agrees to at one point may, in fact, turn out to subjugate him later. Moreover, since specific desires can be for anything and for any amount of it, focus on the actual desires that comprise an individual's sovereign interest may make it impossible for all to agree to anything and may thus subvert the possibility of identifying subjugation for everyone.

These five considerations together show that the question we must pose cannot be an empirical question of what actual rational people will agree to. It must be a theoretical question about what it would be reasonable for people to agree to under certain hypothetical circumstances. The necessary hypothetical circumstances correspond to the five reasons just given for why actual agreement will not suffice.

First, because requirements override the recipient's inclinations and judgments and are normally asserted when the recipient disagrees, we must ask whether it would be reasonable for all to agree to some particular requirement (judged against all potential alternative requirements) as a way of resolving conflicts of judgment that they may be on either side of but do not now know which side. Thus we imagine everyone as if they were deciding on principles to govern their conflicts of judgment in the future, in ignorance of which side of those conflicts they will be on. Since subjugation must be identified for everyone, it cannot matter which side of some requirement any particular individual is on. To eliminate the effect that knowledge of which side one was likely to be on would have, we imagine people as ignorant in this respect.

Second, because actual agreement may be a function of successful conditioning to accept some principle, we must ask whether it would be reasonable for all to agree to this principle, when they did not already accept any particular moral principles. Thus, we imagine everyone as if they were deciding on principles, while ignorant of the moral principles that they do,

74

in fact, accept. This hypothetical restriction is already implied in the recognition that the suspicion of subjugation can only be rebutted by reason operating without assuming the validity of any moral principle in advance.

Third, because we want to know what it would be reasonable for people to agree to rather than what they will actually agree to in light of their actual knowledge and reasoning ability, we must pose our question assuming these are perfect. Thus, we imagine everyone as if they were deciding on principles, possessing all relevant knowledge (knowledge of everything that might bear on their choice, except for those constraints on knowledge that are included in these hypothetical conditions) and perfect reasoning ability. This does not imply that anyone has such unrealistically high levels of competence; rather, what is fully and completely reasonable for people to agree to must be what they would agree to when they had the knowledge and competence to make fully and completely reasonable choices.

Fourth, because even the most rational actual agreement will be a function of the initial condition in which alternatives are offered up for possible acceptance and because those initial conditions may be the result of other—possibly subjugating—requirements effectively imposed on people, we must pose our question as if people were choosing all the rules that govern their behavior at once. Thus, we imagine people as deciding on the full set of requirements in a condition in which they do not accept or occupy—or know that they do or will accept or occupy—any arrangement that implicitly embodies any unagreed-to moral requirement.

Fifth, because the specific desires indexed by someone's current judgment of his sovereign interest may change over the course of his life and because focus on the actual desires that comprise an individual's sovereign interest may subvert the possibility of identifying subjugation for everyone, we must pose our question in a way that is independent of the particular desires that make up people's sovereign interests. Thus, we imagine people deciding on requirements in light of the knowledge that they have some sovereign interest with its characteristic urgency but without knowledge of the particular desires that constitute their particular sovereign interests. I shall have more to say about this condition below. For the moment, it suffices to note that, since people must agree on what is compatible with everyone's pursuing his sovereign interest, each person's pursuit of his sovereign interest will be agreed to up to the limit of compatibility. Consequently, no one can expect to gain more by insisting on the satisfaction of his particular desires than he can by insisting on his ability to pursue his sovereign interest, whatever it is, up to the maximum compatible.

The imagery of the social contract and the state of nature embodies these hypothetical or imaginary conditions. But far from leaving current reality and reaching some imaginary state of nature of dubious relevance to the present situation, we have arrived at the need to pose this question theoretically, hypothetically, and thus under imaginary conditions, as a result of determining what is necessary to ask whether present arrangements are subjugating.

Say that someone tells another that he must not steal. Entering the natural context, we see this as potentially an attempt at subjugation. Since principles of this sort are implicitly—and in actual fact—addressed to everyone, we are asking not only whether this is a case of subjugation but whether holding people to this principle generally subjugates them. To determine this, we ask whether the principle requiring people not to steal is one that it would be reasonable for all to agree to in light of their sovereign interests. Because a rule against theft might be a means to subjugate non-owners of property, we ask this imagining that people do not know the things that would indicate to them which side of this principle they were likely to be on. Because people may have been conditioned to accept the prohibition against theft even though it may be subjugating, we ask our question imagining that people do not know their moral convictions. Because people may make mistakes of fact or logic in deciding what to agree to, we ask our question imagining the parties as perfectly competent reasoners with all relevant knowledge. Because the fact that some own property and some do not may determine different people's attitudes toward theft, and because ownership of property embodies a moral principle that itself might be a means to subjugation, we ask our question imagining that people are deciding on all their governing principles from scratch. Finally, because people may judge in terms of desires that will change and because focus on particular desires may make agreement impossible, we ask our question imagining that the parties know that they have sovereign interests about which they care deeply, but of whose component desires they are ignorant. If it would be reasonable for all people, in light of their sovereign interests, to agree—when fully rational and possessed of all relevant knowledge—to be bound by rules that include a rule against theft, when they must agree to all the rules by which they will be bound, not knowing which side of the rules they will find themselves on, not knowing their existing moral convictions, and not knowing the components of their sovereign interests, then it follows that the requirement not to steal is nonsubjugating.

The various conditions that make this a matter of theoretical rather than empirical agreement all stem from a single source, which, in our affection for individual freedom, we may easily overlook. This is all the more likely in view of the discussion of the importance to people of their judgment and authorship in determining and performing the actions that will serve their sovereign interests. We tend to think that, when a person is minimally sane and not deceived, what he freely accepts (where this has the commonsense meaning of what he accepts when not coerced) becomes automatically morally authorized by that acceptance. But this is itself a moral belief. Since it is in principle possible to be subjugated by something that we freely accept in fact, whether actual uncoerced acceptance overrides subjugation in any given instance is an open question. The apparent order of things is the reverse of the real order. The capacity of actual free (that is, uncoerced) acceptance to override subjugation must itself be proven by a theoretical argument. The test of that argument cannot lie in whether its conclusions are actually freely accepted.

Accordingly, the authorizing power of actual free acceptance must be the conclusion of an argument proving that actual free acceptance is the surest and safest means to identify what is not subjugating. This is just what we do when we attach minimum sanity, lack of deception, and so on, as necessary conditions for actual acceptance to have its authorizing power. We attach such conditions because implicitly we grant actual uncoerced acceptance its authorizing power subject to what would be reasonable, and these are the minimum conditions that it would be reasonable for us to insist on before viewing actual free acceptance as morally authorizing.

Once again we are confronted with the alliance of freedom and reason. Freedom is not the absence of coercion, but the presence of reason. It is, Aristotle writes, "when their acts are reasonable that men especially hold that they are their own acts, and they have been done voluntarily" (*NE*, ix:8, 278). The assertion that actual acceptance is voluntary and thus overrides subjugation is based implicitly on a theoretical and hypothetical argument proving that it would be reasonable for everyone to accept it as such. In making this theoretical argument, we must give due weight to the fact that people's sovereign interests are desires to lead the lives they actually judge they desire.

If we keep this in mind, we will spare ourselves the most common errors about the social contract. Since the social contract takes the test of moral principles to be whether they would be agreed to hypothetically, it is easily mistaken as claiming that such choices bestow moral authorization on those principles, in the way that we commonly take actual uncoerced acceptance to bestow authorization. This leads to three objections. First, it is objected that only actual choices authorize, so hypothetical ones do not. (That it would be reasonable for you to sell me your car for one thousand dollars does not authorize me to take your car and leave the money.) Second, it is objected that hypothetical choices can only authorize in hypothetical circumstances. (That it would have been reasonable for us to agree to some principles in the state of nature only authorizes those principles in the state of nature.) Third, it is objected that the principle that choices bestow moral authorization is itself a moral principle and thus that the neutrality of the social contract as a method for warranting moral principles from scratch is compromised. (One form of this objection, raised by Hume, is that the social contract establishes moral principles as tacit promises and thus pre-supposes the moral principle that promises create moral obligations [*EPM*, 95].)

All of these objections are avoided if we understand that the acceptance in the contracting situation is purely theoretical. It is not an act that autho-rizes anything. It is not an act at all, not even an imaginary one. In normal life, we take a person's choice as having authorizing power insofar as it is a separate act that he performs after he has been presented with an argument for the choice, indeed, even after he has granted the validity of the argument. His choice has authorizing power because it is a distinct engagement of himself. In the contracting situation, by contrast, the acceptance is not a separate act after a valid argument is made. It is just a way of saying that the argument is valid. To say that a principle would be accepted by a reasonable person is nothing but a dramatic way of saying that it would be reasonable for that person to live according to this principle. It adds to that reasonableness no separate authorizing engagement. Consequently, none of the three objections voiced in the last paragraph hit their target. The social contract is not aimed at passing off hypothetical acceptance as real autho-rization. It is aimed at determining whether a set of principles are subju-gating. It does that by asking whether those principles would be reasonable for people to live by. It asks this by asking whether people would agree to them in some hypothetical circumstances. It does the latter, because the question itself is theoretical and thus necessarily hypothetical.

Although the question is hypothetical, it is about the reasonableness of principles to the actual people governed by them. Any formulation of the contracting situation aimed at determining whether present asserted require-ments are subjugating existing people will specify hypothetical conditions on the acceptance to be argued for and thus call upon us to imagine those conditions. Such conditions will normally limit the knowledge of the parties in the contracting situation, because it is only as knowledge that anything can enter this theoretical argument about what would be reasonable to ac-cept. What we must insure is that only those hypothetical conditions nec-essary to pose this theoretical question about the principles that govern actual people are built in. As long as this is so, the conclusions reached are valid for actual people. In order to determine whether some principle really subjugates people, we must, paradoxically, launch an argument about what it would be reasonable for them to agree to under imaginary conditions. "Sometimes," the central character in Edward Albee's play *Zoo Story* says, "it is necessary to go a long way out of your way in order to come back in the right direction."

Recognition of this fact will help us avoid another problem that dogs contractarianism—namely, the problem of gambling. Because, according to our first hypothetical stipulation, people do not know which side of a principle they will be on, it might seem that, in determining what is rational to agree to, they should be allowed—as normal people actually making such decisions would normally be—to make some estimate of the odds of ending up on one side or the other and use this to determine whether or not to agree to the principle. For example, it would seem that if a principle, say one allowing lies to be told to people over seven feet fall, were compared to one insisting on truth-telling to all, then a person (hypothetically ignorant of his own situation) might consider the unlikelihood of his being over seven feet tall and the gains of being able to lie to such people and then rationally accept a principle that permits this rather than a general prohibition on lying.

Thinking that such rational gambling on the odds is appropriate in the contracting situation is a very common misinterpretation that comes from misconceiving the point of the state of nature and the social contract. I shall have more to say about it in part 2, since it is the Achilles' heel of Rawls's theory and a clear example of how justice as reason's answer to subjugation provides Rawls's theory with a badly needed foundation. For the present, note that allowing gambling undermines the capacity of the social contract to test for subjugation. Consider the example of the principles just mentioned. It will presumably be reasonable for everyone to accept the exception about lying to people over seven feet tall, even though each has a slight chance of ending up the seven-footer. But that cannot show that the seven-footer's position would be reasonable for *him* to accept. At most, it would show that it would be reasonable for people to accept the risk of ending up a seven-footer in light of the gains possible if one does not end up a seven-footer. The reasonableness of a gamble in the contracting situation shows only the reasonableness of taking the gamble; it cannot show the reasonableness of accepting losing that gamble unless one has actually gambled. If the point of the contract is to determine whether the occupants of existing arrangements are subjugated, then this can only tell us that any particular seven-footer is not subjugated if he freely took the gamble of being seven feet tall. Since existing seven-footers never had any chance of being a different height, nothing is said about whether they are subjugated by this rule.

Moreover, we want a way of determining whether all the outcomes to   79 which agreeing to a principle may lead are free of subjugation. Allowing gambling subverts this purpose because—as the case of the seven-footers illustrates—no matter how bad some outcomes are, if they are few enough and the countervailing gains large and likely enough, the risk of ending up in the bad positions can always be reasonably accepted. Accordingly, it will be impossible to distinguish arrangements that subjugate a very few people for the benefit of many from arrangements that are free of subjugation entirely. To determine whether anyone at all is subjugated by a principle, principles must be considered as if in accepting them one was accepting occupying all the outcomes they will produce. So understood, a principle that would be reasonable, compared to all the possible alternatives, for all to agree to is truly reasonable for all the people presently governed by it. Accordingly, under the first hypothetical stipulation, in which people are taken as ignorant of how they will be affected by any principle to which they may agree, I include a general ban on gambling on whatever probabilities people can extract from the knowledge they are imagined to have. I shall have more to say about the exclusion of gambling from the contracting situation in chapter 5.

Deprived of knowledge of how they in particular will be affected by any candidate principle, people must evaluate it as if they could be anyone. From this it follows that the only restraints they will allow on their pursuit of their sovereign interests are those they would want applied to others to protect their own. Thus they will, as Hobbes saw, naturally be content with as much liberty against others as they would allow others against themselves. This may seem to some to be a liberal bias in the test. Moreover, the fifth hypothetical stipulation, prohibiting knowledge of the details of anyone's sovereign interest, may seem to bias the agreement against certain kinds of moral principles—for instance, one that requires imposing some religious orthodoxy on everyone. If everyone will only find it reasonable to agree to what will enable her to promote her sovereign interest, whatever it turns out to be, people will not find it reasonable to agree to having some orthodoxy forced on everyone. But this is no real bias—or rather it is the bias of the test of subjugation and that, if my arguments are sound, is justice's own "bias." What this reflects is that principles that must be forced on other people irrespective of whether they value them are unlikely to satisfy the requirement of reasonableness to all and thus overcome the suspicion of subjugation. Since we know this in advance from the shape of the test itself, this is no bias unless the test is not really the appropriate test of morality. Any test will favor some outcomes over others. That this can be seen in advance implies no bias, anymore than that we can know that an unskilled person cannot pass a test of skill implies that such tests are biased against unskilled people. If the test itself is reasonable, then the fact that it will favor some outcomes over others shows that the test is effective, not that it is biased.

At issue here is something often missed by those who complain of the meagerness of justice or liberalism or who suggest that social contract theories are prejudiced against the communal values that people have. If people have certain values, they will not need to be forced to act on them. Rather, they will either be moved spontaneously to act on them voluntarily or will come to do so when presented with accurate information. They may need to protect themselves against the effects on their judgment of prior beliefs or habituation to certain relationships, but this is provided for by the second and fourth considerations indicated above. Moreover, they may want to protect themselves against times when they are substantially deranged or otherwise clearly unable to understand their own interests, but since knowledge of these possibilities is included in the third consideration, they are also provided for. For reasons indicated earlier in the chapter, these possibilities will make reasonable only very limited and temporary intervention. Leaving these aside, then, protecting people's capacity to act on whatever values they have protects their capacity to act for communal and any other values, as long as they really have (or freely come to adopt) these values. The only values that would not be protected would be values that required for their realization that others be forced to serve them, though they do not really have them—and this I take to be justice's own bias. Those who would erect communal values into moral requirements are in a dilemma: Either people have (or would freely adopt) these values and then need not be required to serve them, or they must be required to serve them and then it is obvious that they neither have them nor would freely adopt them. I shall have more to say about this in chapter 3.

I conclude that requirements that it would be reasonable for all to agree to when they are imagined to be in the natural context, free of beliefs in the validity of any moral principle, perfectly rational and possessed of all relevant knowledge, unaware of the actual relations in which they stand or how they in particular will be affected by any principle under consideration and unable to gamble on this, and not knowing the specifics of their sovereign interests but concerned to promote their general ability to pursue it whatever it is, are nonsubjugating. I take all these conditions to be summed up in saying that a principle or requirement is the outcome of the social contract and thus that the social contract is the way to determine what is and what is not subjugation. Since justice eliminates subjugation, it follows that the social contract is the way to determine what is and what is not just. I take it then that acting justly is acting according to those requirements it

81

would be reasonable for all people to agree to in the contracting situation. Hobbes was right.

So understood, however, justice is reason's weak answer to subjugation—weak because, while reason distinguishes between justice and subjugation, it does not (here) require that we pursue justice and avoid subjugation. For that, at this point, we must add the antisubjugation assumption. But the assumption is a natural one, one that is hardly to be denied by anyone concerned to act morally, and scarcely to be denied openly by anyone at all. Indeed, even those who do not accept it cannot fail to recognize that, since people will tend to resist what they regard as subjugation, acting on the assumption amounts to an equilibrium solution to conflict in the natural context—the way to end the war of all against all when people doubt one another's moral claims. Accordingly, the weak answer is by no means impotent. It represents the shareable conditions of peace among people whose moral aims are or may become different. Here, too, Hobbes was right.

Moreover, even without being able to show that the antisubjugation assumption is a requirement of reason, we can say that the weak answer has profound moral implications: It places all those who affirm the obligation to avoid subjugation under a duty to impose no moral requirement on anyone unless they can show either that it would be rational for all to agree to it under the conditions embodied in the social contract or that it is directly required by reason. Any moral principle that cannot satisfactorily pass one of these tests must be put forth only as a moral recommendation by anyone sincerely committed to avoiding subjugation.

We can close by bringing justice back together with the other three of Plato's cardinal virtues—prudence, temperance, and fortitude. If justice is acting according to principles that it would be reasonable for all to agree to in light of their sovereign interests, it is acting according to those principles that best enable each person to realize his sovereign interest to the greatest extent possible compatible with the same for everyone else. The four virtues then amount to the conditions (social in the case of justice, individual in the case of the remaining three) that best enable everyone to lead the life he judges that he desires.

Chapter 2: *Reason and the Internal Social Contract*

> When I confront a human being as my Thou . . . ,
> then he is no thing among things nor does he consist of
> things.
>
> He is no longer . . . a dot in the world grid of
> space and time, nor a condition that can be
> experienced and described, a loose bundle of named
> qualities. Neighborless and seemless, he is Thou and
> fills the firmament. Not as if there were nothing but he;
> but everything else lives in *his* light.
> —Martin Buber, *I and Thou*

From External to Internal Social Contract: Hobbes, Locke, and Rousseau

Instituting a sovereign transforms a group of people into a commonwealth by establishing a civil authority that can make and enforce societywide decisions over the dissent of private citizens. We saw that Hobbes advocates absolute sovereignty because, in the absence of civil authority, every individual is a danger to every other or, at least, every individual has reason to treat every other as a threat, which makes everyone a real danger to every other. As long as this threat persists, people cannot be expected to observe ordinary moral restraints, much as we normally do not blame people for what they do under threat of death or serious bodily harm. Thus, according to Hobbes, the existence of a sovereign to protect everyone against everyone else is a necessary condition of people acting morally at all.

This is the case, even though, as we noted earlier, Hobbes held that a shadow morality exists in the state of nature. The tendency to self-preservation itself determines both a "natural right," which prescribes what people are at liberty to do, and a "natural law," which prescribes what people are obligated to do. Since, for Hobbes, natural right is what a person cannot be bound to refrain from and since people cannot be bound to refrain from doing what they think will preserve their lives, by natural right a person may do anything he thinks is needed to preserve his life. Because the war of all against all is the greatest threat to that preservation, the first and

83

fundamental law of nature dictates that a person do what is needed to achieve lasting peace so long as doing so does not endanger his life. As long as each holds a natural right to do anything he judges needed for his self-preservation, all people are threats to each other and the war of all against all persists. Consequently, as we saw earlier, the first law of nature leads to a second: *"that a man be willing, when others are so too . . . , to lay down this right to all things, and be contented with so much liberty against other men as he would allow other men against himself"* (*L*, chap. 14).

Hobbes identified this second law of nature with the Golden Rule of the Gospel, which he states as: "whatsoever you require that others should do to you, that do ye to them." Hobbes derives nineteen laws of nature, including the obligations to keep one's covenants ("the fountain and original of justice"), to show gratitude for gifts, to punish only for future good, to avoid pride and arrogance, to treat people equitably, to submit disputes to impartial judges, and the like, all of which are indicated to us by natural reason as means to maintain peace and thus preserve our lives. Hobbes held all nineteen to be summed up in the Golden Rule, now stated negatively—Do not that to another which you would not have done to yourself—and which he maintained is "intelligible even to the meanest capacity" (*L*, chap. 15).

Though these nineteen natural laws have the familiar look of moral rules requiring people to limit pursuit of their perceived self-interest, they cannot be an authoritative morality in the state of nature. They always bind *in foro interno*, that is, in our consciences. In effect, this means that we are bound to try to bring about a world in which it would be rational for us and others to act on the natural laws. Since acting on the natural laws is only rational when all are subject to a sovereign, we are not, while in the state of nature, bound by the natural laws *in foro externo*, that is, with respect to our actions. It would be contrary to self-preservation for anyone to restrain himself morally when he could not be sure that others would not take advantage of his restraint: "For he that should be modest and tractable and perform all he promises in such time and place where no man else should do so should but make himself a prey to others and procure his own certain ruin, contrary to the ground of all laws of nature, which tend to nature's preservation" (*L*, chap. 15). Even the obligation in foro interno is hardly a full-blooded moral obligation; it functions more like the indications of prudence. "For the laws of nature . . . in the condition of mere nature . . . ," wrote Hobbes, "are not properly laws but qualities that dispose men to peace and obedience" (*L*, chap. 26).

None of these laws can bind actions until people lift themselves out of the state of nature by giving up their natural right to everything they judge necessary to their preservation and empowering a sovereign to hold everyone to this surrender absolutely. If they surrender less than absolutely, with any strings attached, each has retained his natural right, and the state of war persists. Each subject therefore must effectively give up any claim to determine his obedience to the sovereign by his own moral judgments. Thus, Hobbes held that the existence of an absolute sovereign, a sovereign beyond the moral judgments of his subjects, is the condition of people's actions being bound by moral obligations.

But, in fact, Hobbes's conclusion was even more extreme: The condition of people being held to moral obligations is an absolute sovereign whose authority *includes determining the content of morality itself*! Aware that as long as people believe they are entitled to make private moral judgments they are likely to act on them, Hobbes asserted it to be a seditious doctrine poisonous to the commonwealth "*that every private man is judge of good and evil actions.* . . . From this false doctrine, men are disposed to debate with themselves and dispute the commands of the commonwealth, and afterwards to obey or disobey them as in their private judgments they shall think fit, whereby the commonwealth is distracted and *weakened*." For "him that lives in a commonwealth . . . the law is the public conscience by which he has already undertaken to be guided" (*L*, chap. 29).

Hobbes held that there are no obligations except by voluntary agreement (*L*, chap. 21), and the fountain of justice is the covenants people make (*L*, chap. 15). Nonetheless, from this starting point, he concludes that the specific obligations of justice are determined by the sovereign. The threat that makes life in the state of nature a condition of war persists as long as people can act on their private judgments, including their private moral judgments. On the basis of these they may act in ways harmful to their fellow citizens or withhold obedience from the sovereign in ways that endanger others or the commonwealth generally. Even if they do not actually act in these ways, they may, and this will give others reason to fear that they will and to protect themselves by preemptive strike, and everyone reason to protect preemptively against this, and so on, setting in motion the escalating process that leads right on up to the war of all against all. Consequently, the very threat that made it unreasonable to expect people to observe moral restraints persists until people give up to the sovereign their right to make their own moral judgments. Morality authored by the sovereign obligates people because it is reasonable for people to agree to establish a sovereign who will determine the rules of good and evil (*L*, chap. 18) and just and unjust (*L*, chap. 26) and "to submit . . . their judgment to his judgment" (*L*, chap. 18), for all the reasons that make it reasonable to agree to establish a sovereign in the first place.

It will repay us to take a closer look at this argument. Let us call a set of moral rules that *do, in fact*, bind people, a "de facto authoritative morality" and a set of moral rules that both *do, in fact*, and *should, in principle*, bind people, a "de jure authoritative morality." By *binding people*, I mean that people tend generally to recognize the obligations, to restrain their pursuit of their self-interest accordingly, and to identify and penalize violations of those obligations by others. By *generally*, I mean not necessarily in every case, but in the large majority of cases, enough so that one could reasonably feel that his own restraint added to general conformity and did not invite violations by others. Bear in mind that a de jure authoritative morality is a de facto one, in that it does generally bind. A de facto authoritative morality may be a de jure one, but it need not be, as long as it is effective, in fact. With this language, we can say that Hobbes claims that there is no de jure authoritative morality in the state of nature because there is no de facto one. If there were a de facto one, then people could be reasonably held to its terms without fear of vulnerability and there could be a de jure authoritative morality.

Hobbes maintains that there cannot be a de facto authoritative morality until people can rely sufficiently on each other's conformity to make their own conformity reasonable. This requires a sovereign with the power to spell out the authoritative moral obligations and hold people to them on pain of sanction. With a sovereign in place, there is de facto authoritative morality; with de facto, there can be de jure. Since following the obligations laid down by the sovereign will bring peace, those obligations amount to a de jure authoritative morality. Believing that the sovereign is necessary to bring about de facto authoritative morality is equivalent to denying that it would dependably come about naturally. Let us call this denial the "assumption of natural moral discord." Call the belief that de facto authoritative morality will dependably come about naturally the "assumption of natural moral agreement." And call the belief that de jure authoritative morality will dependably come about naturally the "assumption of natural de jure moral agreement."

Hobbes's argument for the necessity of the sovereign is based on the assumption of natural moral discord: "*Good* and *evil* are names that signify our appetites and aversions, which in different tempers, customs, and doctrines of men are different. . . . Nay, the same man in divers times differs from himself, and one time praises—that is, calls good—what another time he dispraises and calls evil; from whence arise disputes, controversies, and at last war" (*L*, chap. 15). Note that this argument for inevitable moral disagreement is somewhat contrary to the implication of Hobbes's statement that the Golden Rule is "intelligible even to the meanest capacity." At the same time, bear in mind that the assumption of moral discord upon which Hobbes's argument rests is not just an assumption about the inevitability of moral disagreement. It is also an assumption about the undependability of people applying moral restraints to themselves at all. Even if people could be expected to converge on the same moral principles, they could not be expected to apply those principles to themselves without a sovereign to protect them against others who might otherwise take advantage. The assumption of moral discord assumes the inevitability of conflict at the level of opinions *and* actions. Since the threat that undermines de facto and de jure morality persists until natural moral discord is replaced with a single commanding moral voice, it follows that the existence of a sovereign who is the author of the content of morality is the very condition of the existence of any morality that anyone ought truly to be bound by.

Hobbes's argument is like a layer cake. On top is de jure authoritative morality; its underlying necessary condition is de facto authoritative morality; the necessary condition underlying this is the authority of the sovereign. What justifies this order of conditions is the assumption of natural moral discord. Because of this assumption, the condition of de jure morality is an absolute sovereign who is the author of morality. But Hobbes's cake is upside down.

To begin to see this, consider that both the assumption of natural moral discord and of natural moral agreement are self-fulfilling prophecies. (Remember that the assumptions apply to actions as well as to beliefs.) If people in the state of nature generally believe there is natural moral discord, then there will be, because it will be foolish for them to restrain themselves according to moral principles. If people generally believe that there is natural moral agreement, then it will seem reasonable to them to conform to the moral principles they see people around them conforming to, and they will, with the effect that it will become more reasonable for others to conform as well, which will tend to make the original belief true. The two assumptions are not only self-fulfilling, but self-expanding as well. The more people come to expect moral discord, the more unreasonable it becomes for them to apply moral restraints and the more moral discord there will be for others to see, the more unreasonable it will be for them to apply moral restraints, and so on, until the war of all against all results. If the opposite process began (either because there was natural moral agreement or because there was believed to be such long enough for the belief to begin to come true), then that would provide the guarantee of protection needed to make further conformity to moral restraints reasonable, which in turn would make it more 87 reasonable for others to restrain themselves, providing more guarantee and then more restraint, and so on, right up to a state of peace—without a sovereign!

Thus, we can undermine Hobbes's argument if we can replace the assumption of natural moral discord with that of natural moral agreement. Because these assumptions have multiplier effects, it is not necessary to assume anything like perfect natural moral agreement to undermine Hobbes. If there were enough of it to generate a common belief in natural moral agreement, that would be enough to provide the guarantees and start the expanding process of voluntary moral restraint in motion. (Hobbes's argument might still show that whoever started this process was irrational in that he took an unwarranted risk—but then we should just thank that person along with the first person who risked appearing foolish by trying to utter words before they had meanings.) For the moment, no more need be noted than that if the assumption of natural moral agreement were true it would provide a route out of the war of all against all without first establishing an absolute sovereign. Hobbes admits as much: "If we could suppose a great multitude of men to consent to the observation of justice and other laws of nature without a common power to keep them all in awe, we might as well suppose all mankind to do the same; and then there neither would be, nor need to be, any civil government or commonwealth at all, because there could be peace without subjection" (*L*, chap. 17).

Recall further that the assumption of natural moral agreement comes in two forms—corresponding to de facto and de jure authoritative morality, respectively. The de facto form simply assumes that people will, in fact, come to agree on their moral judgments, though which ones they agree on will just be a matter of historical chance—much as people come to agree on the standard spelling of words though what they agree on is just a matter of historical chance. The de jure form assumes that people will, in fact, come to agree on a particular set of moral judgments that are true. In either case, de facto or de jure, the assumption of natural moral agreement includes the assumption that people will dependably make their actions conform to their moral judgments, even at the expense of their self-interest, and enforce them on potential violators.

In discussing Hobbes in chapter 1, I mentioned that his theory contained an even more profound flaw than we considered then. We are now in a position to take this up. The deeper problem with Hobbes's theory is that no sovereign can exercise power alone. The notion that people surrender their power to the sovereign once and for all is a fiction and a misleading one. It suggests the image of marionettes all handing over their strings to one person who thereafter controls their movements. This does not correspond to the way political power is actually exercised in human common-wealths, or even could be (short of science fiction fantasy). The sovereign's power is the power to command, and the power to command is continually dependent on the willingness to obey. Even punishments that the sovereign may threaten for disobedience depend on the willingness of his lieutenants to carry out his commands, which in turn depends on the willingness of a substantial part of the populace to go along with their doing so, and so on. Hobbes's argument that the sovereign cannot be party to the covenant be-cause he must already be empowered for the covenant to be binding (*L*, chap. 18) can be turned around against Hobbes: The sovereign's power cannot be the source of his subjects' obedience, since they (or a substantial number of them) must already obey for him to have power.

Conformity to rules cannot be the product of the coercive power of the sovereign, because that power is itself the product of conformity to rules. Once a political system is in place, it may be risky for any individual to disobey the sovereign's commands. But this is not a risk caused by power literally in the sovereign's hands, but rather the high likelihood that others will obey the sovereign's command to punish violators. If a large enough number of his subjects decide not to, they could not be forced to do so. This is why the commonwealth is not the automaton, operating independently of the natural persons that make up its parts, that Hobbes had in mind in writing of "that great *Leviathan* called a *Commonwealth* . . . which is but an artificial man" (*L*, Intro.).

Sovereign power exists only if a substantial number of people can gen-erally be depended upon voluntarily to agree to, conform to, and enforce some rules determining how they should behave, irrespective of their desires. But, then, the existence of sovereign power itself depends on granting the assumption of natural de facto moral agreement. And since this is equivalent to assuming the existence of de facto authoritative morality without a civil authority to enforce it, we see that, rather than the existence of sovereign power being the necessary condition of de facto authoritative morality, de facto authoritative morality is the necessary condition of the existence of sovereign power. If we grant that the sovereign is necessary to end the war of all against all, it follows that de facto authoritative morality is a necessary condition of ending the war of all against all—directly opposite to the sequence Hobbes conceived. In fact, de facto authoritative morality *is* the end of the war of all against all, at least in the form of the threat of overt violence, and this shows that the war could be ended without establishing a sovereign authority. As the Bob Dylan song has it, "to live outside the law, you must be honest."

There is more. As Locke saw, the state of war survives the installation   89 of Hobbes's sovereign. It exists even during the sovereign's establishment of peace. Since cessation of hostility is always subject to the sovereign's arbitrary will (because nothing prevents him from undertaking violence at any moment), there is never reason to assume that peace will last a moment more, and thus there is the same need for preemptive protective action as existed before the institution of the sovereign. This makes it clear that the objectionable feature of the war of all against all is not violence but subjection to the desires and power of others; violence is only a manifestation of a subjection that can persist even though overt violence ceases. The real danger in the state of nature, then, is not war but subjugation; war is only its continuation by violent means. Or, equivalently, the nonviolent subjection of each to the desires of others is the war of all against all carried on by peaceful means, at least in the extended sense that in this condition, as in open war, people are limited in what they do to one another only by what is physically possible.

If this is so, then it follows that the existence of a de facto authoritative morality is not itself enough to end the war of all against all permanently. It can achieve a temporary cessation of overt hostilities, but when the war of all against all is understood in its wider sense, as including even the nonviolent subjugation of people to the desires and judgments of others, de facto morality provides no security. A de facto morality might actually dress the desires of some people in the garments of sanctity and continue the subjugation of some to the desires and power of others by becoming, in effect, if not in conscious intention, the very means of that power. Given that people's desires and judgments may conflict, they will be inclined to question any existing de facto morality, even their own, and particularly to suspect that it is being used to promote other people's desires at their expense. Consequently, the existence of a de facto authoritative morality is subject to constant attack, suspicion, and doubt. As such, its authority is rendered shaky, and the security it is supposed to provide weakened.

The only way a de facto morality could inspire the necessary confidence to keep its own authority dependable would be if it represented that set of moral principles to which, irrespective of their suspicions and conflicting judgments, rational people are bound to return. And if there is such a morality, one that will withstand challenge and doubt, it must represent the resting place toward which all rational moral questioning tends. Which is to say that it must be compelled by rational argument, certified true by passing the Cartesian test of doubt. Thus, there is no way out of the war of all against all unless the de facto authoritative morality truly distinguishes exercises of power that constitute subjugation from those that do not. De facto authoritative morality can only end the war of all against all permanently if it dependably approximates de jure morality. People, by exercising their reason, must naturally arrive at de jure moral agreement.

To bring a real end to the war of all against all, in or out of the state of nature, then, there must be de jure authoritative morality, as Locke saw: "Force without right upon a man's person makes a state of war both where there is, and is not, a common judge" (*ECG*, sec. 19). The danger in the state of nature is not violence but injustice, and the cure for the war of all against all is not peace but justice. Locke turns Hobbes's argument rightside up. De facto authoritative morality is the condition of ending the war of all against all; de jure authoritative morality is the condition of a de facto authoritative morality able to do so.

This is a striking conclusion—particularly because de jure authoritative morality is only possible if human beings, using their reason, can be depended upon to arrive at true moral beliefs. It amounts to claiming that the very possibility of stable human society depends on human beings being able to identify true morality with the use of their reason and their being disposed to act on it. Naturally, this is not to say that every existing society is truly moral. The attempt by the members of any existing society to arrive at an understanding of morality will be vulnerable to all the errors that assail fallible human beings. Rather, the claim identifies a necessary condition of perfectly stable societies and a tendency built into the nature of imperfectly stable ones. Any society that is stable—not fraught with inner dissent, overt or suppressed—is one in which the morality of existing human relations is for the moment not doubted. To the extent that they come into doubt, the society is destabilized. Any stable society is a resting point of moral doubt, a moment during which people believe that they and their fellows are capable of identifying moral truth by their own faculties. Any stable society is based on the belief that people are arriving at moral truth by use of their reason and acting on it.

What Hobbes discovered was that stable social existence depends on an act of trust, which he understood as people's trust in one another's peacefulness. What he failed to see was that no political arrangement that did not already presuppose that trust could make that trust rational. (The parallel with Descartes—who could find no ground for trust in reason that did not presuppose that trust—confirms the link in their undertakings that I suggested at the outset.) The trust that Hobbes sought could not be made rational by empowering someone to enforce it, since that requires trust in the enforcer and his lieutenants. Moreover, while Hobbes was right in thinking that social existence depends on trust, he was wrong in thinking of it as trust in people's peacefulness instead of as trust in their sense of justice. Relationships of subjugation could be peaceful, and as long as this is possible, they would be unstable as well. They would perpetually invite "corrective" aggression. Thus, stable social existence depends on a deeper trust, on belief in the capacity of one's fellows to determine what justice requires and in their disposition to act on it, even at their own expense. And the possibility of a truly stable society, of ending the war of all against all permanently, presupposes that this belief is true.

Interestingly, Hobbes seems to have recognized as much, albeit obliquely. We saw that Hobbes's sovereign has no effective obligations to his subjects. What Hobbes saw was that the subjects have no effective obligation to refrain from rebelling against the sovereign. Since the only obligations that Hobbes allows are those backed up by the sovereign's power, the decision to use one's private power against the sovereign's is already a decision to risk the sovereign's power and thus cannot be bound by it. As soon as one is prepared to brave the sovereign's power, the obligation to obey him is no more than the obligation to obey the law of nature, which holds that one should try to establish a sovereign by covenant and honor the covenant—but this binds only in foro interno. Consequently, Hobbes held that the grounds of the sovereign's rights must be instilled in people by education, "because they cannot be maintained by any civil law or terror of legal punishment. For a civil law that shall forbid rebellion (and such is all resistance to the essential rights of the sovereignty) is not, as a civil law, any obligation, but by virtue only of the law of nature that forbids the violation of faith; which natural obligation if men know not, they cannot know the right of any law the sovereign makes" (*L*, chap. 30). This amounts to recognition that the sovereign's power ultimately rests on the prior existence of de jure authoritative morality among his subjects. It implicitly constitutes recognition that the end of the war of all against all, with or without the sovereign, depends on de jure authoritative morality among people.

Much as the significance of Descartes's discovery lay in recognizing that the possibility of science depended not on the knower's faith in God but on the knower's trust in his reason; so (equally contrary to appearances) the significance of Hobbes's discovery lay in recognizing that the possibility of society depended not on the citizens' faith in a sovereign but on the citizens' trust in their fellows' reason. But, unlike faith in God, trust in our own and our fellows' reason is trust in something within the reach of our knowledge. Accordingly, it is the philosopher's task to show that (or whether) this trust is well placed. In the social realm, this requires determining the truth of the belief that human beings have the capacity—reason—to discover what justice requires and the disposition to act on what they discover.

For this belief about human reason to be true, at least two conditions must obtain. First, there must be an asymmetry between human morality and human reason: We can determine whether any prevalent moral principle is reasonable; but we cannot apply the process in reverse—appealing to some widely accepted moral principle to determine what is reasonable—since appeal to any moral principle might be appeal to some principle only accepted de facto and thus unable to withstand doubt. Reason must be the final word on the content of morality. Second, each normal person exercising his reason must find the same principles of justice. These two conditions together imply that justice must be nothing other than what is reasonable for everyone and that each person exercising his reason must arrive at the recognition that what reason requires for him is what is reasonable for everyone. This means, in effect, that each person using his reason will come to judge his actions by the standard of whether they would be reasonable to every rational person. Ending the war of all against all requires, then, not simply an external contract established among human beings. It requires that the social contract be built into each separate rational individual as the very structure of his reasoning about how to act, and of course, that each is disposed to act on the results of that reasoning. The upshot of contractarian theory is that stable societies presuppose trust in the existence within each person of an internal social contract.

Insofar as the social contract embodies (as I shall argue later in this chapter) the Golden Rule, we can say that Hobbes perceived this necessity at least dimly, since he maintained that the laws of nature (comprising the "shadow morality" in the state of nature) could be summed up in the Golden Rule, which is "intelligible even to the meanest capacity" (*L*, chap. 15). These laws of nature can be gotten by "everyone from his own reason," because they are inherently "agreeable to the reason of all men." The laws of nature agreeable to the reason of all men are "contained in this one sentence approved by all the world: *Do not that to another which you think unreasonable to be done by another to yourself*" (*L*, chap. 26). In fact, it is because of this accessibility that "Ignorance of the law of nature excuses no man, because every man that has attained to the use of reason is supposed to know he ought not to do to another what he would not have done to himself" (*L*, chap. 27).

But Hobbes only hinted that reasoning agreeable to all is built into the reasoning of all. It remained to prove that it is, and we can understand Rousseau's version of the social contract theory as a step in this direction. Rousseau took up the problem of authority at the point at which it was left by Locke and Hobbes. Hobbes held sovereign authority over citizens to be necessary because of the danger to freedom of leaving things to people's judgments, and Locke held sovereign authority over citizens to be dangerous to freedom if it was not subject to people's judgments. Rousseau accepts

93

both notions: He holds (with Locke) that "be the constitution of a government what it may, if there be within its jurisdiction a single man who is not subject to the law, all the rest are necessarily at his discretion" (*DOI*, 29). And he holds (with Hobbes) that no sooner does a person "subject another to his private will, than he departs from civil society, and confronts him face to face in the pure state of nature" (*DPE*, 124).

Rousseau's solution lay in relocating the distinction between the state of nature and civil society (that is, society subject to civil law) *within* each individual, as a distinction between two capacities in which he can act— his capacity to act according to his private will and his capacity to act according to the general will. A person exercises the former capacity when he reasons and acts in light of his private interest, and he exercises the latter capacity when he reasons and acts in abstraction from his private interest (*DPE*, 122–23). Although this latter capacity is learned from being subject to civil law, it is nonetheless natural to his reason, since what the law teaches him is "to act according to the rules of his own judgment, and not to behave inconsistently with himself" (*DPE*, 124). Correspondingly, the distinction between subject and sovereign is also a distinction within each individual, depending upon the capacity in which he acts: "The words subject and Sovereign are identical correlatives the idea of which meets in the single word 'citizen'" (*SC*, 237). Rousseau took the whole people in a nation to be the one and only sovereign and understood individuals to have sovereign authority insofar as they acted as parts of that whole in light of the general will. The same individuals were subjects insofar as they acted in light of their private interest. The authority of the sovereign is the authority of the individual (in her general capacity) exercised over herself (in her private capacity). Since no one is unfree who exercises authority over herself, such authority is no threat to freedom. Accordingly, Rousseau can slip between the horns of the Hobbes-Locke dilemma. He can make the commonwealth subject to the citizens' judgments—and as long as they will ascertain and act on the general will, this does not reproduce the dangers of the state of nature.

Rousseau's views on the state of nature and civil society are notoriously ambivalent. He is, for example, profuse in his praise for the constitution of his home city of Geneva—the *Discourse on the Origin of Inequality* is dedicated to the Republic of Geneva—and yet he asserts in that same essay that "the history of civil society" is the history "of human sickness" (*DOI*, 28ff. and 51). In contrast to Hobbes, Rousseau took the state of nature to be naturally peaceful and held that the war Hobbes saw there was, in fact, the product of the conflicting interests that people only begin to have as the result of society—though by *society*, here, Rousseau does not yet understand

94

"civil society," but a spontaneous association of human beings governed by instinctive morality and not yet by law (*DOI*, 65, 82, 106). He took society to emerge not as an escape from the disabilities of the state of nature, but as a result of the inherent tendency of human beings toward self-improvement, which, by leading people to desire products that only cooperation could provide, leads as well to greater possessions, greater inequalities, and ultimately to the conflicts of interest that necessitate the law—that is, the establishment of civil society (*DOI*, 76–92).

Rousseau saw prelegal society as "the happiest and most stable of epochs." It was destroyed only by revolutions in material civilization, particularly in metallurgy and agriculture, which produced an abundance that could not be resisted, even at the cost of mutual dependence and servitude: "It was iron and corn," wrote Rousseau, "which first civilized man, and ruined humanity" (*DOI*, 83). And yet there is no turning back. Rousseau is resigned to civil society and sees his task as that of determining the conditions that might make it not such a bad bargain after all. Although human beings, writes Rousseau, "become unhappy and wicked in becoming sociable . . . , yet we should not think that there is neither virtue nor happiness for us and that heaven has abandoned us without remedy from depravity. We should rather try to extract from the evil itself the remedy which can cure it."[1]

What is needed "is to find a form of association . . . in which each, while uniting himself with all, may still obey himself alone, and remain as free as before. This is the fundamental problem of which the social contract provides the answer" (*SC*, 174). And the essence of the contract is that: "*Each of us puts his person and all his power in common under the supreme direction of the general will, and, in our corporate capacity, we receive each member as an indivisible part of the whole*" (*SC*, 175). With this act, a "corporate and collective body" is put in place of "the individual personality of each contracting party." This corporate body is, in the first instance, not yet a full civil society with a government and the rest—it is the organization of the people into a single body which can, in turn, give itself a government. It is a change in people's souls: "The passage from the state of nature to the civil state produces a very remarkable change in man, by substituting justice for instinct in his conduct. . . . Then only . . . does man . . . find that he is forced to act on different principles and to consult his reason before listening to his inclinations." Although the transformation is not without cost or risk, it must be judged positive, even wonderful: "Although, in this state, he deprives himself of some advantages which he got from nature, he gains in return others so great . . . that, did not the abuses of this new condition often degrade him below that which he left, he would be bound to bless continually the happy moment which took him from it for ever, and, instead of a stupid and unimaginative animal, made him an intelligent being and a man" (*SC*, 178).

In precontract society, human beings were moral by instinctive compassion (*DOI*, 67). With the contract and the inner change it represents, they become moral by reason. Despite its perils, this inner change brings with it nothing less than that "moral liberty, which alone makes [one] truly master of himself; for the mere impulse of appetite is slavery, while obedience to a law which we prescribe to ourselves is liberty" (*SC*, 178). But this requires that the actual law that governs society express the general will. If it does not, then some are subject to the private wills of others; if it does, then all are free, even if we are forced to conform to it, since it is that by which we are "secured against all personal dependence" (*SC*, 177). The general will is the only way in which all can be ruled without anyone being subjugated by anyone else.

Rousseau did not so much solve the Hobbes-Locke dilemma as recognize what shape the solution must take. If the sovereign is the citizenry ascertaining and acting according to the general will, then the sovereign is neither beyond accountability to the citizens nor subject to the undependable private judgments of the citizens. But this solution is only successful in the degree to which we can depend on people's ability and disposition to abstract from their private interests in determining the general will—and Rousseau ran into his greatest difficulties in trying to design institutions that could be "guaranteed" to reach truly general decisions. For our purposes, however, it is interesting to note that Rousseau treated this capacity to ascertain the general will as a process of reasoning, natural and accessible to everyone, and inscribed in the very reasoning that leads to the contract itself. Insofar as people are led by rational recognition of their conflicting interests to form themselves into a unity, they are led to reason as if they were a single body with a single will. Rousseau believed that, insofar as the people "regard themselves as a single body, they have only a single will which is concerned with their common preservation and general well-being. In this case . . . , the common good is everywhere clearly apparent, and only good sense is needed to perceive it" (*SC*, 247). What is lacking from Rousseau's argument, however, is an account of human nature that would show that people can, in fact, be depended upon to think of themselves as a single body after the need that moves them to create civil society is quieted. Rousseau goes some distance beyond Hobbes in justifying the trust that social existence requires by asserting that morality is a natural tendency of human reasoning, but he does not go far enough to prove it. This task fell to Kant, whose theory we shall take up in due course.

96

The Puzzle of the Rational Necessity of Morality: Critique of Benevolence, Utilitarianism, Idealism, Neo-Hobbesianism, and Universalizability

To show morality to be the natural tendency of reason, it will not suffice to demonstrate that reasoning beings tend in fact to arrive at similar moral judgments. Reason is not like a muscle that might take on habitual ways of acting. Reason is a process of testing beliefs about what exists and how to act. If morality is to be the natural tendency of reason, morality must emerge as the point at which beliefs about action that survive reason's tests converge. To show that morality is the natural tendency of reason, we must prove that acting morally is required by reason. And this is a puzzle as old as philosophy.

It is generally agreed that it is reasonable for people to act on their self-interest. Morality, by contrast, seems to require acting contrary to one's self-interest, either positively acting in the interests of others at the expense of one's own or at least limiting one's pursuit of one's self-interest to make way for the pursuit by others of theirs. The puzzle, then, is how it can be required by reason that a creature for whom acting on self-interest is reasonable act contrary to his own interests.

This puzzle must be distinguished from a related but less difficult one— how acting morally is compatible with being reasonable. Why is it not irrational, even crazy, for a self-interested being to act for interests that are not his own? The harder puzzle is that of how it is unreasonable *not* to act morally. How is acting morally required by reason? The harder puzzle includes the easier. Showing that reason requires acting morally entails that acting morally is compatible with being reasonable. Since the trust that social existence presupposes is that people can be depended on to arrive at and act on the same moral beliefs, the harder puzzle must be solved: Only if acting morally is required by reason can morality be the dependable tendency of reason—as opposed to a mere option for it.

It will not do to assert that the puzzle is illusory, that acting morally is really acting in one's long-term self-interest. No doubt this is often enough true. Those who act immorally risk retaliation and may contribute to increasing the likelihood of their own victimization at the hands of other immoral actors. But morality asks of us more than is necessary to avoid these outcomes; otherwise, aged or terminally ill people who would not live long enough to suffer the negative consequences of their immoral actions would have no obligations. Or, to take an example from Plato's *Republic*, someone who possessed the ring of Gyges (which enables its wearer to become invisible), or some equivalent means to keep his transgressions

97

secret, would have no obligation not to transgress. Morality seems to require more than prudence with regard to one's own future. Unless morality turns out to be something much different from what it seems, then, the puzzle is a real one.

There are five major strategies for solving this puzzle: benevolence, utilitarianism, idealism, neo-Hobbesianism, and universalizability. The five strategies are varieties of two broader approaches, the first four aiming to show the substantive reasonableness of morality (that acting morally serves some interest or inclination that reasonable beings have) and the last aiming to show that morality is demanded by the formal requirements of practical reason (that deciding to act morally is required if the reasoning by which one determines how to act is to be logical). In this section, I shall take up the five strategies in order. We shall see that the first four are unable to solve the harder puzzle and show that reason requires morality. The fifth seems to prove that reason requires morality but, in fact, proves that reason's requirements parallel those of morality—they are a pale and lifeless image running alongside morality, lacking the force necessary to account for the way that moral requirements require.

The strategy of *benevolence* attributes to people a motivation to promote the interests of others (see, for example, *EPM*, 42–51). If people have such a motivation, it is part of their sovereign interest. Recall that sovereign interests are not necessarily egoistic or selfish. They may be characterized by interest in the well-being of some or all other human beings, or even of all other sentient creatures. If this is so, then acting in the interest of others, as morality requires, is surely reasonable. But this cannot show that reason *requires* such acting in the interest of others, because for it to require that, it would have to override contrary inclinations, mandating other-interested action when one was not inclined to act benevolently. To establish that we are required by reason to act for others' interests, we would have to show that we are required to act benevolently even when we are not moved by benevolence. This shows the general fallacy in thinking that moral requirements are based on people's benevolence: Benevolent people desire to serve the interests of others. If benevolent action is required, it must be required precisely of those who do not desire it. But then people's benevolence cannot be the ground of a moral requirement to act benevolently.

Similar comments apply to T. M. Scanlon's attempt to defend contractarian moral theory (he calls it "contractualism") by claiming that it represents a compelling account of basic moral motivation. "According to contractualism," Scanlon writes, "the source of motivation that is directly triggered by the belief that an action is wrong is the desire to be able to justify one's actions to others on grounds they could not reasonably reject."[2]

This desire is not really a plausible candidate for the source of moral motivation. It is necessary to note this, since I shall argue later that contractarianism rests on a rational requirement to act on grounds that all could reasonably accept and that justification constitutes giving such grounds. But on my view, these conditions are derivative. They are not the source of moral motivation, but (as I shall argue in the next section) rationally required by the knowledge gained through identifying with one's fellows. And this difference between what is source and what is derivative is important. If one accepts Scanlon's account because one unconsciously recognizes that what people cannot reasonably reject is what does not harm their interests, then concern for other people's interests is one's source of motivation and concern for their agreement (or nondisagreement) is derivative. To take Scanlon seriously then, one must believe that what motivates people to be moral is a desire that other people be able to agree with one's reasons independently of why this is a good thing for those other people. And this, particularly since it is not a desire for other people's actual agreement with one's reasons (as Scanlon points out, people may actually accept what it is not reasonable for them to accept), is a quite unlikely candidate for the source of moral motivation. If, by contrast, Scanlon's motivation is derived from a desire to promote or not harm the interests of others, then it boils down to an attenuated form of benevolence. Accordingly, it can give us no rational requirement to be moral, since that would require showing it to be required that we act as if we had this motivation even when we do not.

Utilitarianism holds that an individual is obligated to do whatever will produce the greatest sum of satisfaction of the desires of all the people (or, in some versions, all sentient creatures) affected by her action, herself included (see, for example, *U*, 6, 16, 25). But the sum of satisfaction is a numerical construct, composed of the satisfactions of the desires of separate individuals—the sum itself exists nowhere, is experienced by no one. This means that the sum has no reality beyond the separate satisfactions of the separate people involved, no matter how well arithmetical summing may hide this fact. Consequently, when a person is asked to act at the expense of her own desires in order to produce the greatest sum of satisfaction all told, she is simply being asked to frustrate her own desires in the name of the desires of some other people. Although it may be right to require this sacrifice, proving that such a sacrifice is right calls for more than showing that the sacrifice satisfies those others, no matter how many they are. This only reproduces the situation in which the suspicion of subjugation arises: Some number of people judge that another should sacrifice her desires so that they can satisfy theirs. Utilitarianism simply restates the question of subjugation in declarative tones, hoping to pass it off as the answer.

I think this shows that utilitarianism cannot generate a binding moral obligation. Philosophers have tended to criticize utilitarianism for yielding moral conclusions that seem intuitively false. For example, because utilitarianism holds that whatever maximizes aggregate satisfaction is right, it allows the possibility that punishment of the innocent or suppression of dissenters may be justified if or when such actions make a large enough number of other people happy—and this seems intuitively unjust. But appeals to intuition cannot sink utilitarianism, since our intuitions may be wrong or (as utilitarians have been quick to argue) tailored for those average situations where repression of individuals reduces rather than increases aggregate satisfaction. If I am right, the critics were intuiting utilitarianism's inability to generate a binding requirement. And this reflects the deeper fact that some people's desires cannot themselves generate requirements on the behavior of others.

It is no accident, then, that benevolence has figured centrally in the arguments of utilitarians. Indeed, some have arrived at utilitarianism by taking morality to be what a perfectly benevolent observer of human society would do. Since such an observer would desire to act in the interests of everyone, he would maximize overall satisfaction, and so on. Needless to say, if human beings were perfectly benevolent observers, they would be utilitarians voluntarily. There would be no need to require them to be so.

Some of utilitarianism's defenders have argued that satisfaction of desires is the only thing that is "good in itself" and therefore that we must maximize it wherever it occurs. But this is based on a confusion. The utilitarian's claim that what is good is what reason requires us to promote is based on the fact that what each finds good for herself—the satisfaction of her own desires—she will find reasonable to promote. But this cannot get us any further than the notion that reason requires each to promote her own satisfaction. When utilitarians call the satisfaction of everyone's desires "good," *good* signifies that property common to those results that different individuals have reason to promote. But then good has lost its tie to what any particular individual has reason to promote. The attempt to defend utilitarianism by calling satisfaction the only thing that is good in itself illicitly elides the distinction between good as what an individual has reason to promote and good as what is common to what individuals have reason to promote but that no particular individual has reason to promote; the generalization is purchased at the price of giving up the claim on individuals. This is equally true of the views of those who, like Sidgwick, shore up their utilitarianism with the claim that the satisfaction of one person's desire is (all other things equal) inherently as good as the satisfaction of any other's.[3] Even if this is true, it means no more than that the satisfaction of one person's desire is as good a reason for him to act as the satisfaction of any other person's desire is for her. To suggest that the satisfaction of any person's desire is as good a reason for me to act as is the satisfaction of my own desire betrays the original way in which the goodness of satisfaction makes it a reason for an individual to act.

What I call *idealism* derives from Plato's own attempt to cope with the problem presented by the ring of Gyges. It is essentially the argument that the just person is the happy person. There is an ultimate convergence of self-interest and regard for the interests of others, because being just is a condition of psychic well-being. There are several problems with this solution. The first is that it is too good to be true. The unjust are not always unhappy, nor are the just always happy. What is more, it seems hard to separate the unhappiness that unjust people may, in fact, suffer from their feelings of guilt. If their suffering arises from guilt, then they must feel they have failed at something required. But then the unhappiness of the unjust (or the happiness of the just) could not be used to establish the reasonableness of the requirement to serve the interests of others because if this was not already reasonable it would be irrational to suffer guilt for failing at it.

Moreover, since unjust acts surely have some attractions, any claim that the unjust are unhappy as a result of the evil they do must mean that the unjust experience *net* unhappiness (a surplus of unhappiness over the pleasures of evil). This claim must either be an empirical one, roughly that the dissatisfactions produced by doing injustice outweigh its satisfactions, or an essential one, roughly that the pleasures of being just are intrinsically better than those of being unjust. The empirical claim seems so inherently subject to contingencies—the chance of getting caught, the success of the unjust acts, how long a person lives after his evildoing, how capable he is of self-deception—as to make it extremely unlikely that it could be universally true. The essential version, however, seems to rest on a moral evaluation of certain pleasures as intrinsically better than others, and that consigns the view to vicious circularity.

Another version of idealism is Aristotelian in inspiration. It holds that individuals have an "essential" or "ideal" self, embodying the norms of their proper functioning. These norms are commonly called "virtues," a word linked etymologically with such others as "virility," and which thus implies the realization of essential powers. We seem to be able to say, in a more or less factual way, that things are good when they serve their functions. A broken watch is a watch, but an accurate watch is a good watch, and a dull knife is a knife, but a sharp one is a good one. The functions of such things are part of their definitions (a watch is something that tells time, a knife

101

something that cuts) and, thus, part of their essences. As such, it is possible to identify an ideal watch or knife and judge how far any actual one lives up to its ideal nature by how well it serves its essential functions. Accuracy is the virtue of watches and sharpness of knives. If we could identify the essential functions of human beings, then, we would have the human virtues, and when they were realized by someone, we could say that he was good. And if these virtues or norms of proper human functioning included serving the interests of others, then reason would require this in the same way that it requires winding watches and sharpening knives.

There are two problems with this approach. First, reason does not really require that we wind watches or sharpen knives. At most, these are required when we need the timing or cutting functions. That is, although identifying the functions of things may indicate their good, it does not itself dictate that achieving or perfecting those functions is good, and certainly not that failing to is bad. It follows that even if we could identify an essential human function, we would not necessarily have something that humans were required to realize. This points to the second problem—namely, that human beings do not seem to have essential purposes or functions. Any attempt to attribute some to them either turns out to take their purpose as something like being happy (and is thus reducible to the Platonic form of idealism, which we have already considered) or reads into them the philosopher's or the culture's picture of proper human functioning. This has the effect of either asserting the norms of proper human functioning dogmatically (they are just what the philosopher believes they are) or relativistically (they are whatever the culture takes them to be), but not rationally. Such cultural relativism is the ironic fate of Alisdair MacIntyre's attempt to reinvigorate the Aristotelian emphasis on the virtues as a corrective to modern-day ethical relativism.[4] Lacking Aristotle's faith in the possibility of finding an eternal list of essential human functions, MacIntyre seeks them in the norms of proper functioning inscribed in the roles available in the actual communities in which we live. But fighting ethical relativism with cultural relativism only produces relativism squared: Why should we believe that the norms embedded in actual communities will give us either moral rectitude or proper human functioning?

It is generally a mistake to think that one could prove that reason requires serving the interests of others by first showing that this is a norm of proper human functioning. The only chance of establishing this as a norm of proper human functioning is by first showing that it is required of human beings—which is to say, one must proceed in exactly the reverse order of the Aristotelian strategy. This is the general lesson in all the forms of what I have called idealism. Idealism aims to show a convergence of the self and morality by reading some moral vision into the constitution of the self. But this necessarily requires that the moral vision be established as rationally required first, or else we cannot know whether the norms of proper human functioning are really normative or merely prejudices. Virtue, like the moral goodness of benevolence, must be derivative in a rational moral theory. Once we have established what people are entitled to, then we can see that benevolence is a moral motivation because it serves ends determined independently to be moral, and then we can see that virtue is a norm of proper functioning because it serves norms determined independently to be proper.

The strategy I call *neo-Hobbesianism* has a number of contemporary proponents. In *The Moral Point of View*, Kurt Baier has maintained that valid moral rules are "in the interest of everyone alike" (*MPV*, 106–9). The moral point of view is that in which actions are evaluated from the standpoint of everyone's interest, much as the pedestrian's point of view lies in evaluating things from the standpoint of those who walk the streets rather than drive. Though I think that Baier is fundamentally correct on this, he does not do much to specify how one determines what is in everyone's interest alike, except to distinguish it from what makes everyone happy or maximizes aggregate satisfaction; and he does not do much to prove that what is in everyone's interest alike is the moral point of view, beyond pointing out that it does seem to be what we mean when we make moral assertions. He does, however, offer an argument for why it is rational to be moral.

Baier grants that being moral often goes against one's self-interest—it is just this that makes the question "Why is it rational to be moral?" so difficult. Following Hobbes, Baier maintains that a world in which people always pursued their self-interest would be a world of unending conflict and thus not generally in people's self-interest. It is therefore necessary to have rules to adjudicate conflicts of self-interest. The universal pursuit "of self-interest must lead to what Hobbes called the state of nature. At the same time, it will be clear to everyone that universal obedience to certain rules overriding self-interest would produce a state of affairs which serves everyone's interest much better than his unaided pursuit of it in a state where everybody does the same" (*MPV*, 149). These are the moral rules, and they have priority over pursuit of self-interest because that is their point in the first place. "The very *raison d'être* of a morality is to yield reasons which overrule the reasons of self-interest in those cases when everyone's following self-interest would be harmful to everyone. Hence moral reasons are superior to all others" (*MPV*, 150). They could not adjudicate conflicts of self-interest without being able to prohibit the pursuit of self-interest in certain situations.

"The answer to our question 'Why should we be moral?' is therefore as follows," writes Baier. "We should be moral because being moral is following rules designed to overrule reasons of self-interest whenever it is in the interest of everyone alike that such rules should be generally followed" (*MPV*, 155). But this answer is circular. Since being moral is doing what "is in the interest of everyone alike," it amounts to saying that we should do what is in the interest of everyone alike because it is in the interest of everyone alike that we do. Baier's argument contains enough truth to refute the charge that a person who sacrifices his own interest on moral grounds is irrational. But that is not enough to show that reason requires individuals to make such sacrifices when they could get away with not making them. And that is what is needed if reason is to establish not just the sanity of being moral but the requirement of it.

Another version of neo-Hobbesianism is presented by David Gauthier in *Morals by Agreement*. Gauthier takes rationality to amount to pursuit of self-interest understood as maximization of one's own utility (*MBA*, 22). For rationality to dictate morality, it is necessary to show that being moral maximizes one's utility. And yet for morality to be thereby dictated, it must constrain one's pursuit of self-interest. Consequently, Gauthier must prove that it is in one's self-interest to constrain one's pursuit of one's self-interest. And that is what he sets out to do. He defends a conception of morality (or justice) as that set of constraints upon an individual's pursuit of her self-interest that make it reasonable for others voluntarily to enter into mutually beneficial cooperation with her (*MBA*, 113). Thus, being moral is not the same as simply pursuing one's self-interest. Nonetheless, Gauthier contends that being moral is dictated by self-interest, because by being moral we make it reasonable for others to cooperate with us and thereby we obtain the advantages of such cooperation. He argues that voluntary cooperation requires that one be willing to share with one's collaborators the surplus generated by cooperation (over what one could have had without cooperation) broadly in proportion to each collaborator's contribution (*MBA*, 150–56). Since self-interest consists in maximization of one's utility, unconstrained self-interest would lead a person to try to gain as much of the surplus as she could, all of it if possible. But if a person tried to do this, others would not enter voluntarily into cooperative ventures with her, thereby denying her the benefits of cooperation. Being moral (constraining one's maximizing) is in one's self-interest, then, because "constrained maximizers can . . . obtain cooperative benefits that are unavailable to straightforward maximizers" (*MBA*, 170).

Gauthier recognizes that this does not yet get us all the way to a rational (that is, utility-maximizing) requirement to be moral (that is, to constrain one's utility maximizing) because it leaves open the possibility that one might do even better by cheating when one could get away with it, since "straightforward maximizers can, on occasion, exploit unwary constrained maximizers." To cope with this possibility, Gauthier introduces a novel move. He shifts from the level of particular choices about particular cooperative endeavors to the level of the general choice about whether one will be a constrained maximizer (CM) or a straightforward maximizer (SM) with respect to all the cooperative endeavors that may present themselves: "We consider what a rational individual would choose, given the alternatives of adopting straightforward maximization, and of adopting constrained maximization, as his disposition for strategic behavior" (*MBA*, 170).

For a person to reap the benefits of cooperative endeavors, others must trust that she is not merely pretending to be a CM, while actually being an SM ready to take full advantage of them as soon as she thinks she can get away with it. The rationality of being a CM or an SM depends on the likelihood of others detecting one's true motives. If people's motives were transparent, it would be rational for us all to be CMs. If people's motives were opaque, it would be rational for us all to be SMs. But rather than being transparent or opaque, human beings are, to use Gauthier's happy term, "translucent." People can neither be certain of being recognized for what they truly are or of hiding it, nor of recognizing others for what they truly are. Thus, Gauthier takes up "the conditions under which the decision to dispose oneself to constrained maximization is rational for translucent persons" (*MBA*, 174).

Gauthier accepts that the gains of exploitation will be greater than the gains of cooperation, but he contends that they will not likely be terribly greater. If there is a high enough proportion of CMs in a population, CMs will have many opportunities to obtain the gains of cooperation and few chances of being exploited. If the ability of people to tell SMs from CMs is great enough, SMs will have few opportunities to cheat and many cases of being denied cooperation. If then there are a sufficient number of CMs in the population and a sufficiently well-developed ability to judge character, CMs can expect to do better than SMs (*MBA*, 174–77). Since the benefits of cooperation are great, successful groups will tend not only to have a high proportion of CMs but also to cultivate the ability to detect other people's motives (*MBA*, 181, 188). Then, it will be generally the case that CMs can expect greater utility than SMs and thus that it is utility maximizing to choose constrained maximization, self-interestedly rational to dispose oneself to limit one's pursuit of self-interest morally.

Suppose that this argument succeeds in its own terms. What does it prove? Because I have argued that there is a personal imperative of self-interest, if Gauthier's argument proves that it is self-interestedly rational to choose to be the sort of person who (when in a population with a large enough number of CMs and a sufficiently well-developed ability to judge   105 people's motives—which I shall assume henceforth so as not to have to repeat) always subjects his pursuit of self-interest to moral constraint, then I shall have to grant—perhaps more fully than Gauthier himself would propose—that his argument proves morality to be required by reason. But Gauthier's argument does not prove that it is self-interestedly rational to choose to be the sort of person who always subjects his pursuit of self-interest to moral constraint because Gauthier has oversimplified the problem in at least three ways that dramatically limit the scope of his conclusion. He has assumed (1) that the alternatives are only two, being a CM or an SM; (2) that the choice between these alternatives is made by anyone with average abilities and opportunities, rather than by particular individuals with differing abilities and opportunities; and (3) that the choice is one that must be made once and for all. I shall take these up briefly and in order.

First, a CM is always disposed to limit her pursuit of self-interest on terms that make it reasonable for others to cooperate with her, and an SM is always going for as much as he can get. When an SM limits pursuit of his self-interest he does so only because he reasons that, in the case at hand, there is no way to get more and get away with it. Such a person will have inevitable difficulties in hiding his motives (given how consistent they are) and in refuting charges about his cheating (since he will probably have cheated on many other occasions). But consider a third alternative, the opportunistic maximizer (OM). He has read Gauthier and been generally convinced by the argument for choosing to be a CM even when there is a decent chance of getting away with cheating. But he holds open the possibility of cheating when rare opportunities present themselves—in particular, when the rewards of cheating are not just high but very high and the chance of nondetection not just decent but excellent. He will likely pass up opportunities that an SM would have grabbed, forgoing utility he might have captured. But the opportunities an OM does take are likely to yield him much and pose a minimal threat to his false reputation as a CM. Moreover, since an OM will have passed up many a moderately appealing opportunity to cheat, it will be harder for people to decipher his true motives and harder to pin the charge of cheating on him if he should get caught. It seems obvious that an OM will gain more than an SM, and very likely more than a CM, because he stands to gain all of the benefits that go to CMs plus a few. It follows that Gauthier has not proven that self-interested rationality dictates being a CM, only that it dictates not being an SM. Moreover, I would suggest that the OM comes closer to the actual psychology of (generally successful) cheats than does the SM and that rare opportunistic cheating rather than constant readiness to cheat represents the real temptation to backsliding that would-be CMs must contend with in themselves.

Second, assuming still that Gauthier's argument works, it implies that an SM of average capabilities of deception stands to gain less utility than a CM of average abilities of detection. But what of an SM with highly developed skills of deception, say, a master con artist? Surely, if her skills are good enough (including skill in judging opportunities), a master SM can hope to do better than the average expectation, and thus possibly better than she would do as a CM. Moreover, Gauthier's argument assumes that SMs and CMs face similar and average opportunities for cooperation with their fellows. But what of an SM with special opportunities, say, a gangster whose co-operative ventures have cheating others as their point? Such a person benefits from cooperating with some precisely because of his willingness to cheat others. This may require that he be a CM with his fellow gangmembers, but not a CM generally. Then, a gangster who is a CM with other gangsters but an SM with outsiders can (perhaps in direct relation to the degree to which the gangsters treat one another and no one else as CMs) expect to do better than a CM with normal opportunities.

Third, Gauthier thinks that he has proven that it is self-interestedly rational to choose to be the sort of person who always subjects her pursuit of self-interest to moral constraint, because he has shown this to be the rational solution to the problem in which a person must choose once and for all whether to be moral or straightforwardly self-interested. I think this is wrong both logically and psychologically.

It is wrong logically, because the rationality of disposing oneself to do X in every case is not equivalent to the rationality of irrevocably binding oneself to do X in each individual case. I do not deny that if it is rational to dispose oneself to do X in every case then it is generally rational to do X in each individual case. But that is all it is, *generally* rational. Further, I do not deny that it may be rational to bind oneself irrevocably to act some way in each individual case (as Ulysses did in order to hear the Sirens in safety)—only that that is not the same as it being rational to dispose oneself to act some way. If the doctor tells me that the next drop of alcohol will kill me, then, if I love life, that will imply that it is rational for me to refuse drink in every individual case. And it will be rational for me to bind myself irrevocably to refuse drink. But suppose that the doctor tells me that unless I keep my weight down I will die. Then, if I love life, it will be rational for me to dispose myself to dieting. But this will not rule out special cases (say, a meaningful celebration with friends) in which it may be rational for me to suspend my diet, on the assumption, say, that I will make up for it later. Precisely because Gauthier has had to move from the level of individual choices to the level of choices of dispositions to choose, he cannot treat his solution as like the alcohol case. It is like the dieting case, and that must   107 leave open the possibility (indeed, it must rationally require the possibility) of continual review of my disposition in order to judge its fittingness in the case at hand. But then the conclusion that it is self-interestedly rational to choose to be the sort of person who always subjects her pursuit of self-interest to moral constraint does not follow from it being rational to dispose oneself so.

I think Gauthier's way of addressing this problem is psychologically wrong because it assumes that one chooses one's character first and then acts it out. But character, like the related recognition of one's sovereign interest, takes shape progressively, over the course of a lifetime. Rather than choosing now and forever the kind of person one is and then just executing that policy choice in individual cases, people are continually confronted with choosing the sort of person they are—or at least with choosing whether or not to ratify prior choices about that. If the formation of character occurred in the way Gauthier's argument assumes, it would be much easier, much less of an accomplishment, to have a good character than it is.

At best, Gauthier has succeeded in proving that, if a person with average abilities and opportunities had to choose once and for all between the two alternatives of morality and straightforward pursuit of self-interest, it would be rational to choose morality because (in the appropriate population) this is the best way to assure oneself of being included in cooperative ventures and reaping their benefits. He has thus proved that (or identified one very powerful reason why) it is generally reasonable for people in the general run of situations to be moral. Although this is no small philosophical accomplishment, it does not get us where we need to get. It does not show that it is always unreasonable to be immoral. And thus it does not show us that being moral is required by reason.

The fifth strategy we take up gets its name from a logical device known as *universalizability*. This is the notion that if I affirm that something is a good reason for some action, I must grant that it is a good reason for that action in any relevantly similar circumstances. If I hold that I should be fed because I am hungry and deny that you should be fed though you are hungry, then, unless there are relevant differences between us—say, that you have refused to work though you are able-bodied or that you are a convicted murderer and there is not enough food to go around—I am guilty of the contradiction of affirming that being hungry both is a good reason for someone's being fed and is not a good reason for someone's being fed. If I hold that you should not be fed even if hungry because you have refused to work though able-bodied, then I must grant that I should not be fed even when hungry had I refused to work though I was able, unless there is yet another

108

relevant difference (which in turn must be universalized), and so on. Universalizability offers a way of showing that reason requires acting contrary to one's self-interest, because if I affirm that my self-interest should be served I must on pain of contradiction affirm that others' interests should be served as well.

The case for universalizability has been put most forcefully by Alan Gewirth in *Reason and Morality*. We saw in chapter 1 that Gewirth argues that each person must affirm her own entitlement to rights to freedom and well-being from others. Given this, Gewirth contends that, via universalizability, each person must affirm the same for all. Gewirth claims thereby to prove that respect for people's rights to freedom and well-being is required by reason because violators of those rights necessarily commit a logical self-contradiction. In response, philosophers have raised doubts about whether violators really do contradict themselves and whether they necessarily do— either of which doubt, if not resolvable, might suffice to sink Gewirth's theory.[5] But although these doubts (including those I raised in chapter 1) represent serious problems for Gewirth's theory, they do not identify the fatal flaw in the universalizability strategy. That flaw is most clearly seen if we grant, for the sake of argument, that Gewirth has succeeded in proving that each person must affirm her own rights to freedom and well-being and that violators of rights are necessarily logical self-contradictors—and then ask what this proof amounts to. I shall do this and shall show that it does not amount to a proof that we are morally required to respect people's rights.

Gewirth's argument does not prove that people are morally required to respect people's rights for the simple reason that logical requirements are not moral requirements. A Gewirthian has no satisfactory answer to a murderer who says "Yes, I've contradicted myself, but that's *all* I've done. What I did was no worse than affirming that a bachelor is married, and therefore you are only entitled to regard or treat me as gravely as you would someone who did that." Even if Gewirth is right, he has not proven that anyone (including the guilty party himself) need regard or treat a murderer more gravely than someone who asserts that bachelors are married. And that means that, even if universalizability is a logical requirement, it cannot be the source of any distinctively *moral* requirement. Preference for one's own self-interest over the interests of others may be arbitrary in a logical sense, but it is not wholly unreasonable for the one whose self-interest it is. He has, at least, the reason that it is the interest of the self he happens to be. To show that morality is required by reason, it will be necessary to support moral requirements with a reason strong enough to override the reason an individual has to prefer his own self-interest. Since the importance of a logical requirement is either small or indeterminate, it cannot do this job.   109

It follows that Gewirth may prove that reason's requirements parallel morality's, but not that reason requires morality in the distinctively moral way.

Summarizing the argument of *Reason and Morality*, Gewirth writes:

> First, every agent implicitly makes evaluative judgments about the goodness of his purposes and hence about the necessary goodness of the freedom and well-being that are necessary conditions of his acting to achieve his purposes. Second, because of this necessary goodness, every agent implicitly makes a deontic judgment in which he claims that he has rights to freedom and well-being. Third, every agent must claim these rights for the sufficient reason that he is a prospective agent who has purposes he wants to fulfill, so that he logically must accept the generalization that all prospective agents have rights to freedom and well-being. (*RM*, 48)

Gewirth calls this generalization the Principle of Generic Consistency (PGC). It is binding because "if the agent denies the generalization, then . . . he contradicts himself. For on the one hand in holding, as he logically must, that he has rights of freedom and well-being because he is a prospective purposive agent, he accepts that being a prospective purposive agent is a sufficient condition of having these rights; but if he denies the generalization, then he holds that being a prospective purposive agent is not a sufficient condition of having these rights" (*RM*, 112). In short, because I must affirm my own rights to freedom and well-being and because others are not different from me in ways relevant to this affirmation, I must affirm the rights of others to freedom and well-being. If I act so as to violate the rights of others then I implicitly deny that they have those rights, and affirming and denying the same proposition, I contradict myself. Even if we assume that this is correct, it does not get us where we need to get. I shall proceed in two steps, showing first that there is a serious defect in Gewirth's theory and then arguing that there is a fatal flaw in the universalizability strategy in general.

When someone asserts A and not-A, we can claim that he has contradicted himself, but we cannot claim that not-A is false. A might be false, in which case not-A would be true. One of the assertions must be wrong, but we do not know which. This reveals the serious defect in Gewirth's argument. From the fact that a person implicitly asserts his own rights and then contradicts himself by implicitly denying the rights of others, it does not follow that he is wrong to violate the rights of others. He may have been wrong to assert his own rights. All we know is that he is wrong to hold both assertions. Even if Gewirth is correct that prospective agents must affirm their own rights, that affirmation may still be mistaken—much as Kant recognized that even though a rational agent must believe he is free it remains possible that that belief is false. If an agent's affirmation of his own rights was false, then his denial of the rights of others would not be wrong. Even if Gewirth has proven that people are logically required to affirm the PGC as their supreme moral principle, it cannot be concluded that they do wrong if they violate this moral principle. This strongly suggests that Gewirth's approach (and for that matter, that of other philosophers—such as R. M. Hare—who appeal to the logical requirement of universalizability without first proving that the assertion to be universalized is true) is way off base: There is simply nothing about the logical relationship between an individual's assertions that can make his actions wrong in the moral sense.[6]

Though serious, this is not a fatal flaw because it leaves intact Gewirth's claim that people are required to govern their behavior by the PGC—given that they must or even that they generally do affirm their own rights. Even if this is true, however, the requirement thus established is not a moral one. And that is fatal for the universalizability strategy generally. The requirement of logical consistency is an impostor that resembles a moral requirement but is not one—a mere look-alike seized upon as a desperate substitute for the real thing.

In Gewirth's view, we cannot affirm directly (without the intermediary of the law of noncontradiction) that violating the interests of others is truly bad. The most we can say is that doing so is wrong because it is inconsistent with one's own affirmation of the importance of having one's own interests respected. There is strictly nothing wrong here but the sheer fact of inconsistency. That inconsistency can gain nothing in importance from what it is inconsistent about, as that would require that we be able to affirm directly that violating the interests of others is truly bad. This is why a Gewirthian has no way to refute a murderer who admits that he contradicted himself, but insists that that is all he did, and thus that he should be treated no more gravely than anyone else who makes a simple logical error.

Moreover, since a person's self-interest is the interest of the one and only self he happens to be, he has a powerful reason for preferring his self-interest. It is implausible to think that avoidance of a simple logical error—the sort one would be guilty of if one called a square round—is reason enough to override this preference. It is more implausible to think that it is reason enough to justify using force to prevent or punish acting on this preference. Since a moral requirement must override self-interest and (at least occasionally) license force against violators, it follows that a logical requirement does not have what it takes to be a moral requirement.

So, even if universalizability yields the conclusion that it is wrong to violate the interests of others, it is only logically wrong—not morally wrong.   111

This applies to all the rights comprised in the PGC. Accordingly, even if Gewirth has proven that it is logically required that we recognize others' rights, he has not proven that it is morally required. Even if Gewirth has succeeded in showing that denial of these rights is self-contradictory, what is morally wrong with this denial must be an error of a different sort than that of contradicting oneself, and the moral requirement to respect these rights must be based on different grounds than the requirement to avoid contradiction.

Universalizability is a logical device that mimics the concern for others that seems to characterize morality. Since a logical requirement is a species of rational requirement, it seems to provide a way in which reason can establish the requirement of being moral. But, at best, the requirement to avoid contradiction coincides with the requirement to be moral; the former is like the latter except that it lacks the seriousness and importance of the latter. Appeal to the logical requirement of universalizability cuts the heart out of the moral life and replaces it with a ghost that happens to resemble it.

Moreover, since it is a logical device, universalizability can only work on statements. Thus, it is not a constraint on how anyone should act; it is a constraint on what anyone may logically affirm about how he should act. In morality, however, actions speak louder than words. The rightness or wrongness of actions constrain what we may affirm about those actions—not vice versa. Reversing this reduces the flesh-and-blood concerns of morality to the watery-thin concerns of logicality—as if guilt at immorality were no more than regret over committing a logical self-contradiction. Only a philosopher could believe such a thing. Anyone who has experienced the pang of moral guilt knows the difference between it and the pain of contradiction. The pain of contradiction just does not hurt enough.

Morality as Reason's Passion: The Moral Imperative of Respect

Morality must either override self-interested reasons or be an illusion. If being moral is required by reason, there must be some constraint on self-interested reasoning that reason itself imposes. This constraint can only be one of two things—a requirement of logic or the necessary implication of the recognition of some fact. Our discussion of Gewirth's attempt shows that it cannot be a requirement of logic, since then we cannot say how being immoral is worse than being illogical. This leaves only one alternative. There must be some fact whose recognition limits the authority of self-interested reasoning and that provides the substantive basis for understanding what is distinctively wrong with being immoral. I think that this fact is the existence of other persons.

I contend that this fact makes reason take the distinctive shape of morality, and that reason necessarily and naturally accepts this charge. By *necessarily*, I mean both that morality is a necessity imposed on reason by the fact of other people's existence and that it is an inner necessity of reason that it respond to this fact by taking the shape of morality. Accordingly, reason's relation to morality is at once passive and active in a way that makes the term *passion*, meaning at once overpowering compulsion and willing devotion, appropriate: *Morality is reason's passion.*

The shape into which reason is brought by the fact of other persons is called "respect," and I maintain that respect is a cognitive attitude required by reason in a world in which some of the objects are human subjects. This cognitive attitude distinctively yields not only a constraint on judgments about action, but a disposition to action as well. Analytic distinctions that have made this seem impossible are the result of thinking that all knowledge is public and impersonal—expressible without residue in third-person propositions.

I shall argue that respect is a rational necessity in a world of human subjects. I argue, as well, that this gives us a way of understanding the nature of conscience, evil, and obligation. In the following section, I shall show that the theory defended in the present section gives us a way of reinterpreting Kantian ethics that confirms the most important of Kant's insights. In the last section of this chapter, I shall show that this account makes good on the requirement that the social contract be established as a built-in tendency and necessity of reason, though much of this will become clear as we proceed in the present section.

That there are persons out there like oneself entails the theoretical judgment that those persons have grounds for practical judgments like one's own. They are rational, mortal, embodied beings with sovereign interests. The world is one in which a plurality of persons are engaged in subjective practical reasoning. They each live the must of sovereign interest and necessarily recognize the truth for them of the personal imperative, "I must realize my sovereign interest," and thus derivatively of "I should promote my sovereign interest as far as possible." Accordingly, they are making first-person determinations about outcomes that matter enough to them in light of their sovereign interests to move them to act to promote or prevent those outcomes, as far as they can. I use the phrase "plurality of persons" to stand for this claim, and I regard the existence of that plurality as a fact in need of no further argument. Moreover, I take recognition of the plurality of persons as the natural effect on a rational person of interacting with other

113

human beings and therefore view any human being who interacts with others and is not at least dimly aware of this fact as incompetent in a way that makes him incapable of moral responsibility.

To hold that practical reasoning is subjective does not mean that it does not occur as an objective fact. The plurality of persons entails that subjective practical reasoning occurs objectively all around us. That this reasoning is subjective means that its nature is altered if it is changed from the first person to the third. Something is lost when "I am hungry" is described as an instance of "someone is hungry." "Someone is hungry" describes a situation in the world in which a lack at one spot can be filled by moving the things from other spots. "I am hungry" describes a particular way in which the whole world lines itself up to my gaze as obstructing or facilitating my eating. *Someone's* hunger occurs at one point in the world I see and can be, so to speak, surgically removed from that world without altering the rest. But *my* hunger colors everything in the world I see with its particular urgency, giving everything a valence as means, obstacle, or callously indifferent to my need.

What I have in mind here is a distinction parallel to that made by existentialists and phenomenologists between my body as it is lived by me and my body as it is known by others: "The body," writes Sartre, "is *lived* and not *known*." It is "the point of view on which I can take no point of view, the instrument which I cannot utilize in the way I utilize any other instrument." "So far as the physicians have had any experience with my body, it was with my body *in the midst of the world* and as it is for others. My body as it is *for me* does not appear to me in the midst of the world"; "the hand which I grasp with my other hand is not apprehended as a hand which is grasping but as an apprehensible object. Thus the nature of *our body for us* entirely escapes us to the extent that we take upon it the Other's point of view." And vice versa: "What for the Other is his *taste of himself* becomes for me the *Other's flesh*" (*BN*, 324, 340, 303, 358, 343). Analogously, a desire lived in the first person escapes us when we take toward it the third-person viewpoint by which it is known by others. But no fishy dualistic metaphysics is necessarily implied here. The distinction can be made without assuming that first and third person refer to different realities, that mind and body are ontologically distinct. (Nagel concurs [*VFN*, 29].) The point rather is that, for the same real desire, description of it as an event in the world does not capture what it is like to have it—it does not capture the unique and pervasive way in which its satisfaction counts to the one who has it. "The *fact* that I want to, viewed from outside," writes Nagel, "has none of the importance of *wanting to*, experienced from within" (*VFN*, 168).

The shift in perspective here is a kind of gestalt shift. Seen as an event in the world, the desire and its satisfaction stand along with those of others as figures on the ground of the public world that is the neutral setting for them all. For the one who has the desire, however, the desire becomes the ground, pushing to the side the desires of others, coloring the world in the nonneutral tones of its insistence. The satisfaction becomes the figure, the irresistible target of action. The sovereign interest asserts its sovereignty in the first person. Self-interested practical reasoning fills the field with its imperative. This is what gives self-interested practical reasoning its imperialistic tendency to view the authority of its own reasons as unlimited. To describe this in objective terms, to take the first person as a case of the third, is to reverse this gestalt shift. It is to locate the first person in a larger world, as one concernful gaze among others. The reverse gestalt shift effectively denatures the first-person reality, much as thinking about one's death in the third person, as "passing away," denatures the real finality of death. The translation to the third person lacks the exclusive, all-encompassing, insisting, urgent, imperative nature of first-person practical reasoning.

If it is true that each individual human subject has a first-person reality that is denatured and distorted if described in the third person, it follows that the only way to understand accurately the nature of the human subjects that populate my world is to imagine having their first-person experiences. I can only understand what the subjective existence of others really is, in fact, if I put myself in the others' shoes. I will not understand what being hungry is unless I imagine myself hungry; no third-person description of lack of food and its operation on the nervous system and so on will give me the whole story. The plurality of persons implies that there are facts one can only comprehend in an undistorted way by identifying with them.

We have already encountered this identification in chapter 1, when we considered the possibility of imagining one were someone else. There I argued that it is possible to do this because one can participate imaginatively in the sheer subjectivity of another human being, without imagining that one's own person was inhabiting him. It is possible to separate subjectivity from self or personal identity, and to identify with another's subjectivity by taking up the partisan practical attitude that constitutes it, allowing oneself to feel what it would be like to have the other's fate as a fate. Feeling this is just feeling the sovereignty of the other's sovereign interest, the urgency with which its commands are uttered, and it is recognizing the truth for that individual of the personal imperative to realize his sovereign interest.

The existence of other persons is the existence of facts that can only be known for what they are by such identification, much as the existence of colors is the existence of facts that can only be known for what they are by looking. Because acting reasonably is acting as far as I can in light of the real nature of the facts, it follows that acting reasonably toward others requires identifying with them.

Moreover, this identifying with other persons is as much a natural tendency of reason as looking is of eyes. Anyone can testify to this from his or her own experience. The simplest tasks of daily life—negotiating one's way through crowds or traffic, for example—would be inconceivable if we did not naturally and unthinkingly view our world from the standpoint of the others in it. What else is shame but the sense of the other's disapproving look, what else blushing but the rising of the blood to meet the feel of that look upon one's skin? It is no accident that the sense of shame—the feel of the other's judging eyes upon one's flesh and the penetration of that judgment under one's skin—is portrayed in the Garden of Eden myth as born together with the knowledge of good and evil. They are, in fact, twins. It is our reason's natural tendency to take and be vulnerable to the viewpoint of the other toward ourselves that equips us to leave unquestioning obedience behind and distinguish good from evil on our own. Those who, like Nietzsche, think that without God there is no morality fail to see that without God there is still human reason. Without the judge, the jury of peers remains. Rational, mortal, desiring creatures are their own natural moral audience.

The decisive fact that makes us moral creatures and makes moral knowledge possible is that another person is a kind of vortex that literally sucks one's reasoning into it and spins it around so that one finds oneself looking out at things from his standpoint. I call this "turning round" by which I comprehend the first-person subjective reality of the other "respect." Respect is, as the word suggests, a way of looking. And while this turning round of respect happens to reason, it is also necessitated by reason, since it is the appropriate way to look at persons so as to grasp their reality, as introspection is the appropriate way to look at oneself, and inspection the appropriate way to look at things.

Identification is not required by respect,[7] nor is respect a result of identification. Respect is identifying with a human subject—it is the particular shape into which reasoning curls itself in order to grasp the subjective reality of another. (I take it, by the way, that there is a kind of identification that reason requires regarding nonhuman animals, though, to the extent that they lack awareness of their mortality, this identification is closer to sympathy than to respect. Although I think that analyzing this kind of identification would show us what reason requires of us in the treatment of animals, I shall, for simplicity's sake, ignore it.) Consequently, I understand respect to be a cognitive attitude that a rational person appropriately and naturally

116

tends to take up toward other persons. This is a necessary cognitive attitude because my world is made up of subjects as well as objects or (to avoid any suspicion of metaphysical dualism) of objects that happen to be subjects, much as some objects happen to be red. Since this cognitive attitude is rationally required in order to understand accurately the reality of other persons, a reality whose existence every rational person recognizes, respect is rationally necessary. Not to respect others is to thwart the natural tendency of one's reason and distort one's conception of the reality in which one acts.

To be sure, this tendency can be blocked. The imperious claims of one's own sovereign interest work against it, and differences between people in race, religion, nationality, or class can come to seem like differences between persons and nonpersons. When we speak of owing others respect or trying to respect someone, and the like, we refer to the effort to resist these blocks. Identification with and respect for other persons can indeed be short-circuited. I claim only that identification is necessary for an accurate understanding of the world in which one acts, though misinformation and self-interest may cloud that understanding—and I claim that the tendency to identification and respect is a natural tendency of reason, not that it is the only tendency or invariably the dominant one.

It cannot be objected that the reasonableness of obtaining an accurate understanding of the world in which one acts is merely a counsel of prudence ("look before you leap") that can be lightly ignored. Accurate understanding of the relevant facts is intrinsic to the reasonableness of any judgment, theoretical or practical. Any such judgment is a judgment that something (a belief or an action) is appropriate under the circumstances—and making such a judgment commits one to wanting one's assessment of the circumstances to be accurate, and therefore to obtaining as accurate an assessment as possible. This is true even when one judges that it is not worthwhile to do anything to check that assessment or that there is not sufficient time to do anything. These judgments, too, rest on an assessment of the circumstances (that the issue is not worth more effort or that time is so short that quick action on a guess is better than spending time investigating), and they too carry a commitment to doing whatever is possible to make that assessment accurate—even if nothing is possible. I take it then that getting as accurate a picture as possible of the reality in which one acts is a basic and inescapable requirement of reason—and therefore that if that reality includes objects that can only be accurately known by identification, then identification is a requirement of reason.

It is by rationally necessary identification with the subjectivity of others that reason shows that something outside of my own subjective reasons limits the authority of my subjective practical reasoning and thus provides the solution to the puzzle of how morality is rationally required. To see what this showing is, I shall consider identification both phenomenologically (describing what the experience is like, how it feels in the broadest sense of "feeling") and cognitively (indicating what it teaches, what truth it reveals). Whereas the phenomenological dimension is important for understanding how identification works, the cognitive ultimately counts, since only if identification leads to a truth that a reasonable person must recognize can it show that morality is a requirement of reason. I take up the phenomenology of identification first.

When I identify with the other, I step into his shoes and feel the force of what matters to him with the same urgency and exclusiveness as what matters to me. This means that, when I engage in practical reasoning about an action that may matter to others, I must consider more than that it matters to others. I must put myself in their shoes and feel for myself the way it matters to them—just the sort of thing that the Golden Rule is continually reminding me to do. Having identified with another, I cannot return to my own shoes with the information and then do what only or mainly matters to me. Turning the experience into "information" transforms the experience I obtained by identifying with the other's first-person experience back into the third person, dilutes its actual urgency, and thus distorts it. Holding fast to the experience in its real first-person urgency will make me want to act in light of what matters to us both.

But identifying with others' first-person experiences does not make them into or add them onto my own first-person experiences. I must let myself feel what matters to others, from where they are and thus from outside what matters to me. This is different from simply adding what matters to them to the things that already matter to me. Identification with others is not experiencing myself as if I were a single composite person whose fate was made up of all the fates of all the individuals my acts affect. That would turn me into the "benevolent observer" of utilitarianism who, experiencing all the desires of everyone, treats them all as her own simultaneously and selects the course of action that maximizes her (= their) aggregate satisfaction. But this way of understanding identification with what matters to others distorts how things matter to them.

Thinking that identifying with others amounts to experiencing oneself as a composite person for whom everything that matters to anyone matters belies the facts because it blurs the nonfungible nature of first-person mattering and thereby denatures its exclusiveness and urgency. If I list all the things that matter to me, it may be reasonable for me to sacrifice some in order to achieve others. But it cannot be reasonable for me to sacrifice all of them. They have a kind of urgency and unsubstitutability as a whole set. This is

118

lost if they are made part of a larger list of what matters to some "benevolent observer." She will treat the larger list as I treated my own, namely, by being willing to sacrifice some items to reach others. But doing this with the larger list, she may find it reasonable to sacrifice all that matters to some people in order to reach what satisfies others. That shows that aggregating the plurality of persons into one composite person distorts the way things matter to people separately.[8] Writes Rawls, "Utilitarianism does not take seriously the distinction between persons" (*TJ*, 27).

Neither does identification lead to altruism, though its effect is to require a certain kind of consideration of other people's interests. Crucial here, again, is the nonfungibility of sovereign interests. Given the irreducibly subjective nature of practical reasoning, the reasons of others remain their reasons. That I must identify with their reasons lets me feel their force but does not make them my reasons. In identifying with the hungry person, I do not become hungry; nor am I moved to act as if I were hungry. I come to feel and understand the particular urgency of hunger and to understand that for the hungry person food matters in just the way it would for me, if I were hungry. Since identification must be true to the reality of other people's experiences, it leaves them as the first-person experiences that they are and adds them on as separate (not aggregated) first-person experiences alongside my own.

Remember Napoleon. When I imagine being him, I do not come to desire that the person Reiman refight Waterloo. I identify with the way Waterloo presented Napoleon with compelling reasons for him to act. Napoleon's ends remain reasons for him to act, as my ends remain reasons for me to act. There is no crossing over here. His ends do not become reasons for me. Rather, I identify with the whole indivisible package "his-ends-as-reasons-for-him-to-act." The nonfungibility of sovereign interests entails that this package cannot be broken up and distributed among separate persons. Identification does not turn the other's ends into the ends of the particular person that I am.

When I identify with the others whom my action will affect, I imagine myself simultaneously being each one of them as a separate and indivisible package of "ends-and-desires-to-act-on-them." While I do this, I remain a person too, and I must not distort my own first-person experience. If it were not for this, identification would naturally lead me to take on the ends of others as my own. But because I identify while remaining the person I am, that result is blocked, and instead I endorse the ends of others for them just beyond the boundary of my own ends. Thus, I feel the pull of their ends and their personal imperatives on *their* actions, the pull of my ends and imperative on *my* actions, and not the pull of their ends and imperatives on

119

my actions. Since I never stop being a separate person from the others, experiencing the pull of their sovereign interests and true personal imperatives on them is experiencing it as a pull from outside my own. The pull becomes a push and boxes me in, taking up normative space on the other side of my own sovereign interest and limiting its imperious claims.

In short, to identify is not to mix my sovereign interest with others' but to experience mine as hedged in by theirs, limited in its jurisdiction, much as the existence of other sovereign nations limits a nation's jurisdiction to its borders. Instead of giving me new ends to pursue, identification with the pull of others' ends limits the authority of my own ends as reasons for my action. It gets me to want to act for my own ends in a way that leaves room for each to act likewise for his own ends. I do, as a result, act in ways that serve (at least indirectly) others in pursuing their ends. But this is not because I am moved to serve their ends—it is because I am moved to moderate my pursuit of my own. And, since respect—as commonly understood—is a way of honoring other people's self-determination rather than of serving their ends, a way of making room for their pursuit of their ends rather than of pursuing their ends myself, identification disposes me to act not altruistically, but respectfully.

The identification I am describing here is part of sizing up the objective situation in which I am to act; thus it occurs before I act and shapes any decision I make about how to act. It is different from any identification that I might engage in as a project for my own purposes, such as companionship. In this way, reason requires that I recognize (what we saw in chapter 1 as) the natural equality of all human subjects. I must decide how to act while according equal urgency to all the sovereign interests with which I identify (including my own). Were I to identify as a project for my own purposes, I would effectively reverse the order dictated by reason—instead of identifying as preparation for deciding how to pursue my purposes, I would decide that first and then, subject to it, identify. If I stick to the order mandated by reason, I will identify first and in light of that determine how to pursue my purposes—and I will accord weight to others' sovereign interests equal to that I accord my own. This should serve to dispel one likely source of confusion. Certain forms of evil, say, sadism, also involve imaginative identification with the other. The sadist takes pleasure in imagining his victim's suffering and longing to escape it. But it should be clear that this is only possible because the sadist identifies for his own purposes. He has not subjected his decision on how to act to a prior identification that gives equal weight to the sovereign interests of the other. Instead of allowing the other's desire not to be hurt to function as a brake on his sadistic purposes, he

120

will imagine that desire as part of his purposes—but only because he has reversed the order that reason requires.

Thus far, I have mainly described the phenomenology of identification and its felt impact on my commitment to pursue my sovereign interest. If this were all there were, however, it would be reasonable to suspect that, although identification is required by reason, its effects on me are psychological ones, mere feelings—as if identification were a kind of rationally induced sympathy. Sympathy is a natural psychological consequence of identification, but I contend that it is not the way in which identification leads to distinctively moral concern for others. If it were, if moral concern for others were no more than a feeling, a psychological consequence of identification, then that concern would still be a brute fact with no warrant as a requirement of reason. Then, even if identification motivated me, in fact, to treat others respectfully, it would not necessitate the conclusion that I truly should. For that, we must turn to the cognitive dimension of identification.

Reason requires me to identify. Identifying, however, does more than move me to feel concern. It positions me to see, from the inside, from the only place it can be seen for what it is, the truth of each person's personal imperative. Seeing this truth—or, more precisely, these truths—my judgments about my own actions are constrained not just by emotional resonance with others but by my endorsement of these truths.

Recall that the personal imperative is not only "I ought to promote my sovereign interest"; it is "I must realize my sovereign interest." This latter is more stringent, since it does not depend on what I can do. *Must* does not imply *can* as *ought* does. I must realize my sovereign interest because if I fail, no matter why I fail, I fail to live a life that answers to my mortality. This distinction between must and ought is important because, if identification led me only to endorse the truth for each of "I ought to promote my sovereign interest," it would entail no limitation on the authority for me of my own sovereign interest. It is possible to believe that I ought to do whatever I can to survive or prosper, while believing that others ought to do the same for themselves, and thus no limit on what I ought to do toward others follows. This is because, since *ought* implies *can*, what the other ought to do can never be more than what he can do. Thus, my endorsement of his doing everything that he ought to do does not imply a prohibition on my acting in ways that restrict what the other can do. By contrast, since *must* does not imply *can*, there can be more that a person must do than what he can do. Thus, restricting what the other can do does threaten to limit him in doing what he must do. Consequently, my endorsement of the other's doing every-

121

thing that he must do implies a commitment to not restrict his ability to do it.

When, therefore, I endorse for each the truth of the more stringent imperative, "I must realize my sovereign interest," I become committed not merely to other people's right to try to realize their goals but to each one's right to an opportunity to succeed—a right limited only by everyone's similar right, including my own. I come to recognize that the authority of my own sovereign interest for my actions is not unlimited. Its writ runs only as far as is compatible with everyone else's. I learn that my sovereign interest has a finite jurisdiction hedged by the equally valid authority of everyone else's sovereign interest. I discover that the imperialistic tendency of subjective practical reason to view the authority of its own reasons as unlimited is an illusion.

This account can be stated in terms of the notion of reason as maximizing coherence. What must be added to that notion is that there is a type of fact (the other subject) that I encounter that resists coherence from my own individual standpoint, precisely because that fact is the living demand for coherence from its own (and to me, alien) standpoint. To accommodate that fact, I must identify with it, and doing that changes profoundly the task of achieving coherence. My planned actions will only be coherent, then, when they are coherent from my standpoint and the other's. I can only accomplish my own reason's goal of maximum coherence by expanding the standpoint from which I seek coherence to include (via imagination) the first-person standpoint of other subjects. The human subject who enters my field of reflection is a kind of coherence leak, a black hole that draws my solitary attempt at coherence outside itself into an attempt to achieve coherence from the other's standpoint as well as my own, and thus ultimately from the standpoint of all subjects.

This requirement that anyone's planned action be coherent from the standpoint of every individual is what the universalizers mistake for a logical requirement. They fail to see that it is required by the facts. Living in a world of other subjects with nonfungible interests as imperative as one's own, one's reasoning literally bangs up against the reality of other persons. The effect of this collision is recognition of the force of other people's sovereign interests claiming their jurisdiction in the world with the same force as one's own and recognition of this force from without as an external fact that limits one's own jurisdiction. The effect of the encounter with this fact is not just feeling; it is knowledge. But it is the sort of knowledge that cannot be translated into a formal principle that the reasoning subject must accept as presupposed by and internal to his reasoning itself. This is what the universalizers do not see. They assume that the only principles that can have jurisdiction over a reasoning subject are those internal to, presupposed by, his own reasoning. Thus, they appeal to the logical principle of universalizability, which is the internal look-alike of identification. But their very fastening upon universalizability reveals that they were already in possession of the truth that identification enables us to see. Otherwise, there would have been no more reason to think that acting according to the logical requirement of universalizability was acting morally than to think that acting according to modus ponens was.

Identifying with others entails endorsing the truth for each of his or her personal imperative. Consequently, I must evaluate all judgments about how to act in light of my accepting that truth for each individual from each one's first-person standpoint—imaginatively in every case but my own. Then, I cannot accept any judgment about how I should act that is not acceptable from the standpoint of each person it affects in light of his recognition of the truth of his personal imperative—as I imaginatively participate in this recognition. I can only find it reasonable to do something if I would find it reasonable from their standpoints while accepting the truth of their personal imperatives. This makes it rationally necessary that my own practical reasoning take place as if a conference were going on in my head, at which everyone potentially affected by my actions was present and had to find my conclusions acceptable in light of the truth to them of their personal imperatives. And when I go beyond reasoning about what I should do in some particular situation that will affect some particular persons, to reasoning about general principles to govern action that may affect everyone, I must only find reasonable what everyone—all recognizing for each the truth of his personal imperative—could find reasonable together. Needless to say, when I do this, I reach the physical limits of my capacity to identify with others imaginatively and must fill out my imagination with reasoned inferences about what such imaginative identification with everyone would lead to if I could do it in fact. In short, reason requires that each individual's practical reasoning take a shape like that of rational contractors who have to agree on principles of action. By requiring identification, reason requires that practical reasoning take the shape of an internal contract.

We can already see the larger shape of any principle that can be found reasonable in light of this requirement. Recall that identifying with another's personal imperative implies a restriction of my own pursuit of my sovereign interest to a space compatible with leaving an equal space for the other to pursue his. Since reason requires that everyone identify with everyone, the truth of each one's personal imperative presses itself upon everyone equally, yielding the imperative: "We should each pursue our sovereign interests to the greatest extent possible compatible with allowing the same for everyone 123 else." I call this *the moral imperative of respect,* or for short, *the moral imperative.* It requires us to treat each other respectfully, to make room for each to pursue his sovereign interest. The moral imperative is true and binding on all rational human beings and governs the choice of any particular principles of action.

Identification does not merely incline or move us to grant this truth. It positions us, so to speak, so that we can see and appreciate the force of this true moral imperative. But like any other truth, it remains true even when one is no longer perched to see it. Thus, while identification teaches us the truth of the moral imperative of respect, we know it to be true whether or not we are identifying in the moment. And this moral truth reflects a truth about the natural world: that beings care about their lives in the way that human beings do is reason enough to allow them to make the best of them, and thus reason recognizes this care as sufficient grounds for entitlement to that allowance. This is the simple truth about morality. What is unusual about this is only that one must identify with human caring as it is lived in the first person to see this truth.

Recognition of the truth of the moral imperative of respect is tantamount to recognition that one ought to limit the pursuit of one's own sovereign interest to the terms of the moral imperative. The reader may understandably wonder how this distinctively moral ought arises from identification with the personal imperatives of others. But it is a mistake to expect an argument from endorsement of the truths of others' personal imperatives to endorsement of the truth of the moral ought. Endorsing the truths of others' personal imperatives *is* endorsing the truth of the moral ought. These are two expressions for the same thing. Recall that throughout identification with others I remain the one who I am with my sovereign interest commanding me as insistently as ever. The moral ought describes the force of my identification with others as it registers within the bounds of my own sovereign interest.

The moral ought is how identification with the sovereign interests of others, who stay other, speaks to the sovereign interest that is one's own and stays one's own. Precisely because this ought comes from beyond one's own personal imperative and limits from without how far one may pursue one's own sovereign interest, it is a *moral* ought. The moral ought is the must of other people's sovereign interests identified with from a distance, endorsed in both its truth and its otherness. Because we are rational mortal beings, morality has real existence in the natural world: *The must of sovereign interest is the shadow cast by never again on now. The ought of morality is that must identified with at a distance, the distance between human subjects. And thereby is learned the truth of the moral imperative of respect.*

124

Consider, now, how this account of identification enables us to say in what conscience, evil, and obligation consist. Conscience is comprised of two Latin roots—*con*, meaning together, and *scientia*, meaning knowing. Conscience is the capacity of knowing together—that is, of arriving at rational conclusions from a plurality of standpoints. On my account, conscience is not a separate faculty. It is the natural consequence for a rational creature of all the evidence she has to believe that she is surrounded by real persons to whom things matter just as much and as really as things matter to her. As people go about their own individual practical reasoning, they are, insofar as they are rational, led by their reason to identify with and acknowledge the imperative force of the sovereign interests of others, and thus to examine their own practical reasoning in light of that of others— that is, from a plurality of standpoints. If we think of the conclusions of people's reasoning as speaking in separate voices in their heads, then the "voice of conscience" is the voice in which the first-person sovereign interests of others speaks when the individual rules on the acceptability of the conclusions of her own subjective practical reasoning in light of the reality of others. The voice of conscience is not, as Freud thought, only the voice of the introjected father. It is the voice of everyone introjected—although during childhood fathers may (and surely in Freud's Vienna did) speak with the loudest voice, with lasting effects on what the voice of conscience sounds like. One could describe the effect of identification as imagining that one was "in the heads" of all the participants at a conference made up of all the persons one's actions might affect, or that they were all "in one's own head." This is conscience—the voice of the internal contract. And, since it is equivalent to recognizing the truth of each one's personal imperative, it is a knowing together.

Evil is the refusal to count the fates of others as if they counted as much as one's own fate counts to oneself. "Vice in general," writes Bishop Butler, "consists in having an unreasonable and too great regard to ourselves, in comparison of others" (*FS*, 154). Evil is a kind of blindness to the reality of other persons, a deafness to their pleas, implicit or expressed. This is why we often think of evil people as treating others as things. Evil is culpable because, insofar as a person is rational, he has the power to understand and consider the reality of others and what it implies. Identification is not only a rational necessity, but a natural tendency of reason. Thus, any normal person has already had this experience many times over by the time he reaches an age at which we hold him capable of moral action. Anyone who grew up without this experience or who lacked the capacity for it would be crazy in a way that would make him dangerous but not morally responsible.

125

This explains why we hold any rational personal responsible for his evil and why we do not allow ignorance of the rules to excuse basic forms of wickedness. They are indeed obvious to any rational person.

Being evil is being unreasonable but not irrational. Being reasonable is acting in accord with the facts; rationality is the capacity to do this. Lacking this capacity, one cannot be blamed for being unreasonable or evil. But any sane person brought up by human beings has this capacity and can thus be blamed for not exercising it.

Evil is done freely. Earlier, I maintained that acting on reason's requirements was being free. That might seem to suggest that the evil person is unfree since he fails to act on reason's moral requirements. But the evil person acts on other requirements of reason, those inscribed in his personal imperative of self-interest. His evil lies in doing that while ignoring the requirements of reason that come from the personal imperatives of others. This is how evil is linked to a disregard for the reality of others as subjects, a disregard that, in effect, lets the imperialistic tendency of self-interested reasoning take over. But this is never due merely to ignorance of the reality of others. It always involves turning from or tuning out others, letting the noise of one's own desires drown them out. This is why we generally think it takes more evil to victimize people face-to-face than from a distance, since at close range it takes a more willful effort to tune out the other; this is why we think it worse to harm another in cold blood than in the heat of passion, since in the latter case we recognize that some of the noise that drowns out the reality of the other is not in the actor's control. That evil involves a kind of inattention to the reality of the other is why evil is often, as Hannah Arendt has said, banal—done by those who let routine obstruct their view of the effects of their actions, rather than by those who aim to do great bad deeds. That technology has increased our ability to affect people whom we cannot see and that bureaucracy has increased our ability not to see those whom we affect give force to the fears of those who find the modern era particularly ominous. But this can be exaggerated—every era has its means of shutting out the reality of its victims. As Sartre writes, "every society chooses its dead."[9]

That evil is willful refusal to face the reality of the other as a subject explains why the eyes are so important in moral relations. More than any other feature, the eyes seem to show the person as a subject having her own experiences, rather than merely as an object of the experiences of others. The eyes look like they are looking. Evildoers normally cannot bear the eyes of their victims, and liars normally avoid looking their listeners straight in the eyes. In both cases, seeing the eyes of the other makes it more difficult to ignore the reality of the other as a subject, as one must to succeed in being evil.

Obligation is the primitive natural nonmoral must of other people's personal imperatives as it comes from beyond the boundaries of my sovereign interest and presses up against the warmer and louder must of my own personal imperative. The strangeness of the moral ought results because it is the nonmoral ought of others hailing me from outside my own nonmoral ought and yet making a claim on me. The rational necessity that makes obligation binding is the rational necessity of facing the reality of other persons for what that reality is. Disregarding one's obligation is acting as if others were not persons in the way that they really are.

Since obligation stems from facing the reality of people's first-person subjective experience, this reality gives importance to the wrongness of defaulting on one's obligations. My argument is thus not vulnerable to the criticism I leveled against Gewirth's theory. Recall that against Gewirth I argued that, if moral obligation is grounded in logical obligation, then failure in the former can be no more important than failure in the latter. It might seem that against my argument it could be said that, if moral obligation is grounded in the reasonableness of recognizing facts for what they are, then failure in the former can be no more important than failure in the latter. Then, as I held that Gewirth cannot prove that murder is worse than calling a bachelor married, I could be accused of being unable to prove that murder is worse than, say, refusing to wear one's galoshes when it is raining. The reason that this criticism will not work against my view, however, is that I do not base the importance of obligation on anything that the actor is held to assert, implicitly or explicitly. Since Gewirth does, for him the importance of obligation can be no more than the importance of being consistent with those assertions. I contend, rather, that the importance of obligation arises because there is a fact—independent of our assertions—that brings importance with it. Importance, mattering, and urgency come with the territory for human beings. Any rational human being brought up with other human beings will come naturally to recognize that this is a fact for all—or else he will fall below the level of competence necessary to be morally accountable at all. Thus evil is disregard of what is truly important and of what one already knows is important. Our duties are not merely logical. They derive from the real way in which things matter to others. Our obligations come from the claims of real people—and, when we respond to them, it is, as William James said, "life answering to life."[10]

Finally, a word must be said about the elusiveness of the simple solution that I have offered to a puzzle that seems as old as humanity. The elusiveness

127

is explained by a key fact in the theory—namely, the irreducible subjectivity and nonfungibility of practical reason. This fact is what gives us the imperialistic tendency to think of our own reasons as the only ones that claim us—and, of course, this is just what also makes us prone to evil. The natural nonfungibility of sovereign interests, or, equivalently, the inherent subjectivity of practical reason, is original sin. It is our congenital susceptibility to the temptation not to recognize how the reality of others limits the jurisdiction of our own reasons. Consequently, when we find ourselves moved by concern for what matters to others, this seems a kind of accident that runs directly counter to what reason itself counsels. We are led, then, to think that feeling rather than reason makes us moral—but then morality appears unreasonable, a brute fact that stares back blankly when asked to present its credentials. All the while, however, we know in our hearts that morality has credentials that would pass the test of reason could they only be found. And so we turn round and round, looking beyond reason for what seems reasonable. On my view, this is just what ought to be expected: Morality speaks with a voice that sounds different from the voice of our own reason because it is the voice of our own reason bouncing off the reality of other persons and coming back to us with the strangely disembodied quality of an echo.

Duty is reason's echo, asserting authority in a strange and yet familiar voice from beyond an individual's sovereign interest. This is why, as Kant saw, the voice of duty built into every human being's reason inspires reverence, an emotion at once humbling and uplifting. I am humbled by the sound of that which transcends my desires in its authority and uplifted by recognizing in its strange resonance with my own reason that I am the vessel of that transcendence. It is quite natural to think that morality comes from a source at once personal and beyond the limits of ordinary persons. And yet that holy voice is nothing but the voice of ordinary persons: "The voice of the people," wrote Rousseau, "is in fact the voice of God" (*DPE*, 122). And Kant wrote: "There was a time when . . . I despised the masses, who know nothing. Rousseau has put me right. This blind prejudice disappears; I learn to honour men."[11]

Kant and the Nature of Respect

In *The Foundations of the Metaphysics of Morals*, Kant writes: "Rational beings are designated 'persons' because their nature indicates that they are ends in themselves, i.e., things which may not be used merely as means. Such a being is thus an object of respect" (*FMM*, 53). Let us call Kant's

128

view that human beings are to be treated as ends in themselves, and never merely as means, the "ends formula." Considering how respect as I have described it is linked to the ends formula will help clarify the claim I am making. If my argument is sound, Kant's claim that the formula is a requirement of reason is vindicated, though not by the route Kant is normally thought to have taken. To establish the link between respect and the ends formula, we must first explicate the formula. This is trickier than it seems because Kant does not merely assert that people are to be treated as ends in themselves *and* never merely as means; he holds that they are not to be treated merely as means *because* they are ends in themselves. The problem is to understand "end in itself" in a way that implies that an end in itself may not be used merely as a means. On the face of it, however, that something is an end in itself seems to imply that it need not be used as a means, not that it may not.

It will be worth our while to view the ends formula in the context of Kant's argument for it in *The Foundations of the Metaphysics of Morals*. There he argues for a supreme principle of morality, the categorical imperative, which is essentially a version of the requirement of universalizability— namely, that we act only on principles that we could will to be universal laws. (Call this the universalizability formula.) He then proceeds to derive four other formulations of this supreme principle, of which the second calls for acting only on principles one could will to be a universal law of nature (the law of nature formula), and the third is the ends formula. (Kant counts the five formulae differently, taking them as three, the first and third of which have alternative forms. I shall continue to count them as five.) In this section, we follow the steps by which Kant arrives at the ends formula in *The Foundations*. In the next section, we shall follow as Kant derives his two additional formulations, the last of which qualifies him as a representative of the social contract tradition. This will throw further light on the nature of respect. What is more, I shall argue that to make Kant's argument work requires something like the notion of identification that I have defended.

Kant starts by asserting that "Nothing in the world—indeed nothing even beyond the world—can possibly be conceived which could be called good without qualification except a *good will*" (*FMM*, 11). Although talents and powers are judged by the consequences to which they lead, people who try to do their moral duty are commonly thought worthy of praise whether they succeed or fail, and people who do not try to do their duty are commonly not thought worthy of praise, even if they happen to produce the same results they would have produced had they tried to act on their duty and succeeded. If this is the case, it follows that the reasons for which a person wills her actions must determine whether she is praiseworthy. Because Kant holds

129

that something can be a person's reason for acting only if it is what truly moves her to will that action, Kant seeks to determine how something could move an individual's will in a way that would redound to her moral credit.

If the desirability of the consequences of my action is my reason for willing it, then this desirability must move me to will it, and that must be because the consequences are desired by me. But if I am moved by the fact that I desire to bring about the consequences, then my willing is indistinguishable in worth from any willing I perform in the service of any end I desire—indeed, it is indistinguishable from what the bad man's will does when he tries to bring about what he desires. It follows that the desirability of the consequences of my action cannot be a reason for acting that bestows moral worth on my will. If I bring about the consequences, not because I desire them but because I should try to bring about these consequences, then something other than the desirability of the consequences must be the source of the motivating power of this *should*.

With the desirability of the consequences put to one side, what is left to motivate me in a way that bestows moral worth on my will is the recognition that something should be done or, in Kant's terms, that it is my duty. Kant concludes that my action only redounds to my moral credit if I will it because of recognition that it is my duty. The rest of Kant's moral theory can be understood as an attempt to determine the conditions under which an individual could recognize and be moved by recognition of his duty without being moved by the desirability of the consequences of doing his duty.

That the distinctive moral value of actions lies in their being willed for the sake of duty implies that the worth of actions lies in the intention for which they are done rather than in what they succeed in doing. Kant calls the intention for which an action is done, the "maxim" of the action. For Kant, a rational agent always acts on some maxim to the effect that action of the sort about to be undertaken is appropriate under the circumstances. If I drink to quench my thirst, I act on the maxim, "if I am thirsty, I should drink." Some dim awareness of this as the ground of my action is what distinguishes it from blind reflex or the instinctive reactions of lower animals. The maxim of an action is subjective—it holds only for the actor—and it is the one that really moves him (or that expresses what really moves him) to the action he undertakes. Maxims may simply move me to serve my desires or inclinations (as in the example of thirst), or they may move me to act morally.

Since whatever is distinctively morally worthy about action lies in its maxim and is independent of the desirability of its consequences, Kant argues that the only way I can act on duty is if I act on a maxim dictated

130

strictly by respect for the (moral) law: "Duty is the necessity of an action executed from respect for law. . . . Now as an act from duty wholly excludes the influence of inclinations . . . , nothing remains which can determine the will objectively except the law, and nothing subjectively except pure respect for this practical law. This subjective element is the maxim that I ought to follow such a law even if it thwarts all my inclinations" (*FMM*, 20). Bear in mind here, since it is so often overlooked in discussions of Kant's ethics, that Kant is not saying that the maxim that moves me to act morally cannot itself make reference to desirable consequences, nor that the appropriateness of a particular maxim to serve in this capacity must be determined without reference to the consequences that acting on it will yield. His point is strictly in reference to what moves the will. With desire for the consequences put to one side, all that can motivate me in a maxim is its form as a (moral) law. Consequently, if my action on a maxim is to count as being done from duty alone, it must be motivated by the form of the maxim as a law.

Suppose, for example, that I am moved to act on the principle "Thou shalt not kill." Preserving life is the matter of this principle; its form is that of a universal law: "Everyone should do X." If I am moved to do so by the desirability to me of preserving life, then no moral worth redounds to my will, since my will does nothing different from when it is moved by anything it desires. If I am moved to act on this principle without being moved by the desirability of its content, then the form of the principle—its sheer lawfulness—must be what moves me. It follows then, in general, that to do something in a way that bestows moral worth on my will, I must be moved by the sheer lawfulness of the requirement of doing that thing. Acting on my duty, then, is being moved by the sheer lawfulness of it. And if it is possible to act on duty, I must be able to recognize my duties from their sheer lawfulness. For that, it must be the case that only certain actions can fit within the form of sheer lawfulness and thus that we can identify our duties by determining which actions can take this form. Consequently, if acting on duty is possible, the clue to whether any action is our duty will be whether we can will the maxim of doing it as a universal law.

Kant does not start by asserting something about the essence of duty. It is more accurate to think of him as starting with the notion that whatever our duty is, unless it can make itself known to us as our duty, it is as good as nonexistent. A person cannot be bound by a duty if he cannot know that it is his duty. But if something is to make itself known to us as our duty, it must conform to the conditions by means of which we could recognize it as such. Recognizing our duty is not like recognizing something inert like a rock; it is recognizing something that can move our wills by our recognition of it. For that, it must be able to move us by recognition of its rightness independent of our inclinations. Thus, we must ask for the conditions that determine how we could recognize—and be moved by the recognition of— rightness, independent of our desires. These conditions will limit what can be our duties, because they will limit what can be known to us as duties. We should, then, be able to find a principle by which our duties can be identified.

Those familiar with Kant's *Critique of Pure Reason* will see that this is essentially the transcendental strategy applied there to scientific knowledge, applied here mutatis mutandis to moral duty. The transcendental strategy essentially starts with some apparently real but puzzling human accomplishment, such as scientific knowledge or moral action, and tries to work back to the conditions, beyond observation, that are necessary to make this accomplishment possible. It is something like attempting to determine the shape of an elusive key by working backward from the shape of the hole in the lock. With respect to science, Kant starts by assuming the possibility of scientific knowledge and then works backward to sketch the shape of the knower capable of having such knowledge. With respect to morality, Kant starts by assuming the possibility of acting on duty and then works backward to determine the kind of thing that duty must be if we are to be able to act on it. But Kant only tentatively assumes the possibility of acting on duty. Not until much later in the argument, satisfied that his search has hit on something that requires us to act morally, does Kant redeem the tentative assumption and claim that we do, in fact, have duties and can act on them. Until then, he argues conditionally: If wills are to have moral worth, then we must be able to will actions for the sake of duty, and so on. Proceeding cautiously in this vein, he asks how we *could* will actions for the sake of duty. What could move a rational person to action when the desirability to him of the consequences of his actions is excluded as a motivation?

Kant answers that it is not just inclinations that move us to act; we are, as rational beings, moved by reason's commands as well. Reason commands us by identifying some action "as practically necessary, i.e., as good" (*FMM*, 34). Here, Kant uses *good* in a sense that is wider than the moral. It applies to things, like physical exercise, that we judge good strictly in terms of our self-interest. Understood in this wide sense, actions can be commanded by reason as good because they are means to some end or because they are good in themselves. The difference between the two commands is that the first depends for its motivational capacity on the individual desiring the end to which the action is a good means, whereas the second does not. But in both cases, reason commands by invoking a universal law valid for any rational creature. Any rational being should do what is a good

132

means to an end he has and should do what is good in itself. Strictly speaking, these would not be commands for a purely rational being, since such a being would act on them automatically. They are commands for us because we are only imperfectly rational—that is, sometimes moved by our inclinations to act contrary to reason. This is as much the case with things that are good as means to our own ends as with things that are good in themselves, as anyone who has tried to give up an unhealthy habit can testify. Consequently, these universal laws or principles are to us imperatives—commands that we withstand temptation and do what reason shows to be good.

If we cannot be moved morally by desires or inclinations, then the possibility remains that we may be moved by one of these imperatives of reason. Inasmuch as reason can recognize actions as good either as means to certain ends or in themselves, the imperatives it issues are either hypothetical or categorical. A hypothetical imperative counsels us to do something because it is an effective means to some end we desire. Thus, it counsels particular action only to one who desires the relevant ends. Exercise is rational *if* one's end is staying healthy. The hypothetical nature of the particular command does not detract from the universality of the underlying law, namely, that every rational creature should do what is an effective means to the ends he desires.

Nonetheless, since we must be moved to our duty independently of our desires, the maxim that moves us to it cannot be a hypothetical imperative. It must conform to an imperative that calls for action as good in itself— that is, a categorical imperative. To determine what this is, Kant maintains that the very concept of it gives us its formula (*FMM*, 43–44). If all desired ends are eliminated, all that is left to motivate our action is the sheer form of the imperative as a universal law. That is, "there is nothing remaining in it except the universality of the law as such to which the maxim of the action should conform; and in effect this conformity alone is represented as necessary by the imperative" (*FMM*, 44). Remember, Kant is not saying that the maxim upon which we act must have nothing in it but the form of law. He is saying that if acting on the maxim is acting on duty, the maxim must move us solely by its form as law. From this, it follows that the categorical imperative—to which our maxims must conform if we are to act on our duty—must be simply the formal requirement of universal lawfulness: "Act according to that maxim by which you can at the same time will that it should become a universal law" (*FMM*, 44), the universalizability formula. He will go on to give four more formulas for this supreme principle of morality.

The universalizability formula works as follows. Suppose I am contemplating stealing something from my neighbor. I test this by whether I can will the maxim permitting me to steal as a universal law, which would of course permit others to steal from me. Since I naturally will the protection of my own belongings, I cannot will this universal law. Thus the contemplated maxim fails the test—acting on it would be acting contrary to my duty. Note that what makes my maxim wrong is not that acting on it would in fact render my own property unsafe. This would make the test of duty into a matter of long-term self-interest. What makes the maxim wrong is that willing it would bring my will into contradiction with itself—and this would make the maxim wrong even if I was perfectly certain that my own property would never be touched as a result of my acting on that maxim.

Later, in *The Critique of Practical Reason*, Kant will maintain that the existence of duty, the claim made upon us to act according to the law itself irrespective of our inclinations, is a sheer datum, a *fact of reason* (*CPR*, 48). At the point at which we are following him in *The Foundations*, however, he still admits the possibility that there is no such thing as a duty, arguing conditionally that, if we are to be able to act on duty, we must get those duties from the categorical imperative. His next step is to argue that this categorical imperative is at least plausible as a source of duties. Here he reformulates the imperative, maintaining that, since "what is called nature . . . is the existence of things so far as it is determined by universal laws . . . , the universal imperative of duty can be expressed as follows: Act as though the maxim of your action were by your will to become a universal law of nature" (*FMM*, 44–45). Kant now proceeds to apply this law of nature formula (his second formulation, by my count) to various actions generally thought immoral, such as suicide and making false promises, satisfying himself that the maxims that lead to them cannot be willed as universal laws.

I shall not take up these applications. Whether or not they work, if Kant's argument ended here, it would be subject to the same criticisms as Gewirth's. That is, the formal requirement of universality may look like morality, may even yield duties, but it cannot tell us what is distinctively important about acting morally.

But Kant's argument does not end here. Still cautiously refraining from any assertion that we do or can act on the categorical imperative, Kant proceeds to ask how we could be motivated by the categorical imperative. Since he believes that every action must be moved by some end, he must determine whether there is an end that supplies a motive "valid for every rational being." Such an end cannot be supplied by desire, as that would make it relative only to those creatures who have the desire, and thus it could not "afford any universal principles for all rational beings or valid and necessary principles for every volition" (*FMM*, 52). The ends of desire can provide only hypothetical imperatives. Moreover, if the end were a product of desire, acting for it would be acting on inclination. To do the job Kant has in mind, he must find an end prescribed by reason itself. Suppose, he writes,

> that there were something the existence of which in itself had absolute worth, something which, as an end in itself, could be a ground of definite laws. In it and only in it could lie the ground of a possible categorical imperative, i.e., of a practical law.
>
> Now, I say, man and, in general, every rational being exists as an end in himself and not merely as a means to be arbitrarily used by this or that will. . . .
>
> . . . rational beings are designated "persons" because their nature indicates that they are ends in themselves, i.e., things which may not be used merely as means. Such a being is an object of respect and, so far, restricts all choice. (*FMM*, 52–53)

Kant takes it that rational beings or persons are ends in themselves that must move all rational agents irrespective of their inclinations. This is the subjective ground of action on the basis of duty, where the universal form of law is the objective ground of it. Interestingly, Kant now speaks of persons as objects of respect, where previously he spoke of the law as the object of respect. Accordingly, he now offers a third formulation (he counts it the second) of the categorical imperative, the ends formula: "Act so that you treat humanity, whether in your own person or in that of another, always as an end and never as a means only" (*FMM*, 54). And he proceeds to apply this to the same acts to which he applied the earlier formulation, to show that it leads to the same judgments about duty.

Here, too, I leave the applications aside. I instead undertake to show how human beings are ends in themselves in a way that demands respect. I shall argue that doing so requires something like what I have called identification and has the implication that the real fact of reason is not the moral law that spells out our duty but the real other human subjects to whom our duty is owed—and whose nature is revealed to us by rationally necessary identification. If my argument is correct, it implies that this third formulation is the core of Kant's doctrine. The ends formula should not be thought of as derivative from the universalizability formula, but vice versa. Though I make no claim about what Kant actually thought, the result of this reversal is a substantive Kantianism (based on the nature of human subjects) in place of the traditional formalistic version (based on the formal lawfulness of rules of duty).

In *Respect for Persons,* R. S. Downie and Elizabeth Telfer try to spell out the relation between respect and the ends formula, and they begin by noting that the formula is obscure because of the strangeness of thinking of persons as ends. Ends are normally objects of striving—things, events, or states of affairs we aim to promote or bring into existence. It seems inappropriate to think of people this way and surely inappropriate to think that this is the paradigmatic way of showing respect for them. Undaunted by this strangeness, Downie and Telfer argue that an end in itself is something valuable "because of what it is," as opposed to things that are valuable because of what they do or the way they lead to other things of value. They claim that a thing that is valuable in itself is something "which should be *cherished* because of what it is," and conclude that respecting persons as ends in themselves means valuing them for what makes them persons.[12]

In their view, what makes people persons is that they have rational wills, which can be analyzed into two components; persons set their own ends for themselves, and they are capable of governing their behavior by rules. As to what is implied in valuing people because of the first of these components, they quote Kant, "For the ends of any person, who is an end in himself, must as far as possible also be my end, if that conception of an end in itself is to have its full effect on me" (*FMM,* 55). They contend that the expression of valuing appropriate here is a kind of active sympathy in which we take the other person's ends as our own. We need not follow their analysis further, since this claim already goes too far.[13]

If respect is taken to involve the adoption of the other's ends as one's own and thus extended to include altruism, it is stretched beyond recognition. Respect involves a certain regard for the interests of others, but not as much as adopting them as one's own. Respect is altruism's cooler cousin. It shows its solicitude for the interests of others in its reserve rather than its enthusiasm. One can respect one's adversaries or even one's enemies without having sympathy with their ends or actively adopting them. Respect is characteristically exhibited by self-restraint, by making way for the other to promote his ends rather than by actively promoting them oneself. It is by refusing to suppress differences, silence disagreements, cross boundaries, undermine competitors, and the like, that respect is shown. Respect is holding one's own interests in check, not serving those of others. This is what is obscured when respect is taken to include altruism. Altruism is taking the other's values as if they were mine; respect is a certain honor paid to the other's values because they are his.

But what then of the relation between respect and treating people as ends in themselves? Downie and Telfer were led to their overstretched conception of respect by misconceiving what is meant by "ends in themselves."

Recall that they started with recognition of the oddness of thinking of persons as ends, since ends are objects to be promoted or brought into existence. They thought this oddness could be removed by taking end in itself to mean "valuable in itself." To be sure, Kant invites this by speaking of ends in themselves as having absolute worth. But this will not do the moral work that Kant assigns it, because he takes recognition of people as ends in themselves as implying that they may not be treated merely as means. It does not follow from the fact that something is valuable in itself that it may not be treated merely as a means. Strictly speaking, all that follows from this is that its value can be realized independently of any further efficacy. It need not be treated as a means in order to have value. If we believe that knowledge is valuable in itself, that would not imply that we were prohibited from using it for, say, the cure of disease. It would only imply that we believed that knowledge need not be used in such ways to have value. That something is valuable in itself makes it possible to treat it not as a mere means—it does not make it necessary. What has to be shown, then, is that in regarding people as ends in themselves one is confronted with an imperative forbidding their treatment as mere means. I contend that we can get this result by emphasizing a different feature of ends in themselves.

An end is any valued object even if it is valued as a means to some other end, as when I value a house because it is a means to shelter. We characteristically think of the objects of our valuing as organized into chains in which each link points to the next: I value my job because it pays my salary; I value my salary because it pays for my house; I value the house because it gives me shelter; I value shelter because it gives me, comfort, and so on. Insofar as any link is valued because it leads to the next (or to others further along), it is a means. Nevertheless, insofar as such a link is valued even as a means, it is an end. Though I may value my house because it is a means to shelter, it is nevertheless an end for me, an object of my valuing. It is common to think of such means-ends chains as if any given means is only an object of valuing because of the end to which it is a means. So understood, such a chain must have an ultimate end that is not itself a means to anything else, otherwise there would be no source for the value that gets passed down the chain from link to link. Since this end does not derive value from yet another end to which it is a means, it is distinguished from the others in the chain by being called an end in itself.

Two features characterize ends in themselves. First, they have value that does not depend on their being means to some value beyond them. Second, they are sources of the value of things that are only valuable for the sake of something beyond them. They are, so to speak, the unmoved movers of the valuable. Downie and Telfer emphasize the first of these aspects and take

137

regarding people as ends in themselves as regarding them as valuable in a way that does not depend on their being means to something else. But this does not exclude treating people as means; it only shows that they have value without that. I think we can get the result Kant has in mind if we emphasize the second aspect and understand regarding people as ends in themselves as thinking of them as able to bestow value on things, irrespective of whether they (people) are valuable themselves. (Of course, they may also be this as well.)

People are ends in themselves in this value-bestowing sense, from their own standpoints, insofar as they have sovereign interests that make it compellingly and nonfungibly reasonable for them to try to obtain the objects of their desires (as indexed by their sovereign interests). Consequently, we regard people as ends in themselves if we view them from their own standpoints—that is, identifying with the commanding and nonfungible nature of their particular ends, recognizing their personal imperatives as compelling and true. From her own first-person standpoint, each person is an end in herself in the sense that her true personal imperative bestows value on things that promote her sovereign interest without reference to any further end or value beyond. I do not claim that this is always how Kant uses the phrase, but I think it accounts for the main thrust of his usage and offers a path to confirming his most important assertions about morality. Most important, it shows the link between treating people as ends in themselves and respecting them.

In a moment I shall have to explain why this interpretation of the ends formula does not dissolve respect into altruism, as Downie and Telfer think. For the present, note that it accounts for the prohibition on using persons as mere means. From the standpoint of his own sovereign interest, every individual naturally rejects being treated merely as a means, since that is being treated with indifference to how the treatment serves his sovereign interest. This is the force of the *merely*, since people do not naturally reject being treated as means as long as their sovereign interests are also thereby served. I do not treat the bus driver as a mere means when I treat her as a means to get home, since her job of driving me serves her ends also. What people reject is having their ends wholly disregarded. This rejection is their personal imperative in negative form. "I must realize my sovereign interest" implies "I must resist the actions of others that subject me to their sovereign interest while disregarding my own." If treating people as ends in themselves is allowing myself to recognize the imperative force of their sovereign interest and the truth of that imperative, it entails that I endorse as a true imperative their refusal to be treated as mere means. And that

138

makes Kant's claim—that people may not be treated merely as means because they are ends in themselves—true.

Moreover, a person's insistence on not being treated as a means is not a demand that others be means to his ends. It is a demand that others refrain from acting as if his pursuit of his ends were unimportant, not that they take his ends as important for them. Thus, it is a demand that others experience the imperative force that his ends have for him, without themselves coming to experience his ends as imperative for them. The demand not to be treated as a mere means is a demand for respect, not for altruism.

The prohibition against treating people as mere means is also a prohibition against sacrificing some people to save others. That people are ends in themselves must imply that they are not substitutable for one another. Kant wrote that an end in itself "is one for which no other end can be substituted" (*FMM*, 53). This makes little sense if "end in itself" is understood as "valuable in itself." If knowledge is valuable in itself, that does not prohibit trading it for something else valuable in itself, say, art; it only implies that we do not have to be able to trade knowledge for something else in order for knowledge to be valuable. There is no reason to think that something valuable in itself could not be substituted for by something else comparably valuable in itself. But such substitutability in the case of persons is precisely what Kant is at pains to reject. If regarding people as ends in themselves is identifying with them, participating imaginatively in the partisan practical attitude of their first-person subjective reality, then it is recognizing the way in which satisfaction of their interests is to them nonfungible, incapable of being substituted for by the satisfaction of other people's interests; it is recognizing their imperative refusal not be sacrificed for others with the same force as their refusal to be treated as mere means.

We can get "regarding people as ends in themselves" to do the jobs Kant assigned it if we understand it as "identifying with people's first-person reality as subjects." Then, treating people as ends in themselves is treating them in the ways that are appropriate in light of this identification. Further, if other persons are facts whose nature can only be understood by identification, then a rational being must identify and must view other persons as ends in themselves. Human beings are the facts of reason that make Kantian morality rationally necessary.

Insofar as I treat people as ends in themselves, I do not stop treating myself that way. Kant insists not just that you treat others as ends in themselves, but all "humanity, whether in your own person or in that of another" (*FMM*, 54). This is why the Kantian formula requires respect not altruism—not that I must promote others' ends as if they were my own but that I must promote mine in a way that is compatible with their promoting theirs; otherwise, I would ignore the urgency of my own ends. To consider altruism as one's duty is to treat all people except oneself as ends in themselves.

To be sure, Kant says that "the ends of any person, who is an end in himself, must as far as possible also be my end, if that conception of an end in itself is to have its full effect on me," and this does suggest altruism. Recall, however, that I spoke earlier of sympathy as the natural psychological consequence of identification. Much as one might describe the trajectory of a missile by indicating where it would land if nothing stopped it first, we can understand Kant here as describing the nature of the identification necessary for seeing the other as an end in himself by indicating the resting point that the identification would reach if all its natural consequences were realized such that it would "have its full effect on me." This does not deny that there might be things that legitimately stand in the way of the full realization of all the natural consequences of identification. For instance, my own ends would legitimately stand in the way, as long as they were legitimate ends: "No one," Kant writes in the *Metaphysical Principles of Virtue*, "has the right to demand from me the sacrifice of those ends of mine that are not immoral" (*MV*, 46). I do not discount my own ends, since I am required to treat myself as an end in itself as well. The effect of identifying with the other is then not to replace some of my ends with some of his but to recognize with full force that outside of my ends are other people caring just as ultimately about their own. Identifying with them, I feel the pull of that caring, which, operating against the pull upon me of my own (legitimate) ends, pulls me in the direction of caring about theirs. Accordingly, if identification had "its full effect on me"—that is, if I had no legitimate ends obstructing its natural tendency—I would come to adopt all the other's (legitimate) ends as my own.

This conclusion accords with *The Metaphysical Principles of Virtue*, where Kant distinguishes the duty to love one's neighbor from the duty to respect one's neighbor. By the principle of the first, people "are directed constantly to approach one another," and "by the principle of *respect* which they owe one another they are directed to keep themselves at a distance" (*MV*, 113). "The duty to love one's neighbor can also be expressed as the duty to make the ends of others (as long as they are not immoral) my own. The duty to respect one's neighbor is contained in the maxim, degrade no man merely as a means to personal ends" (*MV*, 114). Kant understands the duty of love as practically equivalent to acting on the "maxim of benevolence; and this maxim results in beneficence" (*MV*, 113), that is, in positive

140

assistance to the other. The duty of respect, however, is "actually only negative," a duty "not to exalt oneself above others" (*MV*, 114).

The Social Contract and Reason's
Strong Answer to Subjugation

Recognition of the fact of the plurality of persons entails the rational requirement that we reason about the pursuit of our sovereign interests subject to limits that are reasonable from all subjective standpoints at once. This is the "knowing together" of conscience. Since "what is reasonable from all subjective standpoints at once" is equivalent to "what it would be reasonable for all individuals to agree to accept," this "knowing together" can be represented by means of the social contract. Recall that the acceptance in the social contract is not a separate authorizing act done in response to what is shown to be reasonable—it simply dramatizes that something has been shown to be reasonable. The appeal of the social contract theory, then, is that it makes vivid the necessary and natural moral structure of our own reasoning and thus the rationally required structure of moral reasoning.

This moral reasoning will of course be aimed at determining what it would truly be reasonable for everyone to agree to accept, not what they, in fact, accept. Since people are imperfectly informed, imperfectly rational, and likely to hold untested moral beliefs, the principles they would actually accept are not necessarily those that are truly reasonable for them to accept, and these would fail to meet the standard implicit in the structure of moral reasoning. Thus, determining what does meet this standard requires posing the theoretical question we formulated about people in the natural context at the end of the last chapter.

But now there is an important difference. At the end of the last chapter, the theoretical question we posed was directed at locating the difference between justice and subjugation. We got as far as identifying the mutually reasonable terms for identifying and prohibiting subjugation, but no further. The result was not itself a rational requirement on our action, since we could not say that everyone is required to agree to what it would be reasonable for all to agree to. To get to that, we needed the antisubjugation assumption—namely, that subjugation was a general evil from which all people were to be protected. Now, however, we have seen that we are required to reason about pursuit of our sovereign interests in terms that it would be reasonable for all to agree to. Thus, it is rationally required that we each limit our actions at that point at which all can pursue their sovereign interests   141 to the maximum compatible with the same for everyone. We recognize the truth of the *moral imperative of respect.*

Since this is equivalent to a rational requirement that, according to the terms for identifying and prohibiting subjugation to which it would be reasonable for all to agree, people not subjugate one another, it amounts to showing the antisubjugation assumption to be a requirement of reason. Since the sovereignty of each person's sovereign interest is equivalent to each person's insistence on not being subjugated, identification with each person disposes one to refrain from subjugating others, and endorsement of the truth of each person's personal imperative of self-interest is recognition that everyone is truly entitled not to be subjugated. The truth of the moral imperative of respect shows the antisubjugation assumption to be true and required by reason. Consequently, it is rationally required that we act according to the principles that all could agree to under the conditions of the social contract: The social contract is reason's strong answer to subjugation.

The content of reason's answer to subjugation is the same in the weak or strong versions. What is different is the authority of the answer. We no longer operate under the assumption of moral inconclusivity. Now that the requirement of respect has shown the antisubjugation assumption to be a requirement of reason, the same principles that constituted reason's weak answer now constitute reason's strong answer. Consequently, I shall not repeat the arguments at the close of chapter 1. There we concluded that requirements that it would be reasonable for all to agree to, when they are imagined to be in the natural context, free of beliefs in the validity of any moral principle, perfectly rational and possessed of all relevant knowledge, unaware of the actual relations in which they stand or how they, in particular, will be affected by any principle under consideration, unable to gamble on this, not knowing the specifics of their sovereign interests but concerned to promote their general ability to pursue their sovereign interests whatever they are, are nonsubjugating. We saw as well that, though determining whether any requirements satisfy this test is posing a hypothetical question that requires imagining the necessary constraints on knowledge and the rest, the theoretical question must be posed to determine whether existing relations are subjugating. The answer thus applies to existing relations and can be extended from there to any potential arrangements. All that is changed now is that the answer is binding on our actions. Acting according to principles that satisfy this test is a requirement of reasoning in light of the facts. As such, it is a requirement of reason that individuals subject their judgments about action to an internal social contract and govern their behavior accordingly.

In the remainder of this section, I shall defend this conclusion in several ways. First, I shall indicate how it converges with the interpretation of Kant's theory begun in the last section and vindicates Kant's own theory of the internal social contract. I go on to show that the internal social contract coincides with the Golden Rule, with the structure of moral justification, and with everyone's real interest in morality. Finally, I shall suggest how justice as reason's answer to subjugation accounts for the meaning of such notions as resentment and degradation. In chapters 3 and 5, I shall present the specific principles of natural and social justice that follow from the internal social contract.

We left Kant in the middle of his derivation of the five versions of the ultimate principle of morality, the "categorical imperative," in *Foundations of the Metaphysics of Morals*. After the ends formula, Kant argues for two more versions of the categorical imperative—namely, one that holds that we are to act only according to principles that respect the capacity of human beings for self-legislation (the autonomy formula) and that we are to act only according to principles that could be legislated by all rational beings for a "kingdom of ends" (the kingdom formula). The last of these places Kant firmly in the social contract tradition. Since the kingdom formula is held to be a requirement of each individual's reason, his is a theory of the internal social contract. I shall show how Kant's argument for the kingdom formula confirms and is confirmed by the interpretation of the ends formula that I defended in the last section.

Kant gets to the autonomy formula (he calls it the third principle) by combining the universalizability formula (the first principle) and the ends formula (which he calls the second principle):

> Objectively, the ground of all practical legislation lies (according to the first principle) in the rule and in the form of universality . . . ; subjectively, it lies in the end. But the subject of all ends is every rational being as end in itself (by the second principle); from this there follows the third practical principle of the will. . . . By this principle all maxims are rejected which are not consistent with the universal lawgiving of will. The will is thus not only subject to the law but subject in such a way that it must be regarded also as self-legislative and only for this reason being subject to the law (of which it can regard itself the author). (*FMM*, 56).

If we take the ends formula to mean that human beings are "valuable in themselves," the natural way to interpret this combination of it with the universalizability formula is this: As rational beings we are required to will actions on maxims that could be universalized (the objective ground), and since human beings are valuable in themselves, we are required to take as   143 our end (the subjective ground) what is valuable in them. Since what is valuable in human beings is their rational nature, which imposes on them the requirement of willing actions on maxims that could be universalized, the combination yields the additional principle that we are to treat people in ways that are compatible with their willing their actions on maxims that could be universalized. The problem with this natural interpretation is that, unless he is drugged, knocked unconscious, or killed, a human being can will to act on universalizable maxims no matter what is done to him. Recall that universality applies to the intention of my action independently of whether my intention succeeds in the world. Bound in chains, I can still will to act on the universalizable maxim that, say, all unjustly bound captives should do what they can to escape. Nothing that anyone does (short of wiping out my reasoning capacity) to thwart my successful action interferes with my willing according to universality. So interpreted, the new principle will be a rather toothless moral prohibition.

Clearly, Kant means more by the autonomy formula than just letting people will to act according to universal laws. He means that they are only to be treated according to maxims that they themselves could reasonably have willed as universal laws. To reach this nontoothless autonomy formula from the combination of the universalizability and ends formulas, Kant must draw more out of the latter than the interpretation just mentioned has him doing. And he does. In the passage just quoted, Kant takes the ends formula to imply that human beings may only be subject to laws that they can regard themselves as authoring. People can only regard themselves as authoring laws compatible with their ends. This is only another way of saying that the ends formula requires not treating people merely as means to the ends of others. I showed in the previous section that we can make this inference from the ends formula by interpreting it as calling for identification. Consequently, adopting that interpretation enables us to reach the nontoothless autonomy formula.

From the autonomy formula, it is a short step to the kingdom of ends. By a kingdom of ends, Kant understands, "the systematic union of different rational beings through common laws. Because laws determine ends with regard to their universal validity, if we abstract from the personal difference of rational beings and thus from the content of their private ends, we can think of a whole of all ends in systematic connection, a whole of rational beings as ends in themselves as well as of the particular ends which each may set for himself. This is a kingdom of ends" (*FMM*, 58).[14]

This is a difficult passage to decipher because in it Kant is using *ends* sometimes to refer to people's particular ends and sometimes to refer to the people themselves; he also seems to abstract from the content of private ends in one sentence only to bring it back in the next. I think, however, that what he means is this: Since according to the ends formula, people can only will maxims on the basis of ends that all could embrace, a world in which people acted according to this requirement would be one in which each person pursued his own private ends in ways that were compatible with other people's pursuit of theirs. Since each person could only pursue ends that everyone could accept him pursuing in light of their own, we can picture this imaginary world while abstracting from the content of people's private ends. We see people instead as subjects pursuing their private ends— whatever those ends are—up to that point at which this blocks the like possibility of the others pursuing their ends. Living according to the rules of such a world is living in a way that accords each person an equal ability to pursue her ends, and thus it treats no one as merely a means to others' ends. But this is only a picture of the kingdom of ends, not yet the formula.

To get to the kingdom formula from this picture, it is necessary to add the autonomy formula. Then the world pictured is equivalent to one governed by laws that everyone could reasonably will for herself and others as universal laws: "Morality, therefore, consists in the relation of every action to that legislation through which alone a kingdom of ends is possible. This legislation, however, must be found in every rational being" (*FMM*, 59).

It is, in short, a necessity of our reason that we subject our actions to the requirement of being compatible with the principles that all human beings (abstracting from their "personal difference" and "from all content of their private ends") could reasonably will for all human beings. Since this is effectively the social contract as the very shape of moral reasoning, this is an argument for the internal social contract toward which Hobbes was groping. Moreover, there is no question that Kant aims with it to vindicate Rousseau's insight that freedom and moral authority could be reconciled if morality were shown to be a natural tendency of reason and the individual shown to be obeying himself when he obeys the moral law. Appropriating for the kingdom of ends Rousseau's claim that the citizen is both sovereign and subject, Kant writes: "A rational being belongs to the kingdom of ends as a member when he gives universal laws in it while also himself subject to these laws. He belongs to it as sovereign when he, as legislating, is subject to the will of no other" (*FMM*, 59). For our purposes, the important point is that Kant's claim that the kingdom formula (that is, the internal social contract) is a requirement of reason is vindicated if we interpret taking people as ends in themselves as identifying with their subjective reality and add to this that such identification is itself required by reason. This lends support to the argument for the rational necessity of the internal social contract that I have presented in this chapter.

Turning from Kant, another consideration that supports this argument is the convergence of the internal social contract with the Golden Rule. The internal social contract has, as Hobbes also saw, the reciprocal shape of the Golden Rule. It is a requirement of reason that people take the standpoint of others toward their own actions and only do that which could be simultaneously accepted by all. The test of the social contract is the test of the Golden Rule applied to the whole plurality of persons. The Golden Rule has, however, a congenital vagueness that must be cleared up before it can serve as a workable moral standard. When we make the necessary adjustments, the convergence between the Golden Rule and the social contract as I have formulated it becomes evident.

The Golden Rule requires me to do unto others what I would have others do unto me. Thus, in any given case when I am determining how to act toward some particular other, I must ask myself what I would want to have done to me by him. But, when I ask this, do I consider *me* as having my traits or his? If I take the first tack and determine my action by whether I would have it done to me with my traits, then I may end up subjecting him (the real him) to whatever quirky traits or tolerances I have. If I am, say, a masochist and he is not, I would be willing to have him do me some violence, and then applying the Golden Rule, I will find it all right to do him some violence that he (with his traits) will not want done to him. This makes the Golden Rule implausible because it amounts to making the other person's actual traits irrelevant (and only mine relevant) to what I may do to him— and then it is pointless to ask me to test my actions by whether I would want them done to me. If we take the second tack and consider what I would want done to me if I had his traits, a related problem arises. The other may want anything, say, that he be someone's slave, or he might be a masochist. Then, if I am to act to him as I would want to be acted toward if I was him, I would have to allow him to enslave or victimize me. This is the mirror image of the first problem, since it amounts to making my own traits irrelevant (and only his relevant) to what may be required of me by the Golden Rule.

To avoid these problems, we must understand the Golden Rule in a way that makes both my traits and the other's relevant. We can do that by asking for what both of us would accept having done (in situations like this) when we could end up on either side (that is, either as doer or recipient of the action) and when we might have either one's desires, traits, and sensibilities. As with the social contract, and for the same reasons, this is a theoretical matter of what it would be reasonable for us to accept, not an empirical matter of what we actually accept. Moreover, to be a workable moral standard, the test will have to be constrained so that some univocal requirement issues from it. Thus, what would be reasonable for each to accept will have to be constrained by the requirement that it be no more than is reasonable for the other to accept. Building these requirements in, we apply the test by asking for what it would be reasonable for us to agree to having done in situations like this, when we do not know which side we were on and which characteristics we had and when neither could insist on more than it would be reasonable for the other to accept. In face-to-face moral conflicts, this might be applied with considerable specificity about the parties' desires, traits, and sensibilities. Applying it generally, however, say, in judging policies or actions that will affect large numbers of people, we must abstract from this detail. What remains is that each will have a sovereign interest that she will be ultimately concerned to promote and whose promotion is for her the measure of the reasonableness of accepting any rule to govern her or other people's actions.

It follows that we can apply the Golden Rule in this wholesale way by asking what actions it would be reasonable for everyone to accept in light of her sovereign interest when she did not know the particular interests that composed it or which side of disputes she would be on, and when none could insist on more than was reasonable for the others to accept. Thus, whenever I act according to what could be agreed to in the social contract, I satisfy the requirement of the Golden Rule, so to speak, writ large.

This further supports the claim that the social contract is reason's own natural tendency, as the Golden Rule is as near to a universally recognized moral standard as there is. Versions of the Golden Rule exist in virtually every major tradition of moral teaching: in Hinduism ("Do naught to others which, if done to thee, would cause thee pain: this is the sum of duty"), Buddhism ("In five ways should a clansman minister to his friends and familiars, . . . by treating them as he treats himself"), Confucianism ("What you do not want done to yourself, do not do unto others"), Zoroastrianism ("Whatever thou dost not approve for thyself, do not approve for anyone else"), Judaism ("Whatsoever thou wouldest that men should not do unto thee, do not do that to them"), and Christianity ("As ye would that men should do to you, do ye also to them likewise" [Luke 6:31]). Among the ancient Greeks, Isocrates is quoted as saying "Do not do to others what you would not wish to suffer yourself," and Diogenes Laertius reports Aristotle saying "Treat your friends as you want them to treat you."[15]

What is more, the Golden Rule is no ordinary moral principle. It neither requires nor forbids any particular action. Rather, it is a kind of test that an individual can apply to any of his actions (or, by implication, to the principles upon which he acts) to determine their morality. That the Golden Rule is a nearly universally accepted test of morality strongly suggests that it corresponds to a natural tendency of reason, perhaps the very structure of conscience itself. If so, that supports my claim that the internal social contract is the natural structure of moral reasoning.

The claim that the social contract corresponds to the Golden Rule runs up against a tradition harking back at least to John Stuart Mill, in which the Golden Rule is said to be equivalent to utilitarianism's principle that the satisfactions of each person are to be counted impartially in calculating aggregate happiness. Mill wrote that "between [the agent's] own happiness and that of others, utilitarianism requires him to be as strictly impartial as a disinterested and benevolent spectator. In the golden rule of Jesus of Nazareth, we read the complete spirit of the ethics of utility" (*U*, 16). This identity between the Golden Rule and utilitarianism's impartiality has recently been argued for in a novel way by Peter Singer in *The Expanding Circle: Ethics and Sociobiology*.

Singer tries to derive an evolutionary warrant for utilitarian moral doctrine from the fact that members of primitive human groups would have had to give reasons for their actions that their fellows could accept: "In a dispute between members of a cohesive group of reasoning beings, the demand for a reason is a demand for a justification that can be accepted by the group as a whole. Thus the reason offered must be disinterested, at least to the extent of being equally acceptable to all" (*EC*, 93). Singer takes this to require that the reason be impartial between the interests of all. "We can progress toward rational settlement of disputes over ethics," he continues, "by taking the element of disinterestedness inherent in the idea of justifying one's conduct to society as a whole, and extending this into the principle that to be ethical, a decision must give equal weight to the interests of all affected by it" (*EC*, 100). The result is the characteristic form of utilitarian ethics: In deciding what action I should take, I am required to consider impartially the preferences of all affected, favoring no preference because it happens to be mine or that of a friend. I then add up all the satisfaction (of preferences) that each action that I might perform is likely to produce, and my moral obligation is to perform the action that produces the greatest amount of satisfaction: "Whatever action satisfies more preferences, adjusted according to the strength of the preferences, that is the action I ought to take" (*EC*, 101). Because this procedure is disinterested and impartial, Singer takes its conclusions as acceptable to all, and thus he takes utilitarianism to be equivalent to applying the Golden Rule, joining company with Mill (*EC*, 135–36).

The flaw in this argument is that, while impartiality in the consideration of what matters to people is surely a condition of the acceptability of one's conclusions to all, there is no reason that all should accept the principle that all should act to promote the greatest aggregate satisfaction because, no matter how impartially this aggregate may be arrived at, its promotion may still require that the satisfactions of some be sacrificed—without compensation—for the satisfactions of others. People have no reason to accept utilitarianism as the principle guiding their actions and those of their fellows toward them because they can have no idea of how they will be treated as a result. In fact, accepting utilitarianism is accepting that there is nothing that may not forcibly be done to one if needed to maximize the satisfaction of others—and accepting that seems downright irrational. What Singer has done is take impartiality, which is a necessary condition of the acceptability to all of moral conclusions, and erect it into a sufficient condition, which it is not.

The requirement of acting according to the principles that would be agreed to in the social contract is not subject to this criticism because it is a requirement that all people (who have not already violated it) have reason to accept at all times. (This does not apply to people who have violated the requirement because they are subject to punishment in ways that they will not necessarily have reason to accept.) Since the requirement is tantamount to a guarantee that each person will have the maximum possibility of promoting his sovereign interest compatible with a like possibility for all, it is always in every person's interest to accept this requirement except when promotion of his interests requires the suppression of other people's like possibility of promoting theirs. For two reasons, this qualifying clause does not undermine the claim that the requirement is truly in everyone's interest. First, the qualification is no more than the minimum condition of anything being in everyone's interest, and it is hardly plausible to contend that insisting on this condition renders the requirement not in everyone's interest. Second, what serves an individual's interests except when his interests require suppression of other people's interests does, nonetheless, truly serve that individual's interests. It just does not serve *all* his interests. He has an interest in not being subjugated, so even in his case his interests are served, though not completely. By contrast, it is not the case that maximizing aggregate utility always serves an individual's interests at least partially.

Because what satisfies the requirement of the social contract is tantamount to what passes the test of nonsubjugation and because everyone has a real present and continuing interest in not being subjugated, it is in everyone's present and continuing interest to accept the principles that would be agreed to in the social contract. Our interest in not being subjugated is our interest in justice. This is why it is to might that right is opposed.

The argument for the social contract is corroborated in another way. Proving that one's action is compatible with the maximum compatible pos-

149

sibility of every separate person promoting his sovereign interest amounts to establishing an airtight justification for what one has done. Consider that a justification is offered to defeat a complaint. A complaint can be one of two sorts: One may either complain that the other has acted contrary to the complainant's values or that he has acted contrary to the complainant's possibility of promoting her values. Call the first complaint "condemnation," and the second, "resentment." To make good on a condemnation, one must show that the accused has failed in some obligation to serve the complainant's values. But given the nonfungibility of people's values, one person's values cannot in themselves have weight for another and thus he cannot be faulted for acting contrary to them. Condemnations are self-defeating.

To make good on resentment, one must show that the accused has undermined in some reasonably blameable way the complainant's possibility of promoting her own sovereign interest. To be reasonable, resentment cannot just be dissatisfaction with the other for not having done more for the complainant, for not having done exactly what the complainant wants, for not having dedicated his life to the complainant, or for not having undermined someone else's possibility of promoting his sovereign interest. One cannot reasonably resent a person for failing to do something that would have been equal grounds for someone else's (including his own) resentment. But then, it is not possible to resent a person reasonably who has acted in a way that is compatible with everyone's maximum compatible ability to promote his or her sovereign interest. Consequently, proving that one has acted in this way justifies one's action by showing that resentment of it is misplaced.

That resentment is defeated by showing that one has acted in a way compatible with everyone's like ability to promote her sovereign interest implies that resentment is always for being treated as a mere means or, equivalently, for a failure to be treated respectfully. Condemnation, by contrast, is for a failure of altruism, and it is because altruism is not a requirement of reason that complaints about its failure cannot be supported by reason. I do not resent someone for having a different set of ideals or ethical or religious views from me; I resent him for thwarting my purposes, standing in the way of my promoting them, or treating me in a way that trivializes what matters to me. In all of these cases, resentment is the attitude of one who aimed to realize his sovereign interest against another who blocked him. Resentment is the form that the energy I would have devoted to my interests takes when it is blocked, forced to take shape as aggressive feeling rather than productive action, forced to inhabit consciousness—as anger—rather than the world.

Since the requirement of the social contract incorporates the test of nonsubjugation, we can say that the shared will to live according to the principles of the social contract is equivalent to mutual respect. Disrespect is the will to subjugate others. Self-respect is the will not to be subjugated by others—the individual's confidence in the validity of her sovereign interest's claim to sovereignty. Resentment is self-respect protesting disrespect.

Degradation is self-respect undermined, disrespect embraced. In contrast to the resentful person who retains the will not to be subjugated, the degraded person has lost the will not to be subjugated. Thus, addiction seems degrading because the addict seems to desire his continued subjugation rather than to desire escaping it, and servility seems degrading since the servile person seems to embrace his subjugation rather than to consider it onerous. Likewise, torture victims are degraded because they are reduced to wanting nothing but to escape pain, and victims of brainwashing are degraded because their wills are broken entirely and replaced with lassitude and passivity. By virtue of a queer belief that sex engaged in by women without desire or affection is an act of submission, many consider female prostitutes degraded because they appear to will their subjugation to men. The belief is queer because it is objectively false (sex can be engaged in by women without desire or affection though still autonomously) and historically true (in light of the cultural meaning that sex has had where women have been subordinated to men). The result of this is that those who argue that female prostitution is degrading and those who argue that it is not are both right, each missing the other's point.

The question of whether the examples in the last paragraph really are cases of degradation depends in part on the truth of numerous empirical claims about what really goes on in each, which we can not evaluate here. It suffices for my point that what is believed about these conditions when one believes (truly or falsely) that they are forms of degradation is in every case that the will not to be subjugated is not just blocked but undermined, robbed from one by others or undone by oneself. Since the will not to be subjugated is just the press of the sovereign interest, each of these is a case of some deformation of the sovereign interest or of the individual's understanding of it. Recall that the sovereign interest is sovereign because it is hierarchical, exclusive, and imperative. The addict and the torture victim are (thought to be) degraded because the hierarchy of their desires has collapsed in the face of the irresistability of a lower-level immediate desire for relief. The servile person and the prostitute are (thought to be) degraded because the exclusiveness of their sovereign interests has given way to deference to the interests of others. The brainwashing victim is (thought to be) degraded because the imperativeness of his sovereign interest has gone limp, its commanding voice reduced to a murmur. It is no accident that the various institutions that have perfected the technology of destroying the self, institutions most powerfully described by Erving Goffman in *Asylums*, have used some mixture of torture, servility, and brainwashing to achieve their ends.[16]

One implication of my argument is that the capacity to feel resentment is a sign that one is not degraded. Likewise, the belief that one is entitled to justification is a sign that one is not degraded. Both are evidence that self-respect lives. Here it is worth pausing to ask a question rarely asked—namely, why does justification work at all? How are words able to work where actions have seemed to fail? The answer, I think, is that justification attempts to use words to make a person understand that an action which has affected him adversely is required from the standpoint of everyone's sovereign interest. Justification is a retrospective invitation to identification. If the justification is a true one and if the listener hears it while identifying with the sovereign interests of his fellows, then, given the understanding produced by the words, identifying with the sovereign interests around him will dispose the listener toward the adverse action as well. True justifications have real consoling power.

The point can be made in terms of the account of reason as maximizing coherence: The appearance of injustice ruptures coherence because it creates a situation that cannot be harmonized with the plans and ends of both the victim and the perpetrator of the alleged offense. Effective justification shows the one who thinks he is victimized that the suspect situation can, in fact, be accepted from a standpoint shared with the alleged perpetrator. It consoles by restoring the coherence that the alleged injustice breached.

This suggests that acting in a way that no one can resent—that is, acting with respect for all—is acting as if everyone were entitled to acceptable reasons for how they are treated. When my reason encounters others and turns round, it faces me as the demand for reasonable treatment in deed and in word. This, in turn, suggests that two of the ways we have corroborated the social contract in this section—namely, by showing its convergence with the Golden Rule and with the structure of justification—have a deeper link: Considering what to do in light of the Golden Rule is applying the test of the social contract prospectively to one's actions, and justifying what one has done to those affected by it is applying the same test retrospectively.

I conclude that the social contract represents the necessary and natural tendency of reason; determining one's actions by its test is a requirement of reason. Since it is the same test formulated at the end of chapter 1, but now as a requirement of reason not dependent for its authority on an independent assumption that subjugation is a general evil, it is reason's strong answer to subjugation. Reason itself insists that all rational creatures refrain from subjugating their fellows and that they subject their relations to the test of the social contract toward that end. This test corresponds to that of the Golden Rule, to the structure of moral justification, and to what is reasonable for everyone to accept insofar as no one may insist on what it is unreasonable for any other to accept. Likewise, the arrangements that pass the test of the social contract serve each person's real current interest in not being subjugated as far as this interest can be served for everyone. Since the social contract corresponds to conscience, it is not only a necessity of reason but a natural tendency of each individual's reasoning. The internal social contract exists. It vindicates the Kantian notion of a kingdom of ends, and it answers the Hobbesian challenge: The trust upon which human society is based is well-placed.

PART TWO

The Principles of Justice

Chapter 3: *Natural Justice and the Natural Covenant*

> When Gentiles who have not the law do by nature what
> the law requires, they are a law to themselves, even
> though they do not have the law. They show that what
> the law requires is written on their hearts.
> —Romans 2:14–15

The Principle of Compatible Liberty

The principles of natural justice are the requirements that hold between any two or more sane adult human beings irrespective of the social relations in which they stand. Thus, they hold between the members of different societies and between members of the same society, although we shall see that the requirements are subject to modification in light of the special social relations in which people within the same society stand. That, however, is a matter of social justice. For example, we shall see that natural justice requires noninterference with the bodies and immediate possessions of others, except to prevent or punish attacks by them. By *immediate possessions*, I mean those things that people take from the natural world for their survival, and beyond that only what they take when there is enough left over for others. I shall argue that no greater right of property exists under natural justice. Consequently, the principles of natural justice do not allow interference with the bodies of others to prevent them from, or punish them for, taking things that people hold beyond their immediate possessions. I shall, however, argue that a larger right of property does exist under social justice. Thus, in a society with a just system of property, the principle of natural justice is modified so that it no longer prohibits punishment for taking what others justly own beyond their immediate possessions. What is important here is that natural justice is not suspended when we enter societies; it is refracted through just social relations and accordingly widened, narrowed, or both as a result.

In chapters 4 and 5 we shall consider how just social structures refract the lines of natural justice. First, however, we must discover the principles of natural justice themselves, in abstraction from this effect. To do so, it   157 will help to imagine people living in more or less primitive conditions—say, in nomadic desert tribes where people own no more than what they can carry and have no more social structure than is necessary for them to move and defend themselves if necessary as a unit—and consider what behavior they can rightly require of one another.

It is no accident that just such tribes played a crucial role in defining our moral traditions. We shall see that the principles of natural justice include the nonreligious requirements in the Ten Commandments. As the principles of natural justice are the conditions of nonsubjugation, so obedience to the Ten Commandments was represented as a duty of the Hebrews, owed in return for having been brought "out of the house of bondage" (Exod. 20:2). Since they took their duties as reciprocation for their liberation, they understood themselves as bound by a covenant. The principles of natural justice do not depend, however, on religious beliefs for their content or binding power; reason alone suffices. This sufficiency of reason was as true in ancient times as it is in the present. Indeed, religion obfuscates the fact of reason's adequacy in the moral realm, as it clouds reason's theoretical competence with primitive beliefs whose major appeal must have been the security they gave people who were largely subject to forces they could not understand. Accordingly, I take the covenant to be a natural rather than a divine one, one between human beings, not between human beings and God—though at the end of the third section of chapter 2 I offered a suggestion as to why it would be natural to understand the former as if it were the latter. Nonetheless, the contribution of religion to the moral development of the human race is immense. The historical role played by religion—such as that of the Hebrew tribes and their spiritual heirs—in codifying and enshrining the moral discoveries of reason is undeniable. With social structure reduced to a minimum, the natural requirements are most clearly seen.

The principles of natural justice are those that pass the test of morality outlined in the previous chapter, when people are thought to share no social structure or a very minimal one. I shall speak of these simply as the principles it would be reasonable for everyone to agree to in the natural context, where "in the natural context" includes the various conditions, limits on knowledge, and so on, that characterize that test. Any principle that passes the test is a requirement of reason; it is also a condition of human relations currently free of subjugation. Thus, I shall speak of principles as nonsubjugating and mean also that they are reasonable for all to agree to (that is, mutually reasonable), and vice versa. Let us then consider the principles that it would be mutually reasonable for people who share little or no social structure to agree to in the natural context.

The truth of the moral imperative of respect entails that the particular principles to which all will reasonably agree must provide each with the maximum possibility of realizing his sovereign interest compatible with a like possibility for all. It is important to see that this is not to be conceived of as if all selves, hovering above the world as disembodied loci of sovereign interests, were determining how to divide things up in a mutually reasonable way. Since sovereign interests are rooted in the first-person reality of each individual's being and since the reasons they provide are nonfungible, what is mutually reasonable is what is reasonable to every single person simultaneously when none can expect that anyone else will find it reasonable to be required to promote anyone's sovereign interest but his own. (If this sounds ungenerous, remember, first, that we are concerned here to determine what can be *required* of people and, second, that sovereign interests can include desires for the well-being of others. All that is ruled out here then is requiring people to act as if they are generously motivated when they are not.) Because of nonfungibility, the requirement of compatibility functions negatively, as we have seen, as an effective prohibition against using others merely as means to one's own sovereign interest.

Consequently, mutual reasonableness does not require subjecting everything in the world, including everyone's bodies, to what would be reasonable to everyone. In the first instance, it requires noninterference with others. Thus the first principle that would pass the natural test of justice is essentially that which Hobbes believed people in the state of nature would agree to: *"that a man be willing, when others are so too . . . , [to] be contented with so much liberty against other men as he would allow other men against himself"* (*L*, chap. 14). Let us call this the *principle of compatible liberty*. Since each wants the maximum amount of liberty to pursue his sovereign interest, this is a principle of maximum compatible liberty.

Note that the principle contains the qualification, "when others are so too." It would not be mutually reasonable for all people to agree to leave themselves defenseless against invasions of their liberty by others. Each individual's own sovereign interest will make it unreasonable for him to forswear the possibility of using coercion against people who violate the liberty it would be mutually reasonable for all to agree to. The principle therefore contains another principle on its underside—namely, that it is mutually reasonable for people to use coercion against people who take more liberty than is compatible with a like amount for others. Let us call this the *right of self-defense*.

The right of self-defense is a right to use force to protect oneself against interference with one's liberty, whether that interference is intentional or unintentional. It allows defensive or even preemptive coercion in either case. It is essentially a principle giving people the right to use what force is necessary to give effect to their liberty against those who pose a threat to it, whether the threat is intentional, accidental, or uncontrollable (such as might be posed by a homicidal maniac). It is not a principle of punishment, because nothing is said about desert or paying back the violator. On the other hand, there is some crossing of the normal classificatory boundaries. Sometimes self-defense is best effected by threatening force before one is attacked. The right of self-defense thus allows the threat (and consequently the use) of force as a deterrent to attacks, and this may make it seem like a principle allowing punishment. Nonetheless, since the force that may be used here is no more than is needed to protect one's liberty and since it makes no reference to the intentional nature of the threats against which it protects, it will serve clarity to think of such force—even when used in a deterrent fashion—as coming under the right of self-defense. Later, we shall see the special considerations that make punishment as such justified.

Strictly speaking, then, the first principle of natural justice is a double principle of the following sort: It is mutually reasonable for all to agree to be bound by the requirement to grant everyone maximum compatible non-interference *and* to agree to allow everyone the right to use force against violations of this requirement. Attention to this double principle shows the subtle way in which the principle of compatible liberty establishes an obligation not unlike that which is normally thought to arise between people who tacitly agree to mutually beneficial self-restraint. The double principle itself is not the object of any tacit agreement. Acceptance of it in the contracting situation is only a dramatic way of indicating that it is mutually reasonable. It is an obligation because it is a requirement of reason, not because in any sense we tacitly accept it.

Although the double principle itself is binding irrespective of how we choose or act, owed to everyone irrespective of how they choose or act, it is also the basis for an obligation owed to people because of how they choose to act. This is because the double principle calls for both mutual noninterference and coercion when that fails. To be sure, it accords priority to the former, since that is what best serves the sovereign interests of all. But when people fail to abide by the former, they create the conditions under which others have the right to use force against them. Consequently, when people do refrain from interference according to the principle, they create the conditions in which the principle itself calls on all to restrain themselves similarly by making it reasonable for them all to do so. Then each person owes noninterference to the others as the price of the peace in which they let him live, where *price* means that which makes the self-restraint of others reasonable. In short, people are required by reason to accord each other maximum compatible noninterference where this is requited, and when it is requited, people owe it to each other as the condition of the noninterference they get in return. I shall assume that people, seeing the requirement at the first level, are prepared to act on it and create the conditions for it on the second and thus that all are required to accord each maximum noninterference according to the principle of compatible liberty.

The principle of compatible liberty requires no action in the service of other people's sovereign interests because that would amount to requiring some to adopt the nonfungible sovereign interests of others as their own and would thus be equivalent to subjugation. The principle does not, of course, prohibit such altruistic acts from being voluntarily undertaken; it simply rules out forced service. One quasi exception to this is the *duty of easy rescue*. This is the duty to assist seriously endangered others when one could do so with little risk or loss to oneself. This is only a quasi exception because it is only a quasi requirement. Normally, a requirement overrides a person's sovereign interest. But the duty of easy rescue has built into it a proviso that assures that the requirement only applies if it is compatible with the sovereign interest of the rescuer. Since the duty only binds when there is no risk or loss, it is only a requirement in the weak sense that it overrides momentary whim or laziness. With the built-in proviso, everyone stands to gain and no one to lose, and thus it clearly serves everyone's sovereign interest to agree to be bound by the duty of easy rescue.

There is one sort of coercion that a person might use justifiably against another, even though it is not a defense against a violation of someone's liberty. This is paternalistic coercion aimed at stopping someone from doing what is contrary to his own sovereign interest. That people are not always accurate judges of their sovereign interests is part of the knowledge available to people in the natural context. A person might have a desire that he is unaware of, think he desires something that he does not, or wrongly estimate how important some desire he has is to him. Consequently, he may exercise his liberty in ways that are at odds with his own sovereign interest. Thus, if someone could show that he was urging a claim that, in fact, served people's real sovereign interests though they did not know it, this would show that his claim was reasonable and not a form of subjugation, though it might imply a temporary restriction of people's liberty.

Given the central importance in sovereign interests of being the judge of one's interests and the author of one's actions, showing that such a paternalistic restriction is not subjugation will require showing that it is necessary to prevent so great a sacrifice of the individual's sovereign interest as to outweigh these powerful concerns. Merely asserting this or believing it sincerely will not be enough. Proof is necessary. And, though difficult, such proof is not impossible—the smaller the requirement and the larger

161

the likelihood of people misjudging its efficacy (say, forcing slightly incon-venient but highly effective safety precautions), the more likely such proof could be provided. The general point is that, leaving aside the abuses to which it can be put, which are a legitimate but separate concern, there is nothing absurd about "being forced to be free," as people who ask to be hypnotized or to be tied to shipmasts to protect themselves against temptation testify.

In general, however, the surest way to avoid subjugation is by giving people the best information available and then letting them do what they judge they should. This is so, first of all, because the tendency to abuse coercive power, which is already present when it is used to protect liberty, is greatly magnified when it can be used to protect people's freedom against what they desire or judge that they should do. When coercion is used to protect liberty against interference, it has the immediate verification that comes from the protected person's recognition that her desires or judgments are being served. When coercion is used to protect people against what they want or judge, this verification is absent and must be replaced by the protector's theoretical inferences. The very same facts that make some people prone not to see their real sovereign interest clearly make other people prone to think they see it clearly, when they are in fact blinded by their own interests.

Moreover, as long as a person is not crazy, she should be able to be convinced that she is making some mistake about what she really desires, when she is presented with adequate information. And, to avoid both abuse and vicious circularity, proving that someone is crazy requires showing more than a tendency to make judgments that others disagree with. Because for each (sane) person the measure of what is reasonable is her sovereign interest, any claim that she has mistaken her desires must implicitly be the hypothesis that upon sufficient evidence she would see her mistake and recognize her true sovereign interest. If she would do this, then she would act voluntarily in light of the new understanding. Thus, the safest way to test any claim that someone has mistaken her sovereign interest is to present her with the relevant information and leave her the freedom to find out her mistake for herself.

That people want to live a life that serves their sovereign interest, of which they are the best though fallible judge, already argues against pater-nalistic interference. This is because the interferer's judgment is susceptible to all the errors of judgment about the sovereign interest of the one he would interfere with, and then some. But there is more. We have already seen that the sovereignty of people in the natural context is three-dimensional. It is

162

not just a flat list of desires, but a dynamic interest in being someone, in judging who that someone is, and in intentionally acting accordingly. Because the urgency of an individual's sovereign interest arises from his recognition of his mortality, satisfaction of an individual's sovereign interest must be such that the individual can recognize the worth to his life of that satisfaction. This means that people want a life that serves their sovereign interest as they judge it. Since human beings are active beings, they understand their sovereign interests primarily in terms of undertakings and accomplishments, rather than in terms of feelings and experiences. These facts also argue against paternalistic interference because, even where the interferer's judgment is correct, he runs the risk of trampling on the fact that people do not just want to live a certain life but to lead a life that seems worthy to them.

The upshot of these considerations is that, although the conditions under which substantial paternalistic coercion would be justified are extensive in theory, those conditions are in actual situations quite limited and easily identifiable. Where they are not easy to identify, the possibility of error and the palpable cost to the presumed beneficiaries argue for favoring liberty whenever there is reasonable doubt. In other words, in the real world in which people may be mistaken about their sovereign interests and others may be as well, the relation between liberty and the absence of subjugation is a practical kinship not a logical one. So understood, I shall take the principle of compatible liberty to include the narrow possibility of justifiable paternalism—namely, in cases in which people are palpably deranged or temporarily "not themselves" or in which interference is minor or temporary and the tendency to misjudgment very large (say, forcing minor safety precautions or delaying suicide attempts to allow second thoughts).

If we take harms, actual or threatened, to be the main ways in which people's liberty is violated, then the principle of compatible liberty finds expression in John Stuart Mill's famous "harm principle": "That principle is, that the sole end for which mankind are warranted, individually or collectively, in interfering with the liberty of action of any of their number, is self-protection. That the only purpose for which power can be rightfully exercised over any member of a civilized community, against his will, is to prevent harm to others. His own good, physical or moral, is not a sufficient warrant" (*OL*, 72–73). Note that Mill also allows paternalistic coercion when there is blatant evidence that a person is not acting in the service of his own sovereign interest: "If either a public officer or anyone else saw a person attempting to cross a bridge which had been ascertained to be unsafe, and there were no time to warn him of his danger, they might seize him and   163 turn him back without any real infringement on his liberty; for liberty consists in doing what one desires, and he does not desire to fall into the river" (*OL*, 151–52).

The principle of compatible liberty embodies a negative concept of freedom, in which the main right of people vis-à-vis their fellows (outside of the dire straits that invoke the duty of easy rescue) is to be let alone. Many people feel certain that morality requires more than this. Such beliefs could lead many to doubt the soundness of the test of morality from which the principle is derived. In defense of this negative freedom, I will say two things now, and more later. First, as I shall indicate in greater detail in the following section, the principle of compatible liberty does not entail the right of property beyond ownership of things for consumption. Thus, though the principle is a libertarian one, it should not be confused with a defense of the moral validity of laissez-faire capitalism. Second, the emphasis on negative freedom does correspond to many of our moral intuitions. For example, we seem to make an important distinction between actively harming people and simply refraining from helping them, even when the results are the same. To cite a famous example, we generally regard it as acceptable (even required) to refrain from using scarce medical resources to save one person when the same resources are the only way to save ten others. On the other hand, we would regard it as prohibited (even terrible) to intentionally kill one sick but surviving person in order to use his organs to save the life of ten others who would otherwise die. Some philosophers have attributed this to an intuitive priority given to the evil of doing positive injury, but it is exactly this intuition that needs to be explained. Others have tried to deal with it by means of complex theories of causation, which try to account for a common intuition by reference to esoteric metaphysics and thus make the intuition less rather than more plausible. The natural test accounts easily for the intuition. Killing the one to distribute his organs to others is clearly a case of subjugating one to the sovereign interests of others because it invades his body for their purposes. Refraining from helping does not and thus is not an act of subjugation.

The principle of compatible liberty amounts to the principle that Kant claims is the Universal Principle of Justice: "Every action is just that in itself or in its maxim is such that the freedom of the will of each can coexist together with the freedom of everyone in accordance with a universal law" (*MJ*, 35). If the argument that leads to this point is correct, it vindicates Kant's claim that this is a requirement of reason. It shows that the Sixth Commandment, "Thou shalt not kill" (Exod. 20:13), is also such a requirement, as are all the other rules against unprovoked violent aggression. These are true requirements of justice with which people may rightly be coerced to comply.

As a requirement of reason, the prohibition against killing is not a general prohibition on the taking of all life, nor even of all human life. It is a prohibition that applies only to those individuals who have a sovereign interest, those individuals whose lives have become their fates. The sovereign interest is rooted in first-person reality. It is not the kind of interest that a creature can have "constructively," say, before the interest is actually there to be served. It is not, for example, in someone's sovereign interest to get born—rather, a sovereign interest is an urgent caring about the life one has, and that exists only once one is aware that one has such a life. To have such caring awareness is to have a self—and an individual aiming to be a self is a person. Accordingly, the principle of compatible liberty prohibits killing those who are persons.

Reasons for protecting individuals' lives must be reasons for protecting those particular lives, not just reasons for promoting life in general. Reasons of the latter sort will lead us to promote some optimum number of living beings but give us no reason not to kill any particular ones as long as they could be replaced. Since dogmatic beliefs in the sanctity of life or of the divine soul cannot be the source of requirements binding on everyone (because they cannot be shown unreasonable to doubt), reasons for protecting particular lives must show that they protect against the sort of loss that it would be reasonable for all to want to be protected against. For a creature who is a person—that is, one aware that she has a particular life before her and who cares about that particular life—the loss of that life is a terrible and ultimate loss. Until a creature cares about her life this way, the loss of life is the loss of a future good. Because it is a loss that precludes the existence of the being for whom the lack of that future good will be a loss, it is a "constructive" loss, like the loss one would suffer in never having been conceived. The loss one "suffers" in never having been conceived is the same as the loss suffered by the infinite number of possible human beings who are not conceived every moment. That loss (like the "loss" you and I suffered when we were not born in the seventeenth century) is literally no one's loss (leaving aside the fact that protecting against this loss would require that we produce as many children as we physically can). Accordingly, while we shall see that human beings are required by reason to continue the human race, they are not required to protect every possible human being against the constructive loss of not becoming a being to whom the loss of life would make a difference.

Personhood is not a matter of definition, but of fact. Though there may

165

be transitional stages in between, a creature either is or is not an individual aiming to be some self, and thus does or does not regard the loss of its life as a terrible loss, and thus does or does not qualify for the prohibition against being killed that is a requirement of reason. It is notoriously difficult to say when this fact obtains. But recall that a person is a particular individual who cares ultimately about becoming some particular self over the course of its lifetime. It is the existence of this caring individual, not the occasional awareness of its existence, that determines when the continuation of life matters in the way that amounts to having a sovereign interest in staying alive. Personhood does not depend on the individual's continuous consciousness of her self, and thus an individual does not cease to be a person while she is asleep or in a temporary coma. These are cases in which the caring individual is, so to speak, temporarily relieved of duty, shut down for the night. What matters is that the individual caring about her self must have really appeared at some point and begun its vigil; it cannot have shut down permanently, such that its vigil is ended. It is between these two points in time that the prohibition against killing exists, and the creature in question can be said to have a natural right to life—or, more precisely, a right not to be killed.

I leave it to others to date these two points, but it is clear that they are not coterminous with the beginning and ending of what is called "life," nor with the beginning and ending of human life. This means that the prohibition does not apply to all living things, nor even to all living members of the species *Homo sapiens,* and it may apply to some higher nonhuman primates, and perhaps to the cetaceans as well. Leaving aside the nonhuman cases, it is clear that the person that is the subject of the sovereign interest has not yet appeared in human fetuses. Thus, they do not qualify for the prohibition against killing, nor do they have a moral right to life. Accordingly, there is no requirement of natural justice forbidding abortion. The reason is straightforward: The loss of the fetus's life is not and cannot be a loss of something that matters to that fetus. Since no individual caring about how that life is lived has yet appeared, there is no audience for which its particular ending is a great and irreparable loss. The fetus's death from its point of view (and thus to us when we try to identify with it) is indistinguishable from the loss it would have suffered had it never been conceived. (I am assuming that the abortion can be performed painlessly, which, since we can kill adults painlessly, certainly seems undeniable.) When all unprovable claims about the fetus's soul and so on are removed as not binding on rational beings, what remains is that the difference between murder and abortion is just the difference between the loss you would suffer now being confronted with your death and the loss you suffered by not having been born in the seventeenth century.

Many people think that the abortion problem can be dealt with by determining whether or not the fetus is a human being, on the principle that all human beings (all members of the human species) are entitled to a right to life. Call this "the species principle." We are only committed to this principle as far as we know what it means and, in particular, what is meant by *human being*. A person who endorses the species principle and who learns that some creatures whose status was previously uncertain actually qualify as "human beings" may rightly wonder whether she still believes in the principle given the new information about its range of application. She may decide that she no longer believes the species principle as such but believes instead that all human beings except these new additions have the right to life. Consequently, even if we prove that fetuses are human beings, we cannot appeal to the species principle to show that they have a right to life, because proving that fetuses are human beings alters the meaning of the species principle and thus calls the principle back into question.

In any event, membership in the human species cannot be a rational ground for a right to life unless there is something about humans that warrants protection of their lives. Some, who have recognized this, have argued that it is the possession of certain traits, such as rationality, ability to enter relationships, and the like, that qualify one for the right to life. These traits are sometimes gathered together under the title of "personhood," and then the question of whether the fetus is entitled to a right to life becomes that of whether it is a person. This strategy moves some distance in the direction of a satisfactory solution. But the advocates of this strategy tend to think of "personhood" as a kind of honorary title, bestowed on creatures because their traits make them valuable in some important way.[1] So understood, the strategy is bound to run into trouble. First, if the value of something is a reason for keeping it in existence, it is equally a reason for bringing similarly valuable things into existence and generally a reason for bringing as many as possible into existence, at least until this interferes with other things of comparable value. Reasons for treating one's diamonds with care are also reasons for mining for new diamonds. This strategy will almost surely lead us to prohibit contraception or even abstinence. Second, what is valuable is inherently replaceable with something of equal value. Thus, this strategy will not guarantee the protection of any particular individual's life as long as he can be replaced by another.

To arrive at a reasonable defense of the right to life, we need to identify

167

some trait of individuals that makes it uniquely important to protect the lives of individuals who are already alive, and that makes it uniquely important to protect the lives of particular living individuals though they could be replaced by similar others (similar even in being particular individuals). In my view, the only thing that can do this job is that an individual cares in an ultimate and nonfungible way about the continuation of his own life. Since such caring is a real fact that comes into existence at a real moment in time, the weight of it is only felt for individuals who actually care and thus who already exist. Furthermore, since the individual cares about his life in a way that rules out his accepting its replacement by someone else's life, concern for this caring is sufficient to account for the protection of individual lives against replacement. Thus, those who argue that the right to life is possessed by persons are correct, not because persons are somehow worthy of the right to life, but because a person is, as Kant says, a being "which is conscious of the numerical identity of itself at different times"[2]— and only to a being with such consciousness can the continuation of its life matter.

This caring about one's life is different from the desire to go on living or the instinct for self-preservation, which are built into all animals. Such a desire or instinct is essentially a behavioral tendency to avoid what threatens life, and we can hardly imagine that anything would have survived in evolution without such a tendency. But without the caring about life, these tendencies are blind, and stifling them painlessly simply ends a natural process without occasioning grief. Caring makes the difference precisely because it is not just a behavioral tendency but includes some conscious sense of the life ahead as a thing whose continuation matters. It is, I believe, because animals do not seem to care about their lives in this particular way, whereas they obviously care about pain, that we generally hold that it is worse to be cruel to an animal than to kill it painlessly—quite the reverse of what we generally believe regarding human beings. If it could be shown that some animals cared about the continuation of their lives in the way we do, I believe that the case against killing those animals would be made. Nor is this what some have called speciesism—that is, holding that animals must be like us to have a right to life. It is identifying a real condition of the mattering of loss of life that happens to characterize us but that would support a right to life in whatever species it turned up. The individual's caring about the continuation of his own life is what makes it a requirement of reason to protect individual lives, because it is that which makes the lives of individuals matter irreplaceably.

Some people oppose abortion because of the troubling thought that they would not now exist had they been aborted. But this is a confusion. A person

168

would also not now exist if his parents had had fruitful intercourse the day or week prior to the relations that produced him. A different person with a different genetic make-up would have resulted. Consequently, a person can be no more troubled about the possibility that he had been aborted than about the possibility that his parents had made love on a different night. These dangers are no different from those endured by every possible un-conceived human being. They only seem troubling when contemplated by a human being already in existence. The loss of life is only a loss to a creature who already exists, and abortion happens *before* such a creature who cares about its particular life exists, and thus is not such a loss.

Some people will be troubled that this argument implies that newborn infants also have no right to life, since the individual that cares about his self surely does not appear immediately after birth. But if newborns do not yet care about their continuation, then it is, in fact, not a terrible calamity to kill newborn infants in the way that it is a terrible calamity to kill adults. If our intuitions or natural tenderness for babies obscures this, then they, and not the argument, must be brought in line. Moreover, the implications of my argument should not be exaggerated. There may be good social reasons to discourage the killing of infants: They generally come quickly to be cared about as the particular irreplaceable ones they are, and there might be a dangerous weakening of regard for human life if we were to treat newborns as dispensable. Furthermore, I shall argue in the fourth section of this chapter that we have a general obligation to continue the life of the human species. These and other reasons may argue for the wisdom of protecting the lives of newborns. As a practical matter, this might most effectively be done by treating them as having legal rights to life, and thus treating killing them legally as murder. My argument does not deny any of this. I claim only that if we find it reasonable to prevent the killing of newborn infants, it cannot be because they have a natural moral right to life.

It is a further implication of my argument that the right to life not only begins some time after the beginning of human life but can end before life ends. When the individual caring about its particular fate shuts down for good—say, because of irreversible brain damage—the prohibition on killing shuts down as well because, again, there is no longer a being for whom the ending of this particular life will be a loss. To keep the irretrievably coma-tose alive is to disconnect our concern for life from what makes life matter to the living. To liken euthanasia of the permanently unconscious to murder honors a ghost of life and dishonors the lives of the real victims of murder.

In all the cases I have just discussed—abortion, infanticide, and eu-thanasia—the ending of life is independent of the will of the individual   169 involved. Nothing is said about euthanasia upon request, nor about the right of individuals to commit suicide. The prohibition on killing does not apply to them, since it stems strictly from the principle of compatible liberty, which is a principle of noninterference. Subject to the possibility of paternalistic intervention, which is larger here than elsewhere because the possibility of irrational judgments with tragic and irrevocable results is greatest, sane individuals have the right to end their lives when they wish.

In sum, it is reasonable for people in the natural context to agree to a requirement that protects for each the maximum amount of liberty compatible with a like liberty for everyone else. Lacking knowledge of their particular desires or the particular ways in which they will be affected by this principle, they cannot have any reason to sacrifice protection of their liberty in order to have the freedom to restrict that of others. Their general interest in promoting their sovereign interest, whatever its contents, is best protected by the principle of compatible liberty. This principle includes the right of self-defense, the quasi requirement of the duty of easy rescue, and allows for paternalistic coercion on very limited grounds. It does not prohibit abortion, infanticide, nonvoluntary euthanasia of the permanently unconscious, or freely chosen suicide.

The Principle of Natural Ownership

The principle of compatible liberty amounts at least to a prohibition against interference with the bodies of others who have not attacked one's own body. Indeed, liberty is, in the first instance, freedom from interference with one's body. Says Hobbes, "when the words *free* and *liberty* are applied to anything but *bodies*, they are abused, for that which is not subject to motion is not subject to impediment" (*L*, chap. 21). The truth in this rather extreme claim is that there can be no freedom, no unsubjugated pursuit of one's sovereign interest, unless there is freedom from interference with one's body, since it is with the body that one moves in the world toward realization of one's interests. Moreover, the body is not just a tool available to the self for the realization of its purposes. The body is that biological individual which by investing itself in the becoming of a biographical self comes to have a sovereign interest. One's sovereign interest is the interest of this enduring body (of which my present body is a phase). A person's consciousness is the consciousness of this body, his purposes are the purposes of this body, and his sovereign interest is the plans he has for what this body will be, do, and experience in its time. "It is, therefore, obvious," as Kant says, "that the body constitutes part of ourselves" (*LE*, 148). And, of course, it is by constraining the body that people are most commonly and easily

170

subjugated. Though an individual may under extreme circumstances choose to amputate a part of his body, holding fast to most people's smallest finger is usually enough to constrain them.

Insofar as the right to ownership is an entitlement to use what one owns without interference by others (as long as one does not interfere with the property of another), the principle of compatible liberty entails that people have rights of ownership over (or property rights in) their bodies. Such ownership or property is private in that the owner is a single person.

Private ownership of the body is the nerve of liberalism. It accounts for the characteristic antipaternalism of liberalism (rejection of laws against using drugs or alcohol, or of laws against any use to which consenting adults may wish to put their bodies), as well as its support for laws against physical assault. It accounts for the opposition of liberalism to invasions of individuals' bodies (forced physical examinations or forced testimony), even where necessary for the apprehension of violent criminals. I think it also accounts for the liberal preference for confinement over corporal punishment, since the former can, in principle, be carried out without laying hands on the body.[3] It accounts for the value given privacy in liberal societies, which cannot adequately be accounted for on utilitarian grounds, since it is a right not to have certain intimate areas of one's life and body observed even unobtrusively and even when there could be no danger to reputation or well-being. Privacy protects against such danger, but it is also a ritual by which people show that they recognize one another as owners of their bodies.[4] If the argument to this point is correct, then the principle of compatible liberty and its correlate, private ownership of the body, are requirements of reason. Their violation amounts to the subjugation of some people by others.

Marxists, of course, will not be surprised to learn that liberalism is the application of the right of private property to the body. They will rush to add that it is just this right that enables the worker to sell himself into wage slavery to the owner of means of production (factories, machines, land). I think this claim contains an important truth, the implications of which must be carefully considered. For the present, however, I am claiming nothing about private ownership of things like means of production. This aside, nothing prevents Marxists from believing in something like private ownership of the body—indeed, it is arguably implicit in their claim that the worker's labor is expropriated by the capitalist. Where Marxists and defenders of capitalism differ is on whether and how far this ownership should be extended to things—particularly to means of production—outside the body. Locke thus plays a critical historical role in the defense of capitalism. He starts from the notion of private ownership of the body and, by a series of steps, extends it to such external things as means of production. All this

171

takes place in the state of nature, prior to the agreement to contract into civil society, so that, for Locke, the right to own things like the means of production is the sort of right that civil societies are created to protect not restrict. Because Locke takes virtually unlimited private property in things (meaning "things outside the body") to be a right under natural justice, directly opposite to the view that I shall defend, it will be instructive to see how far we can follow Locke before we must part company with him.

Defenders of private property, even those who draw their inspiration from Locke, commonly argue that the right to own property is a necessary means to the protection or promotion of liberty. For Locke, however, the relationship between these concepts is curiously reversed: Property is the more general notion, and it includes liberty as one of its instances. People, writes Locke, leave the state of nature "to unite for the mutual preservation of their lives, liberties and estates, which I call by the general name— property" (*ECG*, 180). To follow Locke's argument, it will help to keep in mind that *property* has both a prescriptive and a descriptive meaning, as do its kin, *own* and *belong*. The prescriptive meaning amounts to the claim that someone is entitled to uninterfered-with use, enjoyment, or disposal of something. The descriptive meaning points to the part-whole relationship. Thus, we say that a tree's branches *belong* to it rather than to some other tree, that some animals kill their prey with their *own* claws, and that sweetness is a *property* of oranges. In an odd way, the prescriptive meaning both is and is not parasitic on the descriptive. When we take some thing as a person's property, we think of it as entitled to treatment as if it were part of him, as the parts of his body are. This suggests the primacy of the descriptive sense. Yet ultimately, unless we take the person as entitled to uninterfered-with use, enjoyment, or disposal of himself, treating something as if it were a part of him will make no difference. This returns us to the primacy of the prescriptive sense. It also explains how liberty is part of property.

There are actually three senses of *property* here, which we should try to keep distinct. First, there is recognition of some things as factually parts of a person, such as the parts of his body. These belong to him (they are his properties) in the descriptive sense. Second, because of some moral belief about the person, we take it that things which are part of him are entitled to special treatment. These are his property in the prescriptive sense, where the prescriptive ownership extends only as far as what is descriptively part of him. Third, since the first two senses are distinct, it becomes possible to ascribe property in the prescriptive sense to things that are not, in fact, parts of the person, such as his land, clothes, or machines. This is his property in a prescriptive sense that extends beyond what belongs to him in a descriptive sense. Because of the link between the first two senses, it is understandable that property in this third sense is treated *as if* it were a part of the person in the standard descriptive sense. The key to all theories of the natural right to property lies in how they pass from the second to the third sense.

Insofar as the prescriptive sense of property means an entitlement to use without interference (so long as one does not thereby interfere with the property of another), then the principle of compatible liberty does prescribe an arrangement in which people are thought of as owning prescriptively what is their own descriptively—that is, their bodies. We can agree with Locke when he says that "every man has a 'property' in his own 'person.' This nobody has any right to but himself" (*ECG*, sec. 27). Since the body is not just a collection of molecules, but a quantity of energy expendable as effort, Locke is right in applying the same to a person's labor. "The 'labour' of his body and the 'work' of his hands, we may say, are properly his" (*ECG*, sec. 27). If the body is owned, then its efforts are as well. Locke then extends this right of prescriptive ownership gradually, moving beyond the frontiers of descriptive ownership:

> The fruit or venison which nourishes the wild Indian, who knows no enclosure, and is still a tenant in common, must be his, and so his— i.e., a part of him, that another can no longer have any right to it before it can do him any good for the support of his life. (*ECG*, sec. 26)

> He that is nourished by the acorns he picked up under an oak . . . has certainly appropriated them to himself. Nobody can deny but that the nourishment is his. I ask, then, when did they begin to be his? when he digested? or when he ate? or when he boiled? or when he brought them home? or when he picked them up? And it is plain, that if the first gathering made them not his, nothing else could. (*ECG*, sec. 28)

On this basis, Locke claims that when a person removes something out of its natural (unowned) state, "he hath mixed his labour with it, and joined it to something that is his own, and thereby makes it his property . . . , *at least where there is enough, and as good left in common for others*" (*ECG*, sec. 27; emphasis mine).

The emphasized portion of the last statement we can, following Robert Nozick, call "the Lockean proviso" (*ASU*, 175–82). Locke's argument seems to be that if the venison or acorns were eventually to be our Indian's by nourishing him, then they must have always been his from the moment the labor of getting his nourishment began. Let us grant this provisionally, and ask why it is qualified by the Lockean proviso. This question is crucial, 173 since the proviso is not attached to the ownership that people have of their bodies—they do not own their bodies subject to there being enough and as good (organs, looks, talents) left in common for others. Thus, the legitimacy of the extension of ownership from the second to the third senses—that is, from the body to the things of the world—hinges on the answer to this question. Locke's answer, as far as he gives one, occurs a few pages later. Explaining how the proviso works to justify an enclosure of land, he writes, "For he that leaves as much as another can make use of does as good as take nothing at all. Nobody could think himself injured by the drinking of another man, though he took a good draught, who had a whole river of the same water left him to quench his thirst" (*ECG*, sec. 33).

The Lockean proviso is necessary, then, because when it is satisfied no other person can plausibly complain of being injured by an appropriation. This need not be applied to individuals' ownership of their bodies, since that ownership injures no one—it is, indeed, the very standard against which injury is measured. This fact gives natural primacy to the prescriptive ownership by people of that which belongs to them descriptively. Once prescriptive ownership is extended beyond this into the things in the world, however, the threat of injury to others appears. This is a threat to the ones deprived by ownership. Since each person has a body which is the home of her sovereign interest, no one is deprived by everyone having property rights in her body. But, of anything else in the world, this is not so, unless of course there is enough and as good left for others. In short, the Lockean proviso is Locke's recognition that—to be accorded the status of a moral right—private ownership of things must be noninjurious to nonowners, and this is not obviously the case in the way that it is with ownership of the body, because ownership of things in the world has potential threatening effects on nonowners that ownership by people of their bodies does not.

Recognition that property ownership must be noninjurious to nonowners derives from the fact that such ownership is a system of behavior in which both owners and nonowners play roles, and the latter must act in ways that seem to run contrary to their sovereign interests. They must refrain from taking and using the things that are held to be owned by others. To justify property in things beyond the body is to show that such a system of behavior is reasonable to everyone. Since it is obviously reasonable to owners, showing that it is reasonable to everyone requires showing that nonowners are at least not injured by it, not made worse off than they would be if they remained only with the system characterized by ownership of their bodies.

A system of behavior establishing ownership of things can injure a nonowner in two ways. First, she may be required to refrain from using something that she needs, or without which some interest of hers will suffer,

174

because it is owned by another. Second, and by virtue of the first, the nonowner may be required to serve the owner in order to get what she needs. That is, a system of private ownership asks people to act in ways that may either directly cause them to suffer deprivation or compel them to labor for others as the price of avoiding that deprivation. Ownership of the body does not pose a comparable danger, since everyone owns a body and the differences between what people own are small. Even if people do face a small risk of needing some part of someone else's body (a kidney, say), or even of having to work for the other (with healthy kidneys) to get it, this risk could only be insured against by establishing a system in which everyone had claims on everyone's body and thus a system of much more substantial risks to everyone.

The appeal of the Lockean proviso is that, when it obtains, ownership of things is no more threatening to others than ownership of bodies. As long as there is enough and as good left for others, no one is injured by another's appropriation, anymore than she is injured by that person's ownership of her own body. When the Lockean proviso can be satisfied, it is reasonable in the natural context to extend the principle of ownership of the body to include those things that people take out of the natural world for the promotion of their sovereign interests.

Where there is not sufficient abundance for the proviso to hold, then it would be reasonable for all to agree that each has a right to take from nature what he needs for his survival. Either there will be enough for all to survive, in which case this right will give them ownership of what they need for survival; or there will not be enough, in which case each will have the right to what he needs in the Hobbesian sense that no moral requirement blocking this will be reasonable for him to comply with. It is thus a requirement of reason that everyone has the right to ownership of his body, his labor, and what he takes from nature for the promotion of his sovereign interest, either without limit when there is abundance enough for all to have whatever they want and can work on, or enough for his survival when conditions of scarcity obtain. I call this the *principle of natural ownership.* I contend that it is the only right of property provided as a matter of natural justice. Any greater right must be defended as an article of social justice.

Note that, by incorporating Locke's proviso, the principle of natural ownership addresses the two threats posed by ownership of things outside the body. It meets the threat of direct deprivation by assuring that there will be enough and as good for everyone else either without limit or enough for survival when no more is possible. It meets the threat that some will be forced to serve others, since everyone will have the alternative of satisfying his needs directly either without limit or as far as his needs can be satisfied

175

at all. Consequently, no nonowner could be said to be forced to labor for owners.

Because much of the world was still wilderness in Locke's time, he thought the proviso still could be satisfied (*ECG*, sec. 36). Actually, however, the proviso is a very strict requirement no longer applicable in eras like ours, in which virtually everything usable and accessible in nature is owned. It should be no surprise, then, that the principle of natural ownership will not justify the property rights that characterize modern capitalist societies. Modern capitalist societies are characterized by ongoing rights of property such that any new person who comes on the scene is confronted with the fact that everything is already owned. Let us call this fact, "exclusive ownership," and note that exclusive ownership precludes the Lockean proviso.

To see the implications of exclusive ownership, consider that the Lockean proviso succeeds in disarming the threats of ownership essentially by making it the case that no one's property is at the expense of another's. Thus, no one has means at his disposal to deprive others of what they need or to compel them to work for him—or, at least, no one has any more of such means than anyone else. Once the Lockean proviso cannot be met because everything usable and accessible is already owned exclusively, this protection is no longer guaranteed by a system of ownership of things beyond what people need to survive. In such a system, nonowners may indeed find themselves subject to owners' power to withhold from them things they need and consequently subject to power forcing them to serve the owner's interests. It was Rousseau who, more clearly than any of the other contractarians, saw the implications of exclusive ownership: "When inheritances so increased in number and extent as to occupy the whole of the land, and to border on one another, one man could aggrandize himself only at the expense of another; at the same time the supernumeraries, who had been too weak or too indolent to make such acquisitions, and had grown poor . . . , were obliged to receive their subsistence, or steal it, from the rich; and this soon bred, according to their different characters, dominion and slavery, or violence and rapine" (*DOI*, 87). Any system of exclusively owned property is, then, a system of differential power that some individuals have to compel others to labor for them, implemented by differential access to the scarce pool of things needed by all.

What this means is that the step from a world in which things are not exclusively owned to one in which they are crosses a crucial moral boundary. Recall that the principle of natural ownership is essentially an implication of the principle of compatible liberty. The latter is a principle of noninterference that forbids forcing people to act in the service of others. But once we pass to exclusive property systems beyond the applicability of the Lockean proviso, we reach systems that are effectively systems of forced labor. The force is not necessarily of the violent sort that is used in forced labor camps or to extract work from slaves. *Force* here means only the leverage to compel the actions of others that one gets by having control of things those others need when all such things are exclusively owned, so that the only way that nonowners can get them is by doing the bidding of owners. In such systems, force of the violent sort will normally be used to protect people in the possession of what they own, and if it is used effectively to this end that is all the violent force that is needed. The leverage of ownership will do the rest.

Recognition that exclusive property systems are systems of forced labor is not meant to condemn them as unjust or, equivalently, as unacceptable to people in the natural context. The claim is descriptive and is meant to point out what is accepted when exclusive property systems are accepted, and thus what burden must be borne by reasons for accepting them. It implies that only reasons capable of making forced labor acceptable can make exclusive property systems acceptable—it does not imply that such reasons cannot be found. Indeed, I shall defend a set of such reasons in chapter 5. My point here is only to mark the crucial boundary that is reached when we consider systems of exclusive property, noting that they require a separate test of mutual reasonableness. Formulation of that test is the business of social justice.

Locke recognized that the sort of property rights that exist in modern societies—countenancing inequality, accumulation over generations by inheritance, and exclusivity—require a separate moral justification beyond the claim that property rights in things derive from mixing one's labor with them. He claimed to find this further justification in people's consent—namely, their tacit consent to the existence of money. Locke had maintained that the right to property in the state of nature is a right to use things before they spoil, since nature is given to man for his enjoyment by God. This is a separate limit on accumulation of property, operating independently of the proviso, at least until money was invented. Since money does not spoil, it makes possible the accumulation of things beyond need. Because people differ in skill and industry, some can accumulate much more than when they were limited to what could be used before spoilage. As people are not limited by what they can use, they can also pass on their property to their heirs, making for a system in which everything is already owned and in unequal amounts. Gold being of little use, Locke took money to have value   177 only by convention, and he took this to imply popular consent. Thus, for Locke, the conventional value of money is evidence that people "have agreed to a disproportionate and unequal possession of the earth" (*ECG*, sec. 50).

Locke takes the "consent" to money to predate the contract that establishes civil society, making the right to unequal and large property holdings a right in the state of nature that people unite into civil societies to protect.[5] Needless to say, this amounts to a right to such property ownership even though everything is owned exclusively, and thus even though nonowners will be forced to work for owners. Consequently, the consent to this right is crucial. Without it, the system would essentially implement a form of slavery, contrary to the natural freedom and sovereignty of human beings in the state of nature, which for Locke dictates that they be free from dominion of any will except where they have consented (*ECG*, sec. 22).

Locke's argument from the conventional value of money to the consent to it, and from there to what it makes possible, is not persuasive. First, that things have value by convention no more implies that people have consented to their having value than that words have meaning by convention implies that people have consented to that. Real consent (the sort necessary to rebut a charge of slavery) must mean that one has had a choice between alternatives somewhere along the line, which does not seem the case for either the value of coins or the meaning of words; tacit consent can only be argued for by showing that it would be reasonable for all to agree to the conventional valuation, not simply by showing that it exists. Second, even if conventional valuation of money (or conventional meanings of words) did imply consent, it would not imply that people had consented to all that endowing things with conventional value (or meaning) makes possible, such as theft (or lying).

With Locke's argument rejected, we can go no further in considering the justice of property rights in situations in which in the Lockean proviso is no longer applicable. This is a task for chapter 5. For the present then, we can conclude that the principle of natural ownership—covering the individual's body, her labor, what she appropriates from nature that is necessary to her survival, and whatever more she appropriates when there is enough and as good for others—is a requirement of reason, and thus of justice. The principle draws out the implications of the principle of compatible liberty and extends it only to such property in things as poses no threat of subjugation to others. The principle serves everyone's sovereign interest and, in the absence of knowledge of the specifics of people's sovereign interests, can be reckoned no threat to anyone in the natural context. Accordingly, it would be reasonable for everyone in the natural context to agree to be bound by it. Thus the Eighth Commandment, "Thou shalt not steal" (Exod. 20:15), applied to the objects of natural ownership, is also a requirement of reason, as well as all the rules prohibiting the taking from people of what is theirs against their will by stealth or fraud. And it shows the wisdom of the prohibition in the Tenth Commandment against coveting the possessions of one's neighbors (Exod. 20:17). Resistance to coveting is the analogue with regard to things owned of the respect due their owners.

The Principle of Trustworthiness

Before it is a moral norm, truthfulness is a functional norm of speech, as accuracy is of clocks and sharpness of knives. That speakers are telling the truth is what must be assumed if speech is to work at all, even if it is to work for liars. Communication aims to transmit beliefs from one mind to another on the assumption that they are truly believed. This is what makes words messages and more than just clues. Clues have meanings, but messages communicate beliefs.

Suppose I find an empty pillbox and take it as a clue that my friend has been ill. To do so, I need make no assumption about what my friend believed he was doing in leaving it lying around or even that he realized he was doing this at all. Clues generate beliefs irrespective of what the clue leaver believes he is doing when he leaves the clue and, thus, to the sorrow of countless fictional villains, independently of whether he knows he is leaving a clue at all. But consider what happens if I find the pillbox on my desk leaning against my friend's picture or against a name on a bookjacket that is the same as his name. Here I may have been left a message, but I can only understand it as a message by assuming that what I see has been done not only intentionally but with the specific intention that I see that it was done intentionally to communicate with me. When, instead of inferring from the pillbox that my friend is ill, I infer from it his intention to make me see that it was his intention (in using this pillbox or any other physical sign) to get me to believe that he is ill, then it is a message.

Clues give rise to beliefs willy-nilly, as dark clouds spark the belief that it will rain. But messages give rise to beliefs only on the assumption that they were intended to do so. In this way, messages establish the connection between the beliefs in one person's head and those in another's that is called communication. But a message can only generate the intended beliefs in the receiver if the receiver assumes that the sender expects him to believe that the sender is being truthful—that is, that the sender believes the beliefs he means to generate in the receiver. Moreover, the message itself is no more than a string of physical signs. Consequently, it must be decoded; the process by which it is decoded is one in which the recipient infers what beliefs the sender must have (and want to transmit) as the best explanation   179 of why he would emit this particular string of physical signs. Communication, in short, presupposes trust in the truthfulness of speakers.[6]

To speak is to assert that one believes something is true and to invite one's listener to accept the belief. This is why philosophers tie themselves in knots over propositions like "Everything I say is false." One cannot say such a thing and mean it without asserting its truth, and asserting its truth is denying its truth. (One can, of course, say it without meaning it, as I just did.) Truthfulness is a functional norm of speech, because communication only works insofar as speakers invite belief in the truth of what they say and hearers are susceptible to the belief-inducing quality of speech.

This is not denied by the fact that some speech is untruthful, either in the form of lies or stories. Lies can only work because speakers implicitly assert that they are speaking the truth and hearers are prone to believe that they are. One cannot lie by admitting that one is lying—unless of course one has reason to think that one's hearer will not believe that. Rather than lying showing that speech does not presuppose the norm of truthfulness, lying is parasitic on that presupposition and could not exist without it. If people did not normally expect their fellows to speak the truth, no one could lie.

Likewise, story telling works not by violating the expectation that speech will be believed but by using that expectation playfully. Story telling (or acting, for that matter) works because words even when known to be false can in the safety of that knowledge produce a kind of imaginary world of "as if" beliefs, a world of make-believe, into which the hearer can enter purely for the fun of it. (George Burns says: "The secret of being a good actor is honesty. If you can fake it, you've got it made.") The lie intends to get the hearer to believe something false without knowing that it is false, and thus upon which he may act. The story intends to get the hearer to give his imagination over to the belief-inducing power of speech knowing that the beliefs to be induced are false, to be enjoyed as such and not acted on as if true. The liar uses the belief-inducing power of speech to deceive, the actor or storyteller to entertain or edify.

That truthfulness is the implicit functional norm of speech has led Jürgen Habermas to think that a moral theory can be derived from the structure of communication itself. This seems possible because, since truth is what should be freely believed, communication aims at the uncoerced consent of its hearers to its content. Communication seems thus to commit us to what everyone could consent to freely, a kind of linguistic invocation of the social contract, as Habermas himself acknowledges. Habermas's argument is the European cousin of Gewirth's and subject to similar criticisms. As universalizability is a requirement of logic and can never get outside logic into the world that makes morality important, so uncoerced consent is a requirement of communication that can never get outside it. Thus, Habermas cannot explain why we are required to act in ways that meet communication's implicit commitment to uncoerced consent. That we are required to act subject to the requirements of communication cannot be proven from an analysis of those requirements. Just as Gewirth has found in universalizability a logical requirement that mimics morality's concern for others, so Habermas has found in communication a commitment that mimics morality's contractual nature.[7]

The requirements of morality are those of living together, not of speaking about living together. The point of truthfulness in communication is different from its point in human relations, and thus we will likely err if we blur the two. In the simplest terms, truthfulness (or the implicit promise to be truthful) is always and equally a condition of communication because it is always and equally a condition of understanding. Thus, for the purposes of communication, untruthfulness (intentional and with the aim of deceiving) is always equally wrong, a falling short of the norm that makes understanding possible. But in the context of human relations, lies run the full gamut from treachery to courtesy, from deceptions that are as harmful and culpable as acts of violence (framing an innocent person) to those that are harmless and unblameworthy (setting the scene for a surprise party) to those that are beneficial and praiseworthy (shielding a child from knowledge that he is not mature enough to assimilate without psychological damage).

This is what makes Kant's categorical prohibition against all lying under all circumstances implausible and makes Kant subject to the charge of irrationality on the grounds that his argument implies that one is wrong to lie even to would-be evildoers in order to prevent their doing great evil to innocent persons. Kant's prohibition follows from his theory that people are required to act only according to principles that they could will to be universal laws without contradiction. To will that lying becomes a universal law is impossible, because if everyone lied then no one would be believed, and then no one could lie. Ergo lying is absolutely prohibited, without distinction of context or content. But Kant has confused the grounds for truthfulness as a norm of communication (which concern what makes lying possible) with the grounds for truthfulness as a norm of human relations (which concern what makes lying harmful).

What makes lying harmful is that people's words are depended on by others when they determine how to act in pursuit of the things that they care about. This dependence locates the moral value not in the abstract correspondence between what the speaker says and what he believes, but in the web of human interdependence of which words are the threads. What

181

matters morally with respect to communication is the way in which people depend on the beliefs it transmits to achieve what matters to them. In this respect, what we owe one another is not truthfulness per se, but trustworthiness, the quality of being such that others can depend on one's messages in their pursuit of what matters to them. I call this the *principle of trustworthiness*. It would be mutually reasonable for all in the natural context to agree to be bound by this principle precisely because each person's pursuit of his sovereign interest depends on having accurate beliefs, and each is largely dependent on the others for those beliefs. Lacking knowledge of the specifics of their sovereign interests or of how they, in particular, will be affected by the principle, their interest in reliable beliefs far outweighs any interest they might have in being free to deceive. Thus the principle of trustworthiness is a requirement of reason and of natural justice.

From this principle a general obligation to be truthful follows because it is the surest way to be trustworthy, inasmuch as the best way to serve the sovereign interests of others is to provide them, to the best of one's ability, with true beliefs. And that means, at least, to provide them with beliefs that one believes. There is a general obligation to tell the truth because hearers may come to rely on virtually anything anyone says. At the same time, the principle of trustworthiness does not blur the distinction between seriously evil and innocuous lies.

Seriously evil lies are those on which people depend in fateful ways. Thus, false promises (lies about one's future action used to get others to act as they might not have desired) and broken promises (which make into lies retroactively one's previously sincere statements uttered to get people to act as they might not have desired), particularly when it is understood that the promisee will do some important action on the basis of faith in the promise, are seriously evil lies.[8] Likewise, framing another or bearing false witness are particularly grievous lies precisely because they will form the basis for fateful action against their victims. In this regard, it is interesting that the Ten Commandments include no blanket prohibition on lying. The relevant commandments, the Seventh and Ninth, forbid adultery and the bearing of false witness (Exod. 20:14 and 20:16). I take adultery to be neither a matter of sex nor of nonconformity with the rules of marriage, but of breaking a promise upon which people open themselves to the vulnerability of wholehearted loving. So understood, these commandments are requirements of reason.

Lies can be innocuous, such as those that make up a great part of politeness. Perhaps a world in which people would say and could take hearing what others truly thought of their clothes or dinner parties would be better

than the one we have, but it is not obvious that it would be terribly better in the way that a world in which people never betrayed, framed, or defrauded others would be. Furthermore, such lies as those told to keep an evildoer from succeeding in violating the sovereign interests of innocent others are morally required by the same concern for the sovereign interests of others that makes trustworthiness required in the first place.

That trustworthiness is grounded in concern for people's sovereign interests also explains why we generally hold that promising places promisers under a prima facie obligation (one that may be overridden by sufficiently weighty considerations) rather than an absolute one (which cannot be overridden at all). If, for example, I have promised you to meet you tomorrow for lunch and I fail to show up because instead I rushed into a burning building to save someone's life, I am not regarded in the same light as if I had simply decided at the last minute to stay in bed. It is not only that I am forgiven my promise breaking. My promise never required me to pass up saving someone's life. I have acted as promised as far as I morally could—and thus have not broken my promise. It is as if when I made my promise there was an unspoken proviso that permitted nonperformance if necessary to do things like saving people's lives. Promises do include such provisos, because it is not just in the abstract correspondence between promise and performance that their value lies, but in the way other people whose sovereign interests matter imperatively to them depend on them. But to act as if the mattering to people of their sovereign interests is important, one must recognize its importance generally or lose sight of what makes promises important in the first place. Accordingly, promises include, as an implication of their own importance, recognition that there are things important enough to override them.

To refrain from saving a life because I had promised to be at lunch would be to value promises themselves more than the people to whom they matter, much as the German generals did who, faced with the impending destruction of their land, refused nonetheless to join the plot to assassinate Hitler because they had given oaths of allegiance to him. Likewise, to tell the truth no matter what the consequences is to value the abstract correspondence between word and belief over the people who trust our words. This in no way implies that we are freed from the obligation to tell the truth anytime speaking truthfully will cause the hearer pain. There is a general and powerful obligation to be truthful, not easily overridden. Human beings have interests other than the avoidance of pain. Much as speaking promises truth, listening begs for it.

To identify with one's hearer is to participate imaginatively in his desire for the truth. This is why it is hard to lie looking straight in someone's eyes. But the hearer's desire for truth is not an undifferentiated impulse; it is calibrated along the hierarchical structure of his whole system of desires. In cases in which the truth makes the difference between being the self that one aims to be and falsely thinking that one is, the demand for truth is at its most insistent. The sovereign interest in being a certain self cannot be satisfied with less than accurate knowledge of those human relations that are central to being that self, accurate knowledge of the beliefs and feelings of those with whom one makes one's way in the world, and accurate knowledge of the judgments that those whose judgments count make about the quality of one's accomplishments. Lies in areas like these merely to avoid pain subvert an individual's most important interests. Other lies are bad in proportion to the centrality of the interests they undermine; since one's judgments about this regarding one's listener are subject to error from many sources, such lies are inherently risky, even reckless, and almost never worth the risk.

Accordingly, there are some things that must be spoken truthfully no matter how painful, and most things ought to be spoken truthfully. Nothing but avoidance of a moral calamity can justify lying to someone who explicitly communicates his desire or need to be told the truth. Likewise, nothing but avoidance of moral calamity can justify lying to those to whom one has explicitly promised the truth, and, thus, lying by those who have explicitly sworn to tell the truth. If creating special expectations of truthfulness did not increase one's obligation to tell the truth, oaths would be superfluous (as they must be on Kant's view). Even where a request for truthfulness or an oath are not present, there is a normal expectation of truthfulness which, combined with the possibility that people will act on one's words, creates a strong general obligation to tell the truth. Nonetheless, some truth telling is self-indulgent, and some is misanthropic. There is a time to speak, and a time to keep silence.

The Principle of Intergenerational Solicitude

The principle of compatible liberty rules out forced service. As such, it holds generally that beyond noninterference people owe one another only what they agree to voluntarily. But like any other principle, this holds only as far as is possible and must be altered as reason requires in the light of what is possible. The natural condition of human beings dictates that one exchange of services is necessary and must get started before voluntary agreement can occur. Unless it gets started no voluntary agreement can occur. This is the donation of service from existing generations to newly born generations and the return of service from adult generations to the elderly. Its nature is determined by the asymmetrical nature of biological time. Each newly emerging generation gets the benefits of the efforts of the previous ones before it can repay them, and before it can be asked to agree to repay them—indeed, as a necessary condition of reaching the point at which it could repay or agree to anything. Moreover, each aging generation comes to need the aid of the younger ones when it no longer has much to hold out in return. The continuation of the species is an investment without a guaranteed return by the parent generation, which will be repaid only if their children come to regard themselves as indebted for benefits they did not ask for or agree to pay for.

Since everyone can expect to be in both positions, it is reasonable for all to provide for everyone in both positions. Thus, it is reasonable to treat the relations between the generations as a kind of rolling debt, in which each older generation owes the younger nurturing and passing down of the accumulated fruits of civilization, and each younger generation owes repayment in the form of support for their elders when their powers decline. In slightly different terms, since it serves everyone's sovereign interest both to be well brought up as a child and to be well supported as an old person, and since the young can only be brought up by their elders and the elders only supported by their juniors (even if this is done wholly by impersonal bureaucracies), serving everyone's sovereign interest will effectively require imposing an obligation on the older generation to raise and provide for the younger, and on the younger, in its turn, to support and provide for the older. Since people in the natural context do not know the relations in which they stand (including whether they are young children or aging parents), it will be reasonable for all to accept this as a requirement on all.

Moreover, the same lack of knowledge of the relations in which they stand excludes from the natural context knowledge of which historical generation one is in. Since it is in the interest of existing people that they were born, it will be in everyone's interest that some number of people continue getting born. Although this will neither obligate all people to have children nor prohibit abortion (it could if the species were in danger of dying out), it will entail a prohibition against stopping the procreation of the human race entirely, reducing it to so small a number that it would be in danger of dying out, destroying the world, or rendering it uninhabitable. In fact, since each existing person comes into a world shaped by the generations before it, it is in everyone's interest that each generation both leave the world at least as good as they found it and, where possible, continue the intergenerational accumulation of accomplishments that distinguish human groups from other animals.

These obligations are summed up as the *principle of intergenerational solicitude*. They are general in nature, but not so general as to leave us   185 without guidance. They provide us with an obligation to continue the human species, though not with a specific obligation on anyone to have children as long as there are enough being born—this is the general obligation to promote human life that I mentioned earlier in this chapter, at the close of the first section. They provide us with an obligation to treat the world with care and to continue the forward march of civilization, but they do not assign particular jobs to specific individuals. They provide each older generation with a duty to provide for, nurture, and educate the young, and each younger generation with a duty to provide for, support, and protect the old, but they do not require that this be carried out only or even mainly within natural families.

The principle of intergenerational solicitude requires all adults to look out for and provide for all children and all grown children to look out for and provide for all older people. But since parents are naturally inclined to provide for their children, they will almost always be better at it and find it less of a diversion from their own interests than anyone else. The principle will thus be best served by parents caring chiefly for their own offspring. Because the young will then come chiefly to owe their own parents repayment for their early nurturing, they will almost always be more inclined to provide for them than for others, and thus the principle will be best served by children caring for their own parents.

Needless to say, the principle of intergenerational solicitude requires that the generations treat each other as befits their situations. In the case of the young, this requires that their elders subject them to control only to prepare them for the task of free and rational pursuit of their sovereign interests. Thus, writes Locke, "The power, then, that parents have over their children arises from that duty which is incumbent on them, to take care of their offspring during the imperfect state of childhood. To inform the mind, and govern the actions of their yet ignorant nonage, till reason shall take its place and ease them of that trouble, is what the children want, and the parents are bound to" (*ECG*, sec. 58). In the case of the elderly, this requires that the young support them not as objects of charity but as having earned their support by their past efforts. It requires that they be treated with that particular form of esteem that regards persons worthy now because of what they did without guaranteed return in the past. This esteem is called honor. Thus, the Fifth Commandment, "Honor thy father and thy mother" (Exod. 20:12), is a requirement of reason. Locke continues, "though there be a time when a child comes to be as free from subjection to the will and command of his father as he himself is free from subjection to the will of anybody else . . . , yet this freedom exempts not a son from that honour which he ought, by the law of God and Nature, to pay his parents, God

186

having made the parents the instruments in His great design of continuing the race of mankind and the occasions of life to their children" (*ECG*, sec. 66).

The Point of Morality, Mutual Respect, and the Principle of Just Punishment

Punishment is a harm done intentionally to another because he is judged to have done wrong. It is commonly thought justified either on deterrent grounds, to persuade people not to commit certain acts, or on retributive grounds, to give offenders what they deserve. I count deterrence as a form of self-defense and thus as already covered by the principle of compatible liberty that allows the use of force against those (and only those) who invade one's liberty, but no more force than is necessary to protect that liberty. I understand punishment strictly as retribution, though later I shall consider how this may include force used against offenders for the purpose of deterrence.

It is a mistake to identify retributivism exclusively with the lex talionis, an "eye for an eye." The lex talionis is one form of retributivism. Retributivism—as the word itself suggests—is the doctrine that the offender should be paid back with suffering he deserves because of the evil he has intentionally done (or attempted to do), and the lex talionis asserts that injury equivalent to that he intentionally imposed (or attempted to impose) is what the offender deserves. Another form of retributivism, which I shall call "proportional retributivism," holds that what retribution requires is not equality of injury between crimes and punishments, but "fit" or proportionality, such that the worst crime is punished with the society's worst penalty, the next worst crime by the next worst punishment, and so on, though the society's worst punishment need not duplicate the injury of the worst crime.

It is my view that, with respect to punishment, natural justice calls for a version of retributivism based on the lex talionis with some admixture of deterrence considerations. A version of proportional retributivism is appropriate for punishment among people sharing a social structure and is the shape that natural justice in punishment takes when refracted through just social relations. Proportional retributivism is a matter of social justice, and accordingly, I will take it up in chapter 5. In the present section, I am concerned only with natural justice in punishment.

Retribution is not to be confused with restitution, at least as this is normally understood. Restitution involves restoring the status quo ante, the condition prior to the offense. Since it was in this condition that the criminal's offense was committed, it is this condition that constitutes the baseline   187 against which retribution is exacted. Thus, retribution involves imposing a loss on the offender that reduces him below the status quo ante. For example, returning a thief's loot to his victim, so that thief and victim now own what they did before the offense, is restitution. Taking enough from the thief so that what he is left with is less than what he had before the offense is retribution, since this is what he did to his victim. What restitution shares with retribution is the aim of rectifying the harm done to the victim. If, adhering to normal usage, we think of restitution as the restoring of goods stolen or the repairing of physical injuries imposed (I shall call this material restitution), then we shall see that there is a particular aspect of victimization that can only be rectified by retribution, and thus material restitution is incomplete rectification. If we expand our notion of restitution to include the restoring of the moral relations in which offender and victim stood prior to the offense (I shall call this moral restitution), we shall see that retribution is necessary for moral restitution.

Hobbes believed that in the state of nature all people had the right to punish offenders, as part of their right to do anything they deemed necessary to their survival. Interestingly, Hobbes did not believe that the sovereign's right to punish is given to him by the citizens when they contract to establish a commonwealth. This would imply that the sovereign was a party to the contract, which we have seen Hobbes at pains to deny. Rather, according to Hobbes, the contractors give up their right to punish, and the sovereign simply retains the right he had in the state of nature. As might be expected, since Hobbes takes the evil of the state of nature to be vulnerability to harm, he is a strict deterrence theorist regarding punishment: "The aim of punishment is not a revenge but terror" (*L*, chap. 28). Among those habits of mind conducive to peace that Hobbes takes to be laws of nature binding in foro interno is included: "We are forbidden to inflict punishment with any other design than for correction of the offender or direction of others" (*L*, chap. 15). Because correction is to be imposed by force and because its point is to keep the offender from offending again, I take correction of the offender—which is sometimes called "reform" and offered as a third justifying aim of punishment—as a method of deterrence.

Locke comes closer to espousing retribution as one of the aims of punishment. This should not be surprising in light of the fact that, for him, the state of nature has a de jure authoritative moral law. Thus, the right of people in the state of nature to punish is not part of their right to do anything. It is their right to execute the natural moral law, which "is in that state put into every man's hands" (*ECG*, sec. 7), since otherwise the law of nature would be in vain. Since Locke, in contrast to Hobbes, takes the evil of the state of nature to be vulnerability to injustice, he takes punishment to be aimed both at restoring justice and at deterring violations; Locke declares that one may punish a criminal "only to retribute to him . . . what is proportionate to his transgression, which is so much as may serve for reparation and restraint" (*ECG*, sec. 8). But Locke stops short of thoroughgoing retributivism. By *reparation* he seems to mean mainly material restitution (remember that this includes repair of injuries, not just return of goods). For example, he takes murder as beyond reparation and thus punishment of it to be aimed strictly at deterrence (*ECG*, sec. 11).

Kant, by contrast, is a strict retributivist, who holds that people must receive harm equivalent to what they have intentionally and unjustly inflicted: "Only the law of retribution (*jus talionis*) can determine exactly the kind and degree of punishment" (*MJ*, 101). Thus, if a man "has committed a murder, he must die." Moreover this punishment is due even when there is no hope of deterring others: "Even if a civil society were to dissolve itself by common agreement of all its members . . . , the last murderer remaining in prison must first be executed, so that everyone will duly receive what his actions are worth" (*MJ*, 102).

Judging from the examples of Hobbes and Locke, it would seem that a moral theory that starts from some version of the state of nature cannot end up with a strictly retributivist theory of punishment. If we imagine the rules of punishment as those that people would agree to in a state of nature, then there is every reason to think that such people will rank their desire for protection higher than their desire for revenge and be more concerned to have crime prevented before it happens than to see criminals suffer after. Moreover, their interest in self-protection is also an interest in having the most moderate punishments that will generally prevent crime, since they may find themselves rightly or wrongly accused of some crime in the future. There is considerable truth in these ideas. As stated, however, they underestimate the considerations that make it rational for people to desire retribution in the natural context. Thus I shall argue that it would be mutually reasonable for people in the natural context to agree to a principle that holds retribution—giving offenders the punishments they deserve—as the necessary condition of acceptable punishment and in which lex talionis and deterrence combine to determine what people deserve as their retribution.

I shall speak here of offenders and offenses, or criminals and crimes, as equivalent in meaning to violators and violations, respectively, of the principles of just relations between people—and without any particular legal connotation. There are many technical problems with the application of the rule of lex talionis, so we must take it as stating an ideal to be approached as nearly as is feasible. Some offenses do not seem duplicable, such as treason, or others that require deception or surprise. Then the lex talionis will require as near as possible an approximation of the suffering caused. Some people think that the impossibility of duplicating some offenses renders the lex talionis pointless. But lex talionis is not a policy; it is a theory of desert. It holds that what people deserve is suffering equivalent to what they have intentionally caused. When we try to give them what they deserve, naturally, we can do no more than impose the nearest feasible approximation to that suffering.

Further, suffering itself is a subjective matter; some people may regard a beating as a worse fate than others do. Of course, if suffering were not something we could measure in some rough but reasonable way, we could not have a theory of just punishment at all. I will thus assume that there are roughly identifiable standard amounts of suffering that anyone can expect any crime to produce and that, unless they have knowledge of people's special vulnerabilities, sane adult offenders are to be taken as causing the standard amount of suffering normally caused by offenses like theirs. The lex talionis (and retributivism, generally) takes just punishment to be a function of what people deserve, and what people deserve is a function of what is in their control. Strictly speaking, the lex talionis calls for imposing on people suffering equivalent to that which they have intentionally attempted to impose on others, whether or not their attempts have, for reasons outside of their control, succeeded—and I shall take it this way also. Finally, it is important to remember that the immediate victim of an offense is not necessarily the only victim of it. His friends and relatives may be caused to suffer as well, and others may endure painful anxiety or restrict their actions out of fear of like fates. Thus, though I shall normally speak of doing to the offender what he has done to his immediate victim, I do so only for the sake of simplicity; such locutions should be taken as shorthand for a more complex statement that would include all the qualifications in this and the previous paragraph.

There is nothing self-evident about the justice of the lex talionis nor, for that matter, of retributivism generally. The standard problem confronting those who would justify retributivism is that of overcoming the suspicion that it does no more than sanctify the victim's desire to hurt the offender back. Since serving that desire amounts to hurting the offender simply for the satisfaction that the victim derives from seeing the offender suffer and since deriving satisfaction from the suffering of others seems primitive, the policy of imposing suffering on the offender for no other purpose than giving satisfaction to his victim seems primitive as well. Consequently, defending retributivism requires showing that the suffering imposed on the wrongdoer has some worthy point. I shall do this by elaborating further on the natural interest that people have in morality as it emerges in the present theory.

We have already seen that the interest that all people have in morality is their natural interest in not being subjugated. The effect of the social contract test is to require that any acceptable morality preserve or promote the freedom of all persons from subjugation by their fellows. This, we might say, is the natural point or aim of morality—or, at least, of the requirements of justice—and this makes the natural structure of justice deontological rather than teleological.

Teleological moral theories normally take the production of good consequences as the decisive feature of morally approved behavior. Utilitarianism is the clearest form of teleological moral theory in that it views all moral requirements as derived from the goal of producing the greatest net sum of good consequences, happiness, or satisfaction. Deontological theories are not indifferent to the consequences of actions. As Rawls says, any theory that did not consider the consequences of actions in judging them would be "irrational, crazy" (*TJ*, 30). Indeed, for moral purposes, actions cannot be separated from their immediate consequences. Lying is not just uttering false words into space but inducing false beliefs in one's listener; murder is not just squeezing a trigger but causing someone's death. What is distinctive about deontological theories is that they take the moral status of actions with their immediate consequences to depend on considerations other than the total goodness or badness of all their consequences, immediate and far-flung. Such theories stress the rights that people have or the duties they owe one another as the basis for determining which actions, with their immediate consequences, are right or wrong. Thus, a teleological objection to murder might appeal to the general unhappiness (pain, grief, insecurity) produced by killing people, whereas a deontological objection will point out that people have the right to determine their own fates, a right that is violated by murder.

Because people in the natural context resist being subjugated by one another, the natural context leads to a deontological moral theory that takes the maintenance of nonsubjugating relationships among human beings as the point of morality, rather than to a teleological theory that might allow the production of good consequences for many to justify subjugation or suffering imposed on others.

From here, we must proceed with care because two different things are implied, each with its own implications. On one hand, people have an interest in not being subjugated, irrespective of the intentions of those who subjugate them. Call this their interest in freedom. On the other hand, people have an interest in their fellows intentionally trying not to subjugate them. Call this their interest in mutual respect. The interest in freedom is served by the right of self-defense with its characteristic indifference to the

191

intentions of invaders of freedom. By contrast, the interest in mutual respect is served by punishment, with its characteristic focus on intentions and thus desert. The interest in freedom is served by deterrence, and the interest in mutual respect is served by retribution.

Earlier, I asked the reader to picture people in the natural context as if they were molecules bobbing up and down in a liquid, where the up and down positions represent their relative power to achieve their sovereign interests. Imagine now a doubling of this picture. On one hand, see it as a picture of the relations among individuals' bodies, understood before as representing their actual liberty or power to act on their judgments about their sovereign interests. On the other hand, see it as a picture of the relations among individuals' wills, understood therefore as representing the degree to which they either respect the equal rights of others to pursue their sovereign interests or arrogate to themselves a right to suppress the sovereign interests of others. In the first picture, the up and down positions represent degrees of relative freedom to move one's body without hindrance from others. In the second picture, the up and down positions represent degrees of relative authority willfully arrogated by some over the wills of others. The interest in freedom corresponds to the first picture—it is an interest in keeping widest scope for unhindered action compatible with the same for all. The interest in mutual respect corresponds to the second picture—it is an interest in maintaining equality of relative authority among wills.

Further, since sovereign interests are the interests that people have for their whole lives, the relations between people are not ephemeral but cumulative throughout their lifetimes. Because knowledge of mortality transforms living into living a life, the relations between any two persons are not just the relations in which they stand at any moment but the relations in which their lives stand, the degree to which each has been able to pursue his sovereign interest over the course of his lifetime relative to the other. This applies in both pictures. In the first—looking at the relations among people as relations among their degrees of actual freedom—if one person subjugates another temporarily, then, even after that subjugation is ended, it remains true that (everything else equal) the first has obtained an increment of freedom to pursue his sovereign interest over the course of his whole lifetime that is at the expense of the freedom that the other has for pursuing her sovereign interest over the course of her whole lifetime. In the second— looking at the relations among people as relations among their wills—if one person intentionally subjugates another temporarily, then, even after that subjugation is ended, it remains true that (everything else equal) the first has willed a degree of authority for her pursuit of her sovereign interest over her whole lifetime that is at the expense of the authority that the other has for pursuing his sovereign interest over his whole lifetime. Call this in both pictures the lasting quality of moral relations.

The interest in freedom combined with the lasting quality of moral relations gives individuals the right to use that much force against those who violate their freedom, intentionally or unintentionally, as is necessary to maintain equal relative freedom among people over their lifetimes. Consequently, people who injure others quite accidentally can still be justly made to compensate for the loss, although no guilt for a crime is imputed.

But when the interest in mutual respect is combined with the lasting quality of moral relations, a distinctive conception of crime and punishment comes into view. It is a distinctively nonutilitarian conception. For the utilitarian, a crime is just a unit of suffering added to the aggregate suffering in the world that the utilitarian aims to reduce, and punishment is a unit of suffering imposed in the short run in the hope of reducing that aggregate in the long run. In light of the interest in mutual respect, by contrast, a crime is an act of disrespect, a manifestation of the will to subjugate others, an intentional arrogation of authority over another. It is an intentional assault on the sovereignty of an individual that temporarily places one person (the criminal) in a position of illegitimate sovereignty over another (the victim). Given the lasting quality of moral relations, the criminal act, though temporary in nature, has the effect of altering relations in a permanent way. Thus, merely ending the crime, returning stolen goods to their owner or repairing the physical injuries he suffered, are not sufficient to rectify the crime. Only retribution, giving the victim authority over the criminal comparable to the authority over the victim that the criminal arrogated to himself, can restore lasting relations of mutual respect.

This picture of the relationship between crime and punishment gives credence to the Hegelian notion—dismissed by most philosophers—that retributive punishment annuls a crime. Hegel wrote that "the sole positive existence which the injury [the crime] possesses is that it is the particular will of the criminal [that is, it manifests the arbitrary ascendance of the criminal's will over that of his victim]. Hence to injure (or penalize) this particular will as a will determinately existent is to annul the crime, which otherwise would have been held valid, and to restore the right" (*PR*, 69). I take this to mean that the right is a certain equal relationship of sovereign authority between the wills of individuals. Crime disrupts that relationship by placing one will above others, and punishment restores the relationship by annulling the illegitimate ascendance.

What makes people suspicious of Hegel's claim is that, since the illegitimate act occurred in the irrevocable past, talk of annulling the offense seems exaggerated. Punishment cannot annul the physical harm that a crime   193 has done; even if that is repaired, the harm that occurred in the past remains a fact—corrected, perhaps compensated, but not annulled. What can be annulled, however, is the criminal's assertion of authority over his victim. This cannot be done simply by reducing the criminal to a position at which he *now* cannot assert authority over the victim, since then the past assertion of authority would remain a feature of the lives of the criminal and the victim and, given the lasting quality of moral relations, not be annulled. The only way to annul it is to take the criminal's assertion of authority itself as setting in motion a like imposition of authority on the criminal. That retroactively transforms the earlier arrogation of authority into its opposite: It makes the criminal's act into one the lasting quality of which is to keep him in the original parity of authority with his victim that his crime momentarily upset. For Hegel, failure to do this amounts to holding the earlier assertion of authority as valid—that is, letting its lasting quality last. Punishment according to the lex talionis cannot annul the physical injury that the victim has suffered at the criminal's hands. Rather, it annuls the indignity and disrespect he has suffered, by rendering the criminal's act of subjugating the victim into his own act of subordination to the victim. Given the lasting quality of moral relations, failing to punish in this way lets the indignity stand though the injury itself is healed.

If this is correct, it explains a number of puzzling facts about the desire for revenge. First, that desire has a way of staying alive—as if the failure to punish the criminal appropriately were tantamount to continuing his offense. Likewise, the satisfaction of the desire has the effect of settling accounts; it brings about a kind of closure that is the next best thing to not having been victimized at all. Moreover, it explains why the desire for revenge is not satisfied when the wrongdoer suffers a comparable fate by accident or unconsciously. The desire for revenge is, then, not so much the desire that the offender suffer but that the relation of wills that he disrupted be restored by imposing the victim's will on him. On these grounds, the desire for revenge (strictly limited to the desire to even the score) is more respectable than philosophers have generally allowed. Thus, Hegel writes that "The annulling of crime in this sphere where right is immediate [that is, where moral practice is unreflective] is principally revenge, which is just in its content in so far as it is retributive" (*PR*, 73).

The point of lex talionis is the reestablishment of mutual respect. If the criminal is rational, then punishment equivalent to the suffering he has imposed should normally force upon him recognition of his equality with his victim, by forcing him to experience what he has done from the standpoint of his own sovereign interest. As we saw in chapter 2, identification is the source of moral obligation. Punishment forces the identification with the sovereign interest of the other that the offender should have been led to by his own reason. This is the truth in the notion that retributive punishment restores the criminal to full membership in the moral community. It is also why the retributivist requires that the offender be sane, not only at the moment of his crime, but also at the moment of his punishment—whereas this latter requirement is largely pointless (if not downright malevolent) for a utilitarian. Since the identification with the sovereign interest of the other is what the offender's own reason should have produced, the desire for revenge turns out to be a desire that the work of reason be completed. It is the desire that the offender be forced to recognize his equality as a person with his victim, not the desire for suffering itself, that constitutes what is rational in the desire for revenge.

Here it is worth noting (particularly in light of the discussion of the Golden Rule in chapter 2) the striking affinity between the Golden Rule and the lex talionis. The Golden Rule mandates "Do unto others as you would have others do unto you," whereas the lex talionis counsels "Do unto others as they have done unto you." It would not be too far-fetched to say that the lex talionis is the law enforcement arm of the Golden Rule, at least in the sense that if people were actually treated as they treated others then everyone would necessarily follow the Golden Rule, because then people could only act toward others as they would have others act toward them. This is not to suggest that the lex talionis follows from the Golden Rule, but rather that the two share a common moral inspiration: mutual respect, the treatment of persons as equally entitled to be free from subjugation. Treating others as you would have them treat you means treating others with mutual respect, because adopting the Golden Rule as one's guiding principle implies that one counts one's rights to impose one's desires on others as no greater than their right to impose their desires on one.

This account explains other features of retribution. What the criminal distinctively violates is the requirement that everyone try intentionally to maintain equal relations of sovereign authority by not interfering when others pose no threat of interference. Thus, what matters is not what the criminal does but what he tries to do. His crime consists in trying to impose his sovereignty over another who has not tried to do that to him. Thus, it consists only in what he intentionally attempts to do. Punishment is not for accidental interferences with others' interests, since these do not assert the authority of one over the other. For accidental interferences, one retains the right of self-defense, but no more. Nor is punishment only for successful interferences, since, if the criminal fails for reasons outside of his control, that

195

does not change that he has arrogated authority over the victim—treated his own sovereign interest as if it had greater right to be pursued than the other's.

Correspondingly, what accrues to the victim of a crime is not a duty to punish, but a right to punish. He retains the right to pardon his criminal. Just as it is the criminal's attempt to arrogate sovereignty over the victim that constitutes her offense, so it is granting the victim sovereignty over the criminal—the authority to determine the criminal's fate—that satisfies his retribution. By virtue of the victim having the right to punish the violator (rather than the duty), the victim's equality of authority with the violator is restored. Thus, retributive punishment effects moral restitution.

A crime is an intentional disruption of the lasting relations of sovereign authority befitting individuals who are all entitled to relations of mutual respect. If it is in everyone's interest to have these relations maintained, then it is in everyone's interest to have these relations restored when they are disrupted. It is, then, mutually reasonable for all to agree that the victims of crimes have the right to rectify their loss of standing relative to the criminal by meting out a punishment that reduces the criminal's sovereignty in the degree to which he vaunted it above his victim's. Accordingly, the lex talionis is reasonable for all to accept in the natural context as determining what offenders deserve and what victims have a right to impose on them. But lex talionis is not the only standard of what is reasonable for all to accept as the measure of what offenders deserve, and thus, it does not supply us with the full principle of just punishment that would be agreed to in the natural context.

Consider how people come to deserve punishment. This in itself is a peculiar fact requiring that people's acts have a kind of contagious moral quality about them such that others come to have moral rights to respond in ways that they would not otherwise be entitled to act. Desert requires that by their actions individuals in some way authorize normally prohibited reactions toward them. Since recognition of everyone's right to nonsubjugating relations and to their restoration when violated is a requirement of reason, we can say that insofar as people are rational they authorize their punishment when they intentionally subjugate others. Then it is plausible to say that punishment is compatible with the autonomy of rational beings; indeed, it is necessary to treating criminals as rationally autonomous beings.[9] This accounts for the truth in Kant's assertion that "any undeserved evil that you inflict on someone else among the people is one that you do to yourself. If you vilify him, you vilify yourself; if you steal from him, you steal from yourself; if you kill him, you kill yourself" (*MJ*, 101). Since Kant

holds that "If what happens to someone is also willed by him, it cannot be a punishment," he takes pains to distance himself from the view that the offender wills his punishment. "The chief error contained in this sophistry," Kant writes, "consists in the confusion of the criminal's [the murderer's] own judgment (which one must necessarily attribute to his reason) that he must forfeit his life with a resolution of the will to take his own life" (*MJ*, 105–6). I have tried to capture this notion of attributing a judgment to the offender rather than a resolution of his will with the term *authorizes*. Note that this account of authorization supports the notion that punishment is a right not a duty. By his acts, a rational being authorizes others to do the same to him; he does not compel them to. Otherwise, we would be required to match everything anyone ever did—good, bad, or indifferent.

The notion of desert has another element in it besides authorization— namely, a measure of the relevant worth of actions that determines the legitimate magnitude of authorized reactions. Since it is mutually reasonable for people to be able to restore the relations appropriate to sovereign persons, much of the measure comes from the crime itself. Thus follow the lex talionis, and the validity of the biblical invocation: "thou shalt give life for life, eye for eye, tooth for tooth, hand for hand, foot for foot, burning for burning, wound for wound, stripe for stripe" (Exod. 21:23–25). It may, however, turn out that a punishment that, as far as possible, matches the suffering caused by a crime does not suffice to deter people from committing that crime. For example, inflicting the pains of being kidnapped on kid- nappers might not suffice to discourage people from kidnapping.[10] Then, the right of self-defense takes over, giving one the right to do what is necessary for deterrence. This right is not limited to intentional invasions of liberty. But when we are dealing with crimes, intention is present, and thus we can say that a person who intentionally violates the principle of com- patible liberty intentionally authorizes others to do what is necessary to defend themselves. Accordingly, though this right comes in from a different principle, it comes under the authorization that characterizes desert and appropriately qualifies the measure of just punishment. Normally, enough suffering as will accomplish the ends of moral restitution will suffice for this deterrent function as well. If it will not, then criminals can be held to deserve—that is, to authorize by their actions—enough suffering to make offenses, in Locke's words, "an ill bargain for the offender" (*ECG*, sec. 12).

Since it is in everyone's interest to be subject to the least amount of punishment that will serve the legitimate ends of punishment, it is reasonable for all to accept the principle that violators be subject to the least amount of punishment that will accomplish the ends of moral restitution and effective deterrence. This *principle of just punishment* holds that the offender deserves and the victim has a right to impose on him suffering equivalent to that which he has intentionally imposed on the victim, plus the minimum additional suffering necessary (if any is necessary) to deter reasonable people from committing such offenses.

Note that this principle does not give free rein to deterrence. It does not permit the use of any and every punishment that will effectively deter crime, such as punishing innocent members of offenders' families. The reason is that deterrence here is invoked by the principle of compatible liberty, which only allows force against those who actually invade or threaten to invade one's liberty. Moreover, the point of morality and the source of punishment's justification is the maintenance of relations of nonsubjugation. Consequently, it would not be reasonable for all to agree to coercing those who have not coerced others, since this would amount to disrupting those very relations that justify punishment in the first place. The retributive aim takes priority in just punishment. Only those who deserve punishment, who have authorized it by their intentional actions, may be punished.

Two remarks are worth making before concluding this section. Some people believe that punishing people for the purpose of deterring crime amounts to using people as means to the ends of others. Such punishment cannot deter the offender to whom it is applied, since his offense has already occurred. It seems, then, that he is punished in order to protect others against the crimes of still others and thus that he is used as a means to the ends of others. This view is based on the assumption that what deters about punishment is the individual instances of it. Then, each instance of deterrent punishment is for the prevention of future crimes done by and to other people, and the punished one is used as a means to the ends of others. My view, in contrast, is that a credible threat of punishment is what deters people, and individual instances of punishment are necessary conditions of this credibility. Since the existence of the credible threat protects everyone against crimes, such punishment as is necessary to keep the threat credible serves everyone's interest and thus uses no one merely as a means to the ends of others.

Finally, the principle of just punishment would permit punishments that many people regard as barbaric. For example, torturing torturers, raping rapists, and killing murderers, would all be just according to the principle. I believe that there are good reasons for refraining from these and like penalties. The implication of my argument for the principle of just punishment, however, is that such reasons must be of a different sort than claiming that such punishments are unjust (in terms of natural justice). Kant says that "no one has ever heard of anyone condemned to death on account of murder who complained that he was getting too much [punishment] and therefore was being treated unjustly; everyone would laugh in his face if he were to make such a statement" (*MJ*, 104). It seems to me that the same could be said of torturers who claimed that torture was more punishment than they deserved, or rapists who claimed that rape was a violation of their rights. This suggests that such punishments are not unjust; they are within the natural right of the victim. But here it is worth noting that punishment is only his right, not his duty. As there can be good reasons not to exercise one's right to free speech to the limit, there can as well be good reasons not to exercise one's right to punish to the limit. We shall see that, once people share a social structure, such reasons become binding.

This concludes our discussion of the principles of natural justice. Given the nonfungibility of sovereign interests and in the absence of a shared social structure, there are no further principles that it would be rational for all human beings to agree to be bound by. This is because the principles of natural justice protect against violence, accumulation of property that could be used to coerce others, and deception. Consequently, any other arrangement that is mutually reasonable can be established by free agreements that will be untainted by suspicion of subjugation. Self-defense and just punishment for violations of the principles of compatible liberty, natural ownership, trustworthiness, and intergenerational solicitude are the only legitimate uses of force, as far as natural justice goes. Since the principles of justice are the moral requirements of requiring, it follows that, in the absence of a shared social structure, natural justice prohibits forcibly requiring any more than these principles. (I am speaking, naturally, of what may be forced on sane adults. Quite a bit more—for example, education—may, indeed must, be forced on children in the name of the principle of intergenerational solicitude.) Any other moral ideal, any other goal of any sort, must, as a matter of natural justice, be promoted only by persuasion and urged only for voluntary allegiance. Having reached the outer edge of natural justice, we must look from the outside at the theory that has brought us here. I shall do this in the following two sections by considering two possible objections to the theory. The first objection accuses the theory of being too naturalistic, the second of being too concerned with justice.

The Naturalistic Fallacy

Any naturalistic moral theory, such as the one defended here, must meet a popular objection to all such theories often described as the "naturalistic fallacy." The core of this notion is that it is always wrong to identify the moral good or right with natural facts or with the possession of some set of natural properties. By "natural facts or properties" is meant things or qualities that can be identified with the tools of natural science—things or qualities that would be included in a complete inventory of existing objects and their properties in an ontology based on natural science. Since "possession of a natural property" is a "natural fact," I shall generally use the latter term and take for granted that it may refer to properties as well as things or processes. The objection is not against calling some natural fact good but against defining good as some natural fact. For example, utilitarianism is accused of the fallacy insofar as it defines good as consciousness of happiness or of satisfaction. It would not be so accused if it simply asserted that such consciousness was good, but then it would not be utilitarianism, since it would need some other definition of good to indicate what was good about this consciousness. In short, statements of the sort "X is good," where X is some natural fact, only run afoul of the naturalistic fallacy if the statements are taken as definitions or, equivalently, as tautologies, such that "X is not good" is a contradiction in terms. When "X is good" is only an attribution of goodness to some natural X (such that "X is not good" is held to be false but not contradictory), the naturalistic fallacy is not committed. Since the objection cuts equally against defining with natural facts either what it is right to do or what it is good to promote, I shall, in the discussion that follows, use *right* and *good* as if each stood for both.

The theory of justice as reason's answer to subjugation seems to be subject to the objection in two intertwined ways: First, I have argued that the nonmoral *ought* is the natural fact of human subjectivity as lived in the first person and that the moral *ought* is the fact of all such lived human subjectivities as they make themselves known to individuals through rationally necessary identification. Human subjectivity is a fact that one must be or imagine being to know, and being or imagining being it entails a positive valuation of what serves its sovereign interest. Second, I contend that identifying with people's sovereign interests one will necessarily judge to be right those actions or arrangements that stand in a maximally facilitating relationship to all people's sovereign interests. Rightness, then, is the property of standing in this facilitating relationship, and that is a natural property. These are intertwined in that the first implies the second. Human subjectivity is a fact full recognition of which entails a valuation—namely, that what stands in a maximally facilitating relationship to all sovereign interests is right.

There are three basic arguments that the naturalistic fallacy is a fallacy. The first, formulated by G. E. Moore, claims that "whatever definition be offered, it may always be asked, with significance, of the complex [natural fact] so defined, whether it itself is good" (*PE*, 15). Take some complex natural fact, such as satisfaction of desire, which is held by some to define good. Moore holds that it is evident that one may still ask meaningfully whether it is good to satisfy desire. Likewise, for any natural fact it is always possible to ask meaningfully whether it is good. But if this is always a meaningful question, then the question must be asking something that is not already apparent from the identification of the natural fact itself. Or, equivalently, if the good were some natural fact, then asking whether that natural fact was good would be tantamount to asking whether the good was good, and that is not a meaningful question. Thus if, as Moore claims, it is always meaningful to ask whether any natural fact is good, the good can never be defined by any natural fact.

The second argument, stemming from David Hume, holds that the good is what should be promoted or done, and thus, identification of something as truly good must move one to approval and eventually to supportive action. But reason, which identifies natural facts as such, claims Hume, "is not alone sufficient to produce any moral blame or approbation"—for that, a sentiment is requisite (*EPM*, 83). "Reason, being cool and disengaged, is no motive to action," Hume continues. "Taste," by contrast, "as it gives pleasure or pain . . . , becomes a motive to action, and is the first spring or impulse to desire and volition" (*EPM*, 88). If reason, which identifies facts as what they are, cannot move to approval or action, it follows that no fact as such can be the good. This is because there must also be, consequent upon the identification of some fact, a responding sentiment of approval that impels desire and volition. But it is always a contingent matter whether, upon recognizing some natural fact, one responds with a sentiment of approval and a disposition to action. Therefore, no natural fact necessarily moves one to approval or supportive action, and consequently, no natural fact can be the good.

The third argument, put forth by R. M. Hare, holds that identification of some natural fact is essentially a description of its features; however, we use terms like *good* to commend ends or actions, and a commendation is different from a description. Commendations, rather than being equivalent to descriptions, are based upon them. Moreover, if calling something good were equivalent to describing some natural fact about it, then it could not be a commendation to call it good. Writes Hare: "If it were true that 'a good A' meant the same as 'an A which is C' [where C is some natural fact, such as the satisfaction of some desire], then it would be impossible to use the sentence 'An A which is C is good' in order to commend A's which are C; for this sentence would be analytic and equivalent to 'An A which is C is C'" (*LM*, 90–91). Commending something that satisfies desire would be equivalent to saying that what satisfies desire satisfies desire and would thus be no commendation of what satisfies desire. In short, we hold something to be good because of its features. For this to be meaningful, calling something good must be different from simply describing its features. That means that the good cannot be identified with any natural facts.

Let us call Moore's argument the "open question" argument, Hume's, the "knowing-to-willing" argument, and Hare's, the "commending-vs.-describing" argument. I shall take them up in order, though what I say about each will sometimes bear on the others. We shall see that our theory must accommodate some truth in the arguments.

The open question argument is easiest to answer because it starts from the appearance that it is always possible to ask meaningfully whether some natural fact is good. But such appearances are notoriously unreliable. It *seems* possible to ask meaningfully, "What is the highest number?" but the question is not meaningful. Much of contemporary philosophy is concerned to show that many questions that seem meaningful really are not. So, such logical empiricists as Moritz Schlick, holding that existence means occupying a verifiable location in space, have argued that "Does God exist?" is strictly nonsense; and behaviorists, like Gilbert Ryle, have argued that asking "What is the nature of mind (as distinct from mental activities)?" is as meaningless as asking where the university is after one has seen all the buildings. It cannot be taken for granted that every question it seems possible to ask meaningfully is really a meaningful question.

Consequently, a naturalist in ethics—one who identifies the good with some natural fact—might reply to Moore that it is not really meaningful to ask whether this fact is good. It only seems to be because in every other case it is meaningful, and this leads to the habit of thinking it always is. To claim, then, as Moore does, that it always is possible to ask whether some natural fact is good is only to disagree with the naturalist on this issue. Consequently, rather than being a logical truth, the open question represents a theoretical claim—precisely the one denied by the naturalist. Claiming that the naturalistic fallacy is a fallacy on the basis of the open question argument begs the question, because it assumes the falsity of naturalism in advance.

The truth in Hume's knowing-to-willing argument is that, in general, our knowledge of natural facts does not necessarily move our wills one way or another. I contend that this is because the standard form in which we have our knowledge of the natural world is as third-person descriptions. In fact, third-person descriptions may, though need not, move us. I believe, however, that the knowledge we have of our own sovereign interests does necessarily move us, because it is knowledge of what we must do to be who we are in the face of our impending deaths. The press of this knowledge comes to us only in the first person. That is, as the *I* who I am and who experiences himself as at stake, I experience the urgency of my sovereign interest as an imperative. This fact accounts for the nonmoral ought of self-interested practical reasoning, where *self-interested* is understood not in the narrow sense of selfish, but in the more fundamental sense of that on which the existence of the self depends.

One can, of course, train herself to think of herself in the third person, and indeed this can be a valuable skill. Dieters, and anyone else trying to free themselves from some compulsion, must treat their errant desires as third-person events—things that are happening to them rather than longings in which they live—in order to overcome the natural power of such facts to move them to action. This possibility, rather than counting against the natural tendency of certain facts to move our wills, is evidence for it. Ascetics may try to treat all their desires in the third person, though I believe that they must ultimately fail because they will necessarily exalt their own desire to conquer their desires. Hegel was right to treat religious asceticism as a form of unhappy consciousness.

Knowledge of other people's sovereign interests must likewise be knowledge of them in the first person. To know them for what they are, I must identify with them from within—as if I inhabited the partisan practical attitude of their subjectivity. Since this opens me to the urgency of their sovereign interests, I am moved to act by this knowledge much as I am moved by knowledge of my own sovereign interest.

If I view the interests of others only in the third person, they will not necessarily move me. They will be events in the world striking me with no particular urgency, or with only so much urgency as I happen to feel about such things. Parallel to asceticism, it is possible to cultivate a kind of general indifference to others, seeing them as mere objects moving in the world, and thus to make oneself capable of considerable evil. The same fact that makes it easier to kill people from airplanes when they look like blindly scurrying ants than to kill them face-to-face makes it easier to hurt people when they are reduced to "cases" by the strange distancing effect of bureaucracies, which are called impersonal because they achieve efficiency by treating everyone in the third person. But in all these cases, it takes positive cultivation or real distance to outweigh the natural tendency to see others as living their fates in the first person just like oneself. Rather than showing that these natural facts do not necessarily move the will to act supportively, these cases show that it is precisely this natural tendency that evil or indifference must overcome.

Since Hume understood knowledge of others strictly on the model of third-person knowledge, he was led to think that sympathy or benevolence was the necessary condition of moral concern. If we could only have third-person knowledge of other people's interests, Hume would be right. The

203

only way I would be moved to act supportively of others' ends would be if I spontaneously desired to benefit others. Serving others' interests would then be a first-person interest of mine. But, as we have seen, benevolence must be derivative in a moral theory, since it cannot supply us with moral requirements. Justice as reason's answer avoids both Hume's knowing-to-willing argument and Hume's need to rely on benevolence because the theory does not limit knowledge to third-person knowledge.

The truth in the knowing-to-willing argument is that natural facts known in the standard third-person way will not necessarily move us to supportive action. The theory of justice as reason's answer to subjugation eludes this objection, however, because it asserts that there is one natural fact that can only be known for what it is either by being it or by identifying with being it in the first person—and doing that necessarily moves the will. Morality does not need nonrational passion to stir us to act because morality is reason's own passion. This view is not exotic. Bishop Butler, for example, took rationality to include "both the discernment of what is right, and a disposition to regulate ourselves by it" (*FS*, 189). Pascal held that the heart has its reasons. My view is that reason has its heart.

Consider now Hare's commending-vs.-describing argument. In justice as reason's answer to subjugation, we can say that what is right about some action, such as refraining from killing innocent people, is that such refraining stands in a complex maximally facilitating relation to people's sovereign interests. Rightness, then, is defined by this relation, and since the ability of an action or a type of action to serve people's sovereign interests more extensively than alternative actions is a complex natural fact, rightness is defined by a natural fact. Calling something right, however, says Hare, is commending it. Thus, if serving people's sovereign interests maximally is right, then I cannot commend an action for serving people's interests maximally. That would amount to saying that what serves people's sovereign interests maximally serves people's sovereign interests maximally. I must either describe the fact that actions serve sovereign interests in this way or commend them for so doing, but not both. Commendation must refer to something beyond the facts that are described. By implication, this entails that commending something for facilitating sovereign interests must refer to something beyond that it facilitates sovereign interests, and thus rightness cannot be defined in terms of that facilitating.

The rejoinder of justice as reason's answer to subjugation to this objection is that commendation and description do indeed differ, but their difference is not that the former refers to something beyond the latter. Their difference is in the standpoint from which they are made: The same facts described from a third-person standpoint are commended (or condemned) when viewed from a first-person standpoint. From the standpoint of an outside observer, I describe the fact that refraining from violence facilitates people's sovereign interests. Occupying my own first-person standpoint or imaginatively participating in that of others, I am no longer neutral. Describing the relation between refraining from violence and our sovereign interests, I necessarily commend refraining from violence. As *is* becomes *ought* in the first person, so *description* becomes *commendation* (or *condemnation*). Hare contends that for commendation to work it must be different from description, and on this I agree. But he goes on to assume that such difference must be a difference in what commendations and descriptions are about, and on this I disagree. The difference between them is on the other end, not in their objects but in the position of their subjects.

A commendatory judgment that something is right is a description of its facilitating relation to people's sovereign interests made from the first-person standpoint, my own as lived and everyone else's as imagined. Since the judgment that an action is right in this way is complex, fallible, and open to new evidence, it is always possible to ask meaningfully of any action whether it is really right. It is even possible from the third-person standpoint to ask meaningfully whether what best serves people's sovereign interests is right, and to answer it meaningfully from the first-person standpoint. This accounts for what truth there is in the open-question argument.

I think it is worth noting that, unless the naturalistic fallacy can be outflanked, moral philosophy is doomed. We have seen, in considering Gewirth's attempt, that moral requirements cannot be established on logical grounds. If this is so, then the only way that reason could identify the moral requirements is if there is some fact, the recognition of which does move the will to commend and act. If the naturalistic fallacy is a fallacy, no such fact can conceivably be found. We are then condemned never to be able to distinguish valid moral requirements from mere means to subjugation, right from might.

It is no accident that our three champions of the naturalistic fallacy—Moore, Hume, and Hare—were, in their own moral theories, unable to generate a binding moral obligation. Hare comes closest, but his obligation is a logical one like Gewirth's, though even weaker because people can avoid it by refraining from making moral claims about their deeds. Hume turned to the sentiment of benevolence, which we have seen cannot generate requirements. If we have the sentiment, we need no requirement to act on it, and if we lack the sentiment, then we have no ground for requiring acting as if we did. Moore was driven to the view that moral predicates are nonnatural facts that are known by intuition. Intuition, as readers of philosophy will recognize, is what philosophers call something that seems to be knowledge but cannot be shown to be knowledge. As such, as soon as a person dissents from another's moral intuition, there are no grounds for deciding between them. Intuition can never supply the grounds for overriding dissenting judgments that moral requirements must have. These failures testify to the fact that, if the naturalistic fallacy is truly as fatal as its champions maintain, it is fatal as well to the moral requirements. No moral requirement can overcome the suspicion of subjugation unless the naturalistic fallacy can be overcome.

The Primacy of Justice and the Precondition of Community

As I stated at the outset, the theory of justice as reason's answer to subjugation maintains that justice has primacy over all other moral ideals. With much of the theory before us, it is now time to defend that claim. I shall make this defense, first, by stating the case for primacy generally and, then, by rebutting the attack on the primacy of justice recently leveled by Michael Sandel in *Liberalism and the Limits of Justice*.

Justice has primacy over other moral ideals because justice guards the boundaries between people. That justice has this boundary-guarding function was recognized by the ancient Greeks, whose term for justice, *dikaiosunē*, derived from *dikē*, meaning "reparation for the transgression of limits."[11] As such, justice spells out the moral requirements of all requiring, moral and nonmoral. In the context of justice as reason's answer to subjugation, the primacy of justice is essentially the claim that the only actions (including refraining from certain actions) that people may be strictly required to perform, on pain of sanction for refusal, are those that insure each person's maximum freedom to pursue his ends (or ideals, goals, or desires) compatible with a like freedom for every other individual. Because the requirements of justice are the requirements of moral requiring, to honor justice at all is to place this requirement above all other ends or ideals.

Justice does not presuppose that people have no higher aims than to avoid being interfered with or that they are not benevolent or merciful. It only mandates that these things be voluntary. Indeed, much as forced benevolence is no real kindness and forced mercy no tenderness, freedom is the medium of existence of the "higher," "fuller," or "kinder" ideals. By establishing the boundaries over which force may not pass, justice keeps love, community, benevolence, and mercy free, and thus alive. Moreover, it keeps moralizing—the human enterprise of morality—moral by keeping attempts to get people to adhere to moral ideals on the right side of the border between right and might.

206   The argument for justice's primacy is this: If people have ideals or can

be persuaded to embrace ideals voluntarily then, as long as they are rational, they will act in pursuit of those ideals without having it required of them. For all intents and purposes, the only conditions under which it will be necessary to require rational people to pursue any ideal is when it is not theirs, or not sufficiently attractive to get them to make it theirs voluntarily. (I take this to include such partial cases as those in which people have—or might be attracted to embrace voluntarily—the ideal but only weakly and are required to act on it more than they want. Here, too, they are required to pursue an ideal precisely at that point at which it is effectively not theirs.) It follows, then, that limiting requirements according to the principles of justice allows people to act on all ends that are theirs (as long as compatible with everyone else doing likewise) and only forbids forcing people to act on ideals that are not their own.

To dispute the primacy of justice by asserting that some other ideal ought to be required of people is to claim that people should be forced to act on that ideal even though it is not theirs, nor able to attract them enough for them to adopt it voluntarily. To make good on this claim one must show that people really should be required to act on this ideal; otherwise one's claim is indistinguishable from subjugating some to ideals held by others. One must either show that the ideal really is in the individual's self-interest (in which case he could be required to serve it only within the limited scope of justified paternalism), or one must show that reason requires that he serve the ideal, even at the cost of his self-interest. This latter comes up against all the difficulties outlined in the second section of chapter 2. More specifically, I contend that the only promising alternatives are universalizability and justice as reason's answer to subjugation. I believe that I have shown that the first does not work and that the second does. If I am correct, then—outside of the requirement not to subjugate people—it is simply impossible to prove that a person should be required to support an ideal that is not his. Any such ideal must be put forth as a recommendation or give rise to legitimate suspicion that it is a means of subjugation without binding moral force. Justice is the requirement that requiring must meet to dispel the suspicion of subjugation. The primacy of justice over other moral ideals *is* the rejection of subjugation.

The theory of justice as reason's answer to subjugation is liberal in that it rejects imposing ends on people against their wills; accordingly, it holds the principle of compatible liberty to be the first principle of justice. The theory is deontological because it is not aimed at maximizing aggregate liberty (considered, say, as the total number of effective free choices) across people, but rather at maximizing liberty for every single person, even if this requires a lower aggregate liberty or aggregate anything else than might be obtainable otherwise. Accordingly, it holds the appropriate relations of non-subjugation to be prior in authority to any other conception of the good. Sandel sees the link between the primacy of justice and "deontological liberalism." He writes: "'Deontological liberalism' is above all a theory about . . . the primacy of justice among moral . . . ideals. Its core thesis can be stated as follows: society, being composed of a plurality of persons, each with his own aims, interests, and conceptions of the good, is best arranged when it is governed by principles that do not *themselves* presuppose any particular conception of the good" (*LLJ*, 1).

In one sense, the primacy of justice is linked to a particular conception of the good—namely, that a good society is one in which people pursue their ends freely. But Sandel uses "conception of the good" to mean what I have called ideals or ends—and I shall thus use the terms *conception of the good, ideal,* and *end* as equivalents. Understood this way, primacy of justice does not presuppose any particular end or conception of the good, because justice is the set of rules that can be required of people, and to presuppose a particular conception of the good is to impose an end on people, when justice holds that the mutual conditions for everyone's free pursuit of his own ends are all that can be required of people. Against the primacy of justice, Sandel raises two main objections.

First, he contends that the primacy of justice over particular ends presupposes the separation of moral subjects from their particular ends, otherwise, there cannot be rules that are reasonable for moral subjects independently of (and thus constraining their pursuit of) their particular ends. Sandel takes this to mean that defenders of the primacy of justice think of human beings as choosing their ends (from a range of possible ends standing before them within reach but at arm's length), rather than as discovering their ends (within themselves, inseparably connected to, or even constitutive of, who they are) (*LLJ*, 58). Since Sandel argues that we are, in fact, inseparable from our ends, he asserts that no such subjects exist, and thus the primacy of justice rests on a false philosophical anthropology (*LLJ*, 19ff.).

This first objection addresses the fact that, in contractarian defenses of deontological liberal theories, the parties in the contracting situation (be it state of nature, original position, or natural context) are thought of as judging what it is reasonable for all to accept when none knows the particular values, desires, or moral ideals that constitute his sovereign interest. Sandel takes approaches like this to presuppose "the notion of the human subject as a sovereign agent of choice, a creature whose ends are chosen rather than given, who comes by his aims and purposes by acts of will, as opposed, say, to acts of cognition" (*LLJ*, 22). This conception assumes that the identity of the person is separate from and antecedent to his ends, and thus it rules out persons with commitments so deep that they constitute their very identity (*LLJ*, 62). Presumably, the alternative conception is the notion of a person whose ends are not chosen by him but found by him as part of who he is. Presumably, such persons would not opt for the primacy of justice. Being inseparable from their ends, they would not find it reasonable to be bound by any ends-neutral principles. They would want, instead, communities designed to nurture the ends constitutive of who they are. Thus, Sandel maintains that the primacy of justice is the enemy of such communities— communities not just chosen by subjects but rather upon which subjects depend for their identity. Its philosophical anthropology is biased against such communities.

Sandel's second objection follows from the fact that the virtue of justice is appropriate in the circumstances of justice, which are the familiar ones— moderate scarcity, individuals with conflicting aims, limited altruism. Sandel maintains that if these circumstances were replaced by what might be called the circumstances of benevolence, in which (with or without scarcity) people were motivated either by common ends or by benevolent feelings for one another, the virtue of justice would be nugatory, as the virtue of courage would be in the absence of danger. The primacy of justice then presupposes the universality of the circumstances of justice and thus a view of society in which the resolution of conflicting claims is always the highest priority (*LLJ*, 30). Sandel takes it that the circumstances of benevolence do exist often enough (in loving families or other communal organizations) and that the circumstances of benevolence are attractive enough so that we may be morally bound to try to establish them. Accordingly, the primacy of justice is neither absolute nor neutral. It is relative to those situations in which the circumstances of justice prevail, and it tilts us toward establishing the sorts of social arrangements in which the circumstances of justice prevail and against those in which the circumstances of benevolence do. Here, too, primacy of justice is the enemy of any community that goes deeper than mutually self-interested partnerships.

Sandel's first objection rests on a mistaken inference from the fact that deontological liberal theories that accord primacy to justice take the principles of justice to be those that it would be reasonable for people to choose when they did not know what their ends were. This does not presuppose that real people are separate from their ends or that their identities are not constituted by their ends. That I have reached deontological liberalism and the primacy of justice from an account of sovereign interests that takes a person's ends as defining what he must do to be himself should be sufficient contrary evidence. Though subjectivity is separable in our imaginations from the particular person one is, it does not follow that they are separable in fact or that one's personal identity is simply chosen. My whole account is compatible with the notion that a person discovers the ends that comprise her sovereign interest and thus determine the self she must be.

Far from positing the dubious anthropology that Sandel saddles it with, the claim of deontological liberalism is only that evaluation of principles from a standpoint of ignorance of one's ends—even when those ends are constitutive of one's identity—is the appropriate way for all people to determine the principles that spell out what can be strictly required of them. Those whose ends are truly constitutive of their nature need no more than the freedom to pursue their ends without interference. They can only want more if they want to force others to act for those ends, even though those ends are not constitutive of those others' identities.

The telling fact is that if people in the contracting situation knew the ends that were constitutive of their identities, it would still not be rational for them to insist on requirements different from those that people who are ignorant of their ends would agree to. Suppose they all knew themselves to have one constitutive end, E. They could then agree to the principle that everyone will be able to pursue E as far as mutually compatible—that is, up to the point that one's pursuit of E blocks another's. However, this will give them no more than a principle that allowed each to pursue whatever ends he has up to the point of mutual compatibility—no more, that is, than the principle of compatible liberty. And the latter principle is free of a danger that the E-principle poses: If anyone living under the E-principle should come to change his ends such that he no longer desires E, he will find himself living under a principle that would allow the others to impose their ends on him. This shows that principles selected in ignorance of one's ends offer everything that principles selected with knowledge of ends offer, plus added protection against oppression.

Moreover, the danger of oppression only grows when we remember that the contracting situation is imaginary and that whoever formulates its hypothetical conditions may be mistaken about the ends that people have. In that case, assuming that people know their ends threatens to yield principles that require some to serve ends that are in fact constitutive of others and not of them. Principles chosen in ignorance of one's ends, by contrast, still allow each to pursue the ends that are constitutive of her. The claim, then, that fundamental moral requirements should be chosen in the absence of knowledge of ends is not a piece of philosophical anthropology or psychology—it is a methodological device of moral philosophy. Instead of presupposing that people are not constituted by their ends, theories that adopt this device presuppose only that even people who are so constituted can imagine

210

not knowing what their particular ends are and that this is the right way to figure out what they may require of one another, while protecting themselves against having others' ends imposed on them.

Sandel's second objection fails in a related way. Benevolence is not an alternative to justice; when it exists, it exists within justice. When people are moved by benevolence to serve one another's ideals, then they act voluntarily. If they do not act voluntarily, then it is false to call their actions benevolent. But if they do act voluntarily, then they act within the limits on force set by justice and thus within what justice permits, not according to some alternative to justice. To assert the primacy of justice is not to slight benevolence, but to insist that it be genuine.

Similarly, the circumstances of benevolence are not alternatives to the circumstances of justice; rather the former exist within and presuppose the latter. If, thinking they are in the circumstances of benevolence, people try to force someone to act benevolently, they will find themselves in the circumstances of justice—conflicting aims and limited altruism. They have always been standing in those circumstances but did not notice it as long as everyone was acting benevolently voluntarily. The circumstances of justice are not simply some empirical situation; they, too, are a device of moral philosophy. They represent the way the social world appears as soon as anyone has to be forced to comply with another's wishes. Since force is an ever-present possibility, so the circumstances of justice are ever present.

Likewise, in modern societies, if members of loving families disagree and one adult tries to force another adult to comply with his wishes, they will find themselves in the framework of the criminal law. Again, this is because they have always stood in that framework even while they did not notice it. Before they came into conflict they were not acting outside the bounds of law, but precisely within what the law permits. The criminal law is not an alternative to the relations between members of loving families; it girds those families round as the ever-present legal limit on their actions toward one another. So, too, the requirements of justice, rather than being alternatives to benevolence, gird it round as the ever-present moral limit on what people may do to each other against their wills.

We see thus the general mistake made by those who think the primacy of justice is opposed to the value of community. The community that is put forth as a moral value in competition with justice must be real community. Real community exists among people in some interpersonal relationship, when each desires not only his own satisfaction but that of the others as well; the satisfaction of the others must be desired as good in itself, not only as a means to one's own satisfaction, as a slave might desire that his master was happy so that his own life would be less miserable. For the

211

parties to some relationship to desire each other's satisfaction as good in itself, the relationship itself must not be forced on some by others. A forced relationship is no more communal than forced laughter is happy or forced religious observance faithful. Since justice limits force to that amount that protects everyone from being subjugated by others, it protects the social space in which individuals can voluntarily embrace a relationship with others. Real community exists only among people who share their relationship from within the very space that justice keeps clear of force. Sandel's benevolent community presupposes justice rather than posing an alternative to it.

Justice, then, is not only invoked by the enterprise of moralizing as its morality; it is invoked by community as its precondition. Since community can only really exist where people are voluntarily moved to act in pursuit of their shared ends, it cannot exist between people some of whom are being subjugated by others. People who believe they share real community must implicitly believe that their relations are not forms of subjugation and thus that they are compatible with justice. This belief is—as we learned from Hobbes and Locke—the content of the trust presupposed by any stable social existence. Community implicitly promises justice much as speaking implicitly promises truth.

Chapter 4: *From Natural Justice to Social Justice*

> The social system is not an unchangeable order beyond
> human control but a pattern of human action.
> —John Rawls, *A Theory of Justice*

To answer the question of social justice, one must first understand the question. That is the aim of this chapter. Coming to understand the question of social justice is coming to understand how societies evoke a question of justice beyond the question of natural justice. Following the clue that has guided us so far, I shall consider how the structure of society raises the suspicion of subjugation in a distinctive way. This will allow us to formulate the question of social justice as the test of that suspicion. Then the question of social justice is essentially that of whether the structure of a society conforms to those principles for the design of social structures that it would be reasonable for all people to agree to in the natural context. I call these principles "the articles of the social contract."

I contend that a social structure is a pattern of behavior by means of which all or virtually all the members of a society effectively force their fellows to limit their actions to a range of acceptable alternatives. We shall see that this structural force works in ways that are analogous to, but not identical with, the way overt force constrains people's freedom. Among other differences, the behavior that constitutes the structure is generally performed without awareness that it is constituting a structure, indeed, without awareness that its effect is to force people to channel their actions within some acceptable range. Nonetheless, since this structure-constituting behavior does effectively force people, it raises the suspicion of subjugation and thus evokes the question of justice. Though the behavior is not necessarily done with the intention of forcing people, the question of its justice is the same as the question of whether it would be just to behave that way intentionally. It then becomes possible to pose the question of social justice as that of what principles—according to which the pattern of behavior constituting the social structure would be performed intentionally—it would be reasonable for everyone to agree to in the natural context.

213

That structure-constituting behavior is not performed with intent is in keeping with the tendency of social structures to become invisible. Consequently, the need to pose the question of social justice also tends to be unseen, even though, as I shall argue, an answer to that question is implicitly presupposed by the judgments of criminal justice that are normally made in a society. Failure to pose the question of the justice of the structure is not a neutral omission: It is equivalent to treating the structure as if it were just. Here we shall see the relationship between the invisibility of social structure and what is called ideology. In addition to bringing out these and other aspects of the question of social justice, I shall in this section show how the question of social justice as understood by justice as reason's answer to subjugation dovetails with the question as understood by John Rawls's theory of "justice as fairness"—while providing a needed foundation for that theory.

Social Structure

As people live together over time, their forms of interaction come to have regular patterns such that they can be said to share a social system. Eventually, the social system comes to have a rigidity that we can call a structure. The system then confronts each individual with the social equivalent of ruts or channels into which he must fit his normally rational self-interested behavior. As Rawls notes, however, a social system is "a pattern of human action" (*TJ*, 102). It is a system in which people are allotted various amounts of authority, freedom, wealth, burdens, or punishments, and this allotting is done socially—that is, by their fellows behaving in certain regular ways: obeying or enforcing (authority), protecting or refraining from interfering with (freedom), protecting or refraining from taking (wealth), shouldering (burdens), imposing (punishments), and the myriad other actions that support those who perform these behaviors.

A social system is a peculiar thing. If all the members of society had knowledge of the behaviors by which they together constitute the society's structure, together they could change the system as they saw fit (within, of course, the limits of physical nature, human psychology, and the compatibility of system elements). But for each individual the system is barely changeable at all. She has little choice but to fit her actions into the channels of allowable action created by the pattern of behavior of her fellows. This constraint results not only because some of her fellows will use overt force to prevent her from overstepping the channels. The constraining of each individual's options is not done just by the official wielders of force, since (as we saw in discussing Hobbes) they, in turn, are dependent on the general cooperation of others in order to wield their force successfully. Ultimately, the constraining is done by everyone who plays his or her role in the patterns of behavior that constitute the social structure. To ask about the justice of the social system is to ask about the justice of the actions by means of which members of society together create a social structure that constrains the actions of each member.

The question of social justice, then, is not so much a different question from that of natural justice as the same question asked about a different subject—or, rather, about the same subject in a different form. We reached the principles of natural justice by asking for those actions that could withstand the suspicion of subjugation. We shall arrive at the principles of social justice by the same route, except that the actions we consider are those that constitute the structure of the social system. These actions differ in crucial ways from those that are the subject of natural justice. To pose the question of social justice, we must chart these crucial differences.

Consider the most striking differences: Whereas the actions considered under natural justice are single acts (such as murder or theft), social justice asks about patterns of action (such as that which sustains a legal system or a distribution of wealth), systems of behavior rather than individual instances of behavior. Whereas the actions that are the concern of natural justice, being single acts, are caused by some individual, those that concern social justice, being patterns of action, are caused by all, or at least virtually all, members of society collectively, though not necessarily equally. Whereas the actions that are subject to prohibition under natural justice are visible acts, noticeable breaks in normal routine, the patterns of action that social justice asks about tend to be routine and thus invisible. Like the smell of the air or the feel of the ground beneath one, they tend to melt into the background and escape notice.

Further, because the actions that concern natural justice are single and visible, those who cause them generally know in advance of doing them that they are causing them and are thus responsible. The patterns of action that concern social justice, in contrast, tend to be invisible, and those who cause them may not know that they do so until it is brought to their attention and the actions are already underway. I shall express this by saying that the actions with which natural justice is concerned are the product of *actual intentionality*, meaning that they have not only been caused by people but have been intentionally caused; I shall say that the actions of concern to social justice are *potentially intentional*, meaning that people cause them but not necessarily intentionally (that is, not necessarily with the intention of causing a social structure or of constraining people's choices—the actions may otherwise be done on purpose) until they are made aware that they do

215

cause them and could alter them. Once they come to know this, potential intentionality becomes actual. I do not mean to imply that by virtue of knowledge people can control their actions completely. They inevitably come up against real limits built into their needs, emotional dispositions, deeply engrained habits, and the real world. I mean only that, with knowledge, whole societies can come to be as responsible for their actions as individuals can be for theirs.

To ask for the justice of the social system, then, is to ask for the justice of the potentially intentional freedom-constraining actions that constitute it. But asking this question is tantamount to asking whether it would be just for all concerned to do intentionally what they have been doing unintentionally. Posing the question is looking at any society as if it were a vast pattern of intertwining intentional actions by means of which everyone constrains the options of his fellows and asking whether it would be mutually reasonable for all to agree to the principles that govern the actions that constitute this (or any alternative) social structure.

Because we must ask this subject to all the same constraints that were appropriate for the question of natural justice (we cannot assume the moral validity of any existing or potential social arrangement, and so on), we must pose our question about the actions that constitute the social structure by imagining them occurring in the natural context—with one important difference: Now in the natural context—as in Locke's version of the state of nature—there are some binding moral rules. The principles of natural justice are recognized as binding by all rational people. How far people act on these principles will depend on how strongly their sovereign interests press against their reason, but all will feel disposed in some measure to act on them. Thus, we pose the question of social justice by asking whether it would be mutually reasonable (in light of their sovereign interests and of the principles of natural justice) for any group of people jointly and intentionally to undertake the normally invisible pattern of freedom-constraining actions that constitute their or any alternative social structure. With this, we are brought to the social contract as reason's answer to subjugation by the social structure. Note that this question is both a way of determining whether any existing society subjugates its actual members and a way of determining the form that any society would have to take to avoid subjugation.

Before saying more about how the question of social justice can be answered, it will help clarify the question if we look more closely at the nature of social structure, the particular way in which it evokes the suspicion of subjugation, and the causes and implications of its tendency to invisibility. Social structure has three dimensions: political, legal, and economic. For analytic purposes, we can think of these as separate systems or substructures, but in reality, they are, like the three dimensions of space, thoroughly interwoven. Locating any individual's position in a full-bodied social structure will require identifying its coordinates in all three dimensions. Since societies have no reality beyond the members that make them up and the relations in which they stand, the reality of each of the substructures is in the last analysis nothing but a regular pattern of human behavior, including appropriate states of consciousness.

The political system is that by which the separate individuals comprising a society are organized so that they can act as a single body. In it, words are uttered that come to be treated as decisions for the group as a whole. Members come to view those decisions as authoritative, expect one another to comply, and with the help of the legal system sanction one another for not complying. Such patterns of behavior range from those in which every adult participates in the making of group decisions to those in which only one person makes them. All forms, however, are systems of behavior in which virtually everyone in society plays a role, at least by acquiescing to group decisions.

The legal system is the pattern by which rules, including decisions made through the political system, get enforced for the group as a whole. Through it, some specifically designated people are allowed to decide what rules bind the group, what constitutes an infraction of those rules, and to use physical force to prevent or punish infractions of those rules, such that others generally comply with these rules and generally support the designated individuals, and no one else, in the use of physical force.

The economic system is the pattern by which the resources controlled by the group are deployed and distributed. It is the pattern of behavior in which particular people are allowed by the rest to decide what will happen to or with particular things in the world, and other people are, with the help of the legal system, sanctioned when they try to interpose their decisions.

It is evident here that the legal system is implicated in the political and economic systems, and it should be equally obvious that these are implicated in it and in one another. The political system may within some range determine who shall dispose over what things, and the economic system may within some range determine who shall have more things to use to influence the political system, and so on.

How does the suspicion of subjugation arise about the social structure? To see this we must subject the authority of social institutions to Cartesian doubt and distance ourselves from the normal effects of habituation to our own social structure. Doing this is equivalent to looking at social structures in the natural context. What we see then is that a social structure is a system of potentially intentional freedom-constraining actions that are pre-

217

sumptive violations of the principles of natural justice: According to the principle of compatible liberty, force may not be used against a person except to prevent or punish coercive interference with another; but the political system involves the use of force by some people to get others to comply with group decisions, like it or not. According to the principle of compatible liberty, any person has the right to use force to prevent or punish coercive interference by another; but the legal system establishes a monopoly on the use of force and uses force against individuals who exercise their right to use force under the principle of compatible liberty. According to the principle of natural ownership, people own only their bodies, what they need to support their bodies, and more only if good enough and as much is left for others—thus no one may be prevented from using anything beyond this; but the economic system entails the use of force against some people to protect other people's property beyond the limits of natural ownership. Each of the systems is, among other things, a pattern of behavior in which individuals are allotted power over other individuals, backed up by threat of coercion. The social structure is legitimately suspect of being a form of subjugation, in much the same way as assertions of moral authority are suspect. Both have the effect that, by the actions of others, people may be reduced in their ability to pursue their sovereign interests, without true justification.

Structural Force

Seen as composed of freedom-constraining actions, a social structure is a forcing mechanism exercised in a distinctively structural way. Structural force differs in two important ways from the cases that we would normally call exercises of force. I shall indicate these differences by saying that responsibility for structural force is distributive rather than individual and that structural force works its effects by limiting choice rather than by eliminating choice. Take, as examples of normal exercise of force, two cases—one in which a person is literally chained in place by his captor and a second in which a person is confronted by a gunman who commands: "Your money or your life." In both of these cases, responsibility for the force is individual; some identifiable individual or individuals constrain the will of the victim. In both of these cases, the force denies its victim any real choice in the situation. This is clearest in the case of the chained individual, who literally has no alternative to remaining where he is. Although the victim in the second case has the alternative of giving up his life, the unacceptability of that alternative for any normal person renders it ineligible—an option, but not a real option—and has much the same effect as a chain. Normal cases of force effectively eliminate choice.

218

In structural force, responsibility for the constraint on people's wills is distributed among all the members of society who play roles in maintaining the social structure. Such people as police or prison guards will play the crucial role of directly threatening or administering violence. As we already saw in discussing Hobbes's sovereign, however, the direct forcers cannot do their work without the general support of the rest—that is, without the help or at least forbearance of the vast majority of the population playing their roles, giving respect or nonresistance to the enforcers, and supplying them with resources.

To get a handle on the distributive nature of structural force, picture a large crowd of spectators who must pass through a human bottleneck as they leave a stadium. I mean *human bottleneck* literally. Imagine that people are standing shoulder to shoulder in the shape of a bottleneck and that the crowd must pass through this human funnel to get out of the stadium. The people making up the human bottleneck are there with varying degrees of intention; some are there minding their own business, and others are there because they want the crowd to have to pass through just this sort of shape. But all are inclined to stay where they are because they want to, believe they should or must, are conditioned to, or some combination of these. If people in the crowd try to break through the human bottleneck, they will at least be resisted, and where they succeed in making an opening, people from other points in the bottleneck will move to seal it up and prevent their passing through. Other bottleneckers will, at least, support this and even offer to lend a hand. The crowd leaving the stadium will find in this bottleneck varying degrees of resistance to their attempts to break through it, but enough so that they will have to adapt their flow to the shape.

We can say that the crowd is forced into a pattern by the structure of the human bottleneck. But responsibility for the force is distributed among the individuals who man the bottleneck structure. They play their roles more or less unintentionally, and none of those who play their roles intentionally could succeed in keeping the crowd in the shape were it not for the rest of the people making up the bottleneck.

Although the crowd is forced to take on the shape of the bottleneck, individuals in the crowd are not forced to take any specific route within that shape. Unlike normal exercises of force, individuals experiencing structural force are not deprived of all acceptable alternatives but one. They are not deprived of real choices but constrained to choose within a range of options. The bottleneck forces people to take routes within its shape but leaves to their choices which of those routes, in particular, they take. They are still forced to walk where they do, but the force travels through their "free" choices.

In structural force, the target of force has some play. Between the forcing structure and its effects there is room for the operation of free and rational choice by the individuals affected. Although people are constrained to the set of situations in the array because alternatives outside the array are either unacceptable or prohibitively costly, they can exercise real choice among those in the array, selecting the one that they find most desirable. Nonetheless, I contend that, as long as the group is constrained such that its members must choose among the situations in the array determined by the structure, all the individuals are "forced into" the particular situations in which they end up—even if they made some free and rational choices on the way. Structural force can operate through free and rational choices because force need not only take advantage of one's fear (say, of dying); it can also work, often more effectively, by taking advantage of one's rationality.

Suppose an outlaw is lying in wait for a stagecoach, which he knows carries six passengers each wearing a gold watch worth twenty dollars and each carrying about that amount in cash. Our outlaw wants to emerge with three watches and sixty dollars but is indifferent about who gives which. He resolves then to offer the passengers a chance to choose which they will give, although if their choices do not arrive at his desired outcome he will rescind the privilege and take three watches and sixty dollars. Stopping the coach, gun in hand, he orders the passengers to give him either their watch or their cash. The passengers are utility maximizers who regard their watches and their twenty dollars as comparably desirable, though each has a decided, if small, preference for one or the other. As luck would have it, their preferences match the outlaw's desired outcome. Three give up their watches, and three their cash.

Now, take one passenger at random who has given up his watch. Is it not the case that he was forced to give up the watch? It seems odd to say that he was not forced to give up his watch because he had a roughly equally acceptable alternative. To say that seems to focus excessively on what happens in the moment just before the passenger handed over his watch and to ignore that the situation had been set up so that there was a good chance that the outlaw, by allowing the passengers to choose freely and rationally, in light of their preferences, would succeed in subordinating their wills to his ends. A person can be forced to do something even if he has rationally chosen that thing from among other roughly equally acceptable alternatives, provided that the whole array of alternatives has been forced upon him.

This will be no news to con artists and authors of spy stories. They know that a free choice can be the last link in the chain that ties a person to a forced fate. It is possible to get someone to do one's bidding by setting up a situation in which doing one's bidding is a victim's most rational choice, even if there are other choices that are comparably acceptable though less rational for him. It is easy to overlook this, since when a person does what is most rational for him because it is most rational, and not just because it is the only thing acceptable, he seems to be acting freely. And he is, as I have already suggested in speaking about the link between reason and free will. Rather than showing that he is not forced, this shows that force can work through his free choice. An intelligent forcer can capitalize on the tendency of individuals, left free, to do what is most rational for them. Since people forced in this way are less likely to see or feel that they are being forced, force that works through people's more or less predictable free choices is more effective because it is less visible. For this reason we must abandon the notion that force occurs only when a person is presented with only one acceptable alternative. Otherwise, we shall miss the way in which social structures force fates on people while appearing to leave their fates up to them.

The various substructures that compose a social structure exert their forces distributively and through limited choice. Consider, for example, the political system. Overt force is exercised against those who refuse to comply with some arrangement for reaching group decisions. This force is not simply the work of the direct enforcers. They themselves are subject to force if they fail to play their roles as enforcers. And all the enforcers are dependent on the general cooperation—at least, acquiescence—of the rest of society. If other members of society joined the resisters, supplied them with weapons, or refused to supply weapons or food to the enforcers, or if other members refused to take part in the established decision-making arrangement, so that the result was chaos, the direct enforcers would not be able to enforce the political system. The responsibility for this is distributive, though it is not necessarily distributed equally among all members of society.

In addition, the effect of enforcing a political system is not normally to constrain all the members of society to one acceptable alternative. Political systems generally allow their members some options within the enforced arrangement for arriving at group decisions; for example, they may allow voting on candidates or programs. Enforcing a political system constrains people to a range of choices among which they can choose freely and rationally. They are forced to choose within that range, and as they do they complete the work of that force. This feature of structural force makes it appropriate to think of social structures as establishing channels into which people must fit their normal rational self-interested behavior, rather than as commanding people to perform specific actions. The political system, and the social structure generally, force people to take certain courses of action in the way that a rough terrain will force hikers to take certain routes. By   221 its obstacles and openings, its dangers and opportunities, the terrain determines the range of feasible routes among which hikers must choose and thus forces them into one of these.

It is likely at this point that a common objection to contractarian theories will be raised—namely, that social structure is being treated as an artificial arrangement that must be forced on naturally asocial people. In fact, runs the objection, social structures are natural human formations that people participate in voluntarily. In response, note first that the view that social structures are coercive does not imply that they are artificial or unnatural, since forcing people to play social roles may be as natural a human response as using force in self-defense. Second, if the objection is to have weight, it must assert that people truly play their social roles voluntarily—merely seeming to will not do, as the appearance of voluntary conformity can be produced by indoctrination or effective conditioning, which can undermine volition and be as subject to the suspicion of subjugation as overt force can. If people truly play their roles in a social structure voluntarily then they do so within the limits of the principle of compatible liberty. But then there can be no real *requiring* of those limits on liberty (beyond the principles of compatible liberty and natural ownership) of the sort that were listed in considering the components of the social structure. For there to be no real requiring of these greater limits, there can be no sanction threatened or imposed for violating them, and everyone must know that his compliance with the greater limits is strictly voluntary. No social structure could operate on these terms. I mean this both as an empirical claim and a logical point. An arrangement that was truly voluntary, in which each person had real and effective freedom to comply as he wished, could not survive as and would not count as a social structure.

For this reason, the nomadic tribe we pictured in the last chapter is no longer an appropriate image for us. Such a tribe has the component systems of social structure in rudimentary form, but they are not developed enough to represent a clear alteration of voluntary relations. Nomadic groups cannot have great disparities of political power. Their members are too visibly dependent on one another to be able to dispense with voluntary cooperation. What authority leaders have is continually subject to members' power to vote with their feet and thus must continually win everyone's approval. This produces a decentralizing tendency that applies equally to legal power, so that, although people may occasionally enforce rules in the name of the group, there will not generally be an established officialdom with special powers for this purpose. Accumulation of property is limited by what people can carry, drag, or drive, and this places a strict limit on the degree to which anyone can own things beyond the limits of natural ownership. Accordingly, although there are, in reality, many gradations in between, for our purposes it will serve clarity to call the rudiments of social structure in a nomadic group a *social order*, and reserve for settled territorial peoples, the term *social structure*. By the latter, I shall understand patterns of behavior that have crystalized in a way that makes them no longer truly voluntary.

In the last analysis, however, this point is not a matter of the definition of social structure nor of the empirical description of actual territorial societies. It is a matter of moral philosophy. We come to view social structures as systems of forced cooperation not because we believe that people would not cooperate in the same way voluntarily. We do so, rather, because we recognize that when we question the justice of the terms of a social system supported by coercion in some form, even where people comply voluntarily so that coercion is never needed, we are inquiring about what people can rightly be required to do. To find what they can rightly be required to do whether they want to or not, we must ask what they can be required to do against their wills, when they are not inclined to cooperate voluntarily. The claim that social structures ought not be viewed as coercive is analogous to the claim that justice ought to be based on benevolence: Since requirements override people's wills, the validity of requirements cannot be tested by assuming a will to comply. Accordingly, even if it were the case that the people did voluntarily the very acts that their social structures required of them, we would still have to assume that they were not inclined to comply voluntarily in order to determine if the requirements of those structures were just.

Ideology and the Invisibility of Social Structure

The very strangeness of looking at social structures as patterns of action presumptively in violation of natural justice testifies to the tendency of social structures to be invisible. This tendency is the product of three causes. First, it seems to be a general law of human psychology that what occurs regularly fades from attention. After a while I am no longer aware of the seat I sit upon, no longer feel the clothes I put on this morning, no longer notice the smell of the air, the weight of the atmosphere, or the music of my own language. The second cause is conditioning. Surrounded by people acting out roles in stable patterns of activity, we come to perceive that as how people naturally are (a fact recorded in numerous languages by the kinship of the terms for *stranger* and *strange*). Society becomes second nature. Its patterns do not seem to be actions undertaken, as much as necessities automatically played out, the natural metabolism of social existence. The third cause is the presence of choice in structural force. Since

223

structural force works on people in ways that leave them still able to choose among options, social structures need not overtly obtrude into people's lives. Looking at their local situation, individuals will see their ability to make a choice as if that were the full reality. And if the social structure is already invisible because of the first two causes mentioned, this experience of choice in their local situation will only seem to confirm that they are not being forced and thus render the social structure that much harder to see. Although this invisibility occurs in various degrees in different societies and individuals, it is an extremely pervasive tendency. What is more, it is not a morally neutral tendency.

Suppose that, within a shared social structure, I see someone take a sheep from a field legally owned by another, and I judge this to be an unjust taking, a theft. For this I must believe that what was taken was not something that the presumed owner had himself previously taken from the presumed thief unjustly. The same observed event will yield a different judgment if I learn that what seemed to me an act of taking what belonged to another was, in fact, the taking back of what the first took without justification. What is crucial here is not only that new facts will alter my judgment. The new facts will alter my judgment by virtue of the judgment I make about those facts. If I judge the prior act of taking to have been unjust, then I shall revise my judgment about the taking I saw. If I judge that the prior act was not unjust, then I shall hold to my original judgment about the act I saw.

The first judgment—that the sheep taking is a theft—is an example of the criminal justice judgments typically made within a society. The question of social justice, by contrast, applies to such questions as whether the original ownership of the sheep (assuming there are not enough and as good to go around for everyone) is just. If we answer this question of social justice negatively, it will have an effect on the validity of typical criminal justice judgments. Interestingly, Kant makes the same point, not about theft but about charity: "Although we may be entirely within our rights, according to the law of the land and the rules of our social structure, we may nevertheless be participating in general injustice, and in giving to an unfortunate man we do not give him a gratuity but only help to return to him that of which the general injustice of our system has deprived him" (*LE*, 194). That our social structure is unjust in a way that has deprived someone of what is rightfully his can transform what appears to be charity into voluntary restitution, as it can transform what appears to be theft into forced restitution. It is neither charity to receive, nor theft to take, what was being kept from one unjustly. It follows that normal criminal justice judgments presuppose (generally affirmative) judgments about the justice of the social structure.

The need to consider these latter judgments is rarely noticed because of the general invisibility of the social structure.

This invisibility is not neutral in its effect because the relationship of presupposition between criminal justice judgments and judgments of social justice is asymmetrical. Suppose that, without considering the justice of the social structure, I make an ordinary criminal justice judgment condemning some observed act, be it sheep taking or bank robbing. Only a negative judgment about the justice of the structure can overturn my criminal justice judgment. Learning that the putative theft was the taking of something owned unjustly will lead me to doubt that the observed act was itself unjust. Learning that the action I observed was not done in response to an injustice leaves my ordinary judgment unchanged. Learning that the social structure is just (meaning, at least, not unjust in a way that is relevant to the observed act) is equivalent to learning that I can ignore the question of the justice of the social structure in making my criminal justice judgment. But, then, ignoring the question of the justice of the social structure when making criminal justice judgments is equivalent to treating it as if it were just. It follows that, when we make ordinary criminal justice judgments without considering the question of social justice, by default we make positive judgments about the justice of the social structure. In the same degree as the social structure tends toward invisibility, criminal justice judgments will perforce ignore the structure and unthinkingly presuppose positive judgments about the justice of the social structure. A typical judgment that someone has stolen something presupposes that the property arrangements that he has upset were just.

That ignoring the social context in one's ordinary judgments of justice has the effect of conferring a positive judgment about the justice of the social structure is the core of what is called ideology. Ideology bestows its positive judgment precisely by our not noticing how the injustice of a social structure alters the justice of individual acts. As a consequence, judgments of natural justice appear sufficient for determining the justice of ordinary acts. This is clear enough from the example of criminal justice. Looking only at whether the criminal has defaulted on his obligations to society amounts to treating him as subject simply to requirements of natural justice (expanded to include the prevailing property relations that have become second nature). This belief that ordinary judgments of natural justice suffice is of a piece with not noticing the social structure as relevant to the justice of individual acts. Both reflect that the social structure has disappeared into the background, becoming part of the natural landscape in which actions take place. Its very disappearance bestows a positive judgment on the justice of the social structure. This is what gives ideology its distinctive power. It works just to   225 the extent that it is not noticed. By this means, rather than by any conscious propagandizing, institutions like those of criminal justice convey a powerful ideological message in support of the justice of existing societies.[1] I shall have more to say about invisibility and ideology in the first two sections of the following chapter.

The Social Contract and the Question of Social Justice

One interesting consequence of the social structure's tendency to invisibility is that the question of social justice has a history. The question could not be widely entertained until people generally began to see their social structures as intentionally alterable. Thus, it only appeared as a live social question, not just a matter of utopian fantasizing, around the time of the birth of capitalism and modern science, in the seventeenth century. By then, the printing press had already created a public consciousness, parliaments were actively tinkering with social relations, economic relations were coming unhinged from tradition and being remade according to freely undertaken contracts, and all of nature was a great machine to be made over in the service of human goals. Human beings could begin to take responsibility for their social structures because they began to see their causal role in maintaining or altering them. It is no accident that seventeenth-century social theorists began to think of society as the sort of thing that could be created by a contract. I take it then that the question of social justice characteristically arises as a live social question when a settled territorial society recognizes that its social structure is an alterable pattern of behavior that is rightly suspect of subjugating some or all of its members in violation of the principles of natural justice.

The means for overcoming this suspicion is the same as we saw earlier. It is necessary to show that people in the natural context, now armed with the principles of natural justice, would all find it mutually reasonable in light of their sovereign interests to agree to be subject to a social structure in some form. A social structure in this form would overcome the suspicion of subjugation and be just. Any other form would be just insofar as it approximated it, and unjust in the degree that it diverged from it.

It might seem that social structures could never overcome the suspicion of subjugation. Whatever would be reasonable for people to agree to, they, in fact, do not agree to be members of a social structure: They are just born into one and find themselves subject to it with few real alternatives outside it. But recall that the question here is always a theoretical one about what it would be reasonable to agree to, not an empirical one about actual agreement. As we saw earlier, the theoretical question is not only necessary

226

for determining whether people are currently subjugated by what they do or do not actually agree to, it is also necessary for determining how far their actual agreement ought to be determinative.

This last point is of crucial importance in considering whether it would be reasonable to agree to some or any social structure. On that, actual agreement is impossible, since the social structure cannot be re-created for each generation. Moreover, even if it could be remade for each generation, the effect would be to reduce drastically the advantages that recommend agreeing to social structures in the first place. This is because a social structure is most advantageous as a stable setting in which to grow from infancy to the maturity needed to agree intelligently to anything. From birth, people get the benefits of unified action from the political system, of protection from the legal system, and of prosperity from the economic system. Accordingly, it would not be reasonable for people to insist on their actual voluntary agreement as a condition for participation in social structures, although they might insist on the right to leave them, once they are grown. If this is so, then the question of social justice is that of whether it would be reasonable for people in the natural context to agree to be subject to an ongoing social structure that it would not be possible for them to agree to actually and, if so, what principles for the design of the social structure would it be reasonable for them to accept. A social structure designed according to those principles, assuming one could be devised, would be just because it would acquit itself of the charge of subjugation.

The principles of social justice are the principles governing social structures to which people would agree subject to the conditions of the social contract—that is, in the natural context, under the appropriate restrictions on knowledge, and so on. Since social structures that conform to these principles do not subjugate their participants, violations of the principles of social justice are wrong for the same reasons as violations of the principles of natural justice. The requirements of social justice are, however, narrower in their scope than those of natural justice. While principles of natural justice spell out obligations owed by all human beings to one another, principles of social justice spell out obligations owed only between members of the same society. This does not mean that the principles of social justice are not binding on everyone. They spell out the standards according to which everyone should govern his actions toward whomever he shares a social structure with, and no one else. In this respect, the obligations of social justice are like the obligations of friendship, obligations that everyone is under toward whomever is her friend and no one else. Though in the larger sense we find both natural and social justice by applications of the social contract theory, I mark the passage from nomadic tribe to settled territorial

227

society, from obligations owed simply to all human beings and those owed one another by members of the same society, and from requirements on particular actions to standards for the design of social structures, by passing from speaking of the natural covenant to speaking of the social contract as such.

That social structures force cooperation beyond the principles of natural justice explains why principles of social justice establish only the obligations owed to each other by the members of the same social structure. Only among the participants in the same system of forced cooperation might benefits be produced to offset the forced extraction of cooperative efforts and thus render them reasonable. In contrast to the principles of social justice (and with minor qualifications for the principle of intergenerational solicitude and the duty of easy rescue), the principles of natural justice—which are obligations owed by all people to all others—require only noninterference. It is reasonable for all people to give and require of one another noninterference, whether or not they share a social structure. But it is only reasonable for people to agree to being required to respect additional limits and provide additional benefits beyond those of noninterference with people who will provide them counterbalancing benefits in return. To require people to provide some level of benefits for others, irrespective of whether they share a social structure in which they are producing benefits for each other, is to open people to the possibility of substantial uncompensated sacrifice for the benefit of limitless numbers of others in the universe. The number of strangers who might make a claim on one, including those from other planets with the characteristics requisite to be members of the moral community, is virtually infinite—and the condition of their need could be so great as to be virtually infinite.

The distinction between natural and social justice embodies the distinction often represented as that between "negative freedom" (freedom from interference) and "positive freedom" (possession of the means to realize one's choices).[2] Negative freedom requires that others not coerce me and the like, whereas positive freedom requires that others afford me the education and resources needed to realize my choices. This way of putting the matter is unsatisfactory because it presents it as a conflict between two ways of interpreting the ideal of freedom, leaving unclear how one determines which sort of freedom one is entitled to and when. In my view, negative freedom corresponds to the requirements of natural justice and is thus what everyone is entitled to irrespective of whether they cooperate. Positive freedom is essentially freedom to use the benefits of a system of forced cooperation and is thus what everyone is entitled to from those with whom they cooperate to produce those benefits. Negative freedom is what everyone owes everyone else naturally; positive freedom is what the members of the same society owe one another. The distribution of the latter is a matter of social justice.

A social structure is a system of collectively coerced cooperation. To prove that it is just, we must prove that it does not subjugate by showing that, in fact, people have more power and resources for promoting their sovereign interests in the positions sustained by the social structure than outside them. But such a proof is only the beginning of the refutation of subjugation. Looked at for its effect on individuals, a social structure is a structure of social positions created by the concerted if unintentional action of all its members. What is important about these positions is that they determine at least the outer boundaries of the life prospects of the individuals born into them, by determining the extent of power and resources available to individuals in these positions for the realization of their goals. Implicit in recognizing that social structures are patterns of action is acknowledging that everyone, by playing his part in the structure, contributes to imposing coercive limits on every individual's pursuit of his sovereign interest. Accordingly, once the suspicion of subjugation is raised, it is not satisfied simply by showing that people are better off in social structures than in the wild. The suspicion that the system is a means for subjugating some to others remains.

What must be proven about any particular social structure, then, is not only that it is not subjugating in comparison with the absence of any such structure but also that the particular social structure itself is not a means for subjugating anyone to anyone else. To prove this, we must ask for the principles for the design of social structures for which each can be given the best reasons, compatible with like reasons for everyone else, compared to any other possible set of principles. The principles that satisfy this test are the articles of the social contract; they are the principles of social justice. Showing that a social structure conforms to them refutes the suspicion of subjugation. A society meeting this test is just because in it no person can complain of subjugation due to the design of the social structure. The social contract is reason's answer to subjugation by the social structure.

The question of social justice, then, is this: What are the principles governing the freedom-constraining actions that make up a social structure that everyone, subject to the conditions of the natural context, could be given the best reasons for accepting, compared to any other possible principles? In chapter 5, I shall try to answer this question.

Justice and Fairness

It is a major contention of this book that "justice as fairness"—John Rawls's version of social contract theory—contains most of the elements necessary   229 to pose the question of social justice correctly, and much of the correct answer. I contend, however, that Rawls, operating within the prevailing skepticism about reason and moral knowledge, has formulated his theory largely on intuitive grounds and thus without a foundation that could guide the construction of the theory where intuitions are vague and that could validate the conclusions of the theory where they conflict with others' intuitions. I shall present the main features of Rawls's theory, its problems and their remedies, beginning in the third section of chapter 5 below. I shall argue that "justice as fairness" is a social contract theory of justice in need of a theory of the social contract, in need of an account of why and how the social contract is the correct shape of moral reasoning; I shall try to show that justice as reason's answer to subjugation supplies this needed foundation for justice as fairness. The appeal of Rawls's theory lies in that he has largely correctly formulated the test for subjugation in social structures, and the truth of his conclusions lies in that reason requires the elimination of subjugation from human relations. Moreover, justice as reason's answer to subjugation paves the way for remedying the weaknesses in Rawls's own formulation. If this is true, however, then we should expect the conception of the question of social justice implied by justice as reason's answer to subjugation to coincide with that implied by justice as fairness. In the remainder of this section, I want to show this coincidence. Doing so will shed light on the question of social justice from yet another, and I think quite revealing, angle.

I have argued that posing the question of social justice requires asking whether, under the conditions of the natural context, the members of a society would agree to perform intentionally the actions that constitute its social structure. This amounts to treating those actions as if they were the ordinary actions people undertake intentionally everyday. Since the actions that constitute a social structure are normally done unintentionally, this involves an inversion of normal moral evaluation. Normally, we ignore the social structure, take it as the given landscape upon which our intentional actions occur, and we apply moral evaluation to those intentional actions. Posing the question of social justice involves treating the actions that we do not usually regard as intentional as if they were intentionally done by the whole society. This inversion is already suggested in the phrase justice as fairness, which carries an air of paradox not lost on its author. In the article bearing this title, Rawls acknowledged that "in ordinary speech, fairness applies more particularly to practices in which there is a choice whether to engage or not (e.g., in games, business competition), and justice to practices in which there is no choice (e.g., in slavery)."[3] Justice as fairness entreats us to consider institutional arrangements that we do not enter by choice as

230

if they were the product of choice and asks us to determine if they would be chosen under conditions that were fair—that is, conditions in which no one could exercise power over others to force agreement.

That principles of collective choice are to be applied to the unchosen contours of social life is carried forth in *A Theory of Justice*. Rawls specifies the "basic structure of society," as distinct from "private associations" or "voluntary cooperative arrangements," as the "primary subject of justice" (*TJ*, 7, 8):

> The intuitive notion here is that this structure contains various social positions and that men born into different positions have different expectations of life determined, in part, by the political system as well as by economic and social circumstances. In this way the institutions of society favor certain starting places over others. These are especially deep inequalities. Not only are they pervasive, but they affect men's initial chances in life; yet they cannot possibly be justified by an appeal to the notions of merit or desert. It is these inequalities, presumably inevitable in the basic structure of any society, to which the principles of social justice must in the first instance apply. (*TJ*, 7)

Rawls gives no satisfactory answer as to why it is appropriate to test these unchosen contours of social life by whether they would be chosen. He gives hints to be sure: "No society can," he writes, "be a scheme of cooperation which men enter voluntarily in a literal sense; each person finds himself placed at birth in some particular position in some particular society, and the nature of this position materially affects his life prospects. Yet a society satisfying the principles of justice as fairness comes as close as a society can to being a voluntary scheme, for it meets the principles which free and equal persons would assent to under circumstances that are fair" (*TJ*, 13). "Unjust social relations are themselves a kind of extortion, even violence" (*TJ*, 343). With these remarks, Rawls comes very close to seeing that requiring a society to satisfy the principles people would agree to under conditions of fairness is equivalent to eliminating subjugation from the relations in that society. When Rawls comes to defend his conception, however, his argument is essentially intuitive. He speaks of describing the choice situation so that it incorporates "commonly shared presumptions," making vivid "restrictions that it seems reasonable to impose on arguments for principles of justice," and then modifying the situation as necessary in order to bring its results in line with "our considered convictions of justice" (*TJ*, 18–19). Rawls's candor here is a model for philosophers. But the result surely cannot claim jurisdiction beyond those who share our commonly shared presumptions, to whom the restrictions imposed on arguments seem

231

reasonable and whose convictions of justice match those that emerge from justice as fairness. It thus cannot generate requirements that would override those whose convictions are contrary; which is to say, it cannot generate requirements at all.[4]

I think the remedy for this lies in seeing that the paradox in justice as fairness is only apparent. Social structures are patterns of behavior that can become intentional if they are not already, since they are, in fact, caused by the members of society. To entertain the question of social justice is to recognize this causal role and, to the extent that the question is entertained by a society, to view the social structure or at least its continuation as a matter of intentional action. The actions that each person does in acting out his social part are—for purposes of evaluation—appropriately viewed as chosen. Those actions are rightly subject to assessment because, by sustaining a social structure, they limit others' ability to pursue their sovereign interests (what Rawls calls their "life prospects"), and thus they evoke the suspicion of subjugation. When these actions are shown to be the sort that all would rationally agree to when none had power over others, they are thereby shown to serve everyone's sovereign interests in a way that overcomes the suspicion of subjugation. A society of which this can be said is then voluntary in the concrete sense that no one in it is being subjugated by another, and a society that fails this test is, to that extent, a form of extortion, even violence. But if the actions that sustain a social structure can rightly be regarded as chosen, and if showing that the actions are the sort all would rationally agree to shows them to be nonsubjugating, and if that shows them to be just, then justice *is* fairness applied to the actions that constitute the social structure. The appearance of paradox arose not because fairness is inappropriate to the actions constituting the social structure, but because the tendency of the social structure to be invisible and seem wholly beyond choice makes it appear inappropriate. I contend, then, that justice as reason's answer to subjugation transforms justice as fairness from *a* into *the* theory of justice.

We ask the question of the justice of the social structure by asking whether the set of actions that constitute it subjugate the participants in that structure. And we ask that by asking whether, subject to the conditions of the natural context, it would be reasonable for them to agree to that structure or, more generally, whether that structure conforms to the principles for the design of social structures that everyone can be given the best reasons for accepting, compared to any alternative principles. The principles that pass this test are the principles of social justice. As we look for these principles, bear in mind that, as a result of moving from judgments about particular actions to standards for the design of social structures, the principles of social justice do not fit into the mold of straightforward commands, as do the principles of natural justice. Though they represent requirements to be sure, the principles of social justice will be more like ideals that social structures must in their overall effect approximate. Thus, judgments of social justice will be complex, requiring the combination and balancing of many considerations. We shall not, therefore, end with a blueprint for the just society, but with a set of ideals against which the justice of existing or proposed societies must be measured.

Chapter 5: *Social Justice and the Social Contract*

> Justice being taken away, then, what are
> kingdoms but great robberies?
> —St. Augustine, *The City of God*

Law, Politics, and the Libertarian Blindness: From Locke to Nozick

Although the question of social justice can be asked about a particular society, its answer will be a set of principles by which the justice of any society—actual or possible—can be gauged. To simplify the task of identifying these principles, think of the three components of social structure— the political, legal, and economic systems—as coextensive, that is, as governing the same piece of land and group of people. This amounts to thinking of social structures as coterminous with states. But since states may, in actuality, contain insular societies within their borders or may be integrated into transnational societies with their own social structure, bear in mind that the focus on the state is a simplification. If we can arrive at the principles of social justice in this way, we can later introduce the modifications necessary to do justice to those cases where social structure does not coincide with the state.

Let us ask whether, and if so on what terms, it would be reasonable for people to agree to be subject to the three substructures that make up a social structure. Because the three are intertwined, answers with regard to each depend in part on the answers regarding the others. Let us turn first to the legal system. When and if we find some form of political system and of economic system acceptable, the legal system will also enforce the rules constitutive of those systems. Until then, however, let us assume that the legal system will be used only to enforce the principles of natural justice. On what terms could a system that forcibly deprived people of their right to enforce these principles themselves be acquitted of subjugating them? Here Locke's answer is compelling: In the state of nature—that is, in the absence of a legal system—freedom from subjugation "is very uncertain and constantly exposed to the invasion of others." This is so for several reasons.

First, because

> there wants an established, settled, known law, received and allowed by common consent to be the standard of right and wrong. . . . For though the law of Nature be plain and intelligible to all rational creatures, yet men, being biased by their interest . . . are not apt to allow of it as a law binding to them in . . . their particular cases.
>
> Secondly, in the state of nature there wants a known and indifferent judge, with authority to determine all differences according to the established law. For every one in that state being both judge and executioner of the law of Nature, men being partial to themselves, passion and revenge is apt to carry them too far, and with too much heat in their own cases . . . , make them remiss in other men's.
>
> Thirdly, in the state of Nature there often wants power to back and support the sentence when right, and to give it due execution. . . . [R]esistance many times makes the punishment dangerous . . . to those who attempt it. (*ECG*, secs. 124–26)

Insofar as it is reasonable for everyone to agree to be bound by the principles of natural justice in the first place, it will be reasonable to agree to the means to their sure and effective enforcement. Since the principles of natural justice prohibit subjugation, the more effectively the principles are enforced the less subjugation there will be. It will then be reasonable for all to agree to be subject to a legal system insofar as it more effectively and securely enforces the principles of natural justice for all alike than they would be enforced privately. Legal systems only overcome the suspicion of subjugation insofar as this is true, and I shall assume that a legal system of which it is true can be constructed. If there are rules constitutive of a political and an economic system that it would be reasonable for all to agree to, the same argument will extend to such a legal system the power to enforce those rules as well.

Turning to the political system, we must ask whether (and if so, on what terms) it would be reasonable for all people to agree to be subject to a system that forced all to comply with decisions made for the group as a whole. If there are rules governing legal and economic systems that it would be reasonable for all to agree to, then the political system must be bound to these if its decisions are not to subjugate people. Accordingly, these rules will function for it as "constitutional limits," effectively unalterable—leaving room for such legal coercion as is necessary for its legitimate purposes and for such taxation as is necessary to provide for them. Political decisions, prohibited from overturning legal and economic arrangements that are not

235

subjugating, would seem to pose no threat of subjugation if they are made with free and open discussion, enriched with the widest information, and subject to real majority rule. The advantage of majority rule is not that a majority is any more likely to judge wisely than a minority, but that any system other than majority rule gives a minority the right to determine the fate of the majority. That would give members of the minority greater power in determining the group's fate than other members have. Requiring a two-thirds vote allows one-third plus one to decide, and requiring unanimity lets one person decide for all. Anything but majority rule gives some people more power than others in shaping group decisions. The advantage of majority rule is that it is, as Winston Churchill said of democracy, the worst form of government except for all the rest.

These remarks are admittedly scant. Adequate treatment of the design of a just political system would require a book of its own. I shall assume that where legal and economic justice can be protected by constitutional limits on political decision making, and where such limited decision making as remains is made by majority rule after full, open, and informed discussion, the advantages of being able to act as a unified group—for the purposes of international relations, defense, promotion of culture, education, scientific research and exploration, long-term husbandry of natural resources including population and land, establishment of health and safety regulations and standard weights and measures, provision of emergency services and maintenance of cities, and undertaking of projects too large in investment and impact to be left to private initiative, such as the building of canals, roads, and railways—serve people's sovereign interests in ways that outweigh their having to go along with the majority when they do not wish to, so that the overall effect is nonsubjugating. I take it that some form of *constitutionally limited majoritarianism* would be reasonable for all to agree to in the natural context.

The hardest problem is posed by the economic system, because it poses a double threat of subjugation. The first, and in some ways less important, is the one it shares with the other substructures. The economic system is a pattern of behavior that includes the use of force to assure particular people of control over things in the world to the exclusion of other people. This use of force is one threat of subjugation. It can, in general, be justified if necessary to promote an otherwise unattainable level of prosperity, since this prosperity, appropriately distributed, could serve people's ability to pursue their sovereign interests enough to outweigh the limits it imposes.

The more profound threat of subjugation in a property system is the one that Rousseau recognized—namely, that once the Lockean proviso can no longer be met, once all resources are owned exclusively, those who own property have socially sustained means to get others to labor for them. A

236

system of exclusive property is a system of forced labor. Because of the negative connotation of the term *forced labor,* it is extremely important to remember that here it refers not to the sort of thing that goes on in the Gulag Archipelago but strictly to the leverage that ownership of property gives owners over nonowners in a system of exclusive ownership. Nothing is said here about whether owners intend to force nonowners, and the question of whether such force can be morally justified is open. Bear in mind also that we are now talking about a right of property beyond that conveyed by the principle of natural ownership. We return here to the moral boundary at which the property right conferred by natural justice ends and speak now of property in systems of exclusive ownership, where everything usable is already owned and there is surely not anything left over to satisfy the Lockean proviso—at least as Locke understood it.

At this boundary, European moral theory forks into two lines. One, following Locke, takes property in things (meaning things beyond one's body or immediate survival needs, even in a system of exclusive ownership) to be a natural right and thus its protection simply as the protection of natural freedom itself. As a natural right, what advantages property may give its owner are thought to be no different than the advantages she gains from any other of her natural gifts, such as her greater intelligence or physical strength. The other line, following Rousseau, takes property to be a power artificially created by society and its protection as the protection of the power of those fortunate enough to own some. Such property is at least suspect as an indirect means of slavery, since those who own little or nothing are effectively forced on pain of starvation or pauperization to work for those who own much. The first tradition looks at property from the standpoint of the owner, the second from that of the nonowner. The first sees it as nec-essary to protect the owner from subjugation; the second sees it as a potential means to subjugate the nonowner. A property system is thus subject to suspicion of subjugation from both ends: Too limited rights of ownership may subjugate owners, but too extensive rights may subjugate nonowners. Accordingly, a property system must prove its justice by proving that it is a system that it would be reasonable for everyone to agree to whether or not she owned property.

Much of the discussion that follows is addressed to this complex problem. Two brief remarks are in order. First, because the legal system will enforce the rules constitutive of the economic system and the political system will function within the constraints of that system, no matter how just the legal or political systems are in themselves, they can be no more just in their effect than the economic system is. If the economic system enforces a form of forced labor that is subjugating, then the legal system, no matter how impartial and effective, will protect that subjugation by protecting the pos-   237 sessions that are a means to it. In the same way, the political system, no matter how open or representative, will reproduce that subjugation because the economic arrangements will give some people disproportionately greater power than others to influence the outcomes of majority decisions.

Second, we saw in the previous section that criminal justice proceedings against thieves are only just on the assumption that the property system from which they deviated is not itself unjust. We can now say more clearly what is at stake here. The property system is a form of legally protected forced labor. If the social structure is a system by which some people are subjugated to others, then the violent reactions of the subjugated, which would otherwise be unjust aggression, are to that extent arguably justified, or at least excusable responses to their subjugation. Accordingly, in an unjust society, those who could but do not alter that injustice bear some responsibility for the criminality in that society. Those who would condemn criminality must turn to the problem of making sure that their society—and particularly its economic system—is just.

These considerations noted, let us proceed down the Lockean fork in European moral theory. Property is viewed as part of its owner's freedom. In the contemporary period, the Lockean line is represented in the theory of libertarianism. This theory holds that any attempt to limit people in the use of property they have accumulated without force or fraud amounts to slavery and is for that reason unjust. In this view, a free enterprise capitalist system, limited only to prohibit force or fraud, is just, no matter how great or unequal the distribution of property that results from it.[1] This position is more extreme than one that defends free enterprise on instrumental grounds, as the most likely to yield a free society.[2] The libertarian defense of free enterprise capitalism is not instrumental but righteous. It defends it as each person's natural right. It holds the right to virtually unlimited accumulation of property as part of each person's freedom and thus holds limitations on property as slavery, irrespective of the practical effects of this or that system. I say "virtually," because we shall see that this position does allow one limit on accumulation—namely, a version of the Lockean proviso. It does not, however, interpret this proviso in a way that answers the Rousseauian objection.

The "instrumental" defense of free enterprise capitalism is compatible with recognizing that property is a threat to the freedom of nonowners. It need only hold that limits on property are an even worse threat and that, all told, free enterprise will likely produce a freer society. This approach need not categorically oppose those limits on property that are necessary to protect the freedom of nonowners. The "righteous" libertarian, by contrast, seeing property as part of owners' freedom, must regard any such limits as

238

unredeemed subjugation. Indeed, Robert Nozick, libertarian capitalism's recent defender, claims that such limits amount to ownership rights in the person limited, in short, to slavery (*ASU*, 169).

Libertarianism is blind to the coercive effect of property on nonowners. Because libertarianism is itself a protest against coercion, we should then expect to find libertarianism guilty of begging the question, assuming in advance that property is not coercive. When we take Nozick's version as an example, we find exactly this, in fact in several forms. For example, libertarianism identifies coercion as physical aggression and prohibits its use against those who have not initiated physical aggression against others (*ASU*, 32–33). Because property can be obtained without physical aggression against others, it is not coercive. But physical aggression is opposed because it coerces, not because it is physical or aggressive or even because it hurts— otherwise the libertarian ought to be a pacifist instead. A prohibition against physical aggression in the name of freedom is not a rejection of physical aggression as inherently evil but as a means to coerce people. Accordingly, a theory that gets its credibility from its defense of freedom must treat physical aggression and coercion as distinct concepts, oppose the former as a means to or a case of the latter, and oppose anything else that is a means to or case of coercion as well. Since such a theory cannot identify coercion with any particular means to it, it must be an open question whether property ownership is coercive, even if ownership does not involve the use of physical aggression against others. If libertarianism treats the latter as a closed question, it assumes in advance that property ownership is not coercive— when that is precisely what it must prove.

The same question begging turns up again and again in Nozick's argument. Nozick's libertarian capitalism includes an "entitlement theory" of property rights built upon the Lockean notion that a right to acquire property arises from mixing one's labor with things in the unowned state (*ASU*, 150– 53, 174–82). Other than this, the only way to acquire property justly is by the free consent of its owner, through gift, bequest, or exchange. With one exception, the validity of the right to property depends strictly on how the property was obtained, with no limit on how much is obtained. The exception is Nozick's version of the Lockean proviso, and for our purposes it will be instructive to consider what Nozick includes under the proviso.

According to Nozick, the Lockean proviso stipulates that no process will give rise to a property right in a thing "if the position of others no longer at liberty to use the thing is thereby worsened" (*ASU*, 178). What this worsening consists in must be defined. It cannot be a matter of violating others' rights to own things, because it is part of the determination of such rights in the first place. It is revealing that when Nozick comes to define the worsening that would bring the Lockean proviso into play, he considers only two possibilities: "Someone may be made worse off by another's appropriation in two ways: first, by losing the opportunity to improve his situation by a particular appropriation or any one; and second, by no longer being able to use freely (without appropriation) what he previously could" (*ASU*, 176). That is, one can be made worse off by another's appropriation by either having less to appropriate oneself, or by having less to use (whether or not appropriated). Nozick rejects the first, since it would make appropriation illegitimate as soon as there was no longer enough for everyone to own a decent piece. This will hardly do for a defense of capitalism. He picks the second and weaker possibility (*ASU*, 176, 178). He then asks whether "a system allowing appropriation and permanent property" worsens the situation of people in this second sense. In response, he adduces the traditional argument of capitalism's higher productivity. In other words, even though there is little or nothing left to appropriate for the vast majority of people, beyond property for personal use, they have the use of more things than they would have had, had private appropriation not been allowed. Thus, as Nozick interprets it, the Lockean proviso is compatible with capitalism, even though it is a system of exclusive property.

Nozick puts a more permissive interpretation on the Lockean proviso than Locke, who seems to have meant by it something rather close to the first alternative Nozick considers. With North America mostly empty and only an ocean away, Locke felt that the proviso in its toughest form was easily satisfied "since there is land enough in the world to suffice double the inhabitants" (*ECG*, sec. 36). He did not feel the same pressure that Nozick does to find a way of understanding the proviso so it can be satisfied in a world in which virtually all natural resources are owned. Nozick's rendering permits this. The only accumulations it prohibits would be those in which a person came (albeit legitimately) to own all the sources of some absolutely necessary natural resource, such as water (*ASU*, 180).

Of greatest interest in Nozick's account of the proviso, however, is what he does not include under it. Nozick limits the alternative renderings of the proviso to two, one that would rule capitalism out aborning, the other which happens to fit perfectly with the traditional justifications of capitalism. Nozick never considers the one way in which a person's situation could be worsened by an appropriation that would seem to be of central concern to a libertarian: An appropriation by one person might lead to a decrease in the freedom of another by increasing the ability of the property owner to dictate the conditions of the other's life and work.

The Lockean proviso—permissively interpreted—is the only constraint on the right of property that Nozick allows, beyond the prohibition against

240

physical aggression. Since the proviso omits reference to how the leverage that property gives might decrease the freedom of others, Nozick takes the right to property as the right to do anything with one's property other than use it as a means to physical aggression against others who are nonaggressive. By default, Nozick effectively defines the right to property as including the right to exercise whatever leverage over others property ownership might give. Defining the right this way is in itself unobjectionable, as long as one is still willing to consider the question of whether granting such a right is compatible with or conducive to freedom. The argument becomes circular when Nozick appeals to the right so defined as an answer to that question!

This occurs when Nozick takes up the question of whether the accumulation of large amounts of property threatens the freedom of workers. He writes, "Some readers will object to my speaking frequently of voluntary exchanges on the ground that some actions (for example, workers accepting a wage position) are not really voluntary because one party faces severely limited options, with all others being much worse than the one he chooses. Whether a person's actions are voluntary depends on what it is that limits his alternatives. . . . Other people's actions place limits on one's available opportunities. Whether this makes one's resulting action non-voluntary depends on whether the others had the right to act as they did" (*ASU*, 262). Nozick defends this last principle by means of a fanciful analogy. We are asked to imagine twenty-six men and twenty-six women, named A through Z and A′ through Z′, respectively, all of whom would prefer to be married than not. Each person's preferences for a mate follow the alphabet, everyone wants most to marry an A (with or without prime depending on gender) and least a Z. If A and A′ marry and B and B′, and so on, this progressively diminishes the range of alternatives for the rest, all the way down to hapless Z and Z′, who have no alternative but to marry their last choices (each other) or remain unmarried (an even worse alternative). Nozick concludes that this does not mean—if they get married—that Z and Z′ do not marry voluntarily, since all the others were within their rights in marrying whom they did. With this conclusion in hand, he returns to the workers: "Similar considerations apply to market exchanges between workers and owners of capital. Z is faced with working or starving; the choices and actions of all other persons do not add up to providing Z with some other option. (He may have various options about what job to take.) Does Z choose to work voluntarily? . . . Z does choose voluntarily if the other individuals A through Y each acted voluntarily *and within their rights*" (*ASU*, 263; emphasis mine).

What rights are these? They are, of course, their property rights. But this makes the argument strictly circular. A libertarian defense of property rights must ask whether property rights threaten freedom as part of deter- 241 mining whether property rights are justified, and thus without already assuming that they are valid. Nozick's argument amounts to claiming that property rights do not limit freedom because they are valid rights. But given the primacy of freedom for libertarianism, the question of whether property rights threaten freedom must be answered first in order to determine if they are valid rights. Otherwise, the question posed by the Rousseauian challenge is begged.

Nozick's theory is a perfect example of the libertarian blindness to the coercive aspect of property. Instead of facing the threat to freedom built into property with open eyes and coping with it, Nozick feels his way along the outer edge of property rights and defines freedom so that it does not rub against that edge. Recognition of the circularity of libertarianism of the sort Nozick defends does not amount to proof that free enterprise capitalism, even of the sort that Nozick's theory would issue in, is unjust. It only proves that the justice of such capitalism cannot be established by the route of treating private property simply as an expression of freedom and ignoring its other side.

The only way to show that such capitalism is just is to show that it would be reasonable for all people to agree to private property not knowing whether they would be owners or nonowners. Only such a demonstration can defeat the suspicion that private property is a means to subjugation. In this regard, it is interesting that Locke was a less extreme Lockean than Nozick. Locke believed that the accumulation of property beyond what one could consume required a separate act of consent (which, as we saw in the second section of chapter 3, he thought he found in the conventional nature of money's value), which the original property accumulated by mixing one's labor with the world did not need (*ECG*, secs. 28 and 36). He thereby admitted, at least implicitly, that the extent of that right must be determined by what would be reasonable for all to consent to. Nozick, by putting a more permissive interpretation on the Lockean proviso, effectively extends the property rights created by "labor-mixing" almost to infinity. This is the most extreme form of Lockeanism; it has the effect of extending the principle of natural ownership beyond the body to virtually any and all the things that people might want to dispose of. It amounts to insisting that the treatment due one's body is due one's things. Taking another's property by force is equivalent to making his body one's own property, and respecting people's property is as essential to respecting their freedom as refraining from assaulting them is. With this extreme Lockeanism, we get the most extreme form of libertarian blindness to the coerciveness of property.

In this section, I have essentially accepted the Lockean arguments for the justice of establishing the legal and political components of social structure. As to the economic system, we followed the Lockean line and found it congenitally blind to the coercive threat of property and thus unable to dispel the suspicion of subjugation. The libertarian blindness is a case of the invisibility of social structure. As the invisibility of social structure inclines us to think that judgments of natural justice suffice, so the libertarian thinks that, in a system of exclusive ownership, only judgments of natural justice are needed. All that matters is that people give and take subject to the principles of compatible liberty and trustworthiness—that is, without violence or fraud. This would be true if all that people owned was what they may own under the principle of natural ownership. It would be true if the existence of property beyond natural ownership conveyed no special leverage. Then, simple free exchange would be free of subjugation and satisfy justice. With exclusive ownership, all this is changed. Free exchanges may manifest structural force working through free choice and are suspect as subjugation. Here, then, ends the Lockean line. We turn now to the Rousseauian line.

Property, Ideology, and the Labor Theory of Moral Value: From Rousseau to Marx

Although the libertarian blindness reflects the general invisibility of social structure, its existence is puzzling nonetheless. Since the differences in power that property brings are so substantial, it is hard to understand why it is not obvious that property conflicts with the freedom of nonowners and why nonowners put up with it as docilely as they normally do. We find only suggestive hints in Rousseau: "Slaves," he wrote, "lose everything in their chains, even the desire of escaping from them: they love their servitude" (*SC*, 167). But this is not enough. What must be explained is why people do not see their servitude as servitude. Here the Rousseauian line is picked up by Marx. Marx developed the insight that systems of property are systems of forced labor into a theory of history in general and of capitalism in particular. He conjoined to this a theory of ideology, an explanation of why normal reasonable people would not see capitalist property as a threat to their freedom.

Before turning to the Marxian theory of ideology, we must first consider Marx's analysis of the workings of capitalism and say something about "the labor theory of value." Marx's labor theory of value is a scientific claim about how capitalism operates. It contends that "socially necessary labor-time"—the average time it takes a laborer, expending a standard amount of energy, to produce a commodity—will determine the value of commodities on the market. This theory is often thought refuted by showing that prices   243 of various commodities do not correspond to the time taken to produce them. But Marx only starts his theory in the first volume of *Capital* with the simplifying assumption that labor-time's determination of value is represented in prices directly. He subsequently argues in the second and third volumes that, though labor-time determines value, the full development of capitalism brings with it processes for distributing that value in ways that make prices diverge from time labored. Other objections have been raised against Marx's theory, and I shall not attempt to respond to them. Rather, I want to give the labor theory of value a different meaning from the one Marx gave it, though I believe it is the meaning that ultimately gives the theory its appeal—and this is a moral meaning.

Instead of thinking of the labor theory of value as a description of how prices are actually determined in capitalism, I want to take it as a theory of what ultimately counts morally in systems of production. Hence, the labor theory of *moral* value. The central claim of this theory is that, for purposes of moral evaluation, economic distributions should first be considered neither as distributions of goods nor of money but as distributions of the labor that has gone into producing those goods, to which money then gives its bearer title. By *labor* I mean a definite quantity of time and energy from the finite sum of time and energy available to an individual over the course of his life. By *first*, I mean to signify that the labor theory of moral value does not claim that it is never important to look at economic systems as distributions of goods. On the contrary, since people obtain goods (including services) in return for labor, a distribution of labor will be justified in light of the distribution of goods to which it is coupled. The claim of the labor theory of moral value is only that what gets justified in light of goods is the distribution of labor. The argument for the labor theory of moral value from justice as reason's answer to subjugation follows.

If all ownership were within the limits of the principle of natural ownership, we could be confident that exchanges between people (whether of things or of labor) were nonsubjugating as long as the exchanges were carried on subject to the principles of compatible liberty and of trustworthiness— that is, without violence or fraud. Within natural ownership, there is enough left over for others to obtain the resources that went into what anyone owns. Thus, for each person there is always an alternative to trading for something; he can try to make it himself. What leverage any owner of something has, then, is strictly a matter of the nonowner's preference for making that thing versus making something else and trading for it. All things equal, this will be a function of which alternative gives the individual what he wants with the least labor. Because, in the absence of violence or deception, every exchanger will generally get what he wants with the least labor, there is no reason to suspect that anyone is being subjugated by anyone else. Under natural ownership, exchanges that occur in the absence of overt force or fraud are just.

This picture of exchanges within natural ownership is how the libertarian sees exchanges within capitalism.[3] Because capitalist property is a system of exclusive ownership, however, it places in the hands of owners an additional leverage over nonowners not present when everyone owns only according to the principle of natural ownership. With exclusive ownership, an owner has additional leverage because she owns something that the nonowner cannot make himself, since everything is already owned. As that means that the very resources necessary to live at all are already owned, the nonowner must work for the owner to get the necessities of life. Since the nonowner must get these things somehow and since he does not have the alternative of trying to make what he needs directly, there is no longer reason to assume that exchanges free of violence and fraud will lead to each person doing the least amount of labor needed to get what he wants. It is at least possible that the nonowner is being required to give the owner some premium that the owner has the power to extract because the social structure assures that nonowners can satisfy their needs in no other way. This possibility suffices to raise the suspicion of subjugation. Since the existence of exclusive property is sustained by the actions of the members of society, the suspicion is that people are acting in ways that force some people to work extra for others. Moreover, this can occur through free exchange. It will be reasonable for nonowners freely to choose working for owners even excessively, when the alternative is not working and thus not earning a living at all. Thus, the leverage in capitalist property can function as structural force, through the free choices of nonowners.

At this point, I assume no more than that capitalist property may be a means to force excess labor from nonowners. This suffices to raise the suspicion of subjugation. How shall we test this suspicion? Since ownership may be the instrument of subjugation because it enables some people to withhold valuable resources as leverage over the labor of others, we cannot assume that, because people are not overtly forced to give up what they own, subjugation is not occurring. We cannot detect subjugation by looking for overt violence, nor by consulting the feelings of exchangers. This works both ways. We cannot assume either that people are not being subjugated because they have agreed without coercion to work for others or that they are subjugated because they have to work for others to get what they need. Rather, we have to see the proportions in which people are working for others and ask whether it would be rational for all people to agree to those or some other proportions. To see the proportions in which people are working for   245 others in an economy, we must look at it as a labor exchange. Rather than viewing an economic distribution as a distribution of goods or money, we view it as a distribution of labor. The goods that one receives for one's labor will be viewed in terms of the labor that went into producing those goods, and the money that one receives will be viewed in terms of the labor that goes into the goods that can be purchased with the money. With the economic distribution viewed strictly as a labor exchange, we can ask whether the exchange is one to which all would reasonably agree. If so, it is not subjugating. If there is some general standard for labor exchanges to which all would reasonably agree, this would be the standard of nonsubjugating distributions.

Labor is the proper measure of what human beings give one another in economic exchanges since labor is just time and energy that might have been spent directly on pursuit of one's sovereign interest and that is deflected into the service of other people's interests in an economy. Indeed, labor is life itself spent. Since all labor is done for some period of time at some level of expenditure of energy, the appropriate measure will be a complex function of these two. We can, however, simplify matters in the following way. We can use time labored as our measure, if we take it as applying to labor done at the average level of expenditure of energy. This will give us at least a rough picture of the actual labor exchanges in a society, since most people will be working near the average level. Labor done above or below the average expenditure of energy can be translated into units of labor-time done at the average level. For purposes of moral evaluation, economic systems should be viewed first as distributions of the labor-time embodied in the goods (or money) that are exchanged. Because suspicion of subjugation makes this view necessary for moral evaluation of any economic distribution and the system of exclusively owned property on which it rests, I call this the labor theory of moral value.

If we understand Marx's labor theory this way, then his application of it to capitalism is a description of the morally relevant reality of economic systems characterized by private ownership of, and free markets in, goods and services. The immediate effect of the free market is that prices come to reflect not so much the actual amount of labor-time (understood as time labored at the average level of expenditure of energy) that is put into a product but the amount of labor-time normally necessary in the society for producing that sort of product (*C*, 1:189, 210). Otherwise, when different people offer the same product for sale they will get different prices depending on how much labor they used in producing it. On the free market, however, no one will pay a higher price for a product that she can get for a lower price. The free market works so that those who put more labor in their

246

products than the normal amount necessary in the society will not get compensated for the extra labor. Accordingly, the market forces the prices of things to reflect the labor-time normally necessary to produce them, rather than the actual labor that went into them. This forces everyone, on pain of not getting compensated for more, to try to produce with the least possible amount of labor-time. Thus, the market has the rebound effect of forcing the actual labor-time that goes into products to approximate the normally necessary amount (encouraging efficiency) or go below it (encouraging technological innovation).

Consider what happens when in this free market some people (through force, inheritance, or prior labor) come to own all the available means of production (land, machines, and other resources on which people labor) and other people own little more than their bodies. Since the means of production are the means of working and thus of living, those who do not own means of production must work for a capitalist who does. Marx calls the worker's ability to labor "labor-power." The worker sells labor-power to the capitalist in return for a wage. Since labor-power is a commodity, its value is also equivalent to the amount of labor-time normally necessary to produce it. Producing labor-power means maintaining a functioning worker. The value of labor-power, then, is equivalent to the labor-time that normally goes into producing the goods (food, clothing, shelter) necessary to maintain a functioning worker at the prevailing standard of living (*C*, 1:171). The worker receives this in the form of a wage, the money necessary to purchase these goods.

The capitalist owns the good produced with the labor he has purchased and obtains the money he pays as a wage by selling what the worker produces during the time for which she is employed. But if the worker only produced goods with a value equivalent to her wage, there would be nothing left over for the capitalist and no reason for him to hire the worker in the first place. Labor-power has the capacity to produce more value than its own value (*C*, 1:193–94). The worker can work longer than the labor-time equivalent to the value of her wage. The amount of labor-time that the worker works to produce value equivalent to her wage, Marx calls "necessary labor." The additional labor-time that the worker works, Marx calls "surplus labor," and the value it produces, Marx calls "surplus value." Surplus value belongs to the capitalist and is the source of his profit (*C*, 1:184–86).

Profit is then equivalent to the worker's uncompensated surplus labor. The worker receives value equal to what she produces with her necessary labor and nothing equal to what she produces with her surplus labor. "This expenditure of labour-power," Marx writes, "comes to [the capitalist] gratis." Thus, "the secret of the self-expansion of capital [that is, the secret of profit]   247 resolves itself into having the disposal of a definite quantity of other people's unpaid labour" (*C*, 1:534). Ownership of means of production yields profit because it enables the capitalist to buy an amount of labor-time with a smaller amount of labor-time and thus get some free. Because labor is the source and measure of value, the value that the worker does receive is nothing but some fraction of her fellows' labor. Under capitalism, the workers produce a quantity of value, part of which they pay themselves with and part of which goes to the capitalist gratis.

For Marx, however, capitalism is not only a system in which workers provide labor without pay, it is also a system in which workers are forced to provide this labor. Workers are not merely shortchanged, they are enslaved. Capitalism is, for Marx, "a coercive relation" (*C*, 1:309). The coercion, however, is not of the direct sort that characterizes traditional slavery or feudal serfdom. Rather, it is an indirect force resulting because capitalists own the means of production and laborers do not. Accordingly, Marx characterizes as "indirect slavery, the slavery of the proletariat," in contrast to the "direct slavery . . . of the black races in . . . the Southern States of North America."[4] Lacking ownership of means of production, workers lack their own access to the means of producing a livelihood. By this very fact, they are compelled to sell their labor to the capitalist for a wage, and thus to provide uncompensated labor, since the alternative is either relative pauperization or absolute starvation.

The compulsion works through free contractual agreement by the worker. Because the agreement is free, both sides must offer the other a reason for agreeing. In order to give the capitalist a reason to purchase their labor-power, workers will have to sell their labor-power for a wage lower in value than the value their labor produces. No matter how free the wage contract is, as long as it occurs in a context in which a few own all the means of production, those who do not own means of production will be compelled to give up some of their labor without compensation to those who do. Thus, Marx describes the wage-worker as a "man who is compelled to sell himself of his own free will" (*C*, 1:766) and capitalism as a system of "forced labour—no matter how much it may seem to result from a free contractual agreement" (*C*, 3:819).

It is no refutation of this that workers in capitalism commonly have some other choices: They can work for the government; they can scrimp and save and try to start small businesses; they can join religious orders; they can go on the dole; they can try to become successful gamblers or even criminals. The force at work here is structural; it need not deny workers all choices. It suffices that workers are constrained to a range of options, of which selling one's labor for a wage will be the most rational course of action. Like the robbery victims in the stagecoach mentioned earlier in our discussion of structural force, they are victims of force.

Credit for the discovery of structural force belongs to Marx, since Marx understands the force in capitalism as structural. For Marx, "capital is not a thing, but a social relation" (*C*, 1:766), and it is a coercive social relation (*C*, 1:309). The social relation of capitalism is not defined simply by private ownership of means of production. It is defined rather by the copresence of owners of means of production and owners of nothing but labor-power: "Property in money, means of subsistence, machines and other means of production," writes Marx, "does not as yet stamp a man as a capitalist if there be wanting the correlative—the wage-worker, the other man who is compelled to sell himself of his own free will" (*C*, 1:766). The relation between these two roles, owner of means of production and owner of nothing but labor-power, is the coercive social relation: "The dull compulsion of economic relations completes the subjection of the labourer to the capitalist" (*C*, 1:737).

Unlike slavery, robbery, or conquest, which include the use of overt force as part of their definition, overt force (at least under normal circumstances) is prohibited from the roles defined by the capitalist social relation. The coercion of the capitalist relation lies not in overt violence or direct force but in the structure of the social relation itself. It is coercive in the same way that a social structure that allotted to one group ownership, and thus control, of all the available oxygen would be. Beyond what was necessary to defend this group against challenges to its ownership of the oxygen, no additional force would be necessary for the coercion to operate. It would operate quite effectively by means of bargains freely struck, in which those who did not own oxygen would have to offer something to the owners to get the chance to breathe. They, too, would be compelled to sell themselves of their own free will. The same can be said of capitalism. Once the structure of capitalist social roles is in place, whenever individuals choose from among the alternatives available within their roles the course of action that best serves their self-interest, the extraction of uncompensated surplus labor is enforced without further need for overt force, except in unusual circumstances.

The example of the oxygen-owning society is instructive in another way. It enables us to see that the coercion in the capitalist social relation is not a function of how the means of production originally fell into the hands of capitalists. Even if all the oxygen came to be the property of a few people in a morally unobjectionable way—say, by being voluntarily handed over to them by everyone else as a gesture of charity and fellow feeling—the social relation between the heirs of the owners and the descendants of the others   249 would still be coercive. Similarly, though Marx describes the original accumulation of capitalist property as a violent act of theft (*C*, 1:714–15), those features of capitalism that led Marx to regard it as a coercive social relation would remain even if the original accumulation had occurred in the most saintly fashion. The overt force with which capitalism was born is distinct from the structural force by which it lives.

That the coerciveness Marx found in the capitalist social relation is a matter of structural rather than overt force is closely linked to a second fact. Unlike the relations between masters and slaves, robbers and victims, or conquerors and subjects, the relation between owners of means of production and owners of labor-power not only does not appear to be a coercive social relation, it does not even appear to be a social relation. The relations between masters and slaves, robbers and victims, and conquerors and subjects appear to their members as social relations, because the presence of overt force makes these relations seem not given by nature but imposed on it. The difference between ownership of means of production and ownership of labor-power appears, in contrast, simply as a given, along with all the other differences that exist among people, such as differences in height or strength. The coercive social relation of capitalism appears instead as a free relation between people who just happen to differ in what they own—hence the libertarian blindness.

To understand Marx's explanation of the libertarian blindness, we must turn to Marx's conception of ideology. Ideology is a set of false beliefs about a society that contribute to the smooth functioning of that society. A Marxian theory of ideology must be a materialist theory, meaning one that traces the false beliefs back to features of the prevailing organization of the production of the material conditions of life. In *The German Ideology*, Marx writes: "If in all ideology men and their circumstances appear upside down as in a *camera obscura*, this phenomenon arises just as much from their historical life-process as the inversion of objects on the retina does from their physical life-process. . . . The phantoms formed in the human brain are also, necessarily sublimates of their material life-process, which is empirically verifiable and bound to material premises."[5] But there is more. That a Marxian theory of ideology must be materialist implies also that it must account for false ideas without assuming that they are caused by some subjective error or illusion. They must arise as a result of normal nondefective use of the perceptual and reasoning capacities by which people form their true ideas about their environment. I shall refer to this latter as the requirement that a materialist explanation must show ideology to be an objective illusion rather than a subjective one. This is essential for a theory of ideology not only because such a theory must not preclude the possibility of the very science upon which it is founded, but, of equal importance, such a theory must accommodate the obvious fact that, even where social relations are most successfully shrouded in ideology, the majority of the beliefs in people's heads—the work is hard, the boss is rich, the sky is blue—are true.

Before we look for a materialist explanation of libertarian blindness in the capitalist mode of production, I want to fix the idea of an objective illusion by analogy with another illusion—that the sun goes around the earth. Any illusion, any erroneous belief that an individual holds, can be stated as a subjective error, but not every erroneous belief arises because of a subjective error. A person who believes that the sun rises above a stationary horizon in the morning makes a mistake. But this sort of mistake differs crucially from the mistake of a colorblind person who believes that a light is green when it is red or the mistake of a person balancing his checkbook who believes that a number is a 4 when it is a 2. In these latter cases, the mistaken beliefs are not merely held by the individuals, they arise in the individuals as a result of a defective perceptual faculty or misuse of a normal one. Correcting the defect in the perceptual faculty or its use will undo the mistake. The mistaken belief that the sun goes around the earth, by contrast, arises as a result of a normal perceptual faculty properly exercised. Neither better vision nor more careful looking will enable an individual to correct this mistake and see that what occurs at dawn is not the sun rising above the horizon, but the horizon tipping down before the sun. This mistake can only be corrected by means of additional knowledge, a true scientific theory of the motions of the solar system.

A materialist theory of ideology must show how the falsity of an ideological doctrine is an objective illusion arising from normal, nondefective perception of the organization of material production rather than from some subjective error. "It is not the subject who deceives himself, but *reality* which deceives *him*."[6] Marx offers the beginnings of a materialist explanation of ideological illusion in his famous discussion of the fetishism of commodities in the first volume of *Capital*. The fetishism of commodities is not, as sometimes thought, a diatribe against consumerism or alienation. It is an explanation of the mechanism responsible for the general failure of members of capitalist societies to perceive the capitalist social relation as coercive or even as a particular social relation rather than as a feature of the natural environment.

Consider how this process occurs. Since commodities are exchanged in proportion to the average amount of labor-time necessary to produce them and since the labor-time that goes into producing any single commodity is a fraction of the aggregate labor of all commodity producers in society, the relative values at which commodities are exchanged express the relations   251 between the fractions of total social labor-time that has gone into them. These values express social relations between their producers and all other producers in the sense that they represent the social division of labor and the portions of social labor that different individuals control. But producers do not see this because the production units are isolated, and thus producers do not meet during production. They meet at the moment of exchange, where they only see commodities being exchanged at certain values. Consequently, each producer sees the social relation between his own labor-time and that of the others not as a social relation between them but as a relation between the values of the commodities they are exchanging. Producers see the fractions of social labor in various commodities as the values of those commodities rather than as indications of their own social relations as producers. Marx writes,

> Since the producers do not come into social contact with each other until they exchange their products, the specific social character of each producer's labour does not show itself except in the act of exchange. In other words, the labour of the individual asserts itself as a part of the labour of society, only by means of the relations which the act of exchange establishes directly between the products, and indirectly, through them, between the producers. To the latter, therefore, the relations connecting the labour of one individual with that of the rest appear, not as direct social relations between individuals at work, but as what they really are, material relations between persons and social relations between things. (*C*, 1:73)

Since the endowment of inanimate objects with animate properties is fetishism, Marx calls this phenomenon, "fetishism of commodities." In it, "a definite social relation between men . . . assumes in their eyes, the *fantastic* form of a relation between things" (*C*, 1:72; emphasis mine).

Though Marx presents the fetishism as occurring between producers who exchange their products on the market, what he says applies equally to the transactions between capitalists and laborers, because "the exchange between capital and labour at first presents itself to the mind in the same guise as the buying and selling of all other commodities" (*C*, 1:540). Since exchange itself is free of overt force, each party can only obtain the other's goods by offering something in return that makes it worthwhile for the other to part willingly with his goods. The only power parties have over one another in exchange is their power to withhold their commodity until something sufficiently valuable to them is offered in return. The unequal power of capitalist and worker, then, appears as their equal power to withhold from exchange what they happen to own—means of production and labor-power, respectively—and their social inequality appears as the difference between the values of these things. Rather than the capitalist appearing as if, by virtue of owning the means of production, he has the power to force the worker to work for him, the capitalist and worker appear as if they are equal in power but happen to own things of different value. This occurs in exchange, because exchange is a moment in the circuit of capital when the power to command obedience and back it up with overt force is suspended.

Exchange, then, is the material basis of the libertarian blindness. The freedom in the exchange situation is real. In fact, freedom in exchange is a necessary condition of the operation of the labor theory of value (as Marx understands it); if people were not free to withhold their possessions (including labor) until they received an acceptable offer, there would be no reason to think that the price for which anything was sold would be proportionate to labor-time rather than to the relative physical strength of the exchangers. Exchange accurately perceived gives rise to the objective illusion of libertarianism with its distinctively ideological blindness to the coerciveness of ownership of the means of production. Marx writes that the sphere of exchange, "within whose boundaries the sale and purchase of labour-power goes on, is in fact a very Eden of the innate rights of man. There alone rule Freedom, Equality, Property. . . . Freedom, because both buyer and seller of a commodity, say of labour-power, are constrained only by their free will" (*C*, 1:176). To complete this explanation of libertarian ideology, however, we need to understand how the sphere of exchange, which is only a part of capitalism, can be the source of beliefs about the whole of capitalism. Why should the experience of freedom in exchange (rather than the experience of taking orders on the production line) determine the beliefs that members of capitalist societies come naturally to have?

Marx offers a clue when he says that the fetishism of commodities results because "the producers do not come into contact with each other until they exchange." Exchange transactions are the salient points of social contact for economic actors in capitalism. They visibly punctuate all capitalist social relations. Every social interaction between individuals in the capitalist mode of production begins with such a transaction (the signing of a wage contract, exchanging labor-power for money) and can be ended with such a transaction (the dissolution of the wage contract). Each of these beginnings and endings is characterized by the absence of either party having the power to command the other's obedience or use violence to get it. Each party knows that he can enter or withdraw from any capitalist social interaction without being subject to the command or the overt force of the other. What constraint either feels is, then, just a matter of what he happens to own, which naturally appears as a feature of his own good or bad fortune rather than a condition

253

coercively imposed by the other. Since exchange begins and ends all capitalist social interactions, they all appear as voluntary undertakings between equal people who happen to own different things. That a worker takes these voluntary agreements as the boundaries by reference to which he comprehends the course of his service to the capitalist is as normal as taking the visible horizon as that by which one comprehends the course of the sun.

Both illusions arise from an accurate perception of a local part of the larger system in which the observer is situated. Just as the earth is taken as a fixed ground against which the sun appears as a moving figure, so exchange appears as the ground upon which capitalist production relations appear as figures as well. The laborer's subordination to the particular capitalist for whom she works appears to be the product of her earlier and continuing consent, whereas that she must work for some capitalist seems like no more than the natural fact that people have to work in order to live. This experience leads workers in capitalist societies to believe that they are free though they take orders most of their waking lives and leads libertarians to believe that capitalism is free because it is free of overt force.

I introduced the analogy of the geocentric illusion to distinguish false beliefs that are products of accurate perception of one's local situation from those that are products of erroneous or faulty perception. The former result not from the presence of subjective error but from the absence of knowledge of the larger context shaping the local situation, from lack of a true scientific view of the whole. In the case of the geocentric illusion, the local situation is shaped by the fact that we live on a planet the movement of which we are incapable of perceiving. Failure to recognize the movement of the earth can only be corrected by means of a scientific view of the whole solar system. In the case of the illusion that capitalism is uncoercive, the local situation is shaped by the fact that capitalist social interactions begin and end with transactions from which overt force is normally absent. This illusion can only be corrected by means of a scientific view of the whole capitalist system that enables one to grasp the structural force in the capitalist social relation.

The local situation that gives rise to the fetishism is characterized by the encounter of a particular worker with a particular capitalist who enter into a specific exchange agreement at a given point in time. Setting this situation in the context of the whole requires seeing the encounter of individual capitalist and worker as a point at which the class of capitalists meets the class of workers and seeing that meeting in the context of the history of modes of production. This larger context enables us to penetrate the illusion that, when capitalist and worker exchange wage-goods for labor-power, they simply exchange what each happens to own. This illusion, writes Marx, "vanishes immediately, if, instead of taking a single capitalist and a single labourer, we take the class of capitalists and the class of labourers as a whole. The capitalist class is constantly giving the labouring class order-notes, in the form of money, on a portion of the commodities produced by the latter and appropriated by the former. The labourers give these order-notes back just as constantly to the capitalist class, and in this way get their share of their own product" (*C*, 1:568).

Seeing the capital-labor exchange as a relation between classes amounts to seeing that the workers are being paid with their own product, and only with part of it. This enables us to see that workers work without compensation. When we notice that what keeps workers in this situation is private ownership of production and notice, as well, that this is a particular historical social arrangement rather than an eternal fixture, we can see that they are forced by that social arrangement to work without compensation. We see also that the context of their individual exchanges is possibly unjust and, thus, that the exchanges themselves are also possibly unjust. As we saw in chapter 4, ignoring the question of the justice of the social context has the effect of treating that context as just (or, at least, not unjust). The perception of exchange, though accurate about what it directly perceives, thus serves the conjoined ideological functions of blinding people to the coercion in property and bestowing by default a positive judgment about the justice of the social structure that provides for that property.

It would be a mistake to conclude that this argument automatically implies that capitalism should be replaced with socialism or communism. Just as we saw that the failure of Nozick's libertarianism does not preclude all attempts to defend capitalism in the name of freedom from subjugation (it could still possibly be defended as instrumental to the greatest freedom), so the truth of Marx's claim that capitalism is coercive does not eliminate the possibility of defending capitalism in the name of freedom from sub-jugation. Capitalism may still provide that form of society, among those actually possible, that is most free from subjugation. If the libertarian error lies in blindness to the coerciveness of private property, the characteristic Marxian error lies in misunderstanding the moral implications of seeing that coerciveness. For two reasons, a person who accepts the validity of the Marxian analysis could quite possibly conclude—in the name of the very freedom threatened by capitalist property—that she ought to support and even prefer the continuation of capitalism in some form for the indefinite, and possibly quite long, future.

First, anyone who wants to replace a system because it is coercive can only consistently wish it replaced with a less coercive system. Such a system must in its actual workings be freer. Nor is a system less coercive than capitalism simply because it eliminates the coercive elements of capitalism;

it must replace them with others that are, in actual and overall effect, less coercive. Whether any system can meet this requirement is an empirical matter, and the evidence of so-called socialist societies thus far does not occasion optimism.

Indeed, there are good grounds in Marxian theory itself for pessimism. Marxism starts from the Rousseauian recognition that systems of exclusive property ownership are systems of forced labor. Marxism concludes that, for everyone to be free, everyone must own all the property. (This is the transposition into economics of Rousseau's political argument that, for all to be free, everyone must be part of the sovereign.) Such a system of ownership can work in two ways. Since labor must be organized in some socially rational way, people will have to do certain tasks. Such a system can work voluntarily where there are no conflicts between what the individual wants to do and what the society needs, or it must be coerced (by the state) where such conflicts remain. Recognizing that it is easier to abolish private property than to abolish the conflicts between individual and social interests, Marxism foresees two stages after capitalism. In the final stage—communism—individual and social interests have converged, and the state is no longer needed because it is no longer necessary to coerce people into working. The state "withers away," and production is controlled voluntarily and directly by the "associated producers." Getting to this final stage, however, requires a transitional stage—socialism—during which, though private property is abolished, the tension between individual and social interest is not yet overcome. Here everyone owns all the property through the instrumentality of the state, and the state forcibly requires the tasks that people do not voluntarily embrace (using the standard capitalist method—making their performance the price of obtaining a living). But this means in reality that the functionaries of the state will have their hands on just that lever of power that the capitalists used to have, only now they will have it in an amount beyond any capitalist's dreams and in the absence of competing owners.

At the very moment that Marx was writing *Capital,* John Stuart Mill was cautioning against the illusion of thinking that—because in popular government the people rule themselves—the risk of oppression is ended by popular government. Governance, however popular, requires that some people exercise power in the name of the whole group. Because the power will have to be exercised in some particular way, even when the group is divided on which way, even popular governance will enable some people to exercise power over, and against the will of, some of the others in society. With actual fallible human beings at the helm, the dangers of power and its abuse survive the advent of popular government (*OL,* 66–68). This applies with

256

the same force when the power involved in ownership of means of production is put in the hands of popular government. There may be a point in history when people (both the state functionaries who guard the power of property and the citizens who must guard the guardians) are so developed rationally and morally that so much power in the hands of state functionaries will be no threat to freedom. But that time is not near, and it is utopianism of the sort that Marx bitterly opposed to ignore that fact. In the canon of contemporary Marxism-Leninism, this sin is called "ultra-leftism": advancing policies that assume the working class is more advanced than it actually is. Marx himself knew it as "idealism": the error of believing that ideas make history, and failing to see that ideas (whether about steam engines or social contracts) pop up throughout history but only take root and have influence when history has prepared the soil. Socialism is not superior to capitalism because it is a better idea. It is only superior if and when people are actually capable of controlling their political agencies so effectively that public control of property does not become a means of worse oppression than private control. Until then, precisely because of the power that Marxists recognize in ownership of the means of production, socialism poses real dangers to freedom.

The second reason that might lead someone who accepts the validity of the Marxian analysis of capitalism to advocate the continued existence of capitalism is the following. Marxism takes progress in history to be a matter of progress in two lines, that of freedom from subjugation of human beings by their fellows and that of freedom of human beings from constraint by the forces of nature. It accepts, therefore, that it may be necessary to coerce people socially in order to liberate them from nature. Capitalism is coercive in the first dimension and—by Marx's own admissions in *The Communist Manifesto* and elsewhere—unprecedentedly liberating in the second. Because coercion is opposed for its effect on sovereign interests rather than for its cause, there is no reason, in principle, to prefer one sort of liberation to the other. The greatest possible total amount of freedom from constraint of both sorts is to be preferred, and a society is to be preferred if it offers the greatest total amount of freedom from human subjugation and natural constraint actually possible at that point in history. Because at this point in history capitalism may represent the least amount of human subjugation necessary to achieve its level of freedom from the forces of nature, capitalism may be the society to be preferred. That capitalism is coercive in its relations of production does not foreclose the possibility that it still offers the greatest total amount of freedom—or that it can be altered in ways that would produce this while still remaining capitalism. Though its property arrangements were coercive, such a capitalist society would be just in that it would

257

be reasonable for all people, owners and nonowners, to agree to it in light of their sovereign interests.

It follows that the Marxian analysis of capitalism can be accepted, the Nozickian one rejected, and the question of the justice of capitalism left open. Once Marx appears, however, the question of justice, and the business of moral philosophy, can never be the same because Marx shows in detail what Rousseau only intimated—that there is a question of appearance versus reality regarding freedom. A society may feel free and yet be subjugating. This is what the possibility of ideology reveals, and this very possibility means that henceforth no theory of justice can escape the responsibility of proving that it has not fallen prey to it. For our purposes, this means that we must assume that the knowledge available to people in the natural context includes Marxian theory, as set forth here in conjunction with the labor theory of moral value, and that they are therefore cured of the libertarian blindness. To argue that there are social structures that it would be rational for everyone to agree to in light of this knowledge is to argue for a society that is just in a way that meets the Marxian challenge. In due course, we shall see what a society must be like to pass the test of the social contract for parties who are not victims of the libertarianism blindness. Before that we must turn to John Rawls's version of the theory of the social contract, in which we will find many features of that test anticipated.

The Need for a Theory of the Social Contract: The Power and Limits of Rawls's Theory of Justice

Rawls replaces the state of nature with an imaginary original position that does not represent a point in time—real or imagined—before the existence of the state. In Rawls's original position, free and rational individuals are to come to unanimous agreement on the principles to govern the design of social systems. Their deliberations to this end are subject to several important conditions that restrict the sorts of arguments that can be made and the sorts of evidence that can be advanced. As with those that characterize the natural context, the conditions that characterize the original position simply set forth the shape that an argument for principles of justice must have. "One should not be misled, then," Rawls writes, "by the somewhat unusual conditions which characterize the original position. The idea here is simply to make vivid the restrictions that it seems reasonable to impose on arguments for principles of justice, and therefore on these principles themselves" (*TJ*, 18). In considering the features of the original position, then, bear in mind that each of these features must have a moral philosophical justification which shows that the restrictions it embodies are appropriate for arguments about justice.

The most pronounced feature of, and thus restriction on, deliberations in the original position is that they take place behind a veil of ignorance. Behind this veil, the parties in the original position are deprived of all knowledge about themselves as particular individuals. They do not know their race, sex, age, abilities, social or economic position, nor do they know what sort of society or what particular historical generation they are in. They do not know their psychological or moral attitudes, their goals or their conceptions of the good (*TJ*, 12 and 137). All other relevant knowledge is allowed. The main moral philosophical justification of the veil is that, with this knowledge excluded, "no one is able to design principles to favor his own particular condition" (*TJ*, 12). This seems a reasonable restriction on arguments for principles of justice.

Furthermore, the parties in the original position do have interests. Each seeks to promote and protect "his capacity to advance his conception of the good" (*TJ*, 14), his capacity to live his life in pursuit of some ends that he deems good, though the veil of ignorance deprives everyone of knowledge of the specific content of their conceptions of the good. Rawls says of the parties "that while they know that they have some rational plan of life, they do not know the details of this plan, the particular ends and interests which it is calculated to promote" (*TJ*, 142).

Finally, the parties in the original position are taken to be mutually disinterested and not envious. Mutual disinterestedness means that the parties do not take "an interest in one another's interests" (*TJ*, 13). Since this feature of Rawls's theory has been widely misunderstood, it is worth pausing to be clear on what it means. Some have thought that the mutual disinterestedness of the parties means that they are individuals who are interested only in their own welfare. Were this so, the parties (and thus Rawls's theory) would be biased in favor of competitive and individualistic social systems and against cooperative and communal ones.[7] But mutual disinterestedness is not a characterization of the kinds of interests that the parties have; it "does not mean that the parties are egoists, that is, individuals with only certain kinds of interests, say in wealth, prestige, and domination" (*TJ*, 13). It means only that each of the parties will insist on having his interests protected, whatever they are, as a precondition for agreeing to any set of principles of justice. The effect of mutual disinterestedness is not to make it rational for the parties to opt for a society suited to people who only or mostly look out for themselves, since they have no reason to believe that they are such people. Its effect, rather, is to make it rational for the parties to opt for a society that protects each one's capacity to promote his or her own interests, whatever these turn out to be. Conversely, mutual disinterestedness makes it irrational for the parties to agree to any society that does not provide this for every single individual. This is the moral philosophical justification for its inclusion as a feature of the original position.

The exclusion of envy plays much the same role as mutual disinterestedness. People who are not mutually disinterested might agree to principles that serve the interests of others but not their own; envious people might agree to principles that sacrifice their own interests so that others have less (*TJ*, 143). In neither case would rational agreement among such people necessarily be to terms that are in the best interest of every individual. Rawls is under no illusion that people are actually mutually disinterested and free from envy (*TJ*, 148), nor does his theory in any way imply that they are. Together mutual disinterestedness and the exclusion of envy constrain the hypothetical agreement in the original position so that an argument showing that a principle would be the rational choice of all the parties is an argument showing that that principle serves the interests of everyone.

Rawls holds that two principles, in "lexical" order, would be the rational choice of the parties in the original position. "First, each person is to have an equal right to the most extensive basic liberty compatible with a similar liberty for others" (*TJ*, 60). Second, "social and economic inequalities are to be arranged so that they are both (a) to the greatest benefit of the least advantaged and (b) attached to offices and positions open to all under conditions of fair equality of opportunity" (*TJ*, 83). The first principle applies only to liberty and holds that it is to be distributed in the largest possible equal shares. The second principle covers all social goods other than liberty and holds that they should be distributed according to the "difference principle"—namely, the requirement that inequalities work to the greatest benefit of the worst off. Since the difference principle is the core of the second principle, I shall generally refer to Rawls's second principle as the difference principle and assume that the rider (b) about fair equality of opportunity is included. Readers should bear in mind, however, that the difference principle per se refers only to the pattern of distribution mandated by Rawls's second principle, not to what gets distributed (in Rawls's case, social goods other than liberty).

The difference principle does not require those who are better off in a just society to give some of what they have to those who are worse off. The principle applies to the design of distributive schemes. If such schemes allow inequalities, then to be just those inequalities must work in the scheme to the greatest advantage of the worst off; how they work is a matter of the design of the scheme, not a matter of the better off giving things to the worst off. The lexical ordering of the principles means that the first principle limits the degree to which the second principle can be satisfied; equivalently, the second principle can only be satisfied in ways that do not violate the first. The first principle, accordingly, has priority over the second such that liberty can only be restricted for the purpose of protecting or increasing liberty, not to increase the quantity of social and economic advantages and not even to improve the condition of the least advantaged.

Rawls introduces the difference principle to give specificity to a broader distributive principle that requires "social and economic inequalities . . . to be arranged so that they are . . . reasonably expected to be to everyone's advantage" (*TJ*, 60). Rawls assumes that in most societies, if those at the bottom are benefited, then those above them will be benefited as well: "If an advantage has the effect of raising the expectations of the lowest position, it raises the expectations of all positions in between" (*TJ*, 80). If this does not happen naturally, however, then we are required to make it happen. To this end, Rawls introduces an expanded version of the difference principle requiring that the condition of everyone in society be improved to the greatest extent possible starting with the least advantaged, and then the next to the least advantaged, up to the best-off group in society. This expanded principle, Rawls calls the "lexical difference principle." It mandates as follows: "In a basic structure with n relevant representatives, first maximize the welfare of the worst-off representative man; second, for equal welfare of the worst-off representative [that is, without reducing the welfare of the worst-off representative], maximize the welfare of the second worst-off representative man, and so on until the last case which is, for equal welfare of all the preceding n − 1 representatives, maximize the welfare of the best-off representative man" (*TJ*, 83). By *representatives*, Rawls means individuals representing the condition of the groups whose level of welfare is determined by the distributive scheme. This expanded principle is included in the difference principle, even when the latter is stated in its simpler form, as in the statement of Rawls's second principle given above.

We should thus think of the second principle as requiring not merely the maximization of the shares of those at the bottom of a distribution but the maximization of the shares of every group on the distributive ladder, starting with those at the bottom and working, ratchet-like, up to the top. By *ratchet-like*, I mean that every level is maximized subject to the constraint of not reducing any level below it. This is not a description of how the distribution is produced, but of *what* is required of it. We do not maximize levels in the sense of giving them the most that is possible; rather, we require that, to be just, each level be the maximum it can be as a result of however the distributive scheme gives people what it does. Although I will generally speak of the difference principle as if it applied to a scheme involving only two groups, the best off and the worst off, the reader should   261 bear in mind that what is said of the worst off applies to all the groups above it, subject to the constraint just mentioned.

Rawls's second principle is strictly aimed at determining the just distribution of benefits among those who cooperate in producing those benefits. If there are people whose efforts in no way contribute to the product we make and distribute—members of a self-sufficient primitive tribe living at subsistence level or citizens of a relatively poor country that is insulated from the world economy—the difference principle does not require that we take some part of our social product and devote it to maximizing the shares of those people. Rawls's representatives receive different size shares from a product that they have cooperated in producing. I shall continue speaking, as does Rawls, as if this referred to shares in the product of a whole society that, in one way or another, all able-bodied, adult members of society contribute to producing.

Though the difference principle does not require all shares to be equal, neither does it allow unlimited benefits to those on top. The greater-than-equal shares of those who are better off are only justified insofar as they are necessary to improve the condition of those less well off. Inequalities may improve the condition of the worst off where the promise of larger-than-equal shares functions as an incentive to more productive efforts, which in turn increase the amount available for everyone's shares (*TJ*, 78) or where the greater shares cover the costs of training and educating the more able members of society so that their gifts are used more effectively to benefit the rest (*TJ*, 102). Presumably, without these inequalities those at the bottom of the distributive scheme would be even worse off.

That inequalities benefit the worst off is a strict requirement. It is not satisfied simply by showing that the inequalities produce some benefit to the worst off. An inequality is only justified if the shares of the worst off cannot be improved by decreasing it. Two things follow from this condition. First, the difference principle is not simply applied within a society's distributive scheme by asking whether its inequalities benefit the worst off. If there is an alternative distributive scheme—for example, in another society that is at a similar level of development—in which the worst off enjoy better conditions than in the first society's distributive scheme, the existence of the latter society demonstrates that the first society's scheme can be altered in a way that further improves the shares of the worst off. Rawls's second principle requires this alteration because, without it, the shares of the worst off are not being maximized. Second, within a society's distributive scheme, if inequalities can be reduced in a way that improves the long-term prospect of the worst off, then the reductions must be undertaken. I say long-term

prospect here, since any redistribution from the better off to the worse off will improve the latter's immediate condition, but if it reduces incentives and thus productivity, it may in the long term worsen that condition overall.

Some of Rawls's characterizations of the difference principle suggest conflicting interpretations. For example, he writes that inequality between the entrepreneurial class and the working class in a capitalist society "is only permissible if lowering it would make the working class even more worse off" (*TJ*, 78). This suggests that, if a distribution were such that the larger shares of those at the top could be reduced with no long-term effect— positive or negative—on the smaller shares below, the larger shares would be impermissible. But the lexical difference principle states that all shares should be maximized, except where reducing them would improve the shares below them. This would permit the larger shares in the case described. Wherever there is such ambiguity, I take the lexical principle to be definitive.

Turn now to Rawls's argument for his two principles. The two principles in lexical order are a special case of what Rawls calls "the general conception of justice," which holds that, "All social values—liberty and opportunity, income and wealth, and the bases of self-respect—are to be distributed equally unless an unequal distribution of any, or all, of these values is to everyone's advantage" (*TJ*, 62). The general conception applies to all social goods including liberty and thus allows trade-offs between liberty and other social values, which the two principles in lexical order prohibit. The two principles are thus the product of a sequence of three agreements in the original position: first, to accept the general conception; second, to factor liberty out of the general conception (under specific circumstances) and give it a principle of its own that accords it inviolable (that is, lexically prior) status while leaving the general conception as a second principle applying to all other social goods; third, to interpret "to everyone's advantage" in the second principle according to the difference principle—that is, as maximizing the share of everyone from the worst off on up. We can understand Rawls's arguments for his two principles of justice if we can understand why he thinks that these three agreements would be reached.

Leaving aside for the moment the problem of gambling in the original position, it appears rational for people in the original position to agree to the general conception of justice. Since they are mutually disinterested, each will insist that a principle serve her interest as a condition for agreeing to it. Since none knows who she will turn out to be in society, the only way to insure this is to insist that the principle secure everyone's advantage. Since the general conception embodies just this as the standard of distributing all social values, it is the natural choice. Indeed, the general conception simply restates the problem of the original position as its solution.   263

It is somewhat harder to see why the parties in the original position would choose to factor the general conception into two principles whose effect is to rule out accepting "a lesser liberty for an improvement in economic well-being" (*TJ*, 152). Here Rawls argues that, "as the conditions of civilization improve, the marginal significance for our good of further economic and social advantages diminishes relative to the interests of liberty, which become stronger as the conditions for the exercise of the equal freedoms are more fully realized" (*TJ*, 542). As economic well-being increases, "only the less urgent wants remain to be satisfied by further advances," and "the fundamental interest in determining our plan of life eventually assumes a prior place" (*TJ*, 542–43). On this basis, Rawls argues that limitations on liberty are only allowed when the general level of well-being does not permit their effective exercise, and then "only to the extent that they are necessary to prepare the way for a free society" (*TJ*, 152). Consequently, the two principles of justice are not for all time. Rawls writes that, in adopting the two principles in lexical order, "we are in effect making a special assumption in the original position, namely, that the parties know that the conditions of their society, whatever they are, admit the effective realization of the equal liberties" (*TJ*, 152). This is not the complete argument for the second agreement. The argument is completed along with the argument for the third agreement, to which we now turn.

It is by no means obvious that it would be rational for the parties in the original position to agree to the second principle of justice—which translates "to everyone's advantage" into the difference principle's requirement of maximizing the share of everyone from the worst off on up—since such maximizing is at the expense of the higher shares and thus places limits on how well people might do if they were among the better off. Rawls argues, however, that the difference principle, along with the lexically prior principle of equal maximum liberty, represents "the maximin solution to the problem of social justice" and that the features of the original position make the "maximin" solution the rational choice of the parties (*TJ*, 152–53).

Maximin is a rule for choice under conditions of uncertainty. According to it, the alternatives we must choose between are ranked by the worst that can happen under each, and the alternative with the best worst possible outcome is chosen. We maximize our minimum outcome. Suppose I do not know whether it will rain or be sunny, and I must decide whether to wear my raincoat. If I do wear my raincoat, the worst that can happen is that it will be sunny and I will be uncomfortably overdressed. If I do not wear it, the worst that can happen is that it will rain and I will be soaked. This is all I need consider to apply the maximin rule. The better outcomes (that I wear my raincoat and it rains, for instance) are irrelevant. Assuming it is worse to be soaked than to be overdressed, maximin requires that I choose to wear my raincoat since this has the best worst outcome.[8]

Rawls acknowledges that maximin is an unusual rule not appropriate for most ordinary choices made in conditions of uncertainty. If it were, rational people would always be wearing raincoats. Maximin is appropriate only in circumstances characterized by very specific features. We can identify these features if we look at the raincoat example and see why maximin is generally not appropriate in such cases, why it is generally unreasonable to dress only for the worst. First, we are almost never wholly in the dark about the magnitude of the probability of rain, and as long as the probability of rain is low enough, it is reasonable to risk leaving one's raincoat home. Second, the best outcome, being comfortably dressed on a sunny day, is sufficiently attractive to make this small risk worth taking. Third, the worst of the possible worst outcomes, getting soaked, is not so dreadful as to be avoided at all costs.

For all these reasons, maximin is not generally appropriate for decisions about how to dress for the outdoors. But what if these reasons do not obtain? If we have no knowledge of the magnitude of the probability of rain, if we do not care that much about being comfortably dressed for the sun, and if, due to a sickly constitution, we are likely to catch our death if we get soaked, then maximin is the correct decision strategy. In short, maximin is appropriate when the person choosing has little or no knowledge of the probabilities of the various outcomes, when he cares little for what he might gain above the minimum he can be sure of by following the maximin rule, and when the worst of the possible worst outcomes are intolerable (*TJ*, 154).

Rawls maintains that all three of these features characterize the choice to be made in the original position and that since the two principles of justice guarantee the best worst possible outcome, they are the parties' rational choice. First of all, "the veil of ignorance excludes all but the vaguest knowledge of likelihoods. The parties have no basis for determining the probable nature of their society, or their place in it" (*TJ*, 155). Second, because the two principles guarantee maximum liberty (under conditions of its effective exercise) and maximum possible well-being for the worst off (and everybody above them by the lexical difference principle), there is little reason for strongly preferring better outcomes. Indeed, the reasons for the priority of the first principle imply "that the persons in the original position have no desire to try for greater gains at the expense of equal liberties" (*TJ*, 156). Third, the outcomes possible under conceptions of justice other than the two principles may well be intolerable, since they may permit either

265

serious infractions of liberty, terrible poverty to the worst off, or both. Rawls concludes that the two principles are the rational choice of the parties in the original position and, therefore, that they are the principles of justice.

This conclusion is, however, undermined by a problem that appears merely technical but that has profound implications for understanding how the social contract functions as a moral theory. I refer to the so-called gambler problem, and considering it will show why Rawls's theory needs a theory of the social contract to guide it and how justice as reason's answer to subjugation satisfies that need.

Rawls's theory is an attempt to offer an alternative to the utilitarian conception of justice, and in defending his two principles, Rawls generally treats a variant of utilitarianism—known as average utilitarianism—as the stiffest competition. For classical utilitarianism, whatever distribution of rights, duties, wealth, and opportunity maximizes the aggregate satisfaction or well-being of everyone in society is just. Since every new person born is likely to add more possible satisfaction to the aggregate, even if there is a bit less to go around for the rest, utilitarianism seems to counsel virtually unlimited growth in population even if per capita satisfaction declines—up to the point at which total aggregate satisfaction declines. Because of this seemingly counterintuitive outcome, utilitarianism is often modified into average utilitarianism, which holds that a just society is one that maximizes the aggregate satisfaction of all its members divided by the number of members. It maximizes average or per capita utility or satisfaction.

This does not mean that every single individual in such a society has the highest possible level of satisfaction or that every individual has an amount equal to the social average. Neither classical nor average utilitarianism specifies any particular distribution of satisfaction as just. Whatever distribution maximizes aggregate or average utility, respectively, is the just distribution. For average utilitarianism, no matter how badly off some people might be, their dissatisfaction can be averaged out by the greater satisfactions of others. A society made up of beggars and maharajahs might have a higher average utility all told than a society of moderately and equally well-off persons. According to the principle of average utility, a society in which some people did extremely well and others did terribly could be just. Because a society that satisfies the principle of average utility must produce the highest possible aggregate well-being (relative to its population), those who do well in such a society are likely to be doing the best that is possible in any society. Consequently, the principle of average utility is likely to appeal to those interested in a chance at making it big.

The contrast between average utility and the difference principle is striking. Since the difference principle requires maximizing the well-being of the least-advantaged members of society, it would seem to appeal most to people mainly concerned to avoid poverty. Indeed, since the difference principle requires that the greater-than-equal benefits of the better off be shrunk to that amount beyond which greater shrinkage, even in the form of direct transfers to those less well off, would no longer improve the long-term prospects of any or all the less well-off members of society, the difference principle would appear to appeal most to individuals for whom the pangs of deprivation are more terrifying than the joys of wealth are alluring. Viewed as the outcome of a collective decision-making procedure, the difference principle looks like an extremely conservative choice that would only be the unanimous preference of a group of abnormally timid individuals. Enter the gambler problem.

Those who raise this problem for Rawls's theory generally argue as follows. Human beings are simply not so timid as to concern themselves exclusively with avoiding poverty and deprivation. Although they may want some security against these outcomes, they will normally accept some risk of poverty or deprivation if the chance of doing better is substantial enough to make the overall package, with its risks and potential gains, a reasonable gamble. Hence, many of these critics argue that, if people in the original position had normal tolerance of risk, they would opt for some form of average utilitarian principle of economic justice. Such critics conclude that the difference principle only issues from the original position if the parties there are artificially assumed to be abnormally reluctant to take risks. If the parties were taken to be normal human beings with normal levels of daring, their rational preference in the original position would be either average utilitarianism or what some writers call "hedged utilitarianism"—average utilitarianism with a guaranteed minimum level of well-being below which no person can fall.[9]

Rawls argues that the parties in the original position will opt for the difference principle because it insures them "against the worst eventualities" (*TJ*, 176). But this puts Rawls in the difficult position of having to explain why people in the original position should be obsessed with this consideration to the exclusion of all others. After all, if one has an equal chance of being anyone in society, then the average utility in that society is the level one can reasonably expect to obtain. Hence, a society that maximized average utility would appear to be quite clearly (almost tautologically) one's wisest bet. Rawls admits this. He writes that, "if the parties [in the initial contracting situation] are viewed as rational individuals who have no aversion to risk and who follow the principle of insufficient reason [that is, assuming an equal likelihood of ending up in one position rather than another in the absence of evidence tilting one way or the other] in computing likelihoods . . . , then the idea of the initial situation leads naturally to the average principle"; he concludes: "The average principle appeals to those in the initial situation once they are conceived as single rational individuals prepared to gamble on the most abstract probabilistic reasoning in all cases. To argue for the two principles of justice I must show that *the conditions defining the original position exclude this conception of the parties*" (*TJ*, 165–66; emphasis mine).

The emphasized words are crucial. On the account of the social contract theory provided by justice as reason's answer to subjugation, I will show that gambling must be excluded in the very design of the contracting situation, if it is to function properly as a model of moral reasoning. Rawls also sees the need to exclude gambling. Instead of trying to show that a prohibition on gambling is a necessary feature of the original position, on par with the veil of ignorance, however, he tries to show that, given the conditions of the original position (without such a prohibition), it is irrational to conceive of the parties in it as willing to gamble. Instead of deriving the exclusion of gambling as a condition necessary to make the original position a valid model of moral reasoning, Rawls tries to derive it from the previously established features of the original position. He uses two arguments. The first relates to the conditions of knowledge in the original position, and the second to what he calls "the strains of commitment." I shall deal briefly with each argument to show that neither is satisfactory.

Rawls introduces a string of questionable assertions to the effect that, behind the veil of ignorance, people in the original position are wholly in the dark about the likelihood that they will occupy any position in society rather than another and about their own levels of risk-tolerance and risk-aversion (*TJ*, 172). Further, they are prohibited from making estimates on the basis of the principle of insufficient reason, and they will have to justify their choices to their offspring (*TJ*, 169). Rawls emerges thus with an overwhelmingly conservative population in the original position, concerned to protect themselves against the worst that could possibly occur. This is implausible for several reasons. First, although people in the original position may have no knowledge about which position they may occupy in the society whose guiding principles they are asked to choose, they would, as its designers, seem able to control the probabilities that would attach to different social positions by building the probabilities into the guiding principles themselves. They could, for example, design a society on the principle that the smartest one-third would be masters and the rest slaves; if they did, there would be no way to keep them from knowing that they had a 66.7 percent chance of ending up a slave. Second, the prohibition against knowledge of levels of risk-tolerance and risk-aversion seems to be an arbitrary limitation on the general knowledge available to people behind the veil of ignorance. Though they do not know their own psychological propensities, they do know general psychological facts about human beings (see, for example, *TJ*, 176). Would not such general psychological information about attitudes toward risk be enough for them to engage in a bit of gambling?

We might imagine that it is in response to just such a question that Rawls introduces his second argument: The parties in the original position must "consider the strains of commitment. They cannot enter into agreements that may have consequences they cannot accept. . . . Moreover, when we enter an agreement we must be able to honor it even should the worst possibilities prove to be the case. Otherwise, we have not acted in good faith" (*TJ*, 176). Thus, consideration of the strains of commitment appears to rule out gambling, at least where there is a risk of an unacceptable outcome. But on several grounds this argument, too, falls short of Rawls's needs.

First, it rests on a conflation of two senses of *unacceptable*. Something might be unacceptable in the sense that one would not freely opt for it or in the sense that one literally could not bear it. Unacceptable can mean either disagreeable or unbearable. The strains of commitment only rule out gambling where there is a risk of an outcome that is unacceptable in the latter sense. One cannot in good faith enter an agreement that includes the possibility of ending up in a position that one literally could not bear, or even that was so close to this that one might be irresistibly tempted to violate the original agreement. But one can in good faith enter an agreement that includes the possibility of ending up in a position that is disagreeable though bearable. Otherwise, we would have to believe that people who, for example, put up their property as collateral for a loan could not do so in good faith. One might not be able in good faith to enter an agreement that includes the possibility of ending up a slave, losing a pound of flesh, or being tortured or killed, but there is no reason to assume that the strains of commitment would make it impossible to agree in good faith to the possibility of ending up in respectable poverty.[10] Thus, the "strains" do not eliminate gambling; they only limit the range of outcomes that can be gambled on. Though the strains of commitment may preclude agreement to average utilitarianism with its bottomless possibility of impoverishment, they do not exclude doctrines like hedged utilitarianism, which pave over this possibility with a tolerable floor below which no one can fall.

Second, different people will surely judge differently the extent to which a possible outcome is unbearable. This makes Rawls's argument irremediably intuitive and dooms his hope of making the argument for the two principles of justice "strictly deductive" (*TJ*, 121). Moreover, since utilitar-

269

ians are, in general, more willing to countenance the inclusion of relatively disadvantaged roles in a society than Rawlsians, the argument is intuitive just at the point at which one can expect the intuitions of utilitarians to diverge from those of Rawlsians and, thus, unlikely to convince precisely those most in need of convincing.

Third, even if the strains of commitment argument were not limited in these ways and even if Rawls could give a convincing account of why people in the original position are deprived of all knowledge of probabilities and of attitudes toward risk, a moral philosophical explanation for these provisions would still be missing. We saw earlier that the features of the original position are justified ultimately because they "make vivid" the requirements of valid moral argumentation for principles of justice. But the appearance of the strains of commitment and the deprivation of knowledge about probabilities and attitudes toward risk as features of the contracting situation seem, at best, a happy coincidence enabling Rawls to combat the gambler argument. The strains of commitment seem particularly ad hoc since the agreement in the original position, being imaginary, ought to pose no psychological problems at all. In any event, neither the strains nor the restrictions on knowledge have any independent moral philosophical rationale comparable to the justification of the veil of ignorance as eliminating the possibility of anyone tailoring principles to his own situation. Thus, even if the strains or the deprivation of knowledge about probabilities and risk succeeded in excluding gambling from the original position, they would give us no understanding of the moral, or moral philosophical, significance of this exclusion. By contrast, we shall see that the theory of the social contract provided by justice as reason's answer to subjugation yields just such an understanding by showing that allowing gambling undermines the capacity of the social contract to identify subjugation.

Without a solution to the gambler problem, Rawls's theory fails. Unless Rawls can show why gambling is to be excluded from the original position, the maximin strategy is undermined. Rational gamblers do not concern themselves exclusively with avoiding the worst that can happen. This may mean, as Rawls himself admits (*TJ*, 165–66), that some form of utilitarianism will be the rational choice of the parties in the original position. What it certainly means is that Rawls's two principles will not be their rational choice. Rational gamblers would not opt for the difference principle with its emphasis on maximizing the share of those worst off at the expense of the shares of those better off. Nor would they agree to the lexical priority of the equal maximum liberty principle that rules out limiting anyone's liberty in return for even substantial gains in material well-being. Moreover, the way in which Rawls has developed his theory makes it impossible for him to deal with gambling in a satisfactory way; indeed, it makes it inevitable that any attempt to do so will look like an ad hoc effort to stave off utilitarianism.

The social contract theory takes as its point of departure a situation that could be real. People could, at some point, sit down and decide among themselves what sort of society they want to have or what principles of justice they want to guide their activities. When philosophers cast this situation into a theoretical device for assessing the justice of social systems, they necessarily transform it into a hypothetical situation. They are then confronted with the question of which features of the real situation should be retained in the hypothetical one and which should not, and they need some rational way of making this determination. For example, in the real situation, people would have knowledge of their personal circumstances, they would be less than perfectly rational, some would be altruists and others envious, they might form coalitions, and their decisions might not be unanimous. All of these are features of the possible real situation that seem inappropriate in the hypothetical counterpart, at least for Rawls. In the real situation it would also be appropriate for contractors to be allowed to gamble if they so chose. Since they would be determining their own destinies and since they would have to live with the consequences of gambles lost, they would surely be entitled to gamble and to have all the knowledge needed to gamble intelligently. Is this feature of the possible real situation to be retained in the hypothetical one?

Rawls's way of dealing with these issues is essentially intuitive. He tries to find the appropriate features of the contracting situation by designing it according to "commonly shared presumptions" and so that the principles of justice that emerge from the contracting situation match our "considered convictions of justice" (*TJ*, 18–19). This procedure may work well enough for the exclusion from the original position of knowledge of particular circumstances or for the requirement that decisions there be unanimous, but it cannot possibly work for the question of gambling. Neither our intuitions nor our most considered moral judgments are refined enough to decide this question. Given sympathy for the disadvantaged on one side and the popularity of utilitarianism and libertarianism (both of which would allow the worst off to be worse off than they would be under the difference principle) on the other, it is evident that we do not have shared intuitions or judgments capable of guiding us confidently either way on whether gambling should or should not be allowed in the contracting situation. Consequently, excluding gambling will not appear as a natural and intuitively plausible restriction and will inevitably appear as an ad hoc restriction designed to exclude utilitarian outcomes. Justice as fairness will not be able to argue successfully

271

against utilitarianism since it will appear to be based on a prior unargued decision to exclude utilitarianism.

The only way out of this impasse is to develop a theory of the social contract theory, one that shows how and when the contract succeeds in modeling moral reasoning properly undertaken. Such a theory would indicate which features are part of the social contract's capacity to model moral reasoning and which undermine that capacity. Justice as reason's answer to subjugation is such a theory. According to it, as we shall see, the appropriateness of the features of Rawls's original position—the veil of ignorance, the interest in pursuing one's ends whatever they may be, and mutual disinterestedness and nonenviousness—stem not merely from commonly shared presumptions, but from the needs of reasoning in a way aimed at identifying subjugation and principles that exclude it. To the extent that I am correct in arguing that reason requires excluding subjugation, then reason is the source of our commonly shared presumptions. That gambling in the contracting situation undermines the capacity of the contract to yield principles that exclude subjugation will provide us with the moral philosophical explanation for prohibiting gambling that Rawls himself cannot supply. I shall take this up shortly. First, however, we must look more closely at the difference principle.

The Difference Principle as the Standard of Nonsubjugating Distributions

In light of the discussions in the first two sections of this chapter, we can say that libertarian capitalists do not notice the way property evokes the suspicion of subjugation and that Marxian anticapitalists do notice it but take the suspicion as its own confirmation. The former do not see how capitalist property forces unequal exchanges of labor, whereas the latter do not see how a system that forces such exchanges can be just. We now turn to this issue. That exclusively-owned property evokes the suspicion of subjugation implies that it must be tested by asking whether it would be reasonable for all people, not knowing whether they would be owners or nonowners, to agree to principles allowing such property. This question is answered by determining what principle governing economic distribution— understood in light of the labor theory of moral value—it would be reasonable for all to accept. I shall argue that the difference principle fills this bill and that something like Rawls's second principle can be deduced from contractarian premises. I say something like Rawls's difference principle in order to signal to the reader that it is not Rawls's second principle of justice that I shall defend, but a principle that requires distribution according to the difference principle. I call the principle that I shall defend "the governing principle of social justice," because I take it to state the logic of any agreement it would be rational for people to reach in the contracting situation regarding the distribution of the benefits of cooperative arrangements. It states the terms that any forced cooperative arrangement must meet to be nonsubjugating.

Because the argument for the governing principle is complex and many-sided, I shall make it in several small steps. Initially, I shall treat the principle simply as one concerned only with the justice of economic distributions. In this section, I shall interpret the principle as applying to economic distributions understood in light of "the labor theory of moral value" and show that this enables us to exhibit the many virtues that Rawls claims for the difference principle but fails to demonstrate. In particular, the principle would be accepted by members of an economic system who recognized that some system of forced labor was necessary to realize their sovereign interests and who wanted to maximize each person's rewards from his labor while minimizing the amount of labor anyone was required to do for anyone else. This means that a system of forced labor that satisfies the difference principle does not subjugate any of its participants and is, therefore, just. With this we can identify the conditions under which capitalism, socialism, and communism—considered strictly as distributive schemes—would be just. In the next section, I shall present a logical deduction of the principle as the rational choice of people in the natural context to govern economic distribution. In the final section, I shall show that the very features that recommend the principle as a principle of economic distribution recommend it as a general principle governing the distribution of all cooperatively produced benefits. Since the principle turns out to be the governing principle of social justice generally, it provides a way to determine the particular principles of social justice.[11]

The difference principle requires redistribution from those who are better off to those who are worse off until that point after which further redistribution no longer increases the long-term absolute size of the shares of those who are worse off. This feature of the difference principle has led a number of commentators to suspect that it is lopsided in favor of those at the bottom of society. Thomas Nagel, for example, finds Rawls's theory resting on the presumption "that sacrifice at the bottom is always worse than sacrifice at the top" or "that sacrifices which lessen social inequality are acceptable while sacrifices which increase inequality are not." And R. M. Hare writes, "A maximin strategy would (and in Rawls does) yield principles of justice according to which it would always be just to impose any loss, however great, upon a better-off group in order to bring a gain, however small, to the least-advantaged group, however affluent the latter's starting point. If intuitions are to be used, this is surely counterintuitive."[12]

Against such criticisms, Rawls maintains that the difference principle is "a principle of mutual benefit" (*TJ*, 102), one under which individuals "do not gain at one another's expense since only reciprocal advantages are allowed." Since it is "one of the fixed points of our considered judgments that no one deserves his place in the distribution of native endowments," the better-off individual is not entitled to claim "that he deserves and therefore has a right to a scheme of cooperation in which he is permitted to acquire benefits in ways that do not contribute to the welfare of others. . . . From the standpoint of common sense, then, the difference principle appears to be acceptable both to the more advantaged and to the less advantaged individual" (*TJ*, 104).

Rawls's argument here is not satisfactory. Even if the better-off or more talented individual is not entitled "to acquire benefits in ways that do not contribute to the welfare of others," it does not follow that he is only entitled to acquire benefits in ways that maximize the welfare of others. Leaving distributions to the workings of the free market also, in effect, forbids anyone to benefit in ways that do not contribute to the welfare of others, since if the market is really free then only mutually beneficial exchanges will be agreed to. The difference between the free market and the difference principle is that the former allows any outcome that improves the exchanging parties' welfares relative to their level before the exchange, whereas the latter allows only that outcome in which the worst-off party's share is the most it can possibly be and the best-off party's is reduced as far as necessary to achieve this. As such, Rawls's argument does not establish the superiority of distributing according to the difference principle over letting the free market run its course, producing what inequalities it may.

Moreover, that the more talented do not deserve their greater talent does not in itself imply that they are only entitled to benefit from those talents in ways that benefit others. That people do not deserve their greater talents supports the notion that they are not entitled to benefit from those talents in ways that make others worse off. But why require any more than this? On the face of it, it seems that Rawls is confusing justice with benevolence and insisting that the more talented have a positive duty to benefit others (regardless of what those others do for them) as a condition of the just enjoyment of the benefits of their own greater talents. It does not seem that the existence of such a positive duty is one of the fixed points in our considered judgments. Even if we grant Rawls that people are not entitled to benefit from their talents in ways that do not improve the welfare of others, then this is surely true for both the more and the less talented. Yet the difference principle, in requiring reduction in the shares of the better off in order to maximize those of the worse off, seems to permit the latter to benefit in ways that do not improve the welfare of others. This suggests that the principle that no one should benefit from her abilities in ways that do not benefit others is only being applied to those with greater abilities and supports the charge that the difference principle is biased in favor of the least advantaged (see, for example, *ASU*, 195). If the principle that no one should benefit from her abilities in ways that do not benefit others is either applied evenhandedly to all groups in society or replaced with the less questionable principle that no one should benefit in ways that worsen the conditions of others, the difference principle seems undermined.

I believe that these charges can be answered, but to do so requires interpreting the difference principle in light of the labor theory of moral value—that is, as governing economic distributions considered as distributions of labor, rather than of goods or money. Remember that *labor* here means time and effort, and, for simplicity, time labored. Goods are products of labor, and money is just paper if it is not an effective claim on other people's labor (in the form of products or services). A distribution of money is a distribution of titles to other people's labor, and a particular distribution of income in a society is a quantitative representation of the proportions in which the members of society work for one another. The implications of this conception are far-reaching. For example, if we take economic distributions as distributions of goods or money, redistributing from the better-off group to the worse-off group according to the difference principle appears to be imposing a sacrifice on the former group for the benefit of the latter. Faced with this, we will naturally ask for a justification for taking from the pockets of the rich to give to the poor. If, however, we understand economic distributions as distributions of titles to the labor of others, the greater shares of the better off will be seen to be made up not of *their* goods or money, but of *other* people's labor. Then we will ask for a justification for allotting the better off even as great a share of other people's labor as the difference principle allows them—and we will be little troubled by the objection that the principle is biased against the better off.

The labor interpretation protects the difference principle against yet other objections. For example, both Sandel and Gauthier argue that determining the rewards that go to talents according to the requirement of the difference principle that the rest of society be benefited to the maximum is based on the dubious assumption that the talents are the "common assets" of the society as a whole rather than of the talented individuals themselves (*LLJ*, 77ff.; *MBA*, 248–54). Whether or not this is true of Rawls's interpretation of the difference principle, it is clearly not true on the labor interpretation. 275

The propriety of determining rewards to talents by the difference principle stems not from who owns the talents, but from who produces the rewards. That the rewards are constituted by the labor of the rest of society turns the question of how high the rewards to talent should be into the question of how much the members of society are to labor for the talented—and that is rightly determined on grounds reasonable to the members of society.

I contend, in fact, that viewing economic distributions as distributions of labor enables us to see the superiority of the difference principle to all alternative distributive principles, including the free market. Further, I shall show that either insisting that the principle that no one benefit from her talents in ways that do not improve the welfare of others be applied even-handedly to the more and the less talented, or replacing it with the principle that no one benefit in ways that worsen the condition of others, supports the difference principle rather than undermining it. Interpreting the difference principle according to the labor theory of moral value shows the difference principle to be truly a principle of mutual benefit, the only principle according to which each benefit conferred by one person on another is matched by a reciprocating benefit. This recognition should dispose of the notion that the difference principle is biased in favor of the least advantaged.

I maintain that the appropriate way to evaluate alternative distributive principles is to view them as different systems of the proportions in which individuals labor for one another and, without assuming the validity of any system of ownership (at least none beyond natural justice), to consider the shares of goods that each such system yields in order to determine which it would be most rational for all to accept. This is of crucial importance to the problem of justifying unequal distributions.

In discussing the justification of unequal distributions, I shall assume that, although the sort of labor that goes into piling huge stones into pyramids or turning bolts on assembly lines may be overtly coerced, labor at above-average levels of talent cannot be coerced effectively. Such labor requires care, attention, cultivation, patience, and self-regulation in degrees that cannot be expected from people who feel they are working against their wills. Accordingly, such labor must either be the individual's spontaneous desire, or it must be perceived by him to contribute to his other desires in a way that spills over onto the labor itself and makes it desired. No defender of capitalism is likely to quarrel with this assumption, and I think that there are grounds in Marxism for acceding to it as well. Most important is that the increase in productivity that accompanies the succession of modes of production in history—from slavery to feudalism to capitalism—is paralleled by a decreasing reliance on open force in the workplace (see, for example, *C*, 1:737). This can hardly be a coincidence, and it strongly suggests that people will work better to the degree to which they see their work as freely undertaken either because it is directly in their sovereign interest or a desirable way to promote their sovereign interest.

On these grounds, it follows that, until such time as the talented work needed in society is exactly what the talented spontaneously want to do, it will be necessary to offer incentives to talented people to draw their talented labors from them. Such incentives will, in general, have to be more than titles or honors, since these can only be granted rarely, if they are to remain meaningful, and even then they bear only a slight relationship to the recipient's sovereign interests. Accordingly, the incentives will have to be material, meaning goods or services. Marxists, at least those who have had to cope with real economies, seem to have recognized this fact. Accordingly, I shall assume that the necessity to grant material incentives to draw out talents is, at least in the present and the foreseeable future, an intransigent fact of human psychology, not eradicated by recognition of its arbitrariness or otherwise easily dislodged. It functions therefore as a fact of nature, to which principles of justice must accommodate themselves, rather than as a creature of justice itself. Like other natural facts, this intransigence may change in time, with important consequences for justice.

Consider how the problem of arriving at a just economic distribution appears in light of the labor theory of moral value. If we conceive of economic distributions as distributions of time labored, we will naturally judge unequal distributions against a baseline distribution in which the goods or money each person receives represents an amount of time labored by others that is equal to the amount of time that he has labored himself. (Since training is also work, we can consider training time as factored into time labored.) It may appear that selection of this as our baseline biases the discussion because it has the effect of requiring deviations from equality to be justified in a way that equality itself need not be. But this starting point is not biased, because it is not selected based on a presumption in favor of equality. It is selected rather based on a presumption against subjugation. It is the baseline that it would be reasonable for everyone in the natural context to agree to use in determining whether subjugation was occurring by means of structural force in an economic system that allows ownership beyond natural justice.

From this baseline, in the natural context, consider how the question of the justice of unequal distributions would take shape. Assuming (for the sake of simplicity) that everyone works the same amount of time, we can say that in the equal distribution that is our baseline, everyone contributes and receives the products of the same time labored, say t hours. We can represent this distribution as a series of exchanges between everyone and

277

everyone else in which each gives and receives t hours labored, in the form of services or products. If an equal distribution can be represented as such a series of exchanges, it can be represented even more simply as an exchange between any two members of society selected at random. Assume that we select A and B, who are exchanging t for t and ending up with equal shares. Against this baseline, A asserts that she is more talented than B and thus entitled to something better than an equal share. She claims that her t hours of labor given to B should bring her in return $t + n$ hours of labor from B. The question of whether an unequal distribution is just, then, comes down to whether and when it would be mutually reasonable for A and B to exchange t hours of A's labor for $t + n$ hours of B's labor.

Remember that A and B are not to be thought of as traders bringing goods from distant zones but as members of a single economic system, a cooperative scheme in which what each gives and gets affects the total amount produced and thus the absolute size of everyone's share. In this light, it will be reasonable for B to contribute $t + n$ hours of labor in return for A's t hours of labor, if the result were to increase output in a way that makes B better off than he was when he was giving and receiving t hours. Of course, it must make B better off in an amount greater than the output of n alone, since he could conceivably have worked the additional n hours for himself and added the resultant output to what he received when all were giving and getting t. Note that talent, here, is any capacity that makes someone able to produce things that other people want in something less than the time it takes people on average.

It will be rational for B to contribute $t + n$ hours of labor to A where the result is to increase B's share by m (a quantity of goods not labor—A's labor for B is still t), where m is the surplus over B's share when he and A contributed t, plus what B could produce for himself with n. Presumably, this could happen where giving B's $t + n$ to A worked as an incentive to bring out A's greater talents in a way that raised overall output and increased B's share by m. We can say that it would be rational for A and B to exchange t hours of A's labor for $t + n$ hours of B's, whenever the increment of n hours to A is sufficient to encourage her to devote her talents to the cooperative venture in a way that results in an increment to B of m goods.

A numerical example will help here. Imagine that a society has only two groups, those with greater than average abilities, the A's, and those with average abilities, the B's. We can then think of the economic distribution in this society as an exchange of labor between an A and a B as representatives of their groups. Assume that A's produce loaves of bread and B's produce cups of sugar and that the average level of output in the society is one loaf or cup per hour labored. Assuming that without special incentive A's produce at the average level, an equal distribution (for an eight-hour day of labor) looks like this:

1. *equal distribution*

	A		B
Measured in labor-time:	8 hours	⟷	8 hours
Measured in goods:	8 loaves	⟷	8 cups

In this case, A and B each contribute 8 hours of their labor to each other, in the form of an exchange of 8 loaves for 8 cups. A receives 1 cup for an hour of her labor, and B receives 1 loaf for an hour of his.

Assume now that with some incentive A can double her output and that the minimum increment that will suffice as an incentive to bring out this heightened productivity voluntarily is a 50 percent increase in what she earns per hour. (Determining what incentives will bring about what levels of productivity is, of course, no easy task. I assume, however, that it is in principle possible by experimenting with different levels of incentive.) Nothing less makes enough of a difference to A. Since B always works at the average level of productivity, this will require B to work proportionately 50 percent more. Since this is the minimum incentive that A will accept and the lowest increase in productivity she gives in return, we can refer to this case as that of the lowest minimum incentive. Under it, the resulting distribution would be:

2. *lowest minimum incentive*

	A		B
Measured in labor-time:	8 hours	⟷	12 hours
Measured in goods:	16 loaves	⟷	12 cups

In this case, A trades 8 hours of her labor for 12 hours of B's (the *t* for *t* + *n* in our previous discussion), in the form of an exchange of 16 loaves for 12 cups. In this case the range of inequality is that A earns 150 percent of what B earns—that is, for a day of labor A receives money sufficient to purchase the products of a day and a half of B's labor. Here A receives 1½ cups for an hour of her labor, and B receives 1⅓ loaves for an hour of his. The exchange is reasonable for A ex hypothesi—we set it at the minimum incentive that A would find reasonable to bring forth her more productive efforts voluntarily. The exchange is reasonable for B because he receives an additional ⅓ loaf for every hour of his work over and above what he had in the equal distribution (the *m* in our previous discussion).

Let us assume further that A can produce even more than 16 loaves in

279

a day. Her maximum productivity is 24 loaves. For this, the minimum incentive that she will accept is a 100 percent increase in what she earns per hour (compared to equal distribution). Since B always works at the average level of productivity, this incentive will require B to work proportionately 100 percent more (compared to equal distribution). Since this incentive is the minimum that A will accept for her new level of productivity, and since this is her highest level of productivity, we can refer to this case as that of the highest minimum incentive. Under it, the resulting distribution would be:

3. *highest minimum incentive*

	A		B
Measured in labor-time:	8 hours	⟷	16 hours
Measured in goods:	24 loaves	⟷	16 cups

In this case A trades 8 hours of her labor for 16 hours of B's, in the form of an exchange of 24 loaves for 16 cups. In this case the range of inequality is that A earns twice what B earns—that is, for a day of labor A receives money sufficient to purchase the products of two days of B's labor. Here, A receives 2 cups for an hour of her labor and B receives 1½ loaves for an hour of his. Once again, for A, the exchange is reasonable ex hypothesi. It is reasonable for B because he receives an additional ½ loaf for every hour of his work over and above what he had in the equal distribution (a higher *m* than in case 2).

Although 16 cups is the minimum that A will take for the 24 loaves she produces in a day, there is a range above 16 for which she could ask that would still leave B better off than he was under equal distribution. If A were to demand 23 cups in return for her 24 loaves, B would have to work 23 hours to get the 24 loaves, and he would end up earning $1\frac{1}{23}$ loaves for each hour labored, which is still better than the 1 loaf per hour he received under equal distribution. Assuming that 16 cups is A's bottom line, were A to offer her 24 loaves on the free market, B would find it reasonable to pay anywhere from 16 to 23 cups in return. We can say that, were these exchanges left to the market, the resultant distribution would be indeterminate in this range, since any trade of 24 loaves for anything between 16 and 23 cups would be beneficial to A and B. Under the free market, the resulting distribution would be:

4. *free market range*

	A		B
Measured in labor-time:	8 hours	⟷	16 to 23 hours
Measured in goods:	24 loaves	⟷	16 to 23 cups

In this case, A trades 8 hours of her labor for anywhere from 16 to 23 hours of B's, in the form of an exchange of 24 loaves for anything from 16 to 23 cups. The maximum range of inequality that could result from these exchanges would have A earning 2⅞ as much as B; for a day of labor A would receive money sufficient to purchase the products of 2⅞ days (23 hours) of B's labor. For A, any of these exchanges are reasonable ex hypothesi; they start at her minimal acceptable incentive and improve from there. Any of these exchanges are reasonable for B because he receives at least 1 1/23 loaves per hour, which is more than the 1 loaf an hour he receives under equal distribution. (I am momentarily ignoring case 2 to keep matters simple. I am also assuming that, whatever the competitive market does to reduce prices, it has done it in setting the price somewhere between 16 and 23, and thus, no further reduction is to be expected.)

Assuming that the four cases discussed are the only possible alternatives, the difference principle requires the third, where A and B exchange 24 loaves for 16 cups. In this case, the inequality between the best-off and worst-off representative persons, A and B, is reduced as far as necessary to maximize the share of the worst off (B gets 24 loaves or 1½ loaves per hour). Were the inequality reduced further, A would not produce 24 loaves a day, and B's share would decline. Were the inequality increased, B would be giving more than 16 hours to A, and B's share (per hour) would decline. Using the notation introduced earlier, we can say that the difference principle permits inequalities—exchanges of t for $t + n$ hours of labor—where n is the smallest increment that will produce the largest m for the worst-off person in the distribution. In the case at hand, n is eight hours of B's labor and m is the surplus of half a loaf per hour that B gets over what he would have had in an equal distribution.

Consider now how the objection that the difference principle is biased in favor of the worse off and against the better off arises and how it is cast in new light by viewing economic distributions as distributions of labor. If A could have gotten 23 cups for her 24 loaves on the market and the difference principle only allows her 16 cups, then this does seem a lopsided affair, since no limitation is placed on B's share, especially since the exchange of 23 cups for 24 loaves would also have improved B's position. Moreover, if our distributive system operates on a free market basis with taxation and transfer payments used after the fact to bring distributions in line with the difference principle, A will first get her 23 cups and then the government will come along, forcibly confiscate 7 cups, and transfer them back to B. At best, this looks like Robin Hood stealing from the rich to give to the poor, and at worst like forcing A to labor for B on terms not of A's choosing.

This is how the redistribution ordered by the difference principle looks if we think of an economic distribution as a matter of individuals' shares in money or goods. If, instead, we view the distribution as a matter of individuals' shares in other people's labor, things take on an entirely different cast. In this light, the 7 cups that A might get on the market (above the 16 allowed by the difference principle) represent 7 additional hours of B's labor for A. What gives A the right to have B labor these additional 7 hours for her? We cannot simply say that she has this right because it would be reasonable for B to agree to it on the free market, since that assumes in advance that free market exchanges are just, which is what we are trying to determine. Such exchanges may simply reflect A's ability to hold her products off the market, and this may be a socially constituted power to extract an extra premium from B. To stay neutral on the question of the justice of market exchanges, we must ask what benefits B derives from working these additional 7 hours for A. And the answer is none. This labor produces no benefits for B that he could not already have working 16 hours to produce the 16 cups that (ex hypothesi) A would have accepted for her 24 loaves.

Considering economic distributions as distributions of labor, it becomes clear that in limiting A to 16 cups from B, the difference principle is not confiscating 7 cups from A. It is prohibiting A from obtaining additional labor from B without benefiting B in return. Labor by B beyond the 16 hours necessary to produce 16 cups results in no additional benefit for B. If, on the market, A can get more than 16 hours of labor from B without conferring additional benefits on B, then this must reflect some advantage that gives A the leverage to extract additional labor from B without compensating it. This is what the difference principle prohibits and why the principle defeats the suspicion of subjugation regarding systems of forced cooperative production.

This way of understanding what the difference principle requires also enables us to see how it is truly a principle of mutual benefit. In setting the distribution at 24 loaves for 16 cups, it assures that A and B are benefited for *all* of the labor that each contributes to the other. We know that A is benefited; ex hypothesi, she finds 16 cups reasonable compensation for producing her 24 loaves. In producing 16 cups, B does only that much additional labor (above the baseline of equal exchanges) for which he receives benefits in return. For A to ask for more is to ask B to work for her additionally for no additional compensation. This is (or should have been) Rawls's answer to the better-off man to show that he "has no grounds for complaint" when his share is limited by the difference principle. He cannot complain because the only limit on his greater share is the requirement that every increment of greater-than-equal labor that others contribute to him must make those others better off as well. In these terms, Rawls could show that the difference principle is "a fair basis on which those better endowed . . . could expect others to collaborate with them" (*TJ*, 103).

We can also now see clearly the difference between the difference principle and free market exchanges. We can represent the range of inequality in our example by the fraction $(t + n)/t$, since A's income is $(t + n)/t$ times B's (that is, A is paid for t hours of her labor enough money to purchase the products of $t + n$ hours of B's labor). Such inequalities are reasonable if they produce a surplus of m for B over what B could have gotten for his $t + n$ hours under equality. We can think of an unequal distribution, then, as an exchange in which B contributes n to A in return for A's m to B. The free market allows any exchange of n for m that leaves both parties better off than before the exchange. (In our example, this means that n can vary between 8 and 15 hours of B's labor, above the 8 hours represented by t.) The difference principle allows only the smallest n that will encourage A to produce m in return (this n is 8 hours in our example). If a larger n will produce a larger m, then the difference principle requires this larger n. (This is why the difference principle requires the third rather than the second of the cases in our example.) The market requires only that the total n yield a surplus of m to B. The difference principle requires that every unit of n from B to A yield an additional unit of m for B. The market would, thus, allow n to go to 15 hours because this total still leaves B with a surplus (an additional $1/23$ loaf per hour). But the difference principle limits n to 8 hours because the units of n beyond this yield no additional unit of m to B. Accordingly, the difference principle limits labor for others to the smallest amount necessary to benefit the laborers themselves, subject to the constraint of having to provide enough benefit to the talented to make it reasonable for them to provide benefits in return voluntarily.

When the difference principle is implemented in a real situation, say, by taxes and transfer, the "money illusion" hides the true nature of the principle. By the money illusion, I mean the belief that the real substance of economic distributions is money (or goods), rather than labor.[13] The money illusion makes it appear that the difference principle, operating by means of taxes and transfers, confiscates A's money (or goods) and gives them to B, when, in fact, it is limiting B's labor for A. This illusion leads to the error of thinking that the difference principle simply imposes sacrifices on the better off for the benefit of the worse off. Once the money illusion is dispelled, the share of the best off is seen to be constituted by the labor of   283 others. Limiting this share is not imposing a sacrifice on the best off; it is making sure that those whose labor constitutes the share of the best off receive compensation in return and give no extra labor that does not receive such compensation. On the other hand, the best-off's share is allowed to rise to that point necessary to make it reasonable for her to work voluntarily in the ways that benefit those whose labor constitutes that share. The more talented person gets her greater than equal share $(t + n)$ only insofar as she gives a compensating benefit (m) to the less talented. The less talented one receives this benefit only insofar as he gives his greater than equal labor time in return as a benefit to the more talented. This shows, I believe, more clearly than Rawls has been able to, how the difference principle is a principle of reciprocal advantage or mutual benefit, compatible with insisting that both more and less talented persons benefit from their talents in ways that benefit others.

Moreover, this provides an answer to the critique of the difference principle leveled by Gauthier in *Morals by Agreement*. Gauthier takes the difference principle to be a standard for distributing "factor rent," the premium that people possessing scarce assets are able to obtain "over and above the full cost of supply, because there is no alternative to meet the demand" (*MBA*, 272). In the case where the scarce assets are special talents, Gauthier takes the factor rent to be the surplus of the actual payment the talented one can command on the market over "the least amount that would induce him" to use those talents (*MBA*, 273). In our example, this surplus is the number of cups of sugar above 16 that A could get on the free market. Gauthier rightly observes that under the difference principle this surplus goes wholly to the least advantaged (*MBA*, 276)—though, on the labor theory, it is more precise to say that this amount of labor *stays* with the least advantaged. Gauthier proposes instead not the libertarian view that the whole surplus should go to whoever can get it on the market, but the seemingly moderate view that it should be divided equally between better and worse off (*MBA*, 277). Compared to this, the difference principle does appear unreasonably to favor the worst off. But once we look at economic exchanges in the light of the labor theory of moral value, then factor rent is not merely a neutral surplus to be divided up as seems fair. Factor rent is other people's labor, and awarding even half of it to the talented effectively gives them the power to have other people work for them beyond what is necessary to induce them to exercise their talents. Gauthier's equal division appears to pass the test of fairness but actually fails the test of subjugation.

In addition to maintaining that the difference principle is a principle of mutual benefit, I stated earlier that the difference principle is compatible with the notion that persons should not benefit from their talents in ways that worsen the condition of others. Again, the money illusion makes it appear that the difference principle confuses benevolence with justice and imposes a positive duty on the more talented to benefit others as a condition of reaping the benefits of their own greater talents. If the difference principle distributes labor rather than money, then it is not insisting that the more talented give some of their money away to the less—it is insisting that the more talented take no more labor from the less talented than they return benefits for. Thus, it prevents the more talented from benefiting in ways that worsen the condition of the less talented by costing the latter more labor without benefiting them in return.

In this way, the difference principle defeats the suspicion of subjugation. The full argument for this conclusion waits upon the demonstration, in the following section, that it would be most reasonable for everyone to agree to the difference principle in the natural context. For the moment, it suffices to recall that the difference principle would not be necessary if—as libertarian capitalists believe—systems of exclusive ownership were not significantly different from natural ownership. Then, actual freedom from violence and fraud would suffice to show that exchanges were not subjugating. Once systems of exclusive ownership are established, however, the danger arises that the very exclusivity of that ownership gives the owner extra leverage to extract service from the nonowner. Since this occurs through exchanges free of violence and fraud, it looks like an exchange between people who, because of their different talents, have different things to offer. What the argument of this section shows is that, if such exchanges satisfy the difference principle, then they are not subjugating, because any additional leverage that might come from ownership (or anything else, for that matter) has been eliminated. That no one labors for anyone else any more than the least amount necessary to make it reasonable for the other to provide him a benefit means that no one can complain of subjugation where the difference principle is satisfied.

The difference principle, as I have defended it here, is an accommodation to the need for incentives to bring out talented labor. This necessity is rooted in human nature, but it could change in history. If such a change took place, the same difference principle would require different principles of distribution in light of this change. We can thus identify the historical conditions under which justice would require capitalism, socialism, and communism. Note that I consider these here only with respect to their characteristic distributive arrangements, leaving aside their legal and political features.

The interpretation of the difference principle that I have given here does not imply that the principle can only operate between people who are actually

285

contributing their labor to the social product, nor does it imply that greater rewards must flow directly and exclusively to those with greater talents. Once a system with the rationale I have outlined got going, there is no particular limit on the size of $t + n$ relative to t, as long as a suitably large m is returned to the worse off. If $t + n$ became so large that an individual could not himself spend it in his lifetime or did not wish to, he could give or bequeath some of it to others who might not have to work at all. As long as this magnitude of $t + n$ was necessary to evoke the m, this would still be justified according to the difference principle, because reducing $t + n$ would reduce m and worsen the condition of the worse off. Moreover, as long as it is reasonable for the worse off to contribute their $t + n$ to those with greater talents in return for m, it will be reasonable for them to contribute their $t + n$ to a scheme that yields them m, even if this means that the $t + n$ does not end up in the hands of those whose talents have gone into m. That is, once economic distributions are seen as distributions of labor, any distribution that satisfies the difference principle by reducing the share of the best-off group as far as necessary to maximize the share of the worst-off group, and the shares of all the groups above them (per the lexical principle), in turn, is a distribution in which no one labors more for others than is necessary to yield him benefits in return. Any such system is one in which people work for one another on nonsubjugating terms.

These last remarks show the conditions under which people would labor for one another on terms that are not subjugating in a capitalist economy. Since the free market is open-ended in its outcomes, it might spontaneously yield the distribution required by the difference principle. More likely, this would have to be achieved by political intervention in the form of redistributive taxation and welfare policies, aimed at reducing inequalities and improving the share of the worse off until the point of diminishing returns. Rawls spends considerable time in *A Theory of Justice* describing the institutions of such a modified capitalist economy (*TJ*, 258–84).

This conclusion might appear to confirm Marxist suspicions that the difference principle is an ideological justification of capitalism, albeit clothed in the garments of the welfare state. In fact, the difference principle is neutral between capitalism, socialism, and communism (understood as distributive schemes). Which of these is just according to the principle depends strictly on empirical conditions. Under appropriate conditions, the difference principle leads to the distributive standards associated with socialism and communism.

In *The Critique of the Gotha Program*, Marx introduces two standards of distribution, one for the first phase of communism as it emerges after capitalism and one for the second or higher phase that emerges when productivity is so great that scarcity is, for all intents and purposes, overcome. Following a long tradition, I refer to the first phase as "socialism" and the second as "communism." Marx's distributive standard for socialism is (with some minor modifications) identical to the one we identified earlier as the baseline of equal exchanges of labor time. At this stage, Marx writes, the laborer "receives a certificate from society that he has furnished such and such an amount of labour . . . , and with this certificate he draws from the social stock of means of consumption as much as costs the same amount of labour. The same amount of labour which he has given society in one form he receives back in another" (*CGP*, 530).[14] Marx's distributive standard for communism is the famous slogan, "From each according to his ability, to each according to his needs" (*CGP*, 531).

Recall that the difference principle allows deviation from the baseline of equal exchanges of labor time when incentives are needed to draw forth the more productive labor of the more talented members of society so as to maximize the share of the rest. Talent is the product of natural gifts plus training. Since the calculation of labor time at the baseline of equal exchanges already includes time spent training and developing one's talents, incentives to the talented in effect reward people for their possession of greater than average natural gifts. I say *in effect* because people are not rewarded merely for possessing greater talents, but for using them in ways that improve the shares of others. Nevertheless, since this amounts to unequal rewards for equal amounts of labor, it results in greater rewards for those who happen to have greater talents. For reasons outside of their control, those with lesser abilities have no chance to receive these greater rewards. Rawls recognizes that fortune in the distribution of natural abilities is arbitrary and inappropriate as a grounds for greater reward (*TJ*, 104). Thus, he requires that such rewards work as incentives to benefit the rest of society, not just talented individuals.

If the difference principle justifies this accommodation to human nature when it is necessary to maximize the share of the worst off, it follows that the accommodation is no longer justified when no longer necessary. In short, if history brought us to a point at which either people were so enlightened as no longer to need inequalities as incentives for more productive labor or production were so efficiently organized that what everyone would do in exchange for an equal share were enough to maximize the share of the worst off, inequalities would no longer be necessary to maximize that share and would thus no longer be allowed under the difference principle. The baseline of equal exchanges of labor time, Marx's socialist principle, would be the standard of just distribution. Under the difference principle, the question of whether justice requires capitalism or socialism is answered by determining

287

if the conditions obtain in which unequal incentives are no longer necessary to maximize the share of the worst off.

In the same way that the difference principle is able to determine whether justice requires capitalism or socialism, so it is able to determine whether justice requires communism. Marx's communist principle is a more perfect principle of equality than his socialist principle; the socialist principle countenances inequalities that the communist principle does not. Since the difference principle requires reducing inequalities as far as necessary to maximize the share of the worst off, it leads from capitalism to socialism when capitalist inequalities are no longer necessary, and it leads from socialism to communism when socialist inequalities are no longer necessary. This is hard to see because the socialist principle appears to be a perfectly egalitarian principle, whereas the communist principle no longer requires equal shares at all. Consequently, some commentators take Marx's move from the socialist to the communist principle to reflect an abandonment of egalitarianism.[15] Marx's explanation for the move indicates, however, that just the reverse is the case. Having stated the socialist principle of equal reward for equal time labored, Marx writes:

> This *equal right* is still stigmatised by a bourgeois limitation. The right of the producers is *proportional* to the labour they supply; the equality consists in the fact that measurement is made with an *equal standard*, labour.
>
> But one man is superior to another physically or mentally and so supplies more labour in the same time, or can labour for a longer time; and labour, to serve as a measure, must be defined by its duration or intensity, otherwise it ceases to be a standard of measurement. The *equal* right is an unequal right for unequal labor. It recognizes no class differences, because everyone is only a worker like everyone else; but it tacitly recognizes unequal individual endowment and thus productive capacity as natural privileges. *It is, therefore, a right of inequality, in its content, like every right.* Right by its very nature can consist only in the application of an equal standard; but unequal individuals (and they would not be different individuals if they were not unequal) are measurable only by an equal standard in so far as they are brought under an equal point of view, are taken from one *definite* side only, for instance, in the present case, are regarded *only as workers* and nothing more is seen in them, everything else being ignored. Further, one worker is married, another not; one has more children than another, and so on and so forth. Thus, with an equal performance of labour, and hence an equal share in the social consumption fund, one will in fact receive

more than another, one will be richer than another, and so on. To avoid all these defects, right instead of being equal would have to be unequal. (*CGP*, 530–31)

It is probably this last sentence that has led commentators to think that Marx's move to the communist principle is a move away from egalitarianism. But note the nature of the defects in the socialist principle that the communist principle is meant to remedy. As the quotation indicates, these defects are the inequalities that result from measuring naturally unequal (that is, differently endowed) people by an equal standard. Interestingly enough, these same sort of defects led from the capitalist to the socialist principle—namely, giving people greater rewards because of their greater natural endowments or, as Marx has it, allowing the latter to function as "natural privileges." The communist principle avoids these defects because it makes each person his own standard: Each person's productive contribution is measured against his own abilities, and his share in consumption is measured against his own needs. Thus, though what each contributes and receives is a different amount, all have their abilities equally taxed and their needs equally satisfied. By comparison, the socialist principle still allows inequalities.

What allows transcendence of the defective socialist principle is the effective conquest of scarcity: When "all the springs of cooperative wealth flow more abundantly—only then can . . . society inscribe upon its banner: From each according to his ability, to each according to his needs!" (*CGP*, 531). The effective conquest of scarcity does not mean the total elimination of scarcity, or, for that matter, of work. It means the reduction of scarcity to that point at which the desire to labor is itself sufficient to motivate whatever work remains necessary for the satisfaction of everyone's needs. Thus, it coincides, for Marx, with the point at which "labour has become not only a means of life but life's prime want" (*CGP*, 531). With this development, movement to the communist principle is possible because it is no longer necessary to force people to labor by making how much they consume depend on how much they labor. Once it is no longer necessary to tie consumption to labor, it is no longer necessary to measure people's contributions and rewards by a common measure. It becomes possible to avoid the inequalities that result from measuring differently endowed people by an equal standard and instead to allow each to be his own standard.

Showing that a property system yields distributions in conformity with the difference principle overcomes the suspicion that any participants in the system are thereby subjugated. This is because the difference principle is really a principle of reciprocal advantage, one that all would accept if all

289

were concerned to maximize the benefits of cooperation while minimizing the degree to which anyone would be required to labor for another. Showing this amounts to showing that the principle is reasonable for those on either side of relationships patterned on the principle. We now turn to the logical deduction of the principle from contractarian premises.

Revising Rawls and Deducing the Difference Principle

About his argument for the principles of justice, Rawls writes: "I should like to show that their acknowledgment is the only choice consistent with the full description of the original position. The argument aims eventually to be strictly deductive. . . . Unhappily the reasoning I shall give will fall far short of this, since it is highly intuitive throughout" (*TJ*, 121). In my view things are not nearly so bleak. I shall argue that, once the exclusion of gambling is seen as essential to the social contract, the difference principle is, in fact, "the only choice consistent with a full description of the original position," and thus a strict logical deduction from contractarian premises of a principle of social justice like Rawls's second principle can be achieved. If justice as reason's answer to subjugation is correct and contractarian premises are the appropriate ones for posing the question of social justice, then what can be deduced from these premises is the correct answer to this question. It is a genuine article of moral knowledge, a true principle of justice.

Let us turn to the exclusion of gambling. We can accomplish this for Rawls's theory, if we take justice as reason's answer to subjugation as the theory of the social contract underlying justice as fairness. As the reader can see by referring to the description of the contracting situation at the end of chapter 1, important features of justice as fairness correspond to those of justice as reason's answer: The original position corresponds to the natural context. The interest in pursuing one's plan of life whatever it may be corresponds to the desire of everyone in the natural context to pursue his sovereign interest whatever it may be. The veil of ignorance embodies the restrictions on knowledge of one's particular interests, moral beliefs, and of how one will be affected by principles selected. Mutual disinterestedness and nonenviousness correspond to the nonfungibility of sovereign interests (and not to egoism or selfishness). The conditions of agreement in the natural context were derived by showing their role in generating principles that eliminate subjugation. Insofar as the conditions of agreement in Rawls's original position correspond to those in the natural context, the features of Rawls's theory can be thought of as conditions necessary to generate principles that eliminate subjugation. This would provide a moral philosophical foundation for Rawls's theory, firmer and stronger than the intuitive grounds he himself provides.

With this foundation, Rawls could have excluded gambling in the very design of the original position by deriving the conditions of the original position to yield principles that exclude subjugation, since, as was already suggested in chapter 1, gambling subverts this capacity. The test of the reasonableness of accepting a principle overcomes the suspicion of subjugation because what is reasonable to accept in light of one's sovereign interest is the reverse of subjugation. This test must be applicable to the principles governing existing societies, and thus it must be capable of determining whether the actual occupants of positions in those societies are subjugated. The social contract only works as a test of subjugation, then, if, because a principle would be agreed to under its imaginary conditions, we can infer that it would be reasonable for all the people who actually end up in any of the positions that principle yields to accept those positions. The inference is not that people actually affirm and embrace their actual fates—rather, that it would be reasonable for them to accept those fates. The trick to the social contract lies in the fact that this inference about the actual situation can only be made on the basis of a theoretical argument in imaginary conditions. But the imaginary conditions must be such as to warrant the inference. This is how I derived the conditions in the natural context, and the conditions of Rawls's original position could have been derived this way. Gambling must be eliminated, because the fact that one would have accepted gambling on ending up where one actually is does not—for one who has not actually gambled—warrant the inference that it would be reasonable to accept being there.

Positions in a social structure are essentially positions into which people are born. That people can, in certain societies, change their positions or improve their conditions should not be allowed to obscure this. That a person may change his situation in one society and not in another reflects that the positions in the first society are characterized by possibilities of mobility that do not characterize the positions in the second, but this is a fact about those positions. That a person born into the American working class has some limited chance of elevating himself to the class of entrepreneurs is itself a feature of the working class position into which he has been born— but that he has been born into a working class position that has such and such possibilities is something he can not change. The question of social justice is, then, raised about the positions in a society with their possibilities of change or lack thereof. With the positions so understood, the occupants of the positions in a social structure should not be thought of as having had any real possibility of ending up in other positions than they do.

It is reasonable to gamble on ending up with an unfavorable outcome, in light of the chance of ending up in more favorable ones. But it is only reasonable to do so if one really has the chance of ending up in the more favorable ones. Precisely this is lacking in the case of the actual positions people occupy in existing social structures. To say of such people that it would be reasonable for them to accept a gamble in which they might end up in the positions they actually occupy is to say that it would be reasonable for them to accept the gamble, not the positions. It implies nothing about the latter, since they never had the chance of being anywhere else.

The imagery of the social contract is misleading here, since it suggests a decision made "before" entering society and, thus, made at a point at which everyone seems to have the chance of ending up anywhere in that society. This gives the false appearance that gambling is appropriate. Once we design the contracting situation as a device capable of testing for subjugation of actual people in existing societies, we see that the notion that the parties decide before entering society is an illusion created because questions about subjugation of existing people in existing societies—who had no chance of ending up anywhere but where they are—must be posed theoretically, and thus hypothetically. Once justice as reason's answer to subjugation is understood as the theory of the social contract theory, as the account of the social contract's power as a model of moral reasoning, then gambling has no place in the design of the contracting situation since it would undermine that power. The gambler problem is an illusion that comes from being taken in by the vivid imagery of the imaginary contracting situation. The illusion is dispelled when we have a theory of the social contract theory that enables us to see the point of this imaginary situation.

Another way to see how gambling undermines the moral philosophical force of agreement in the contracting situation is as follows. In order to show that a social structure is not subjugating to all its members, we must be able to show that all its positions would be reasonable for each of their actual occupants to accept. Since a person occupies his position individually, this requires that the positions be reasonable to accept individually. But gambling makes the choice of principles in the natural context a question of whether it is rational to accept the positions determined by those principles as a package deal. That is, when I accept the possibility of gambling on some outcome X, I do so as part of accepting a gamble on a range of outcomes, A to Z, of which X is one possibility. If X is truly undesirable, the rationality of accepting the A to Z package with X a possibility lies not in the acceptability of X, but of the whole package of possibilities of which X is one. Moreover, accepting the A to Z package with the possibility of undesirable X is rational to the degree to which I am not likely to end up in X. Thus, far from signaling the acceptability to me of every outcome including X, acceptability to me of the A to Z package signifies the acceptability to me of the low risk of having to accept X. This is as far from accepting ending up in X as crossing the street is from throwing oneself in front of a truck. Gambling passes off, as acceptance of an undesirable position, the acceptance of the reasonableness of risking that position, when this latter is a reasonable risk only insofar as it is reasonable to expect not to end up there. That is virtually the opposite of accepting the position, and it is surely not enough to defeat the suspicion of subjugation with regard to positions in a social structure occupied by real people.

Further, suppose gambling were allowed in the natural context and suppose that people there were choosing between two alternative social structures. If people had to choose between a society in which everyone would have a life of decent wage labor and one in which 1 percent of the population would be born into lifelong miserable slavery while 99 percent would live better than decent wage laborers, they might not be willing to take the one-in-a-hundred risk. But suppose this latter alternative were changed so that one tenth of one percent would be slaves, and there was thus a one-in-a-thousand chance of being the slave, or so that one one-thousandth of a percent would be slaves, so that there was a one-in-a-hundred-thousand chance. Eventually, it would be reasonable for everyone to prefer this to the wage-labor alternative, since we normally take one-in-a-hundred-thousand chances of worse fates for much less, say, when driving a car. Let us assume that, when we reach this level of risk of turning out to be the slave, it is reasonable for the parties in the natural context to agree to the society with slaves over the wage-labor alternative. Can we infer from this that it would be reasonable for the person who actually turns out to be the slave to accept his fate? Remember that it only became rational to accept the society with slaves as the likelihood of ending up the slave was decreased from a one-in-a-hundred, to a one-in-a-thousand, and finally to a one-in-a-hundred-thousand chance. Without change in anything about the slave position, just by the addition of other positions alongside it—which the actual slave never had a chance of occupying—the principle providing for the slave position became acceptable.

Generalizing from this, if the number of better positions increases, it will eventually be reasonable for gamblers to accept a package that includes the most terrible of outcomes, as long as they are few enough. Gambling would eliminate the possibility of distinguishing cases in which a small number are subjugated from cases in which none are. The choice made by gamblers is not a choice to accept all the positions in a society but to accept a package deal that includes some positions that they would not accept otherwise.

Gambling rolls back that very feature of the social contract by which Rawls took it to be an advance over utilitarianism. Utilitarianism allows the misery of some to be justified by enough satisfaction to others, even though this in no way improves the position of the miserable. The social contract outflanks this possibility by making the choice of principles a unanimous one made by separate individuals. But gambling reintroduces the possibility that individuals might rationally and unanimously opt for a situation in which the misery of some is justified by enough satisfaction to others, even though this does not improve the condition of the miserable. Gambling does this because allowing everyone to accept a principle based on how many more chances it offers of doing well than of doing miserably effectively justifies imposing miserable fates on some by the number of good ones that will be enjoyed by others. By allowing people to find package deals (which include unacceptable positions) acceptable, gambling neutralizes the effect of requiring unanimous agreement by separate persons in the contracting situation.

In sum, an argument that people would accept some principle when they could gamble on how they would be affected by it is not equivalent to an argument that all would accept all the ways they could be affected by it. Gambling eliminates that feature of the social contract that enables it to test the suspicion of subjugation.

If the contract is understood as a way of posing and answering the question of subjugation, gambling must be excluded in the very design of the contracting situation. To do this, I shall assume that it is never rational for an individual to gamble on inestimable probabilities. Then, we can eliminate gambling by requiring—as a feature of the contracting situation, on par with requiring ignorance or unanimity—that people judge the reasonableness of accepting any principle to govern their social structure by imagining that they have a literally inestimable chance of ending up in any of its positions. This excludes assigning a fifty-fifty chance to indeterminate or unknown probabilities. Moreover, since what one can be sure of in accepting a principle is that one will have at least its worst position, a decision to accept a principle on these terms is equivalent to accepting ending up in all the positions that the principle may yield. This is necessary and sufficient to defeat the suspicion that those positions subjugate their actual occupants.

This opens the way for completing Rawls's abandoned project of a strict
logical deduction of the difference principle: Assuming alternative distri-

butions for the same size population with the same level of technology and resources, any distribution in which one might do better than the best-off person in a difference-principle distribution must also be a distribution in which one might do worse than the worst-off person in a difference-principle distribution. Things are actually a bit more complicated than this because a distribution could fail to satisfy the lexical difference principle, though its worst-off and best-off positions were the same as those in a difference-principle distribution, if some of its middling positions were worse than their counterparts in the difference-principle distribution; or it could fail to satisfy the difference principle though all its positions were comparable to those in the difference-principle distribution, if it had more individuals clustered in its worse positions than the difference-principle distribution had in its. Nonetheless, the general point remains: A distribution not based on the difference principle can only have positions in it that are better than those in a difference-principle distribution if it also has positions in it that are worse than those in the difference-principle distribution because, if there were a distribution with better positions than the difference-principle distribution and no worse ones, then it would be the true difference-principle distribution.

Since people in the natural context must realize their sovereign interests, they have an interest in securing for themselves the greatest possibility of realizing their sovereign interests. Consequently, it would only be rational for them to prefer a distribution not based on the difference principle to a difference-principle distribution, if it would be rational for them to gamble on being in its better-off positions and not in its worse-off ones. With the probabilities of these outcomes literally inestimable, no rational gambling is possible. And then, the difference principle is their only rational choice.

This conclusion holds even when the alternative is a strictly egalitarian distribution. Bear in mind that the difference principle would yield an equal distribution if no inequalities were necessary to improve the worse-off shares. Where the difference principle does not require equality, then no one in the difference-principle distribution will be worse off than anyone in the egalitarian one, but some of those in the difference-principle distribution will be better off than some of their counterparts in the egalitarian society. It would not be rational to opt for an egalitarian distribution over the difference principle, then, since the difference principle guarantees everyone at least what they could have in the egalitarian scheme, and some will do even better.

By the same token, the difference-principle distribution most fully overcomes the suspicion of subjugation. Unlike any alternative, including a strict egalitarian distribution, in the difference-principle scheme no one has less than she possibly could because others think she should have no more or

295

so someone else can do better than she. None is disadvantaged in any way by the social structure itself (as distinct from the inescapable fact that people's shares must be limited by their fellows' shares in any distribution and that in any distribution someone must end up in each of its places).

In the natural context, before any notions of entitlement or distribution are accepted as valid, one can only consider advancing his sovereign interest from the ground up. The testing of all distributive principles must start from a position in which one is, in effect, entitled to nothing. It must first ask what is the smallest share above nothing that a given principle offers and then what shares it offers beyond that minimum. Once gambling on one's chances of not ending up with one of the smaller shares that a distribution offers is ruled out, the best way for everyone to assure themselves of realizing their sovereign interests as far as possible is by selecting the distributive scheme that has the highest worst share, and then (without that being reduced), the highest next-to-worst share, and then (without that being reduced), the highest next-to-next-to-worst share, up to the best share. Rawls describes precisely this in stating the lexical difference principle (*TJ*, 83). Once no one in the original position can advance her interests by gambling on not ending up in some relatively disadvantaged position, the difference principle restates the problem of identifying the distributive scheme that most advances everyone's interests in the form of the solution. Given the conditions of the contracting situation with gambling excluded, the difference principle follows by strict logical deduction.

The deduction works because there are only two grounds upon which it might be rational for an individual to choose a distribution in which some have more, at the cost of others having less, than the difference principle would allot them. These grounds are either the belief that some deserve more or that it would be rational to gamble on ending up with more. Rawls sees that the first of these beliefs must be eliminated from the contracting situation because the situation is aimed at determining grounds of desert and cannot effectively presuppose any. I have argued that the second belief must be eliminated because allowing gambling subverts the capacity of the contracting situation to identify subjugation. With both beliefs eliminated on clear moral philosophical grounds, the only remaining rational consideration is to maximize the share of which one can be sure by agreeing to the difference principle.

This contractarian deduction proves that the difference principle is the standard for nonsubjugating economic arrangements. Once the possibility of structural force working through choice is recognized, we need a standard to determine whether free exchanges are, in fact, conduits of subjugation. The difference principle is that standard because, under its terms, everyone has the most he can have without reducing the share of others who have less than he has. Without independent grounds of desert, the claim that I am being subjugated because others already worse off than me are not made still worse off is not a claim that it would be reasonable for all people to honor. Moreover, as we saw in the previous section, the difference principle means that everyone gets the largest possible share of the social product in return for the least possible amount of work for others. Because no one is being forced to work excessively for another by a property system that satisfies the difference principle, such a system is not subjugating.

The Governing Principle of Social Justice and the Articles of the Social Contract

I contend that the final truth about justice—natural and social—comes down to this: Whether or not people cooperate to produce benefits, they owe each other noninterference, easy rescue, respect for natural ownership, trust-worthiness, intergenerational solicitude, and punishment no greater than lex talionis and deterrence require—and these are owed to everyone equally. Where people do cooperate to produce benefits, they owe each other distribution of the benefits and efforts that went into producing them according to the difference principle. So far as human beings treat their fellows according to these principles, they are acquitted from the charge of subjugation.

I mentioned these two summary principles at the beginning of this book. The first of the two principles sums up the requirements of natural justice, and the second, those of social justice. The second principle, which I shall state in greater detail in a moment, I call the *governing principle of social justice*. To get from these principles of justice in general to the specific principles of social justice—which I call the articles of the social contract—we must see how the requirements of natural justice interact with the governing principle of social justice.

The requirements of natural justice hold among all people, whether or not they share a social structure. The two summary principles are not alternatives, the first stating what people owe each other outside of society and the second what they owe inside. Rather than being supplanted by the principles of social justice, the requirements of natural justice are refracted through the requirements of just social structures and altered as necessary to make room for the latter because the principles of social justice have a status analogous to that of a contractual agreement in the natural context. If two people in the natural context agreed on an exchange of goods now for services later, the one who gave the goods would have the right to use force

297

to get the other to give the agreed-upon service should the latter refuse to honor the agreement when it came due. (The agreement is binding because of the principle of trustworthiness, and force against the defaulter would be justified by the principle of just punishment.) Were there no agreement, this use of force would violate the principle of compatible liberty. With the agreement, that principle must allow for the way the agreement has altered the moral relations of the parties to it. Likewise, the requirements of social justice can be thought of as voluntary and binding undertakings within the requirements of natural justice, and thus, in a similar fashion the latter must make room for the former. But except for this accommodation, the original requirements of natural justice hold as stated.

Among people who share a just social structure, the natural principle of compatible liberty becomes the right and duty of noninterference. I call this social version of the principle of compatible liberty, the *principle of social liberty*. This principle does not contain all that the principle of compatible liberty did. It does not, for example, contain the general right to use force that was part of the latter, because in a just social structure, except for immediate self-protection, use of force to protect people is rightly taken over by the legal component of the structure. Legal protection is the product of a cooperative scheme, and the benefits of it must be applied according to the governing principle of social justice. I shall say more about what this means shortly.

For the moment, we can say that the main principles of social justice are the principle of social liberty (where forced cooperation is not necessary) and the governing principle of social justice (applied to the systems of forced cooperation that constitute the social structure). These are the first and second articles of the social contract. We arrive at additional articles of the social contract by seeing how the remaining principles of natural justice are refracted through a just social structure—that is, through legal, political, and economic arrangements that satisfy the governing principle of social justice. Before we get to that, however, we must state the governing principle in full.

In the previous section we saw that the difference principle is the rational choice of parties in the natural context when gambling is eliminated so that they must agree only to positions all of which it would be reasonable to accept ending up in; in the section before that we saw that the difference principle is a principle of reciprocal advantage in which forced labor is reduced to the minimum necessary to maximize shares in the benefits produced by it. These are two distinct but convergent ways in which the difference principle is shown capable of dispelling the suspicion of subjugation regarding systems of forced cooperation. We considered this with respect to economic cooperation, but that is not the only arena in which people cooperate, nor are economic goods the only benefits they cooperate to produce. Since the people in the natural context have an interest in being able to pursue their sovereign interests, they have an interest in all the conditions that serve that pursuit, which I shall call "the conditions of sovereignty."

By the conditions of sovereignty, I understand those cooperatively produced things that generally enable people to realize their sovereign interest, whatever its constituent desires. Thus, where the phrase refers, for example, to economic goods, commodities, and services, it does not refer to some specific batch of them but to the general availability of a large range of them that people can choose from and obtain. The general availability of a large range of goods should suffice to give everyone access to the things he needs to realize his sovereign interest to the greatest extent possible compatible with the same for the rest. Moreover, this enables us to simplify the conditions of sovereignty with respect to wealth. Instead of having to determine the particular things that different individuals need for their sovereign interests, we can assume that each has an interest in the greatest possible claim on the large range of goods that is available—which is to say, the largest possible money income. But the conditions of sovereignty are not limited to economic goods. They also include the benefits produced by the legal system, namely security, and those produced by the political system, namely those that promote culture, education, safety, health, and development.

Accordingly, people's interest is not simply in maximizing their share of wealth, but in maximizing their share in the conditions of sovereignty, in general, of which wealth is one. Maximization here is not measured simply by the quantity of such conditions but by the contribution that the conditions make to people's ability to subject their lives to their desires as indexed by their sovereign interest. Since these other benefits are produced by systems of cooperation other than the economic, the burdens of cooperation are not just those commonly understood as labor. They include all the sacrifices in the pursuit of one's sovereign interest that make possible the legal and political systems. We can say that everyone's overall interest regarding cooperative endeavors lies in maximizing her net share in the conditions of sovereignty, where this means her share in the conditions that enhance her capacity to pursue her sovereign interest minus the sacrifices in that pursuit that go into producing those conditions. The very same arguments made in the last two sections apply, thus, to all the cooperatively produced conditions of sovereignty. What people would agree to as a principle governing all cooperative arrangements and the design of all social structures follows: In the design of social structures, inequalities in the distribution of the co-operatively produced conditions of sovereignty are just insofar as they maximize everyone's net share in these conditions, starting from the worst-off individual (the individual with the smallest net share in the unequal distribution) and proceeding upward (ratchet-like) to the best-off individual. Where everyone's net share in the conditions of sovereignty can be maximized without inequality, no inequality is just. This is the governing principle of social justice, the second article of the social contract. The principle of social liberty, affirming the right and duty of noninterference, is the first. These are the two main principles of social justice.

The two main principles are reminiscent of Rawls's two principles of justice. Note that this is not the same comparison that I made at the beginning of the book when I pointed out the resemblance between Rawls's principles and the two summary principles of justice. As in that case, however, when we compare Rawls's principles to the two main principles of social justice, the differences between the two sets of principles are at least as important as the similarities. First, Rawls's two principles are distinguished by the nature of the benefits distributed, his first principle distributing liberty, the second, goods. The main principles of social justice, in contrast, are distinguished by how the benefits are produced, the first concerning those produced without cooperation, and the second, those produced with. This distinction cuts across the distinction between Rawls's two principles, so that liberty turns up in different ways in both of the main principles. Liberty per se, corresponding roughly to what is called "negative freedom"—the right not to be interfered with except to stop one from harming others—is everyone's right equally according to the first of the main principles; the conditions of effective liberty, however, corresponding roughly to what is called "positive freedom"—the right to those legal, political, and economic enhancements of effective choice that are produced by social cooperation—are subject to the difference principle according to the second main principle. For example, while everyone is equally entitled to noninterference from his fellows, the police protection that secures this is a cooperative endeavor the benefits of which must be distributed according to the difference principle. Bear in mind that the difference principle only allows inequalities where necessary to improve everyone's share beyond what equality would provide. Where such inequalities are not necessary, the difference principle mandates equal distribution—and this is generally the case with such cooperatively produced legal benefits as security. I shall say more about this shortly.

That the main principles are distinguished by how the benefits they distribute are produced rather than by the nature of the benefits means that the main principles have no priority relations, lexical or other. The two can be realized together, since they do not apply to benefits in conflict. Accordingly, they are equally and simultaneously required. There is a priority relation that parallels Rawls's, but it is not between the two main principles, but rather within the benefits covered by the second of them. As societies advance technologically, the contribution to people's sovereign interests from additional economic goods declines relative to the contribution from political and legal benefits (cf. *TJ*, 542–43).

Considered as conditions of sovereignty, at the earliest levels of development material goods have priority over political participation. The latter amounts to participating in the direction of the group's destiny, and that serves my sovereign interest because my destiny is part of the group's. Nonetheless, at early levels of development the increase in the ability to subject one's life to one's desires that comes from the conquest of starvation and disease far outweighs the increase that comes from the ability to participate in the direction of the group's destiny. Indeed, such participation is hardly possible until the former conquest is established. After a certain point, however, additional material goods add smaller and smaller increments to one's ability to subject one's life to one's desires, while institutions that allow one to have impact on the direction of the group's destiny add greater and greater increments. At this point, establishing such institutions is in everyone's interest. Once such institutions are established, decisions on further trade-offs between political participation and material goods will be made through them. Just institutions of political participation, once established, retain a superiority over all other arrangements in the society. In contrast to Rawls's principles, however, none of this applies to liberty as governed by the first main principle. That is an absolute requirement of natural justice, and it waits on no level of development for its validity.

Like Rawls, I believe that all of the so-called advanced nations of the world have reached the point at which it is in everyone's interest to establish institutions of political participation. Thus, for these countries the governing principle dictates institutions that ensure every adult an equal say in the making of law and the charting of policy. This requires such political liberties as freedom of expression, but in a stronger form than they are normally thought to have. Freedom of expression is not merely one's right to speak one's mind without interference—one already has this right as a principle of natural justice. The freedom of expression required by political justice is the establishment of institutions that provide all citizens with the widest range of information and with a forum in which they can communicate with one another to arrive at truly public decisions. Our current institutions, in which a small minority of people control the mass media and the flow of information to the populace, are far from the institutions that political justice requires. In a just society, mass communication must be communication among the masses, not merely to the masses. Establishment of the kind of communication system in which people could actually communicate among themselves and reach their own decisions, combined with effectively functioning democratic institutions that provided the right to vote, hold office, and recall elected officials, would require a political system, unlike our own, in which access to mass media and public office was available to all, irrespective of their wealth. The priority of institutions of political participation over material goods means that economic arrangements would have to be designed (or compensated for) so that they did not undermine the equality of access to mass media and political office.

The second difference between the main principles and Rawls's conception concerns property rights. Since Rawls distinguishes his two principles according to the type of benefit—liberty and goods, respectively—he is prey to the libertarian blindness to the coerciveness of property. He is open to the Marxian critique that his two principles represent as a natural fact the division of society into the political and the economic that is peculiar to capitalism and that—by suggesting that coercion occurs only in politics—obfuscates the coercive aspect of economics.[16] I have not argued that a capitalist society cannot be just—only that its justice cannot be assessed without considering the coerciveness of property, and Rawls's conception does this, in effect. The main principles, by contrast, do not, since both are concerned to eliminate subjugation. An economic system only satisfies the second main principle insofar as it maximizes everyone's share in the cooperatively produced conditions of sovereignty. Economic systems are to be judged by their overall contribution to people's ability to pursue their sovereign interests, of which goods are only a part. If one system enhances people's ability to pursue their sovereign interests by supplying them with abundant goods at substantial costs to their ability to choose their work or place of living, another system, though producing less goods, might yield a greater overall contribution to the conditions of sovereignty.

A few additional differences between the governing principle and Rawls's second principle are worth noting. The lexical version of the difference principle is included explicitly in the statement of the governing principle. The governing principle does not speak only of maximizing the worst-off person, but of maximizing each position from the worst-off up, subject to the constraint of not reducing the shares of anyone below. Further, Rawls's principle applies to groups, and when he speaks of "representative persons," he means individuals as representatives of the various groups on the socio-economic ladder. The governing principle refers, in contrast, to individuals,

302

not as representatives of groups but as particular individuals. Parties agree to the principle in the natural context as individuals, and they will insist on having their shares protected as individuals. Only in this way can what is agreed to in the contracting situation eliminate the subjugation of every single person. No doubt Rawls has specified his principle in terms of groups because of the enormous practical problems involved in developing distributive policies aimed at giving each individual his rightful share. If this is so, however, it is a matter of the practical constraints on achieving the requirements of justice, not of the requirements themselves. One might object that applying the principle to individuals would require continual interference with people's liberty to keep rectifying the divergences from the principle that would result as people chose to invest or purchase with their rightful shares (see, for example, *ASU*, 163). That the governing principle calls for maximizing shares in conditions of sovereignty in general will be enough to limit this interference at the point at which it threatens to undermine what it is aimed at promoting.

We are now in a position to move from the main principles of social justice to the additional principles of social justice included among "the articles of the social contract." The additional principles are essentially principles for designing social structures so that they conform to the main principles, and they embody the remaining requirements of natural justice as these are refracted through a social structure so designed. Accordingly, we turn first to the substructures of which the social structure is composed.

Although the legal system is aimed at protecting everyone's equal right to freedom from interference, the actual protection it provides is the result of a cooperative endeavor and thus subject to the governing principle. For the most part, this requires equal protection of everyone. In general, one person's area of freedom from interference ends where another's begins. Protecting one person more than another will reduce the other's freedom, implying that maximization according to the difference principle requires equality. Legal protection is not like wealth; as a rule, it cannot be increased overall by allotting unequal shares. Nonetheless, on some occasions unequal protection will maximize freedom for all. Greater protection of law enforcement agents, judges, or witnesses, for example, as well as of those in more dangerous areas or those who are particularly vulnerable or unpopular, may be justified to maximize legal protection for all people beyond what straight equal protection might provide. With these qualifications, equal protection under the law is an article of the social contract.

Similar implications follow for the political system. I have held that some form of constitutionally limited majoritarian arrangement for reaching group decisions will be reasonable for all, since it will equalize and maximize each person's share in the direction of the group's destiny without violating those legal and economic arrangements that are necessary to prevent subjugation. Here, too, equal distributions will be the rule, particularly with respect to opportunities for political participation. One person's political power, like liberty, begins where another's ends, and thus, greater-than-equal shares for some normally means reducing the shares of others. Nonetheless, inequalities necessary to facilitate political decision making, such as special powers and immunities granted to legislators, will be justified if the overall effect maximizes everyone's share in the conditions of sovereignty. With these qualifications, equal right to effective political participation is an article of the social contract.

We have already looked extensively at the question of economic justice. Since the economic system is a double system of coercion, it needs a double dose of the difference principle to justify it. It employs coercion both in the sense that force is used to establish some system of property beyond natural ownership and in the sense that any system established is a system of forced labor. Our discussion of the difference principle as a principle of the justice of economic distributions alone generally addresses the second form of coercion. In speaking of the justice of capitalism, socialism, and communism, I only considered them in this light. But even a system that distributes labor and goods according to the difference principle may still interfere with people's freedom at another level—that of their choices about what work to do or where to do it. This latter consideration would have to be evaluated in conjunction with distribution in light of the governing principle, to see which system yields the maximum shares in conditions of sovereignty distributed according to the difference principle. This is an enormous task, in which I have aimed only to state the standards, not to apply them.

Stateless communism is not on any realistic agenda for the foreseeable future. And neither capitalism nor socialism put ownership of property directly in workers' hands; the former obviously not, the latter because it vests such ownership in the state. In neither system, accordingly, is labor unforced. If a socialist and a capitalist system could both equally satisfy the difference principle with respect to the distribution of labor and goods, the question between them would depend on whether the socialist state could be made democratic enough to give more people more real freedom to control their destinies than they have in the free market—or vice versa. The ease with which socialists assume that state control is real popular control is matched by the ease with which capitalists assume that legal freedom to accept or refuse work on the free market is real freedom for everyone to choose where he works and what he does. The issue depends on looking at what really happens without ideological preconceptions. If a socialist and a capitalist society cannot equally satisfy the difference principle with respect to the economic distribution, then the system in which the worst-off economic shares are lower will only be superior if it provides its members the largest overall package of conditions of sovereignty distributed according to the difference principle. Both systems would have to have legal and political systems that conform to the principles indicated in the previous paragraphs.

The remaining articles of the social contract derive from the remaining principles of natural justice. In a shared social structure, the right of people to make contracts that the state will enforce and the duty of the state to enforce these stem from the principle of trustworthiness. Truthfulness is required from those given special powers in the legal and political systems, as otherwise the coercive actions of those systems cannot be kept subject to popular scrutiny and control. In some circumstances the sovereign interests of all the members of a nation will be served by their leaders engaging in secrecy and deception, particularly in foreign relations with potential belligerents. This must always be thought of as a last resort, kept to as short duration as possible, and eventually subjected to public review. There is an evident analogy here between official deception and paternalistic coercion. Both are, in principle, inherently justifiable and, in fact, inherently dangerous. Both are to be engaged in only when there is obvious need, only for a limited time, and with the requirement that they eventually be justified to those who have been deceived or coerced.

In a shared social structure, alongside the principle of intergenerational solicitude is added a duty of loyalty to the whole society that is responsible for producing the conditions of one's sovereignty. Insofar as the nation provides the conditions of survival and more through its cooperative endeavors, it is, as Socrates observed in the *Crito*, like one's parents. Consequently, the duty of loyalty becomes that of patriotism. But only a just society can be said to contribute as a whole to each of its member's conditions of sovereignty. If the society is unjust, then some parts of it will be working counter to those conditions. Accordingly, societies are owed patriotism to the extent that they are just. To the extent that societies are not just, allegiance is owed to the smaller groups that do wholeheartedly support the individual—his ethnic group, his community, his family. The duty of loyalty includes, moreover, a general obligation to support one's fellow members of a just society in meeting life's dangers. Thus, the duty of easy rescue under the principle of compatible liberty is extended in a just society to require general institutions for the protection of the needy and vulnerable, as a duty of social justice.

Any more coercion than is necessary to support the principles just   305 enumerated is in violation of the principle of social liberty. It follows that in a just society, as David Richards has suggested, the "demonstrable harm" principle—that force not be used against a sane adult except to prevent harm to others—will function as a constitutional limit.[17] Using coercion to prevent sane adults from doing what they wish with their bodies, including putting drugs in them and selling themselves for the sexual pleasure of others, violates the first article of the social contract. Accordingly, there must be general recognition of individuals' right to privacy. The only just restrictions on actions that do not harm others (aside from those necessary to protect the immature against things they are incapable of assessing) will be a very limited allowance of paternalism to keep people from clearly going against their own desires. Such paternalism can at most be a minor restriction or a temporary delay—nothing that could keep a sane person from doing to and with himself what he truly wishes, no matter what the rest of society thinks about his judgment. Naturally, there is plenty of room for people recommending to their fellows what they view as the wisest course.

In a shared social structure, the principle of just punishment becomes that of proportional retributivism. Recall that this is the view that the punishments in a society's table of criminal penalties should be such that the worst crime is punished with the worst punishment, and less bad crimes with proportionately less severe punishments; proportional retributivism does not require that punishments equal the harm done in the crimes. The principle of just punishment was established as an article of natural justice on the grounds that it was reasonable for everyone to agree to the least amount of punishment necessary to achieve the aims of restoring moral equilibrium between criminal and victim (retribution per se) and to prevent reasonable people from committing such crimes (deterrence). Outside of society this establishes for each person a right to exact the lex talionis and whatever more is necessary for reasonable self-protection. Inside a society, these same grounds lead to proportional retributivism, because the existence of a social structure, particularly the handing over of punishment to the legal system, brings additional considerations to bear on what it is reasonable for people to agree to.[18]

Most important, punishment inflicted by the legal system is done in the name of the society as a whole, bestowing a powerful endorsement on the punishment it administers. This has an important effect on the moral development of members of that society, particularly on the young. Administering the lex talionis, closely matching punishments to crimes, amounts to endorsing acts as cruel as those of the worst criminals. This is heightened in its effect because social systems are relatively permanent, whereas encounters between individuals who do not share a social structure are oc-

306

casional. Whatever a society does in the way of punishment, it announces as general and continuing policy. The existence of a social structure makes it possible for less severe or extreme punishments to achieve the goal of restoring moral equilibrium between victims and criminals. The same legitimacy that allows a society to act in the name of the whole enables it to establish the meaning of its punishments, as it can set the value of its currency—neither, of course, with complete freedom. A society can establish a table of punishments such that the worst punishment on it, because it is the worst thing this society is willing to do even to those who deserve more, is equivalent in meaning or significance to the crime, and thus capable of restoring moral equilibrium between victims and criminals. Naturally, for this to be credible, the punishments must be such that reasonable people will regard them as comparable in gravity to the crimes for which they are administered. Such punishments would still be just since they are the least amount needed for the purposes of retribution and deterrence that make it reasonable for all to agree to principles of punishment. Since the society has an interest in refraining from endorsing, even as punishment, the cruelty of criminals, it will then tend to reduce its table of punishments to the least cruel acts that can accomplish retributive and deterrence aims.

One might object that punishment less than the lex talionis is unjust to the victim, since the right to punish arises initially from his natural right to restore moral equilibrium. But since the justifications of proportional retributivism and lex talionis stem from what it would be reasonable for all to agree to in the natural context, the reductions in punishment involved in the former arise from the same source as the victim's right. Reduction in punishment below lex talionis stands to the victim's right in a relation analogous to that in which legitimate reasons for overriding promises stand to the rights of promisees. The obligation to keep promises can be overridden when breaking the promise is necessary to avoid severe damage to other people's ability to pursue their sovereign interests. In such cases, we do not think that the promisee's right to have the promise kept has been violated. Rather, that right has been respected as far as moral considerations linked to the basis of that right itself allow. Analogously, proportional retributivism respects the victim's right to lex talionis as far as moral considerations linked to the basis of that right itself allow.

This ends our discussion of the articles of the social contract. If they seem more schematic and less definite in their implications than the articles of the natural covenant, that was only to be expected. The latter concern particular actions and can be stated as fairly straightforward commands. The former concern the design of social structures and thus express ideals,   307 the realization of which depend on complicated patterns of human interaction. Accordingly, we conclude not with a blueprint for a just society but with a statement of what must be proven to prove that any society is just: Its legal, political, and economic systems must provide the best possible package of conditions of sovereignty, distributed according to the difference principle in light of the cooperative efforts that go into them. Such a society must also avoid all coercive interference with its citizens beyond what is necessary for the operation of these systems. Free speech, freedom of movement, full political participation, official truthfulness, respect for privacy, decriminalization of so-called victimless crimes, equal and effective legal protection, and civilized punishments just to criminal and victim are necessary conditions for any society meeting this test. Beyond this, I shall not venture. Telling human beings which society is just is not the business of moral philosophy. Instead, it should provide people with the instruments by which they can tell. Determining which society produces the best overall package of conditions of sovereignty is a complex and controvertible matter. But recognizing that this is what must be proven to prove the justness of a society enables reasonable people to evaluate and to resolve the differences in their judgments.

Conclusion: *Visions, Moral, Metaphysical, and Religious*

> Asked by a pagan to teach him the Torah while the
> questioner stood on one foot, Rabbi Hillel answered,
> "What is harmful to you, do not do to your fellow.
> That is the whole Torah; all the rest is commentary. Go
> and learn."
> —*Babylonian Talmud* Shabat 31a

I have concentrated only on that part of morality that concerns justice—those things that can be required of human beings by their fellows. I do not claim that these requirements add up to a whole moral vision. There are surely forms of voluntary cooperation that would enable human beings to flourish beyond what justice strictly requires. Nonetheless, justice should not be thought of as a thing apart from this flourishing. Insofar as human beings flower on the ground of freedom, justice guards that ground. Insofar as human beings flower in the soil of community, justice tends that soil. Justice makes possible a social order that people can truly be said to share freely. Since it is one in which no one is subjugated, a just social structure is one that all people can call their own, one whose terms all people can openly affirm, a society in which members can look one another in the eyes and speak honestly about the conditions under which they share their fates. Seeing in the social structure a system of cooperation aimed at enabling each to realize his aims, they can feel from one another respect and toward one another affection, a kind of civic friendship out of which all can take deep pleasure in the flourishing of their fellows, even those whose names they do not know. To me, this is an appealing moral vision.

At this point I shall attempt to locate this vision in that larger map that philosophers always have in the back of their minds. I shall start with metaphysics and move from there to religion.

I believe that philosophy will end with a fully naturalistic view of reality. Indeed, I am convinced that eventually the worldview of natural science will be accepted as a complete ontology. By this I mean a fully reductive materialism, in which every phenomenon can be explained without residue as the product of subatomic particles and the way they interact. I do not mean that all the properties of larger wholes are properties of their parts, any more than the wetness of water derives from the wetness in hydrogen or oxygen. Rather, the properties of larger wholes can be explained by reference to the properties of their parts, as wetness can be from the properties of hydrogen and oxygen and the bonds they form. No unexplainable properties emerge mysteriously at higher levels of complexity. Since this view of the destiny of philosophy is far from universally accepted, I have written this book without assuming its truth. It is, then, worth pausing to consider what would change about my argument were this ontology to be generally recognized as true.

I do not believe much would change. We would recognize that morality is a kind of equilibrium toward which physical systems of the sort that we are—"reasoning machines" that can represent to themselves their desires and their impending deaths—tend. Some people think that this would destroy morality, dissolve our ideals into a shower of subatomic particles worth no more than so much dirt. But I think the reverse. We would learn that our deepest moral longings are nature's own and that our belief in the reality of morality was always true. The crucial properties of first-person experience, caring, reasoning, and judging, would not be denied by this ontology; on the contrary, it would explain how they arose as properties of the physical systems that we are. Greater knowledge may bring with it recognition of new, even higher, obligations than those now visible. But knowing fully what being a human subject is will continue to require being one, or imagining being one. This knowing will still dispose one to judge and act in the ways that I have tried to spell out. Thus, with the completion of an ontology based on the scientific worldview, knowing what human subjects are will continue to generate moral obligations that are as binding as ever. So much for metaphysical speculations.

This book is about religion in that it claims that the core of the morality carried by the Judeo-Christian religious teaching is built into human reason (this applies, I suspect, to the teaching of many other religions as well— about which I remain silent so as not to reveal my ignorance). I have tried to explain why it would be natural to hear the moral voice of reason as the voice of God. I have even suggested a naturalistic version of original sin. If I am right, morality was always the voice of reason, but since the irresistible authority of that voice was heard while its source was not understood, it was, in the childhood of humankind, personalized, its authority hallowed. Chapter 3 began with an epigraph from St. Paul that I take to be the recognition within the horizons of religious consciousness that the moral law, taken as revealed to the Jews by God, is, in fact, built into the reason of every human being. Having thrown out these suggestions, it seems only fair to give the reader a hint about the overall view of religion that lies behind them.

Speaking of these religions as historical events (rather than in terms of the technical details of their theologies), we might say that Judaism represents the discovery of rational morality as holding between the people with whom one actually lives and whom one can trust to reciprocate and that Christianity represents the discovery that rational morality can stop at no barrier short of the whole human race. Thus, Judaism represents the discovery that reason requires and justifies mutual trust in one's fellows' understanding of and disposition to do justice. Christianity teaches that this trust must be offered to everyone in the hope that it will one day be reciprocated and that until then one must turn the other cheek. One must love not only one's neighbor but one's enemies as well. Trust offered before there is reason to expect it to be reciprocated is faith. If my argument that the internal social contract is built into all rational human beings is correct, then this faith is justified. The Jewish covenant then represents the trust in justice directed to one's actual community, and Christian faith represents this trust directed to the virtual community of humankind. Accordingly, each has its strength—insistence on justice here and now for Judaism and on universal inclusivity for Christianity; each has its own corresponding danger—narrowness and acquiescence, respectively.

That the Jews have outlasted all the powerful states that tried to destroy them shows how the Jews are a "chosen" people. In the Darwinian sense, they have been selected because the survival value of mutual trust is greater even than possession of political power. The survival of the Jews conveys, accordingly, a message of importance to all humankind, and no small threat to those who hide behind the instruments of force. But also, insofar as the effect of the historical Jesus was the spread throughout the world of the recognition that the trust underlying rational morality must extend to all human beings, then Jesus was surely a messiah.

I take all this as an encomium to religion, not a slight to it, but since religion has already lost its claim to account for the natural world, this encomium may seem to deprive it of its last remaining claim. I think not. What is essential to religion is neither a particular worldview nor the claim to be the ultimate moral authority. Not even belief in God is essential, as certain forms of Buddhism show. What is essential is belief that there is something worthy of reverence. This belief can not only withstand but be supported by a naturalistic worldview. Respect is given with eyes level, reverence with eyes upwards. The object of respect is the human subject. The object of reverence is the sacred. The sacred is so good as to be better   311 than the best. The only thing that can fit this description is whatever is the ultimate source of there being a best at all. The human subject is the object of respect because it bestows value on things, thereby designating a better and a best; the sacred is the object of reverence because it is the source of there being human subjects and a world of things for them to value. Consequently, the role of the sacred, historically attributed to God, can in a naturalistic worldview be attributed to the natural universe itself. Indeed, many of the attributes traditionally applied to God apply to it—the universe is omnipresent and omnipotent, the source of all that is good and beautiful, and like God of old, it bears a puzzling complicity in the existence of evil that does not detract from its goodness, and it contains our destinies without compromising our freedom.

To see the natural universe as the ultimate source of the best is to be moved to a kind of love for it that, in embracing one's own limits as part of what is loved, is a kind of reverence. And, having such love of the natural universe, one might hope, with a little luck and a little help from one's friends, to experience one's life as a gift, to recognize one's death as no more than the outer dimension of that gift, to see the very imperfections of finite existence as a kind of perfection, to feel honored at being able to tend the universe during the time one has, and to feel joy at being able to live according to the moral law inscribed by it in one's brain and heart, and thus to live a life that might fairly be described as blessed.

Notes

CHAPTER 1: *Subjugation and the Natural Test of Morality*

1. J. W. Gough, *The Social Contract: A Critical Study of Its Development*, 2d ed. (London: Oxford University Press, 1957), 127.

2. Gough, *The Social Contract*, 2, 26–28, 34, 134; cf. Harold J. Berman, *Law and Revolution: The Formation of the Western Legal Tradition* (Cambridge: Harvard University Press, 1983), 298–99, 306; and Quentin Skinner, *The Foundations of Modern Political Thought* (New York: Cambridge University Press, 1978), 2:129–30.

3. St. Augustine, *The City of God* (New York: Modern Library, 1950), 112.

4. See Harry Frankfurt, "Freedom of the Will and the Concept of a Person," *Journal of Philosophy* 68 (January 1971): 5–20; and Charles Taylor, "Responsibility for Self," in *The Identities of Persons*, ed. A. O. Rorty (Berkeley: University of California Press, 1976), 281–99.

5. Bernard Williams, *Problems of the Self* (Cambridge: Cambridge University Press, 1973), 26–45.

6. Robert Nozick makes this point with an interesting thought-experiment; see *ASU*, 42–45.

7. Friedrich Nietzsche, *The Gay Science*, trans. Walter Kaufmann (New York: Vintage, 1974), sec. 270.

CHAPTER 2: *Reason and the Internal Social Contract*

1. Jean-Jacques Rousseau, "The General Society of the Human Race," in *The Social Contract and Discourses* (London: Dent & Sons, 1973), 161.

2. T. M. Scanlon, "A Contractualist Alternative," in *New Directions in Ethics*, ed. J. P. DeMarco and R. M. Fox (New York: Routledge & Kegan Paul, 1986), 49. Scanlon distinguishes what people cannot reasonably reject from what it would be reasonable for them to accept, but I shall ignore this distinction since it is irrelevant to the point I want to make.

3. Henry Sidgwick, *The Methods of Ethics*, 7th ed. (London: Macmillan, 1930), 382.

4. Alisdair MacIntyre, *After Virtue* (Notre Dame, Ind.: University of Notre Dame Press, 1981).

5. See the many fine essays, and Gewirth's replies, in *Gewirth's Ethical Rationalism*, ed. Edward Regis, Jr. (Chicago: The University of Chicago Press, 1984).

6. The most important difference between Hare and Gewirth is that Hare denies that human beings must affirm their own rights. Hare is content to say that they normally do affirm them (or something broadly equivalent thereto), and then, logical consistency (the requirement of universalizability) requires them to affirm the same of others. Because of this feature of Hare's approach, he is constantly dogged by the impossibility of proving the immorality of the so-called fanatic or the amoralist—people who either are willing to have their own rights violated or who refuse to talk in moral terms at all. If I am right, however, it follows that these problems are small beer. Hare's real problem is that, even if there were no fanatics or amoralists, nothing about the sheer consistency of people's claims could determine the moral status of their acts. Hare has developed his theory in several books, the most recent of which is *Moral Thinking* (New York: Oxford University Press, 1981). On his differences with Gewirth, see Hare's "Do Agents Have to be Moralists?," in Regis, *Gewirth's Ethical Rationalism*, 52–58.

7. Cf. Bernard Williams, *Problems of the Self* (Cambridge: Cambridge University Press, 1973), 236.

8. Hare mistakenly takes universalization to require such aggregating. See, for example, Hare, *Moral Thinking*, 109–11. This is a mistake because universalization requires that my actions be such that I can accept them while treating the way people value their fates and desires consistent with how I value mine, but aggregation distorts how people value their fates and desires and thus undermines that consistency.

9. Jean-Paul Sartre, *Critique of Dialectical Reason*, trans. Alan Sheridan-Smith (London: NLB, 1976), 783.

10. William James, "The Moral Philosopher and the Moral Life," in *The Writings of William James*, ed. J. McDermott (New York: Modern Library, 1968), 618.

11. H. J. Paton, *The Categorical Imperative* (London: Hutchinson's University Library, n.d.), 42, 64.

12. R. S. Downie and Elizabeth Telfer, *Respect for Persons* (London: Allen & Unwin, 1969), 15, 18, 29.

13. Ibid., 24, 28. Downie and Telfer use a slightly different translation than I do.

14. I am modifying the translation here slightly, to read "kingdom" where the translator has put "realm."

15. Robert Ernest Hume, *The World's Living Religions* (New York: Charles Scribner's Sons, 1959), 276–78.

16. Erving Goffman, *Asylums* (New York: Anchor, 1961).

CHAPTER 3: *Natural Justice and the Natural Covenant*

1. An example of this approach is Mary Anne Warren's "On the Moral and Legal Status of Abortion," *The Monist* 57, no. 1 (January 1973): 43–61.

2. Immanuel Kant, *Critique of Pure Reason*, trans. Norman Kemp Smith (London: Macmillan, 1963), 341.

3. See Michel Foucault, *Discipline and Punish: The Birth of the Prison*, trans. Alan Sheridan (London: Allen Lane, 1967), wherein the history of the supplanting of corporal punishment by confinement is traced, though its causes are left obscure.

4. I argue for this view in "Privacy, Intimacy and Personhood," *Philosophy & Public Affairs* 6, no. 1 (Fall 1976): 26–44.

5. Kant, by contrast, held the existence of private property to depend on an act of consent by the members of civil society after the latter is established; see *MJ*, 65.

6. See Daniel Dennett, "Conditions of Personhood," in *The Identities of Persons*, ed. A. O. Rorty (Berkeley: University of California Press, 1976), 186–87; and H. P. Grice, "Utterers' Meaning and Intentions," *Philosophical Review* 78 (April 1969): 147–77.

7. See Jürgen Habermas, *Legitimation Crisis* (Boston: Beacon, 1975), 89, 113; and Habermas, *Communication and the Evolution of Society* (Boston: Beacon, 1979), 97, 184, 205.

8. See Alan Donagan, *The Theory of Morality* (Chicago: University of Chicago Press, 1977), 92–93.

9. Cf. Herbert Morris, "Persons and Punishment," *The Monist* 52, no. 4 (October 1968): 475–501.

10. See Ernest van den Haag, "Refuting Reiman and Nathanson," *Philosophy & Public Affairs* 14, no. 2 (Spring 1985): 166–67.

11. F. E. Peters, *Greek Philosophical Terms: A Historical Lexicon* (New York: New York University Press, 1967), 38–40.

CHAPTER 4: *From Natural Justice to Social Justice*

1. I take this up in detail in *The Rich Get Richer and the Poor Get Prison: Ideology, Class, and Criminal Justice*, 3d ed. (New York: Macmillan, 1989).

2. Cf. Isaiah Berlin, "Two Concepts of Liberty," in *Four Essays on Liberty* (Oxford: Oxford University Press, 1969), 118–72.

3. John Rawls, "Justice as Fairness," *The Philosophical Review* 67 (1958): 179.

4. In recent writings, Rawls has moved away from attempting to ground his theory intuitively in our "commonly shared presumptions" and "considered convictions" and has characterized the theory in more pragmatic terms as what is fitting and workable in such pluralistic societies as our own. See John Rawls, "Kantian Constructivism in Moral Theory," *Journal of Philosophy* 77 (September 1980) and "Justice as Fairness: Political not Metaphysical," *Philosophy & Public Affairs* 14, no. 3 (Summer 1985): 223–51.

CHAPTER 5: *Social Justice and the Social Contract*

1. To be sure, libertarians end up in other places, and so there are libertarian socialists, and the like. I shall understand by libertarianism, however, only the libertarian capitalist strain.

2. I take this to be roughly Hayek's and Friedman's position; see, for example, F. A. Hayek, *The Road to Serfdom* (London: Routledge & Kegan Paul, 1976) and *Law, Legislation, and Liberty*, 3 vols. (Chicago: University of Chicago Press, 1973, 1976, 1979); and Milton Friedman, *Capitalism and Freedom* (Chicago: University of Chicago Press, 1962).

3. The picture also corresponds to the market under the conditions that lead Gauthier to describe it as "a morally free zone," since for this the market must be perfectly competitive, which, in turn, means that no one can benefit from any scarcity (*MBA*, 83–112). I will have more to say about this below.

4. Letter to P. V. Annenkov, December 28, 1846, in Karl Marx, *The Poverty of Philosophy* (Moscow: Progress Publishers, 1955), 163.

5. Karl Marx and Friedrich Engels, *The German Ideology*, parts 1 and 3 (New York: International, 1963), 14.

6. Maurice Godelier, "Structure and Contradiction in *Capital*," in *Ideology in Social Science*, ed. Robin Blackburn (Glasgow: Fontana/Collins, 1977), 337. The efforts of members of the Frankfurt School to explain ideology in Freudian terms as irrational embrace of authority or in existential terms as anxious flight from freedom are examples of "subjective illusion" explanations of ideology. See Martin Jay, *The Dialectical Imagination: A History of the Frankfurt School and the Institute for Social Research, 1923–1950* (Boston: Little, Brown, 1973).

7. See Milton Fisk, "History and Reason in Rawls' Moral Theory," in *Reading Rawls: Critical Studies of* A Theory of Justice, ed. N. Daniels (New York: Basic, 1975), 53–80.

8. The example is adapted from Brian Barry, *The Liberal Theory of Justice* (London: Oxford University Press, 1973), 89–90.

9. My formulation of the gambler problem is a composite drawn from many sources. See, for example, R. M. Hare, "Rawls' Theory of Justice," and Richard Miller, "Rawls and Marxism," in *Reading Rawls*, ed. Daniels, 81–107, 206–30; Barry, *The Liberal Theory of Justice*, 87–107; and Robert Paul Wolff, *Understanding Rawls* (Princeton, N.J.: Princeton University Press, 1977), 160–77. On hedged utilitarianism, see Miller, "Rawls and Marxism," 223.

10. Rawls's argument would surely preclude agreement to any serious punishment system and thus have to imply that serious punishment was always unjust.

11. The remainder of this section is a revised version of my article, "The Labor Theory of the Difference Principle," *Philosophy & Public Affairs* 12, no. 2 (Spring 1983): 133–59.

12. Thomas Nagel, "Rawls on Justice," and Hare, "Rawls' Theory of Justice," in *Reading Rawls*, ed. Daniels, 13, 107. See also Wolff, *Understanding Rawls*, 173–74.

13. Marx writes, "it is . . . this money-form of the world of commodities that actually conceals, instead of disclosing, the social character of private labour, and the social relations between the individual producers" (*C*, 1:76).

14. Actually, Marx holds that workers will receive for their labor an amount of goods produced by an equal amount of labor after deductions for the general costs of administration, public goods such as schools, and funds for those unable to work have been made (CGP, 529–30). Since we can think of these deductions as purchasing goods or insurance for everyone, they can be taken as an indirect return to individuals of labor equal to what they contribute and thus as not altering the fundamental principle.

15. For example, Allen Wood, "Marx on Right and Justice: A Reply to Husami," *Philosophy & Public Affairs* 8, no. 3 (Spring 1979): 292.

16. This is the division into state and civil society that Hegel took to be the highest expression of freedom (see, for example, *PR*, 28) and that Marx criticized as a mechanism of oppression (in "On the Jewish Question," in *The Marx-Engels Reader*, 2d ed., ed. R. Tucker [New York: Norton, 1978], 33–35).

17. David A. J. Richards, *Sex, Drugs, Death, and the Law* (Totowa, N.J.: Rowman and Littlefield, 1982), 17–33.

18. I am indebted to my colleague Robert Johnson for the suggestion that the conditions of just punishment of criminals by states might be different from the conditions of just punishment of criminals by their victims.

Index